Begin to sample some of the public-domain and Shareware programs discussed in this book immediately . . .

Order the *Public-Domain Software and Shareware* programs disk today!

The *Public-Domain Software and Shareware* disk (MS-DOS format) contains an excellent collection of useful utilities and entertaining games. Because the files are archived, you actually receive several diskettes worth of programs. Included are such programs as Arcmaster, a full-featured archive file management system; DPROTECT, a disk drive protection scheme; Privacy, an encoder/decoder program that allows you to encode your files; SWAPNAME, a file that allows you to swap the file names of two existing files; the game Spacewar, and much more.

To order, return this postage-paid self-mailer with your payment of $20, plus sales tax if you are a California resident, to: M&T Books, 501 Galveston Drive, Redwood City, CA 94063. Or, call toll-free 800-533-4372 (In CA 800-356-2002). Ask for **Item #48-8**.

YES! Please send me the *Public-Domain Software and Shareware* programs disk for $20 _____

California residents add applicable sales tax _____% _____

TOTAL _____

_____ Check enclosed. Make payable to M&T Books.

Charge my ____ VISA ____ MasterCard ____ American Express

Card # _____ Exp. date _____

Name _____

Address _____

City _____ State _____ Zip _____

7017

Public-Domain Software
and Shareware, Second Edition

M&T BOOKS

Public-Domain Software and Shareware

Second Edition

Untapped Resources for the PC User

Rusel DeMaria and George R. Fontaine

M&T BOOKS

M&T Publishing, Inc.
Redwood City, California

M&T Books
A Division of M&T Publishing, Inc.
501 Galveston Drive
Redwood City, CA 94063

M&T Books
General Manager, Ellen Ablow
Editorial Project Manager, Michelle Hudun
Editors, Sally Brenton, Dave Rosenthal
Cover Art Director, Michael Hollister
Cover Designer, Joe Sikoryak
Cover Photographer, Michael Carr
Production Artists, Lynn Sanford, Beth Auten

Library of Congress Cataloging-in-Publication Data

DeMaria, Rusel, 1948–
    Public-Domain software and shareware.

    Includes index.
    1. Business—Computer programs. 2. Free computer
software. 3. Microcomputers. I. Fontaine, George R.,
1960–   .   II. Title.   III. Title: Shareware
HF5548.2.D435 1988   650'.208'5536   88-8551
ISBN 1-55851-014-1
ISBN 1-55851-011-7 (pbk.)

91   90   89   88   4   3   2   1

To Shareware pioneers everywhere, but also to Theodore Sturgeon, an inspiration in the art of writing; to my dad, and to my family, especially Marsha, Shan, and MAX! —DM

This book is dedicated to Paige, whose love and inspiration kept me going throughout the project—I love you! And Baby (our cat), who kept my lap warm during my long hours at the keyboard. —GRF

Trademarks and Copyrights

Contents

PART II: APPLICATIONS

PART III: SOURCES

Introduction

This book is about public-domain and Shareware programs. It is designed to save you time, effort, and dollars in several ways:

- by showing you how to find excellent products at low prices.

- by providing information about Shareware written by professionals in the Shareware world.

- by providing reviews of some of the best and most important Shareware and public-domain products.

- by helping you find and utilize major sources of good programs.

The book is divided into three main sections: *Basics, Reviews,* and *Sources.* The *Basics* section is a primer on telecommunications, and contains information we feel you'd like to know. Even if you are an expert telecommunicator, you may find parts of the information in the *Basics* section interesting and new.

The *Reviews* section contains real product reviews of everything from simple, but very useful, utilities to full-fledged applications. By using the information provided in the *Reviews* section, you should be able to tell if a product is right for you.

The *Sources* section of the book details how and where to get public domain and Shareware. If you are new to telecommunications, or just don't know where to find good software, this section will provide you with several alternatives, including instructions on how to establish accounts with some of the major bulletin-board services, how to locate their software, and how to download it.

The book also contains several informative essays from Shareware professionals that will give you insight into the world of Shareware marketing. We did not tell these people what to say. We invited them to talk about Shareware in their own words. It is a way to give Shareware professionals a chance to speak to you. Look for these essays throughout the book.

Why this Book?

Why a book about software whose average price is well under $50? Isn't it easy enough to download some programs, look them over, and then get rid of any you don't want? Why a book about public-domain and Shareware programs?

Let's start more or less at the beginning. The IBM PC came out in 1981. The idea of public-domain software was well established in mainframe circles and on other computer systems like Apple, Commodore, and CP/M machines, but it took the IBM PC to create a wide-spread demand for free computer programs.

Over the years, the number of public-domain programs grew, and some of the more sophisticated computer users exchanged files at group meetings, between themselves, and through local bulletin boards. Enter The Source and CompuServe, large commercially run BBSs where people could telecommunicate, exchange files, etc. Still, the average computer user knew little or nothing about the public domain.

Then enter attorney and programmer Andrew Fluegelman and programmer Jim Button, pioneers thinking along similar lines. Their common idea: Shareware. Try before you buy. Trust the consumer. Believe in the honor principle.

Fluegelman successfully marketed PC Talk according to the Shareware principle, as did Button with his original PC File. Others also joined as they saw the concept working, and some were successful.

Shareware was alternately called Freeware and user-supported software. The concepts were essentially the same, but the names were different. Today there is a tendency toward uniformity, as Shareware becomes a better known commodity.

In 1983, we began the Royal Hawaiian Software BBS on an IBM PC with a dual ten megabyte Bernoulli Box. We were excited by the opportunities afforded by telecommunications, and curious about the world of software being distributed that way. We didn't know if our BBS would last, or go the way of many other boards.

Our board has run 24 hours a day ever since. It has grown, transformed, and evolved, and it remains constantly busy. In the course of running our BBS, we have seen people use and share software freely. We've seen how public-domain and Shareware products can enhance the computer environment. Anything that successful and that active must have something going for it.

For the past few years we've written a weekly newspaper column and many commercial product reviews for computer magazines. We've acted as developers and consultants for businesses and individuals, and we have worked with user groups and private software companies. We've seen public domain and Shareware grow both in quantity and in quality. We've also heard many misconceptions and prejudices expressed about PD and Shareware, despite (or maybe because of) this growth. We have continued to support the free interchange of PD and Shareware.

This book is an attempt to answer complaints, dispel some myths, and help spread the word about good programs that deserve to be used. This book makes it possible for more people to find great software without paying an arm and a leg, or risking more than the cost of a phone call.

Public Domain vs. Shareware

The public domain is a democratic concept. It's the area where all of us share equally. Anything in the public domain is free. That includes peoples' writings, music, and now computer programs. Many generous people have spent their time and effort to create programs, utilities, and even games for the public domain. These programs are free.

It is important to note, in passing, that some public-domain material is protected against alteration or commercial use. It still doesn't cost anything, but copyrights may apply.

The Commercial World

On the other hand, commercial programs designed to make a profit are sometimes bankrolled by immense corporations, designed by teams of experts, crafted by some of the best programmers, and marketed through huge advertising campaigns. Many of those programs are excellent. Some of them are not. Most of them are fairly expensive because of research and development costs, licenses, and marketing. Big companies have big overhead and big appetites for profits.

Smaller companies make for-profit software as well. They compete in a difficult arena. Their expenses are large; usually so are their debts. Some can make very little profit because of the considerable overhead that accompanies software marketing and development these days.

Many excellent development teams have turned away from self-marketing, but produce software that more successful companies market. This leads to mega-software houses and to a less open, less responsive atmosphere. The mega-companies do, however, present some advantages. They can bankroll talented developers, find and market excellent products from other developers, and, if they're good at what they do, encourage and demand excellence in their products.

There is, however, an alternative that provides some excellent choices.

Shareware

Have you ever purchased a commercial program for $300 or $400 and found you didn't like it or couldn't use it? How long did it take to choose it in the first place? Whose opinion did you rely on?

If you purchase a commercial program that you really don't like, you probably can get your money back—after going to who-knows-what effort. Wouldn't it be better to get a program that a) costs less, b) you could try before you put out any money, and c) you could find no farther away than your own telephone line?

This is the concept behind Shareware. Many of the programs listed and reviewed in this book are Shareware. Shareware does not mean public domain. Shareware programs are commercial programs that feature the advantages listed above. Look at these factors again:

a. *Costs less*. With little or no advertising budget, without a huge staff oriented toward commercial distribution, and generally with a smaller number of people demanding a share of the profits, Shareware developers can cut their costs dramatically and pass the savings on to you.

b. *Try before you buy*. You don't put your money in anyone else's hands until you decide you want the product.

c. *Shop by phone*. Most Shareware can be found on bulletin boards, both local and commercial, or from catalogs who sell disks for nominal fees. With access to a modem or phone, you can choose among thousands of programs from the comfort of your home or office.

Some readers may think, "Sure, there's lots of Shareware and public-domain software around, but it's mostly junk, or something I don't need. I'm too busy to weed out the garbage."

We agree. There is too much out there, and much of it is either substandard or out-dated. Up to now, no one has really attempted to do the weeding for you. That's what this book does. With very few exceptions, the programs in this book are of excellent quality. The exceptions are noted. We have attempted to give you enough information about each program for you to know whether it will be useful to you.

Most software catalogs and BBSs don't have the space to provide a full review of a product. We hope you'll find that this book provides that service. Some catalogs screen programs extensively before listing them, but even so, they contain a great number of programs. How do you know which ones are for you? Again, this book attempts to give you the necessary information.

In this book you'll find essays by some of the professionals in the Shareware market—people like Jim Button, who was one of the originators of the Shareware concept; Bob Wallace, whose PC-Write is one of the most successful Shareware products; and several others in the Shareware marketplace, including major sysops and catalog librarians. These are people who see hundreds of Shareware products every week. We hope you'll find these articles entertaining and informative.

We, the authors of this book, support both traditional commercial software and Shareware. We feel that there is a place for both. But we want to stress that Shareware is an excellent marketing method, nothing more. As it is with any product, success comes to those with good products, good product support, and good timing (*see* Bob Ostrander's article, *Shareware Authorship*, elsewhere in this book).

We've attempted to find some of the best programs—the ones that you'll find useful, stable, and well programmed. Some of those reviewed here are simple utilities; others are full-featured applications that compete with more traditional commercial products for your patronage. Some generate yearly gross sales in the millions. Others are free. But they are all either public-domain or Shareware programs, freely copyable and freely distributed.

Enjoy!

Note on
Shareware Versions

Wherever possible, we have tried to work with the actual version of a product you would get after sending in money for it. This implies that Shareware is a marketing principle, not a way of getting free software. For instance, there are several advantages to registering a Shareware product. In most cases, you get a bound manual. In other cases, you may receive additional modules that enhance the product. In the case of some major products, the bound manuals, quick reference sheets, and additional utilities alone are worth the Shareware price.

In some cases, we have reviewed the Shareware version of a product. We have done this most often when, a) there was little difference between the distributed and the registered versions, and b) we had to work with the distributed versions alone for reasons of time.

We want to stress that we did not review *crippleware*—products that are intentionally limited and do not function fully in their distributed state. Only in rare occasions does the concept of crippleware seem valid, and most people in the Shareware community frown on it. On the other hand, a product enhancement that comes with registration is fine.

A Dissenting Opinion

We believe that Shareware is marketing, that people should treat all Shareware as try-before-you-buy commercial products; that keeping Shareware and not paying for it is software piracy. Although this is the prevailing opinion, some proponents of Shareware say that it should work entirely on the honor principle, and that no coercion should be associated with it. These people see Shareware as an alternative to commercial motivation; primarily as a moral stand, and secondarily as a profit-oriented enterprise.

That debate is beyond the scope of this book. We support people's right to make money from their efforts. At the same time, we support the idea of morally motivated marketing. Each Shareware author is different, and each writes Shareware for slightly different reasons. None, we think, would send back a check sent in appreciation of his work, but some may find money a less compelling motivation than others.

Shareware vs. shareware

You will notice some discrepancy among authors as to whether the word shareware should be capitalized. Some spell it *Shareware,* others *shareware.* We have decided to capitalize the word in an effort to distinguish it as a legitimate type of software. We don't have the term in our Webster's, so we'll just have to decide for ourselves. When some authors do not capitalize the word, it is not a misprint.

Ratings

A lot of people have asked us why we don't rate the programs reviewed in this book. The answer is simple. Out of literally thousands, we consider all the products in this book to be good. We might think they could be better, and we'll say so, but all are useful and among the top programs.

We don't really believe in ratings anyway. Though they are convenient to read, they are often arbitrarily given, and we prefer to give legitimate information over arbitrary numbers. Most major products have an information box along with the review. This box summarizes our feelings about the product.

Limits of Liability and Disclaimer of Warranty

The Authors and Publisher of this book have used their best efforts in preparing the book and the information contained in it. These efforts include the development, research, and testing of the programs to determine their value. The Authors and Publisher make no warranty of any kind, expressed or implied, with regard to the documentation contained in this book. The Authors and Publisher shall not be liable in any event for incidental or consequential damages in connection with, or arising out of, the furnishing, performance, or use of the programs reviewed in this publication.

This Book is not Finished

This book may never be finished. New public-domain and Shareware programs are constantly appearing, while existing products undergo revision. This book must be forever incomplete, but it has been written and placed on the market within a few months—and the products mentioned here are good already. If they change, they will get better. If better programs come out in the meantime, hopefully, we'll include them in an update for you. This book is incomplete for another reason—there are simply too many programs and too many opinions. We may have left out some of your favorite programs, or we may have left out a whole area of programs that you feel is important. If so, you can help—fill out and return the survey included in this book. We'll try to incorporate your input into our next book. If you are a programmer or developer who wants to distribute public domain or Shareware, send it to us. If we like it, we'll try to help distribute it in any way that we can. You can send your programs to:

M&T Books
501 Galveston Drive
Redwood City, CA 94063

Acknowledgments

We would like to thank several great people and organizations that helped us to produce this book. Without them, it would have been nearly impossible. With the help of those that follow, it was merely monumental:

CompuServe for giving us a press account to make it possible to be on-line without being on edge (and also for the introductory subscription included with the book);

GEnie for the same thing as CompuServe—thanks;

PC SIG for their loan of a CD ROM player and their library on same (and other contributions);

Bob Ostrander from Public Brand Software for his advice and significant contributions;

PDN Newsletter (Tim Mullen) for letting us reprint some of the reviews that first appeared in that publication;

Nelson Ford from The Public (Software) Library for allowing us to reprint some of his thoughts;

Vernon Buerg for sending me some great utilities (some his and some not);

Greg Salcedo for becoming our resident Accounting expert and contributing several reviews to the book. Greg is a systems analyst and designer working for Rainier Bank in Seattle. He has been a controller, designer of banking and securities systems, and is also the author of several fine Shareware utilities for Borland's Paradox.

U.S. Robotics for supporting sysops everywhere with generous prices on their modems, and for the loan of a 2,400 baud device that's been indispensable in preparing this book;

Microcom for letting us use their high speed modems;

NEC Home Electronics for helping us obtain decent video display and EGA equipment;

Amdek for a second CD ROM player;

to all the public-domain and Shareware authors, whether or not they contributed directly to this book. It is their work that is represented here;

and to **Andrew Fluegelman** and **Jim Button** for pioneering.

The Royal Hawaiian
Software BBS

Our RHS RBBS is on-line 24 hrs a day, 7 days a week. We want to thank our BBS users. It is from them that we got much of our software early on, and they are still a great source of interesting and unusual programs. Their support has helped us keep going these past few years.

We welcome comments, software, or any interesting dialog. If you have something you want to share with us, please call our board:

RHS RBBS—(808) 871-5651

Settings—8, 1, N (1,200; 2,400; 9600 baud).

Part I

Telecommunications Basics

1

Telecommunications Basics

Starting Out

Finding and using public-domain (PD) and Shareware products always implies
telecommunications. Even though there are some fine catalog services and user
groups that offer these products inexpensively and conveniently, telecommunications is still one of the most common ways to find and obtain PD and Shareware.
At the end of this book, you can read about how to establish service with some
of the large commercial bulletin board systems as well as how to work with local
BBS.

The next few chapters are devoted to information about telecommunications and
related subjects. We've divided these subjects into the following categories:

1.   Telecommunications Basics.

2.   Protocols.

3.   Libraries, Archives, and Zoos.

4.   Trojans and Hacks.

We recommend that you read Chapters 1 and 3. If you are interested in learning more about the growing number of telecommunications protocols in use, read Chapter 2. We recommend that you look over Chapter 2 briefly in any case. Chapter 4 is a discussion of illegal and tampered programs. If you plan to do some downloading, take a look at this chapter. It contains warnings about potentially dangerous programs.

You only need four items to begin telecommunicating: a computer, a modem (modulator-demodulator), communications software, and a telephone line. With these, you can begin to "reach out and touch" a lot of people, ideas, services, *and* a lot of software. If you already own a computer, for less than $200 you can increase your communications gateway to include the world. With these four items and a minimum of knowledge, you gain access to the free interchange of ideas and information only possible in the Age of Communications.

(If you are already pretty knowledgeable about telecommunications, you may want to skip this chapter.)

We assume that you have some information about your computer system already. For more terminology, see the Glossary at the end of this book.

Terms

Modem. A modem is a device that intercepts electronic information from a computer, translates it into a series of sounds, transmits those sounds (usually over a phone line) to another modem which receives the information, translates it back to electronic information, and sends it to the receiving computer. Modem stands for MOdulator-DEModulator because it modulates computer information to telephone sounds, then demodulates it back again.

Serial. Serial ports and serial cables are used to connect modems (and other devices) with computers. During serial data transmission, information is sent in streams or packages of data, like a train with many boxcars. There are various factors such as word length, stop bits, parity, protocol, and baud rate that must be set correctly for serial transmission to occur. You define these settings using a telecommunications software package.

It's not really necessary to understand all the technicalities of parity, stop bits, and word length. In fact, it is fairly technical and has nothing to do with obtaining good PD and Shareware products. As a guideline, however, you will generally set a telecommunications package to either 8 bits, 1 stop bit, No parity; or 7 bits, 1 or 2 stop bits, and Even parity. There are exceptions, but one of these two settings will access any BBS in the country. The most common setting is 8, 1, N which is necessary for transferring files using Xmodem. For more information on Xmodem, see Chapter 2.

Bytes and Bits. A bit is a standard unit of computer measure. It is one instruction, one on/off, one 1 or 0. Eight bits make a byte. A kilobyte is actually 1024 bytes. 64 kilobytes is expressed as 64K. A megabyte is 1,024,000 bytes.

Baud Rate. Baud actually means bits per second. It is a measure of speed like miles per hour. It means the number of bits (see above) that are transferred per second. Baud rates are measures of communications speed, but the actual transfer rate of information may vary with line conditions and other factors. Basically, common baud rates are 300, 1200, and 2400. 1200 is four times faster than 300, and half as fast as 2400. At higher baud rates, bad telephone line quality has greater effect. So if a download is unsuccessful because the line is "dirty," then it might work better at a lower baud rate.

Carrier Tone. When a modem detects that the phone on the other end has made a connection, it sends a high pitched tone called a carrier tone. It then waits for an answering tone. The two tones are high pitched sounds, but when they establish a link, the sound changes to a hissing sound (like white noise or the sound of an empty television station). You know that a modem link has been established when you hear the hissing sound.

Download. Downloading is receiving data from another computer. When you download a file from a BBS, for instance, you move a copy of that file from the BBS storage to your disk drive. In many ways, it is the same as copying the file from one disk to another, but with remote computers doing the copying.

Upload. Uploading is the opposite of downloading. When you send a file from your computer to another system, that is uploading.

Log On. To establish connection with a bulletin board service. This usually involves entering your name and personal password after you have established a connection (see Carrier Tone, above).

Log Off. To end the connection with a bulletin board service.

Logon. The word logon refers to the information you provide a remote connection or service. In most cases, this is your name (or handle) and your password. A handle is a nickname or pseudonym you may use on a bulletin board in place of your real name. Many BBS users like to log on using a handle. The sysop (system operator) of the board generally needs to have a user's real name on file, however.

What is Happening?

When you hook up a modem to a computer, you use a special cable called a serial cable. (*Note*: There are exceptions to this. See the *Glossary* for definitions of Acoustic, Internal, and External modems). This cable is called serial because it passes information in a series of electronic pulses. For instance, when your computer sends information to another computer across the country, it first sends a series of pulses along the serial cable to the modem. The modem then translates the electronic signal to sound pulses which are relayed down the telephone line to a receiving modem. At the other end, the pulses are re-translated and passed on to another computer.

Each telecommunication program has a manual explaining how to use it. Whatever package you use, try to become familiar with its commands and how it handles modem settings and file transfers.

See also duplex, full duplex, and half duplex in the *Glossary*.

A Sample Communication Session

Although it is not feasible to illustrate all the possible events or occurrences that you might experience when working with telecommunications, this section will take you step by step through a typical session of downloading software. For more information on how to sign on to and work with several bulletin board systems, see Section III, Sources.

We've chosen to illustrate a sample session using Qmodem and our RHS RBBS service. The steps illustrated here will be similar to those you will employ if you use other software, or log onto a different service.

To begin, you will want to boot your computer by turning it on. You should also confirm that your modem is on. This won't be necessary if you use an internal modem.

Suppose you keep Qmodem on your C: drive in a directory called \TELECOM.. From the DOS prompt, you would enter:

```
C:>cd \telecom
```

Press Return to complete the operation. Now that you are in the *TELECOM* directory, you want to run the Qmodem program:

```
C:>qmodem
```

Press Return to complete the operation.

After a few seconds, the title screen will display, then the program will load. The first thing that Qmodem (and most telecommunications programs) will do is send some commands to "wake up" the modem. You should see the word "OK" on the screen. This is the standard response from the modem and indicates that it is ready to begin communications.

If this is the first time you have used Qmodem (or any other package), you will want to set up a dialing directory for the numbers you will ordinarily call. You may also want to use the program's setup program to establish defaults for both the appearance of the program (color and other screen settings) as well as the telecommunications defaults (type of modem, speed and other default settings).

To add an entry to the dialing directory in Qmodem, press Alt-D (the Alt key and the D key simultaneously). You will see the default Qmodem Phone Book. Qmodem comes with one entry already filled in. This is the number of Forbin Project bulletin board (the home base, so to speak, of Qmodem).

The new Qmodem phone directory.

```
┌─[ Qmodem Phone Book ]─────────────────────────────────────────────────┐
│ Page  1 of C:\TELECOM\QMODEM1.FON                                      │
│ [D]             Name                    Number       Comm     Script   │
│   1 The Forbin Project PCBoard BBS    1-319-233-6157  1200-8-N-1        │
│   2                                                   1200-8-N-1        │
│   3                                                   1200-8-N-1        │
│   4                                                   1200-8-N-1        │
│   5                                                   1200-8-N-1        │
│   6                                                   1200-8-N-1        │
│   7                                                   1200-8-N-1        │
│   8                                                   1200-8-N-1        │
│   9                                                   1200-8-N-1        │
│  10                                                   1200-8-N-1        │
│                                                                        │
├─[ Options ]───────────────────────────────────────────────────────────┤
│                                                                        │
│        C - Clear Entry(s)          O - Other Information               │
│        E - rEvise Prefix Codes     R - Revise this Screen              │
│        L - Load new FON File     PgUp - Show Previous Page             │
│                                  PgDn - Show Next Page                 │
│                                                                        │
│        Dial Number(s)  -or-  Menu Options  -or-  [Esc] to Exit         │
│        ) -                                                             │
├────────────────────────────────────────────────────────────────────── │
│ ░░░░ Enter number(s) to dial  -or-  Phone Book commands  -or-  [Esc] to Exit ░░░░│
└────────────────────────────────────────────────────────────────────────┘
```

The directory entry for The Forbin Project is typical of the entries in other communication program dialing directories. Here are the different parts of the entry.

Name. The name is entirely up to you. It can be any name which identifies the directory entry for you. You could call it *Fred*, or the *Royal Hawaiian RBBS*, or *My Favorite System*. It doesn't matter.

Number. The number is the full phone number of the service you are calling. This should include the area code and number, and a prefix code if necessary. The prefix codes are defined on a separate screen. Press E to see the list of available codes. In Qmodem, you can define up to 5 different prefix codes for long distance companies or special switchboard dialing sequences. On a normal switchboard, for instance, you may have to dial 9 to access an outside line. You may want to create a prefix code that dials 9, then pauses a specified length of time, then continues with the long distance code, and finally the area code and number. You might assign the prefix character, + to mean *9,* and the - character might be assigned to your long distance codes (with appropriate pauses). A typical dialing string of this type to call our RHS RBBS in Hawaii might read:

```
+,-8088715651
```

Setting prefix definitions in Qmodem.

```
=[ Qmodem Phone Book ]
 Page  1 of C:\TELECOM\QMODEM1.FON
 [D]                 Name             Number       Comm      Script
  1 The Forbin Project PCBoard BBS  1-319-233-6157  1200-8-N-1
  2                                                 1200-8-N-1
  3                                                 1200-8-N-1
  4                                                 1200-8-N-1
  5                                                 1200-8-N-1
  6     =[ Revise Prefix ]
  7     Current Phone Prefixes :
  8
  9     + 1
 10     - 9,,
        !
=[ Optio @
        #

        Enter the Prefix to change or [Esc] to Exit -


        Dial Number(s) -or- Menu Options -or- [Esc] to Exit
        >
```

Communication Settings. Once you have entered the phone number, you will define the way the communications session should be established. You will want to provide numbers for the baud rate, the data bits, the parity, and the stop bits. In most cases, you will be prompted for this information, although, in some packages like Qmodem, you are simply expected to enter it without prompting.

You should enter the maximum baud rate that both your equipment and the remote equipment can handle. If you are unsure, 1200 baud is generally a safe guess. Later, when you log on, you'll learn how to adjust the baud rate while on line, in case you guess wrong.

Many commercial services maintain separate telecommunication lines for different speed access. Many local BBS can handle speeds up to 9600 baud. You can always log on at a lower baud rate, then, when you know what baud rate is best, change the baud rate in your dialing directory to the appropriate value.

In the case of The Forbin Project entry in Qmodem, notice that they have settings of 1200-8-N-1. This means 1200 baud, eight data bits, no parity, and 1 stop bit. Though this sounds confusing, the good news is that this setting will work well for almost every circumstance, and, other than the baud rate, you will probably use these settings all the time.

The completed phonebook entry.

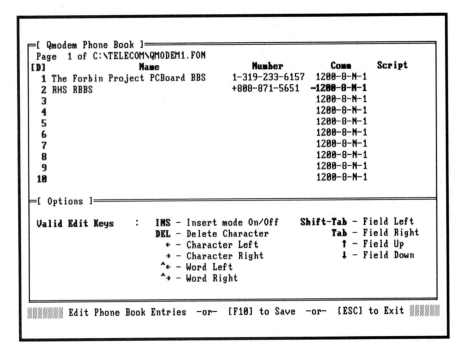

```
=[ Qmodem Phone Book ]══════════════════════════════════════════════
  Page  1 of C:\TELECOM\QMODEM1.FON
[D]              Name                 Number        Comm     Script
  1 The Forbin Project PCBoard BBS  1-319-233-6157  1200-8-N-1
  2 RHS RBBS                        +800-871-5651  -1200-8-N-1
  3                                                 1200-8-N-1
  4                                                 1200-8-N-1
  5                                                 1200-8-N-1
  6                                                 1200-8-N-1
  7                                                 1200-8-N-1
  8                                                 1200-8-N-1
  9                                                 1200-8-N-1
 10                                                 1200-8-N-1

=[ Options ]════════════════════════════════════════════════════════

 Valid Edit Keys   :   INS - Insert mode On/Off   Shift-Tab - Field Left
                       DEL - Delete Character          Tab - Field Right
                         ← - Character Left             ↑ - Field Up
                         → - Character Right            ↓ - Field Down
                        ^← - Word Left
                        ^→ - Word Right

░░░░░░░ Edit Phone Book Entries  -or-  [F10] to Save  -or-  [ESC] to Exit ░░░░░░░
```

Script. Many telecommunications programs include a powerful script programming language. These languages can be used to automate uploads and downloads, call a number at a specific time, or automate your logon (name, password, etc.). If you have script for the number you are entering here, you will want to enter the script name on the phone book entry.

Try creating a new phone book entry. Before you begin, define any special outside codes you may need by pressing *E*, then the code character you want to define, then entering the appropriate information. Remember, long distance access codes will require pauses, and you may need to experiment with them to discover how much of a pause to enter, and where.

1. Press R to Revise this screen.

2. Use the cursor keys to position the cursor at the first blank entry.

3. Type RHS RBBS and press Tab.

   Type in the phone number with any special codes you need. If you are dialing direct and ordinarily need to use a 1 to access long distance, you may need to preface the number with a 1 (or define one of the codes to equal 1).

4. Type any prefix codes, then 808-871-5651. Press Tab

5. If the next section reads 1200-8-N-1, you can leave it alone. If your modem will support a higher baud rate, you could replace the 1200 with another number up to 9600.

6. To tell Qmodem you're finished, press F10 and your new entry will be saved. Press Esc if you wish to back out without saving the new entry.

Now that you have entered a phone number, practice entering some other numbers that you want to use. Next, you will want to dial a number.

To dial a phone number from the dialing directory, press the number associated with that entry, and then press Return. If you can, experiment with a local number--one that won't cost you any money as you learn.

Calling RHS RBBS at 1200 baud.

```
Qmodem SST Version 3.1a Production  Compiled October 31, 1987.
Copy ┌[ Dial / Re-Dial ]══════════════════════════════════════════
     │ Dialing : 8715651        Desc. : rhs-1
Regi │ Script  :   [blank]      Last On : 07/13/88   Total Calls : 12
     │
Only │ Started : 16:46:54       Clock  : 16:46:54   Attempt Num.: 1
Scre │ Modem   :
Scro │ Status  : 53  Seconds remain until Cycle
     ├[ Dialing Queue ]═══════════════════════════════════════════
Qmod │  #   FON    Directory Description              Phone Number
AT E │  1 : 5      rhs-1                              8715651
OK   │  2 :
     │  3 :
     │  4 :
     │  5 :
     │  6 :
     │  7 :
     │  8 :
     │  9 :
     │ 10 :
     └────────────────────────────────────────────────────────────

    ▓▓▓ [C]ycle Next ▓ [K]ill Current ▓ [E]dit Queue ▓ [X]tend Cycle ▓ [Esc] Exit ▓▓▓
```

Once you dial a number, Qmodem displays a screen that helps you see the status of your call. Some programs display more or less information about your call-in-progress. Generally, when you establish a successful connection, you will hear the carrier tones match up, and you will see the word *CONNECT* (or something similar) on your screen.

You will probably have to wait a second or two while the modems talk to each other and establish the connection. You may want to press Return once or twice to help the other system identify yours. This helps the other system see how fast the incoming information is going, helping it determine the baud rate to use.

Next, on a typical system, you should see a prompt asking you for information. If you see odd, senseless characters (know as garbage) on the screen, you may have the wrong baud rate. The exception is Tymnet access. For more on Tymnet, see Section III, Sources, in the section about CompuServe log ons.

If you are connected at the wrong baud rate, chances are you attempted to call in at too high a rate. In most programs, you can still adjust the baud rate. In

Qmodem, you can do so by pressing Alt-P and selecting from the list. Try a baud rate lower than the one you initially tried.

Connected at 1200 baud.

```
Qmodem SST Version 3.1a Production  Compiled October 31, 1987.
Copy┌─[ Dial / Re-Dial ]══════════════════════════════════════════
    │  Dialing : 8715651       Desc. : rhs-1
Regi│  Script  :  [blank]      Last On : 07/13/88   Total Calls : 12
    │
Only│  Started : 16:46:54      Clock  : 16:46:54   Attempt Num.: 1
Scre│  Modem   : CONNECT 1200
Scro│  Status  : Connected!  Press any key to continue!
    ╞═[ Dialing Queue ]════════════════════════════════════════════
Qmod│  #   FON    Directory Description          Phone Number
AT E│  1 : 5     rhs-1                           8715651
OK  │  2 :
    │  3 :
    │  4 :
    │  5 :
    │  6 :
    │  7 :
    │  8 :
    │  9 :
    │ 10 :
    │
    └──────────────────────────────────────────────────────────────
```

Eventually, you will get the correct baud rate and you will then have the opportunity to enter your logon information. Once you have done so, you will be connected with the host computer system.

You should read everything that you see on the screen carefully, and follow any on-screen instructions. Some BBSs require that you register the first time you go on-line. Some systems do not allow you to access files the first time, and you must register and then wait for the sysop to clear you and grant you access to the system.

For the purpose of this run through, suppose you are registered and have normal access privileges on the BBS. You enter your name and password and the system recognizes you. Now you may want to read mail. Bulletin Board Systems get their name from the fact that they are a great way to correspond with one or more people, sometimes in widely separated areas. Reading and answering on-line mail is easy, though the methods vary from one system to another.

Reading mail on the BBS.

```
Caller # 22416  # active msgs: 39  Next msg # 41  Last msg read: 38

USERS: used 176 avl 310  MSGS: used 39 avl 165  MSG REC: used 192 avl 831
Upload disk has 14163968 bytes free

 179 min left

MAIN command <?,A,B,C,D,E,F,H,I,J,K,O,P,Q,R,S,T,U,V,W,X,1,2,3,4,5,6,7>? r;9
Message base MAIN

Msg # 9    Dated 04-15-88 03:42:35  Security: 0
 From: TRENT BLACKBURN
   To: SYSOP
   Re: YOUR BOOK Received 19:06:37 on 06/13/88

HELLO.  I AM IN CHARGE OF SOFTWARE PROCUREMENT FOR A COMPANY HERE IN
SEATLE, AND I JUST WANTED TO THANK YOU FOR WRITING SUCH AN EXCELLENT
REFERENCE ON PUBLIC DOMAIN/SHAREWARE.     THERE ARE NO OTHER BOOKS AROUND
QUITE LIKE IT...PROBABLY GLOSSBRENNER COMES CLOSEST.    ANYWAY, YOU DID
A WONDERFUL JOB AND I HOPE YOU MAKE MILLIONS IN ROYALTIES!  GREETINGS
FROM THE CITY OF RAIN.

More [Y],N,NS,RE,T,C? -
 ANSI   ONLINE   1200-8-N-1 ║ [Home]=? ║ ◄=◄ 8        ʃ        ↑    ║ 00:00:53
```

Often you will want to save the messages you receive. All communication programs have a "capture" mode which will save the activity in your session to a file. If you want to save your mail or other messages, find the command to turn capture on. Read the message on screen, then turn capture off to end the process. In Qmodem, pressing Ctrl-Home toggles capture mode on and off.

You will need to provide a filename for the captured information. Be sure to use a name that will have meaning for you. You can use people's names or dates to identify messages, like *Joe9.txt* or *0914Gen.txt*.

Once you finish with the mail and other messages, you will probably want to download some files. Find the file section of the service you are using. See Part II, Sources, for more information on finding the file area on several different types of service.

Once in the file area of an on-line service, you can list the available files. Each service has its own commands to control listing files. Follow the menus or prompts, or read help files to learn how to list them. There is some service specific information about listing files in Part III, Sources.

Listing files on screen.

```
PCQUOT.ARC      104449   07-09-88   Create sales quotes for salesman (IBM)
$TOKTRX2.ARC    179281   07-09-88   portfolio manager for PC
ESTIMATE.ARC     50177   07-09-88   construction estimation program
CONTRAR.ARC     147457   07-09-88   stock portfolio manager
EP25.ARC        164865   07-09-88   project management program for PC
1040.ARC        293377   07-09-88   1040 tax program for PC
EZFORMSX.ARC    274177   07-09-88   forms creation system for PC
ALL-TSS.ARC      96257   07-09-88   directory list for programmers bbs
EQUIP.COM         3073   07-07-88   Simpler equipment reporter/checker
CHECKIT.ARC      31745   07-07-88   Exc. listing of your equip. options
BUTRFLY.GIF      75777   07-07-88   Beautiful GIF pic of butterfly
VGIF34.ARC       43089   07-07-88   Fast, flexible GIF viewer for EGA/VGA
SORRE28.ARC     103681   07-03-88   Newest Version game of SORRY. GREAT!
SOUND1.SIT         513   06-30-88   bRoyal Hawaiian Microphone file
MR200.ARC       221101   06-29-88   Mind Reader W.P. ver. 2.0 (IBM)
PFROI.ARC       190858   06-29-88   Portfolio Manager (IBM)
MAHJONGG.ARC     41089   06-28-88   ega-mahjong
NP.ARC          115713   06-24-88   notepad, simple database (DOS)
NYET.ARC         18433   06-24-88   version of Tetris (USSR) game DOS
MATHLAB.ARC      81921   06-24-88   <description unavailable>
COMIC.ARC       121857   06-24-88   fine EGA game for PCs
MARIE2.PQC       36353   06-23-88   PART 2 OF MARIE1.PQC
BANKING.ARC      96001   06-22-88    home finance for 1 check acct.
MORE: [Y],N,NS, or file(s) to download? -
 ANSI    ONLINE    1200-8-N-1 ▓ [Home]=? ▓ ◄=◄ 8        ⌐          ↑   ▓ 00:01:58
```

Remember, you can quickly capture a file listing by turning the capture mode on before the list begins to appear on your screen. You can then log off, examine the listing with an ASCII editor or word processor, pick the files you want, then return to the system to download them. This saves on-line time. Some systems have their file listings already in a formatted file. If you can download one of these files right away, you may be able to examine the available files in a word processor or database. The best way to do it is to use a database system so you can select the files you want, sort them, print them out, and otherwise manipulate the list.

Back to the on-line system: When you know the file you want, enter its name or identifying number and wait until the remote system tells you the file is ready for downloading, then initiate the file transfer. Qmodem (and several other programs) use the PgDn key to start a download. You will probably have to select the appropriate transfer protocol. Xmodem or Xmodem CRC are safe choices when in doubt.

Starting to download NYET.ARC using Y-Modem protocol.

```
BUTRFLY.GIF     75777   07-07-88  Beautiful GIF pic of butterfly
VGIF34.ARC      43009   07-07-88  Fast, flexible GIF viewer for EGA/VGA
SORRE20.ARC    103681   07-03-88  Newest Version game of SORRY. GREAT!
SOUND1.SIT        513   06-30-88  bRoyal Hawaiian Microphone file
MR200.ARC      221101   06-29-88  Mind Reader W.P. ver. 2.0 (IBM)
PFROI.ARC      190058   06-29-88  Portfolio Manager (IBM)
MAHJONGG.ARC    41089   06-28-88  ega-mahjong
NP.ARC         115713   06-24-88  notepad, simple database (DOS)
NYET.ARC        18433   06-24-88  version of Tetris (USSR) game DOS
MATHLAB.ARC     81921   06-24-88  <description unavailable>
COMIC.ARC      121857   06-24-88  fine EGA game for PCs
MARIE2.PQC      36353   06-23-88  PART 2 OF MARIE1.PQC
BANKING.ARC     96001   06-22-88   home finance for 1 check acct.
MORE: [Y],N,NS, or file(s) to download? nyet.arc
Searching for file...
Non-ASCII required for nyet.arc

Protocol:
A)scii, X)modem, C)Xmodem/CRC,
X)ermit, Y)modem, W)xmodem, N)one? y
FILE SIZE:  19 blocks  18433 bytes
Transfer time: 3 min, 6 sec
YMODEM SEND of nyet.arc ready.  <Ctrl X> aborts
-
 ANSI    ONLINE   1200-8-N-1 ▓ [Home]=? ▓ ◄=◄ 8       Г      ↑  ▓ 00:02:34
```

Entering the name and path of the file to download.

```
BUTRFLY.GIF     75777   07-07-88  Beautiful GIF pic of butterfly
VGIF34.ARC      43009   07-07-88  Fast, flexible GIF viewer for EGA/VGA
SORRE20.ARC    103681   07-03-88  Newest Version game of SORRY. GREAT!
S╒[ Download File (receive) ]═══════════════════════════file
M│                                                       (IBM)
P│
M│
  ╒[ Download File Allocation ]══════════════════════════════
  > C:\ARC\NYET.ARC─



B│                                                       acct.
M│
S│
N│

Protocol:
A)scii, X)modem, C)Xmodem/CRC,
X)ermit, Y)modem, W)xmodem, N)one? y
FILE SIZE:  19 blocks  18433 bytes
Transfer time: 3 min, 6 sec
YMODEM SEND of nyet.arc ready.  <Ctrl X> aborts

▓▓▓▓▓▓▓ Enter/Edit Filename, [+] to Search Screen -or- [Esc] to Exit ▓▓▓▓▓▓▓
```

Finally, you should enter the filename (and path, if necessary) of the file you want to save. It does not always have to have the same name as the file you are downloading although generally you will want to use the same name.

Most programs will show you information about the progress of your download, any errors that occur, and sometimes the approximate length of time it will take. One piece of information you may find useful is the number of blocks in the file.

The download in progress at 9600 baud using Y-Modem 1K blocks.

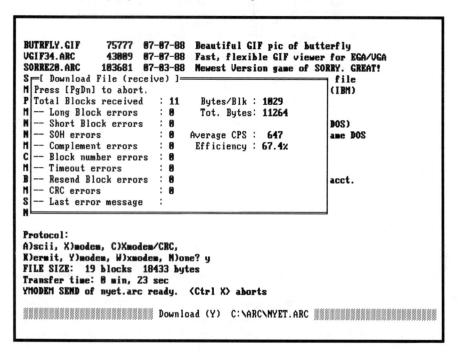

Blocks are discrete portions of the file that are sent one at a time. Remember the definition for serial transmission. The blocks are like the boxcars in the transmission. Each one is bordered by a "coupling" of information that identifies it and helps the receiving computer to determine if all of the block arrived in good order or if there was a problem. Block size varies with different protocols, so don't be surprised if you try a download with Xmodem and it contains many more blocks than a similarly sized file downloaded with Ymodem, which uses larger blocks.

At any rate, if you are downloading a file containing 150 blocks, and your telecommunication program displays the number of blocks received, that is a good way to tell if the download is almost complete.

Exiting Qmodem.

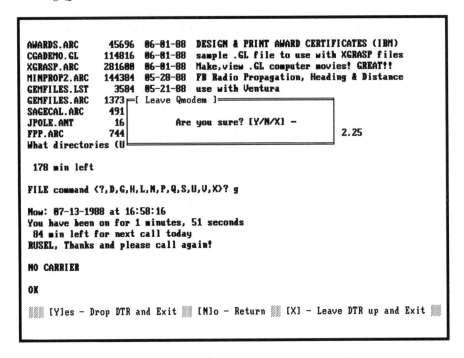

```
AWARDS.ARC      45696   06-01-88   DESIGN & PRINT AWARD CERTIFICATES (IBM)
CGADEMO.GL     114816   06-01-88   sample .GL file to use with XGRASP files
XGRASP.ARC     281600   06-01-88   Make,view .GL computer movies! GREAT!!
MINPROP2.ARC   144384   05-28-88   FB Radio Propagation, Heading & Distance
GEMFILES.LST     3584   05-21-88   use with Ventura
GEMFILES.ARC     1373 ┌─[ Leave Qmodem ]════════════════════════════┐
SAGECAL.ARC       491 │                                             │
JPOLE.ANT          16 │          Are you sure? [Y/N/X] —             │
FPP.ARC           744 │                                             │  2.25
What directories (U └─────────────────────────────────────────────┘

  178 min left

FILE command (?,D,G,H,L,N,P,Q,S,U,V,X)? g

Now: 07-13-1988 at 16:58:16
You have been on for 1 minutes, 51 seconds
 84 min left for next call today
RUSEL, Thanks and please call again!

NO CARRIER

OK

▓▓▓ [Y]es - Drop DTR and Exit ▓▓▓ [N]o - Return ▓▓▓ [X] - Leave DTR up and Exit ▓▓▓
```

Generally, when the download is complete, you will return to the host where you left off. You can then download another file, list files again, return to a message section, or even log off. Typical log off commands are *bye* and *g* (for goodbye).

To exit Qmodem, press Alt-X. Other programs have their own exit commands.

That's about all there is to a typical communication session. The specific commands will vary from one program to another, but the basic tasks and operations will remain the same.

2

The
Protocols of
Telecommunications

This chapter is for those who are new to telecommunications, or whose understanding of file protocols and telecommunications terminology is hazy.

In order to take full advantage of the services mentioned in this book and obtain free software and Shareware, you must be able to "download" to your computer. The term "download" means to transfer a file from a host computer, like a BBS or commercial service (CompuServe, GEnie, Delphi, Source, etc.) to your home computer. The transfer is done by sending the file data in a special way so that your modem program can decipher it and save it to your computer. Depending on the communication program you are using, you may have several protocols available.

ASCII

An ASCII file transfer is the equivalent of typing information from one system to another. The information in the file must be in ASCII (American Standard for Coded Information Interchange) format. ASCII files are sometimes called text files and often have the file extensions *.TXT* or *.ASC* (sometimes *.DOC*, although this extension is also used by many word processors for proprietary files). Most program files are binary files, not ASCII text files, and cannot be transferred using the ASCII file protocol. Another disadvantage of ASCII file transfers is that there is no error checking. So if there is a transmission problem during the transfer and a portion of the file gets garbled, the host will not re-send the damaged portion of the file and the transfer will be inaccurate.

So what is the advantage of the ASCII file transfer? ASCII file transfer is easy to use, and with most terminal programs, you can usually see the data as it's being received from (or sent to) the host computer. ASCII file transfer is necessary when uploading and downloading text messages from BBSs on commercial systems like MCI mail.

As an example, suppose you are a traveling representative who uses a portable computer to communicate with the home office via MCI mail. The most efficient and cost-effective way to use MCI is to type your message off line using your favorite word processor, then save the file as an ASCII file. Now, call the service and transfer the file to the host using the ASCII method. Likewise, if the home office has left a message for you and your terminal does not support screen capturing, you can use the ASCII file transfer method to capture all the incoming data, save it to disk, and read it at your convenience.

Xmodem

It was a quick hack I threw together, very unplanned (like everything I do), to satisfy a personal need to communicate with some other people. ONLY the fact that it is done in 8/77, and that I put it in the public domain immediately, made it become the standard that it is . . . People who suggest I make SIG-NIFICANT changes to the protocol, such as 'full duplex,' 'multiple outstanding blocks,' 'multiple destinations,' etc. etc., don't understand that the incredible simplicity of the protocol is one of the reasons it survived to this day in as many machines and programs as it may be found in!

—*Ward Christiansen*

Xmodem is a block-oriented error checking protocol. It (along with several variants) is the most widely used telecommunications protocol. Xmodem transfers one file at a time, and can handle any file type, including *EXE* and *COM* type files. This protocol was released into the public domain over ten years ago by its creator, Ward Christiansen. It uses two-way communications and either a checksum or cyclic redundancy check (CRC) for error checking.

How does checksum work? The transmitter takes the data and divides it into 128-byte pieces and places them in Xmodem packets. A packet contains a header character, followed by a sequence number, a complement of the sequence number, 128-byte data elements, and a one-byte sum of all the data bytes in the packet. The receiver then receives the packet and compares the sum sent with the packet to the sum it calculates. If they are not the same, the receiver sends a message to the transmitter, to re-send the packet.

CRC is very similar to checksum. Instead of using an 8-bit checksum, it uses a 16 bit CRC character (CRC/16). The CRC/16 algorithm treats all 1,024 data bits in an Xmodem packet as an integer, multiplies that integer by 2^{16} and then divides that 1,040th bit number by a 17 bit prime number. The lower order 16 bits of the remainder becomes the 16 bit CRC. CRC is a newer and more effective error checker, and should be selected when available over the older checksum method.

Xmodem requires transfers to be performed with 8 data bits, 1 stop bit, and no parity. If you have your terminal program set to any other setting, Xmodem will not work. Fortunately, most terminal programs will allow you to change the settings, or will change the settings for you.

Some commercial systems like CompuServe, GEnie, etc. have trouble meeting the timing sequences of Xmodem. This can result in abnormal file transfer interruptions which can be annoying, especially if you are downloading a very long file and the transfer is aborted half-way through. Xmodem has no feature to allow you to pick up where you left off in the transfer, so if this happens, the only thing you can do is start the transfer again. Some communication programs, like Procomm, have "relaxed" Xmodem settings which allow longer delays and decreases the "time out" errors primarily responsible for abnormal terminations.

Modem7

Modem7 is a variant of Xmodem. It allows batch transfers of files. Typing the file name, *ANYFILE*, instructs the host system to send all files called *ANYFILE* with any extension. This is accomplished because the host sends the file name before sending the file.

Telink

Telink is also an Xmodem/Modem7 variant which adds the file size and creation date information to the file that is being transferred from the host system. You can usually find Telink on FIDO BBSs. It also allows batch transfers.

Ymodem

Ymodem is another Xmodem variant. Its biggest advantage is that it supports longer data blocks of 1024 bytes, and thus speeds up the data transfer time. Some versions of Ymodem will also allow batch transfers.

WXmodem

WXmodem or Windowed Xmodem is another variant of Xmodem. It provides a sliding window protocol and other features like Kermit discussed below. WXmodem can be found on Peoplelink Information Service and newer versions of RBBS-PC.

Zmodem

Zmodem is another derivative of Xmodem. It sends the whole file in one continuous stream. At the end of the transmission it will re-send any part of the file transmission that was bad. In addition, Zmodem can restart a file transfer at the point of failure. Zmodem can be very fast, but is not available on very many systems.

Kermit

Kermit is a packet-oriented protocol developed at Columbia University and is available on many different types of systems. Kermit uses a technique called 8th-bit quoting which allows it to transfer binary files between 7- and 8-bit systems. In some versions, Kermit can support multiple file transfers.

The latest version of this protocol includes data compression, file attributes, and sliding windows. The most significant of these features is the sliding windows.

A sliding window allows full duplex transmissions—in other words, you can send and receive data at the same time. The Xmodem type protocols all use half duplex transmissions—they must wait between each block sent, for a reply from the host, which wastes a lot of time. Full duplex protocols can send a continuous stream of data while receiving replies concurrently—greatly increasing file transfer efficiency. So far, sliding window Kermit is available on The Source, TCOMM BBS, and PC-HOST BBS. Mainframe versions are under development and should be available soon.

CompuServe B

This protocol is available on the CompuServe Information Service and is similar to the Xmodem family. It sends 512 byte blocks and has built-in delay settings which help eliminate the time out errors that occur when using Xmodem with this system. This protocol asks for the computer's file name, and then sends the file.

Other Error Correction and File Compression Protocols

The information in this section is technical, contains more than its share of telecom buzz words, and is of interest to people who want to use high speed telecommunications—particularly those who are in the market to buy a modem that can handle transfers of 2400 baud or greater. **None of the information in this section is necessary to make effective use of public domain and Shareware.** *It is only placed here to help those who need this information. Further, this situation is constantly changing, and standards are being set, new protocols being developed, even as you read this!*

Higher baud rates have demanded more sophisticated technology. Modem manufacturers and telecommunication experts are continually trying to find ways to transfer data faster and more accurately. At faster speeds, errors creep in, so the standards that worked well enough with 300 and 1200 baud sessions start to fray a little at 2400 and above. Basic telecommunications standards are set by the CCITT (the International Telegraph and Telephone Consultation Committee), as close to a governing body as you can find in the telecommunications arena. The standard for the 2400 baud devices outlines the way 2400 baud devices send and receive data. It is called V.22bis, and it is universally adopted. This means that any 2400 baud modem should be able to communicate with any other.

While the "experts" once claimed that no one could reliably telecommunicate at speeds greater than 300 baud, they have been proved wrong time after time. However, the capacity of the current technology to handle even higher rates seems to be eroding. Above 2400 baud is the next emerging option, the 9600 baud modem. Unfortunately, the CCITT standard for 9600 baud communications, V.32, is expensive to implement, and modems adopting that standard cost in the range of $2000. Compare that to the Hayes compatible 2400 baud modems which can be found for not much more than $200, and you might ask yourself, "Who needs it?"

An earlier 9600 baud standard was V.29, but that standard is somewhat limited. For one thing, it is a half-duplex standard when used on normal dial-up two-wire telephone lines. This means it can only transmit information in one direction at a time. At higher speeds, half-duplex communications are inefficient. Special dedicated four-wire lines could be used for full-duplex operations, but the majority of modem users want to use normal phone lines.

One of the most important innovations currently available is MNP (Microcom Network Protocol) from Microcom. Although there are several error checking protocols and other schemes to add advanced features to modems, MNP has become the de facto standard using the V.29 protocol at high speeds—at least for now. MNP allows modems to simulate some of the functions of the more expensive V.32 modems at half the price, or less. MNP actually comes in several versions ranging from MNP Class 1 to MNP Class 6.

MNP Class 1 is a very simple scheme that does little. It's basic level error checking operates in half-duplex (one direction at a time) and is not commonly found on modems in the United States.

MNP Class 2 is a substantial improvement over Class 1 because it allows full-duplex transmission, causing significant improvements to the data throughput. Class 2 is also relatively inexpensive to implement.

MNP Class 3 does something significant, though somewhat technical. It turns the asynchronous communication into a synchronous one, using a technique called synchronous framing (see asynchronous in the Glossary). Thus, the communication goes asynch-synch-asynch as the modems strip the start and stop bits from the transmission, resulting in data throughput improvements. According to Microcom, using synchronous framing can improve the effective baud rate by up to 20%. For instance, a 2400 baud connection might achieve real rates of around 2600 bits per second (bps). The importance of this method is that it improves reliability, speed, and efficiency.

MNP Class 4 uses synchronous framing and adds Adaptive Packet Assembly and Data Phase Optimization. Adaptive Packet Assembly involves the size of the packages (remember the boxcars?) that are sent during transmissions. If the quality of the telephone line is very good, larger packets will be assembled and sent. If there is a lot of excess noise on the line, smaller packages are sent. By sending smaller packets on noisier lines, fewer errors will be able to creep in, and fewer retransmissions will be required. Data Phase Optimization is Microcom's fancy term for an improved protocol that requires less information to be sent with each data packet.

Microcom Network Protocols Class 1 through Class 4 are in the public domain, and any modem manufacturer can use them. The remaining MNP classes are not in public domain, but several modem manufacturers have licensed them.

MNP Class 5 adds data compression which uses a sophisticated algorithm to reduce the amount of data that is sent over the communications lines. The data compression routines actually adapt to data content, to achieve up to 2 to 1 compression on text files (though somewhat less on binary files). Compression combines duplicate characters (like tabs and spaces) while taking very common characters (the letter e, for instance) and changing them to something that requires less time to transmit. At their most efficient, Class 5 modems using data compression can achieve effective transfer rates of up to 19,200 bps when connected at 9,600 baud. However, this is a best-case scenario, and is probably not achieved in practice very often.

MNP Class 6 includes all that has preceded it, but also adds something called Statistical Duplexing, Microcom's proprietary method of simulating full duplex operations by quickly switching the direction of the transfer. Also known as "Ping Ponging," this method is used by other modem manufacturers like Hayes, Multi-Tech, Telebit, and others, though it is given different names by different companies. Using the Ping Pong technique, terminals and computers think they are communicating simultaneously in both directions because the modems switch directions so quickly.

Another significant improvement in MNP Class 6 is Universal Link Negotiation which allows MNP modems to connect at the highest common speed automatically, and either adjust upward or downward depending on line conditions. Other MNP classes also perform some upward and downward adjustments, but Universal Link Negotiation allows very sophisticated adjustments, not just of speed, but of modulation techniques as well. Universal Link Negotiation also allows non-MNP modems to connect with MNP modems without problems. In fact, the RHS RBBS (871-5651) has been using a Microcom AX/9624c Class 6 modem for several months, allowing other MNP modems to establish "reliable" high-speed connections while ordinary modems connect as usual.

While MNP is by far the most common new protocol, and is supported in modems from Microcom (of course), Racal-Vadic, Ven-Tel, AT&T, Concord, Codex, US Robotics, and many more, there are other protocols. One of the most efficient is called V.32, but V.32 modems are very expensive (in the $2000 range).

Another protocol is used by Hayes Microcomputer Products, Inc. in their V-Series modems. This protocol uses a powerful synchronous protocol (LAPB or Link Access Procedure Balanced) and adds start and stop bits to it using Hayes' AFT (Asynchronous Framing Technique). Although this may seem to perform the opposite function as that of the synchronous framing technique of the MNP protocols, there are some powerful technical arguments for the adoption of the LAPB and AFT combination. Hayes also has its own data compression techniques and other enhancements, making their V-Series modems powerful. One drawback is that Hayes' lack of support of MNP means the V-Series modems won't take advantage of MNP enhancements, and vice versa. So owners of Hayes V-Series modems can't take advantage of their modem's special features when connected with any other modem. Nor can owners of MNP modems take advantage of all their special features unless the other modem has the same class of MNP implemented.

When it comes down to it, most people won't need to communicate at 9600 baud (or higher). Only people who have heavy telecommunications needs over long distances will benefit enough to make a current purchase desirable at this time. This includes heavy ":point to point:" users, like businesses that regularly communicate data from one office to another; or heavy BBS users who connect via long distance to upload and download files. Typically, these users will find that files requiring, say, 20 minutes to download at 1200 baud, will download in a couple of minutes or less (depending on data compression and other factors). Of course, there are those of us who just want to have the most current technology to work with. But trying to keep up with telecommunications technology over the next few years promises to be an expensive proposition.

Don't look for the "packet switching" dial-up networks like Tymnet and Telenet to provide 9600-baud service any time soon either. This means that most people using CompuServe, GEnie, MCI Mail, and other major services will not benefit from the new technologies, at least not immediately. Probably these major services will move up to 9600 baud and above some day—when there are universal standards and a big enough installed base of high-speed users. (There are some test installations in major cities; you can check with the service you use for availability.)

Unless you really need a high-speed modem, a 2400-baud modem probably offers the best price-to-performance ratio at the time this book is being updated. On the other hand, I don't mean to imply that there is anything wrong with wanting one if the 9600 baud devices. I'd take one any time I could get one. They really perform well, and if it's something you can use, don't be shy. Get one. If you don't really need it though, you might prefer to save your cash for something else. Certainly there will always be something else. In computers, that's a given.

3

The Facts About Archives, Libraries, Zoos, and Squeezed Files

Most of the files that you see on public information services like CompuServe, GEnie, and BBSs have been transformed by using one of the public-domain or Shareware utilities like SQueeze, ARChive, LiBRary, or ZOO. This transformation fills a two-fold purpose: to compress the files and thereby minimize downloading time; and to combine several files into one easy-to-manage file. Any file that you obtain in a transformed state must be restructured to its original form before it can be used. Each transformed file is identified by a unique file type extension (the file type extension consists of the last three letters after the dot or period (.) in the file name). These file type extensions are:

.?Q?   for squeezed files (the middle letter of the file type is a Q, the other letters can be anything)

.LBR   for files libraried with *LU.EXE*

.ARC   for files archived with *ARC.EXE* or *PKARC.EXE*

For instance, you can easily identify an *ARC* file by its extension, e.g. *filename.arc*. Similarly, a squeezed file would appear as *filename.dqc* or *filename.cqm*.

SQPC.COM and *NUSQ.COM* are used in conjunction with each other. *NUSQ.COM* is used to unsqueeze, or expand files that have the letter Q in the middle of the file type. These files have been squeezed or compressed with a program called *SQPC.COM*, or some similar program. By using this type of program, a file can be reduced from 5 percent to 60 percent of its original size, depending on the distribution of data in the file.

LU and its relatives (*LUU*, *LUE*, *LUP*, *LUT*, *LU86*, and *LAR*) maintain libraries of files. Since *LU* programs don't squeeze files as they are placed in a library, most people squeeze the files using *SQPC* before placing them into the library. Otherwise, library files behave pretty much like *ARC* files (below).

ARC is used to create and maintain file archives. An archive may contain one or more files that are grouped together into one big file, and may be separated at a later time, intact. *ARC* will automatically compress the files it archives, and will expand them during extraction. You can also add comments to an archive entry, check the integrity of an archive, and benefit from other valuable utilities that are not found in library programs.

ZOO is a newer archiving program similar to *ARC*, but the archive files it creates are not compatible with *ARC*. *ZOO* will sometimes produce a smaller archive file than *ARC* and execution is faster than *ARC*. (Please refer to the reviews that follow). *ZOO* can also produce archive files with long path names in them (directory names, as well as file names).

Archives and Libraries can also be extremely useful for archiving unused programs, as well as backing up hard disks. For example, suppose you use a presentation manager once a month for producing a single graph from a Lotus 1-2-3 worksheet. And let's say that the presentation manager takes up about 1 megabyte of disk space. Now, you have three options:

1.   You can erase the subdirectory and the presentation manager and re-install it every time you need it.

2.   You can leave it installed on your disk; but it takes up a megabyte of your disk space which could be used for other things during the course of a month.

58

3.   You can archive the directory into one single file which may take up 40 percent less disk space, or approximately 400k; this option, though a compromise, is an equitable solution, since it frees up disk space and at the same time reduces the amount of time needed to re-install the presentation manager once a month.

SQPC ver. 1.31
Vernon Buerg

SQPC is file compression utility. It creates a compressed (SQueezed) copy of a file. With this version, you run the program from the DOS command line and specify a file name which may include the drive letter, path name, and wild card characters. The resulting output file contains a *Q* in the middle of the file type. For instance, *filename.exe* becomes *filename.eqe* and *filename.doc* becomes *filename.dqc*. SQPC can compress a text file by up to 60 percent and binary *EXE* files by 10-20 percent. Using a */D* in the SQPC command instructs the program to delete the original file after it has been squeezed. For very small files, the file size may actually be larger than the original file, because decoding information is stored in the file.

Although this program works very well, it is somewhat outdated and is usually passed over in favor of *ARC* or *ZOO*. It may be useful, however, if you have a single, moderately large file that you would like to reduce before sending over a modem and you don't feel like creating an archive for it. Since SQPC is so easy to use, you can compress a file or two on the fly without having to remember any commands or digging through a manual.

NUSQ ver. 1.10
Cliff Sharp

NUSQ is a utility for expanding squeezed files (those that have a *Q* in the middle of their file types) into their original uncompressed state. These files have usually been squeezed by either the SQPC or NSQ programs.

The program is written entirely in assembly language. As with LU86, this program has an interesting history of development, which began with a C version that was written by Richard Greenlaw. This version was then converted to work with several different processors.

The program has two operating modes, Command and Interactive. In Command mode, a single instruction is passed from the command line (the DOS prompt) which invokes NUSQ. The Command mode will support wild cards in the file names which makes it especially useful for multiple squeezed files.

In Interactive mode, the program allows you to specify only those files which you want processed without reloading the program each time into memory. In other words, the program executes one command, and waits for another. The program does have built-in overwrite protection, which prompts you before it overwrites an already existing file. For those of you who don't like this feature, instructions are provided detailing how to disable the feature using the DOS DEBUG program.

The manual is adequate and provides examples of how to use the program. Overall, the program performs satisfactorily.

This program is a must for those programs which have been squeezed or compressed with either SQ or NSQ. Out of all the versions tested, this one appears to be the most stable and bug free.

LU86 ver. 4.05

Library Utility 86 (LU86) is a program that allows you to combine multiple files into one library file. It does not compress or reduce the size of the files placed into the library, nor does it contain any bells or whistles. This is understandable, considering the long history that the LU format has had and how this evolution has spawned the newer utilities like *ARC* and *ZOO*.

Gary Novosielski designed the LU format and wrote the first programs supporting the LBR files. He has continued to support and improve the LU format by distributing a file of the official LU format definition. However, this program had its beginnings in the UNIX program *LAR.C*. Tom Jennings translated the program into a C language that MS-DOS machines could understand and called it *LU.C*. Paul Homchick, taking this program as a base, revised it to make LU86.

Running this program is pretty straightforward. At the DOS command line you type:

```
A>lu86 [option] [library file name{.lbr}] [file]
```

Options for this program include:

- displaying a directory list of a library.

- extracting all files from a library.

- extracting only specified files from a library.

- adding or creating a library—this option also allows you to add files to an existing library; the date and time stamp of the file is also read and included in the archive.

- deleting files from the library.

- reorganizing a library—this option creates a new library file with only the active members of the old library; reorganization gets rid of space lost from delete and duplicate file name update operations.

The library file name can be any valid DOS file name. If you leave the extension off, it will automatically default to *LBR*.

File... represents the file names of the files to be added or manipulated by the library program.

With the newer versions of this program (Version 4.0 or later), a CRC (Cyclic Redundancy Check) is performed when a file is added to or removed from a library. If the CRC fails, a warning message is displayed, indicating that the library file may be corrupt.

This version of LU86 does support wild card type file definitions (i.e. *.exe*). The program is rather slow. It took the program a full twelve seconds to archive a 57k ASCII document on an IBM AT. Another annoying feature requires you to tell the program how many slots it should reserve for the library. On a lengthy file list, this can be quite a bother since you have to count the number of files to be added to the library. If you miscalculate, you have to reorganize the library before you can continue and update the the library with the remaining files.

The documentation that is included with this release is adequate, but may prove to be a bit much for the computer novice, since the document is rather technical.

This library utility is about the best available for handling LBR files. However, you should think twice about adopting the LBR file format for your archiving needs, or using this utility for everyday archiving purposes since it is slow and does not provide the compression and reduction features that the ARC-type utilities provide. In addition, LBR files are not efficient and require maintenance when they are updated.

ARC ver. 5.21

System Enhancement Associates
21 New Street
Wayne, NJ 07470

Shareware: the messages states, "If you like this program, and find it of use, then your contribution will be appreciated. You may not use this product in a commercial environment or governmental organization without paying a license fee of $35. Site licenses and commercial distribution licenses are available. A program disk and printed documentation are available for $50."

ARC is designed to help you create and maintain file archives, and is the most widely used program of its kind. An archive is a group of files, often squeezed, and then placed into one file in such a way that the original files may be recovered when needed. ARC differs from other library utilities, such as LU86, in that it compresses the files being archived so that the resulting file takes up a minimum amount of space. ARC uses three storage methods when files are added to an archive:

1. no compression; the file is stored as is.

2. repeated character compression where repeated sequences of the same byte value are collapsed into a three-byte code value.

3. dynamic Lempel-Zev compression where the file is stored as a series of variable size bit codes which represent character strings.

ARC determines which storage method is best, depending on the type of file being archived.

ARC is invoked from the DOS command line in the following format:

```
A>ARC [options] [archive name] [files...]
```

The options for ARC include:

- adding and deleting files from an archive.

- extracting files from the archive.

- listing and running programs from an archive.

- testing and converting an archive.

- encrypting and decrypting an archive along with other options that make ARC more versatile than other library utility type programs.

Archive name represents the name of the resulting archive file. If you leave the extension off, the program will automatically place the ARC extension on the file name.

Files... represents the files you wish to add or manipulate in the archive.

The manual included with the package is quite complete and describes each feature in detail. The only feature that is missing is an interactive version of ARC that would allow you to perform several archiving tasks without having to rerun the program for each new command.

This program is Shareware, and contributions are requested from the general public. Government and commercial users are required to pay a registration fee of $35.

ARC is the most widely used archiving utility available today. You'll find it in every kind of BBS. ARC may not be the best, but as the the most widely accepted archive utility, it is a must-have program for anyone interested in PD and Shareware programs.

PKARC ver. 3.5 *

PKWARE, Inc.
7032 Ardara Avenue
Glendale, WI 53209

Shareware: Similar agreement to ARC (above); $20 contribution; $45 gets you one free update.

Undoubtedly, PKARC is one of the fastest archiving utilities available today. It is also quickly becoming the standard archive utility and is supported by more front-end utilities and other Shareware enhancement products than any other archiving system. Similar in nature to the ARC program described in this chapter, PKARC boasts one of the highest compression ratios using "Enhanced Dynamic Ziv-Lempel-Welch Crunching and Squashing." In addition, the program supports archive commenting (which allows you to enter comments about a file being archived), 16-bit Cyclic Redundancy Check (CRC), configuration file option, multitasking and network support, and a superior file buffering system.

Though PKARC uses its own compression and squashing scheme to provide up to a 50 percent increase in compression when compared with ARC, it is still upwardly compatible with ARC files. Unfortunately (some may say fortunately), the extraction program, PKXARC, is not included as a part of the main program, and must be run separately. PKARC is invoked from the DOS command line:

```
A>PKARC [compatibility options] [options] [archive name]
[file name...]
```

The compatibility options allow the archive to be compatible with ARC. The format and choices regarding these compatibility options can be confusing for a novice and are the program's major pitfall. And since PKARC creates the same file type extension as ARC (.ARC), it can be even more frustrating for the user who downloads a file thinking that ARC will unpack it, only to find an error message about a bad file header. We recommend that the author use a different file type extension so that users know that an archive is packed using the superior PKARC format (some people use .ARK or .PKA extensions to label archives

---

* **Note:** The newest version of PKARC is 3.6 There are some definite enhancements to the product. However, if you use one of the popular front-end products like ARCTOOLS, ARCMASTER, LARK, NARC, or PKXTRACT, you may want to be sure that you have an updated version of the front end before switching from PKARC 3.5 to version 3.6. PKARC also comes with a MAKESFX program that will create self-extracting archives (see SEZ later in this chapter).

created with the squashing algorithm—the only one not compatible with ARC). Some systems, such as GEnie, have banned all archives created using PKARC's squashing compression to avoid confusion.

The documentation provided with the program is technical and assumes that the user is already familiar with archives.

Despite the compatibility problems, PKARC is a fast and efficient archiving utility. This program would be a welcome addition to anyone's collection of archiving tools. And since PKXARC is compatible with ARC and PKARC files, you may want to obtain this set just for the fast de-arcing utility that is included.

ZOO ver. 1.5
Rahul Dhesi

ZOO is an archiving utility similar to ARC and PKARC. However, ZOO takes a different approach when creating archive files, so none of the ARC or PKARC files are compatible with ZOO. There are several conversion utilities available that will convert an ARC file into a ZOO format and vice versa.

ZOO files can be recognized by the word ZOO in the file-type extension. ZOO works in the same way as other archiving utilities. Commands are entered from the DOS command line, with options, and the program executes. When files are added to an archive, they are compressed using the Lempel-Ziv compression algorithm.

ZOO offers some features that are not found in the other archiving utilities:

- a comment may be attached to a file and listed in a directory listing of the archive.

- enhanced wild-card features where a * can be used anywhere in the file name and character ranges (i.e., a-d) can be used as well.

- long file names (greater than 11 characters) and the path of the file can now be stored in a ZOO archive.

ZOO performs faster than ARC but slower than PKARC. The file sizes of archives created with PKARC are smaller than ZOO. However, ZOO may be a better program due to the organization of data within the archive file. The design allows for quicker directory listings, better portability to other machines, and compatibility with future versions of ZOO. So, even though this program is not the fastest, it is a consistent and reliable performer, and is better designed.

If you obtain files from a service with the ZOO extension, then you have no choice but to use this program to extract the files from the archive. You will find that using this program in a daily environment will have benefits, due to its stability and overall reliability. Out of all the archiving programs tested here, we felt this one to be the top of the line. Be aware, however, that many people do not have ZOO, and that ARC is still the most common and safest program to use for distributing archives. For internal use (to archive your own programs and save disk space), we recommend ZOO.

SEZ vers. 2.20
Steve Manes and Rahul Dhesi
Public Domain

One further use of Zoo files occurs in conjunction with the SEZ utility. SEZ is designed to convert a Zoo archive into a self-unpacking file. The procedure is simple, and version 2.2 only adds another 2924 bytes to the original Zoo file. The syntax is:

```
SEZ file makefile
```

In the example, *file* is the original Zoo archive (*FILE.ZOO*) and *makefile* is the resultant program (*MAKEFILE.EXE*). Simply typing *MAKEFILE* at the DOS prompt will unpack the files and save them to disk. The authors warn, however, that if any error message indicates a bad CRC, the files should not be used, as they are probably corrupted.

This utility makes it possible to pack and shrink files into a Zoo archive and distribute them without the need for anyone at the other end of the distribution to have the Zoo program. You may have seen some messages on bulletin boards saying "self-unpacking file." Now you know what that means.

SEZ is one example of a self-extracting archive utility. There are other programs designed to perform the same function for other archive programs. We feel that SEZ is especially important for people who want to use the ZOO extractor, since ZOO is not as commonly distributed as the other archives like ARC and PKARC.

4

Practicing
Safe Shareware

This chapter is about the unpleasant side of computer software. In this chapter, you will find mention of a host of illegal and/or destructive programs. We want you to know, from the outset, that you are unlikely to encounter any of these programs if you are careful where you 'shop.' However, we understand the concern that the average user has, especially considering the attention that has been paid to viruses lately.

We repeat, this chapter is only for your information, and we consider the other parts of this book to be much more important. We hope you will ignore most of this chapter. We suggest scan the rules and suggestions herein, but don't be overly concerned about the general subject. The problems of trojans and viruses has been over-blown. Don't let rumors and ill-conceived news reports stop you from getting the best out of your computer system.

Safe Shareware

Yes, it's inevitable that comparisons will be made between safe sex and safe Shareware. That's because, in many ways, the threat of a computer virus is similar to the threat of a disease.

Though computers aren't living creatures, they are susceptible to attacks by sneaky programming code which can cause various kinds of havoc in a given system. We have nothing good to say about people who spread these diseases, but there are some precautions you can take to prevent having to deal with them. First of all, there is the master rule:

BACK UP! BACK UP! BACK UP your files! And do it *before* you try a suspect program. If you do it *after*, any virus will, in all likelihood, be backed up too.

Here are our Safe Shareware suggestions:

1. The cardinal rule: KNOW YOUR SOURCE! Know where you got the program from. Be familiar with the BBS or service that you use and satisfy yourself that nothing is passed by them without thorough testing.

1a. A corollary to rule 1 is to GO THE EXTRA STEP. Call or write the author of the program that interests you and ask him or her where you can obtain a clean copy. If you haven't access to a source of a copy, chances are the author will send you one.

Sometimes you will have to run the program to find information about the author, but most often you can find the information you require from the text files that accompany the product. If you do have to run the program to find out who wrote it, run it on a floppy disk with your hard disk protected.

2. DON'T BE THE FIRST ONE ON YOUR BLOCK TO DOWN-LOAD A NEW PROGRAM, unless you are completely sure of its source. This is especially true of local BBS where the sysop may simply be too busy or otherwise unable to personally check every upload. In the case of commercial services like CompuServe and GEnie, the screening is more reliable, but...

3. THERE IS NO 100% SAFE METHOD OF PREVENTION! Whether it's Shareware, PD, or commercial software, the potential exists for a virus or other nasty code to hide awhile, then appear. Some sysops and other experts examine the code itself to search for these hidden time bombs, but it is a very difficult task. It is, unfortunately, a fact of life that computers are vulnerable to infection.

4. PROTECT YOUR SYSTEM. You can achieve some small measure of protection by setting the archive bit on system files (like COMMAND.COM and the hidden BIOS files) to (P)rotected. In addition, you may be able to partially protect yourself by using one of the many anti-virus programs available, but you must use these with caution. For instance, recently someone took a legitimate anti-virus program—FLUSHOT3—and released a contaminated version of it with the document display program, *FLU4TXT.COM*, carrying the virus code. This program would destroy your hard disk.

One maker of commercial software who has released an anti-virus program is Paul Mace. Mace Virus is one program that may help, and there are many others on the bulletin boards.

5. DON'T PANIC! It sounds pretty awful, but it really isn't that bad. Most viruses show up in a short time, and people in the PD and Shareware community are quick to identify them. The chances that you will actually encounter anything damaging are slim. In fact, George and I have not encountered any known viruses on our machines, despite an extremely active participation in Shareware and PD software on the PC and on the Macintosh. The main reason is probably that we know our sources very well in almost all cases.

We offer this information, and that which follows, as public service. We don't want to give energy to destructive and illegal activities of this kind. There is too much that is good and constructive about computers, and it is a shame to cast a shadow over such a creative arena. Though we can offer no guarantees, our experience has convinced us that Shareware is not only safe, but economical and fun, too!

The Dirty Dozen

This chapter is dedicated to identifying some potentially dangerous and illegal public domain software products in circulation today. Though the list I have included is not complete, it does give the reader an idea of what to lookout for. The list was obtained from GEnie Information Service. It was compiled by a group of individuals who are committed to providing information about illegal or dangerous software in the public domain. Before the list is presented, you should be aware of a few terms that are used by computer enthusiasts and are also used in the list.:

TROJAN (T)   These programs *purposefully* damage a user's system upon their invocation. They almost always will shoot to disable hard disks, although they can destroy other equipment too.

HACKED (H) An unlawfully modified copy of an otherwise legitimate public domain or user-supported program. It is illegal to distribute a modified copy of someone else's work without their permission! All modified programs must contain this permission, either in the program's display or documentation.

CAUTION (C) Programs labeled in this manner may or may not be trojans; the question is unresolved. Use caution when running these programs!

PIRATED (P) This is an illegal copy of a commercial, copyrighted program. Examples: a cracked (de-protected) game, a compiler, editor or other utility, or a Beta test copy of a program under development. In the latter case, the program in question may never make it to market due to the piracy! In the case of games, there's a tendency for the pirate to patch a clumsy "PUBLIC DOMAIN" notice over top of the original copyright. *ZAXXON.COM* is a prime example.

MISC (M) This is miscellaneous illegal software and/or text. The best definition, aside from that, that I can think of is that it's *not* pirated software.

You shouldn't see any of these titles on any of the commercial systems such as GEnie, Compuserve, etc. Fortunately, these systems have professional SysOps who review each title before it's placed in the public directories. Also, these systems usually have complete personal information about the users of their systems for billing purposes. This discourages most from contributing these types of programs on commercial-based systems. But, nothing is fool-proof, and there is always a chance that a program could slip by, so here are a few final pointers on what to look for:

1. Never assume that a public-domain program will work the way it says it will.

Many of the programs that are distributed in the public domain have not been thoroughly tested, and may, either unintentionally or intentionally, cause damage. You should always test a newly acquired program on a blank diskette first before copying it to your hard disk. Power off your hard disk, or use one of the public domain titles mentioned in this book to temporarily write-protect your hard disk during the testing phase.

2. If the public domain program looks too good, it may be pirated.

Though there are many talented programmers who contribute many, many hours to creating their masterpiece for public domain, most public domain software lacks the appearance of commercially written software. For example, I have personally seen some of the pirated Atari games floating around on some non-commercial BBSs. Its really ironic that someone would alter the cover page to read "Public Domain by Atari." Now why would Atari release a commercial game into the public domain?

3. If all else fails, trust your instincts.

If you practice good common sense in acquiring public domain software, you can't go wrong. Stay away from BBSs that appear to offer too much for free or encourage pirating. Acquire programs that can be potentially dangerous to your data, like disk compression routines, from reliable sources like the services mentioned in this book. See the other suggestions at the beginning of this chapter.

Special thanks to Tom Neff, Eric Newhouse, and Gerhard Barth of Dirty Dozen, on BBS, for providing the list of software in this chapter.

Safe Shareware—Consider the Source!
by Marshall W. Magee

This article is also reprinted to further define the situation, and was written by Marshall Magee, the author of Automenu and President of the Association of Shareware Professionals.

There is much concern about a new phenomenon within the personal computing world—that of software "viruses." These modern day plagues are becoming more publicized every day, with news that major Fortune 500 companies (IBM, EDS, Aldus, AT&T, etc.) and even smaller businesses have been "hit." Damages usually range from relatively small messages appearing on-screen to the complete and total erasure of a hard disk system.

The first question to ask ourselves is **"What is a virus?"**

Viruses usually show up as abnormalities in program code that disrupt or interfere with the normal operation of a computer system. These "trojan horses" are placed into the code on purpose, with the perpetrator knowing full well of the potential dangers that lie ahead.

Sometimes these viruses are outgrowths, or "mutations," of otherwise proprietary programs, sometimes used to maintain system integrity and security. Copy-protection schemes, modified only slightly, can become deadly to a disk by removing file directories and file allocation tables in an instant.

Another question to ask is **"Where do viruses come from?"**

Some reports have placed origins of these "diseases" from as far away as Pakistan, but their geographic starting point is hardly important—what we really want to concentrate on is their *logical* origins.

Within large software organizations, many programmers work on different modules of code. There are few safeguards to avoid possible contamination by "logic bombs" or timing sensitive abort routines that can shut down a system, or flash messages on the screen ("Peace On Earth"). With cases like this already documented, it becomes more important *where* you buy your software, and *who* you buy it from.

Viruses do *not* come from Shareware—in fact, the vast majority of confirmed cases of viral attacks have been reported by users of *commercial* software. These attacks are not only found on micros, but also on minis and mainframes. There is also no guarantee that by avoiding Shareware you will avoid viruses—there is just *no relation* between the two.

"What else could be causing my computer problems?"

If the files were downloaded from a bulletin board or other electronic service, there is always the potential for file integrity to be compromised through "glitches" on the phone line. Some files are even downloaded without using error-correcting protocols like X-Modem or Y-Modem, and these may well be incomplete or corrupted (at best).

Running a corrupted file on your computer may cause unpredictable results, like screen blanking, or total system freezes, but hardly ever will any permanent damage be done. Restarting the system is usually all that will be required. Some users have obtained files using improper transfer formats and then blame their problems on viruses because it's the simple thing to do.

"What are the facts about viruses?"

Fact #1

Viruses still account for an amazingly small percentage of actual computer system failures, and most of those are caused by commercial software programs and their attending "copy protection" schemes. It is because viruses are such hot topics at this time that they garner so much attention. To date they have caused several dozen problems based on a population of over seventy-five million computers in use domestically.

Fact #2

Avoiding Shareware is no guarantee of avoiding viruses, but avoiding questionable dealers *is. Know your publisher!* Shareware is a growing, thriving element of high technology, and is open to underhanded acts of sabotage as much as any segment of the computer industry. To blame these viral problems on Shareware is not only irresponsible, it is entirely ignorant, and unfortunately, some of those in high places (i.e., computer publication editors) have already chosen to go on record by placing the blame in the wrong places.

Fact #3

Copy protection schemes and bug-ridden commercial software are more responsible for the vast array of user-related problems than are viruses, or trojan horses, or logic bombs, or whatever you want to call these diseases. Shareware offers so many positive advantages over other types of computer software that it is far too easy to point the finger and blame it for the ills of userdom.

Fact #4

Bulletin board systems (BBS) and other electronic file transfer services are protected from infection simply by having the System Operator review all the uploaded files before making them available to users. If the programs are mailed on diskette to the Sysop or disk duplicator, there is far less chance of contamination through improper transfer protocols or deliberate sabotage. Users should be made aware that some efforts are in order to protect themselves, but definitely *not* at the expense of the authors who have made the fruits of their labor available to all users for the price of a phone call!

Fact #5

Yes, it is true. Viruses are *such* a hot topic that some companies are going so far as to publicize events which have never occurred, in hopes of garnering free advertising. This is almost as bad as the virus problem itself. So when you read a story about a software "hit," consider the source. Maybe everything you read isn't true.

The Dirty Dozen List

NOTE: If no file extension is supplied, that means that the file has been circulating under many different extensions. For instance, BALKTALK has been seen with extensions of: *.EXE*, *.COM*, *.EQE*, *.CQM*, *.LBR*, *.LQR*, and *.ARC*.

<u>VIRUSES</u>

Name	Size	Category	Notes
COMMAND.COM	?????	V	This is a traditional Virus. Originating in colleges and universities across the nation, this virus will embed itself in *COMMAND.COM*. Once there it will copy itself onto four floppies before scrambling your FAT and initiating a format. Beware!

<u>TROJAN HORSE PROGRAMS</u>

Name	Size	Category	Notes
ANTI-PCBT		T	The story behind this trojan horse is sickening. Apparently one RBBS-PC sysop and one PC-BOARD sysop started feuding about which BBS system is better, and in the end the PC-BOARD sysop wrote a trojan and uploaded it to the RBBS SysOp under *ANTI-PCB.COM*. Of course the RBBS-PC SysOp ran it, and that led

to quite a few accusations and a big mess in general.

ALTCTRL.ARC	T	This program reputedly trashes boot records. Other than that, I know nothing about it.
ARC513.EXE	T	This hacked version of SEA's *ARC.EXE* appears normal. However, it writes over track 0 of your [hard] disk upon usage, destroying the disk's boot sector.
ARC514.COM	T	This is completely similar to *ARC* version 5.13 in that it will overwrite track 0 (boot sector) of your hard disk. Also, I have yet to see an *.EXE* version of this program.
BACKALLY.COM 64512	T	This sophisticated trojan will axe your FAT table after a couple of months of usage. Beware the delayed trojan! BACKALLY *may* only work on floppy disks, but that sounds unlikely. Debug has shown that BACKALLY formats a track at one point as well as reading in the amount of freespace on your disk. It may only wipe out full disks, like *NOTROJ*. Please, be wary! An included *.BAT* file comes with a request for donations to "SomeWare" located in Fredericksburg, VA. Look out for other products from SomeWare!
BACKTALK	T	This once beneficial utility will write/destroy sectors on your [hard] disk drive. Use this with caution if you acquire it, because it's more than likely that you got a bad copy.

CDIR.COM	T	This program supposedly gives you a color directory of files on disk, but it in fact scrambles your disk's FAT table.
COMPRESS.ARC	T	This trojan, dated April 1, 1987, destroys FAT tables. COMPRESS is executed from a file named *RUN-ME.BAT* and is advertised as a "Shareware 'ARC' from Borland!"
DANCERS.BAS	T	This trojan shows some animated dancers in color, and then proceeds to wipe out your [hard] disk's FAT table. There is another perfectly good copy of DANCERS.BAS on BBSs around the country; apparently the author altered a legitimate program to do his dirty work.
DEFENDER.ARC	T	This trojan both writes to ROM bios and formats [hard] disks. The Duplicators claim credit for this trojan; beware of other products by them. Also, do not confuse this trojan with DEFENDER by Atari. The latter is a pirated program.
DISCACHE.EXE	T	This program uses direct BIOS routines to write to disk. Apparently, those BIOS routines will scramble your FAT table. Please see *DISCACHE.WNG*, a file that I'm looking for myself, for more information.
DISKSCAN.EXE	T	This was a PC Magazine program to scan a [hard] disk for bad sectors, but then a joker edited it to *write* bad sectors. Also look for this under other names such as *SCANBAD.EXE* and *BADDISK.EXE*.

DMASTER	T	This is yet another FAT scrambler.
DOSKNOWS.EXE	T	I'm still tracking this one down— apparently someone wrote a FAT killer and renamed it DOSKNOWS.EXE, so it would be confused with the real, harmless DOSKNOWS system-status utility. All I know for sure is that the *real* DOSKNOWS.EXE is 5376 bytes long. If you see something called DOSKNOWS that isn't close to that size, sound the alarm. More info on this one is welcomed—a bagged specimen especially.
DPROTECT	T	Apparently someone tampered with the original, legitimate version of DPROTECT and turned it into a FAT table eater.
DROID.EXE54272	T	This trojan appears under the guise of a game. You are supposably an architect that controls futuristic droids in search of relics. In fact, the program copies *C:\PCBOARD\PCBOARD.DAT* to *C:\PCBOARD\HELP\HLPX* if PC-Board SysOps run it from *C:\PCBOARD*
EGABTR	T	BEWARE! Description says something like "improve your EGA display," but when run it deletes everything in sight and prints "Arf! Arf! Got you!"
ELEVATOR.ARC	T	This poorly written trojan suggests in the documentation that you run it on a floppy. If you do not run it on a floppy, Elevator chastises you for not reading the documentation. Regardless of what disk you run it on,

			Elevator will erase your files. It *may* format disks too; be careful.
EMMCACHE	????	C	This program is not exactly a trojan, V. 1.0 but it may have the capability of destroying hard disks by: A) Scrambling every file modified after running the program, B) Destroying boot sectors. This program has damaged at least two hard disks, yet there is a base of happily registered users. Therefore, I advise extreme caution if you decide to use this program.
FILER.EXE		T	One SysOp complained a while ago that this program wiped out his 20 Megabyte HD. I'm not so sure that he was correct and/or telling the truth any more. I have personally tested an excellent file manager also named FILER.EXE, and it worked perfectly. Also, many other SysOps have written to tell me that they have, like me, used a FILER.EXE with no problems. If you get a program named FILER.EXE, it is probably all right, but better to test it first using some security measures.
FINANCE4.ARC	??????	C	This program is not a verified trojan, but there is a file going around BBSs warning that it may be trojan. In any case, execute extreme care with it.
FUTURE.BAS		T	This "program" starts out with a very nice color picture (of what I don't know) and then proceeds to tell you that you should be using your computer for better things than games and graphics. After making that point, it trashes all of your disk drives, starting with disk A:. Not only does Future scramble FATs, but

it also erases files. As far as I know, however, it erases only one sub-directory tree level deep, thus hard disk users should only be seriously affected if they are in the "root" directory. More information about this is especially welcome.

MAP	T	This is another trojan horse written by the infamous Dorn W. Stickle. I believe that there are legitimate MAP.EXEs floating around.
NOTROJ.COM	T	This "program" is the most sophisticated trojan horse that I've seen to date. All outward appearances indicate that the program is a useful utility used to *fight* other trojan horses. Actually, it is a time bomb that erases any hard disk FAT table that IT can find, and at the same time it warns: "another program is attempting a format, can't abort!" After erasing the FAT(s), NOTROJ then proceeds to start a low level format. One extra thing to note: NOTROJ only damages *full* hard drives; if a hard disk is under 50% filled, this program won't touch it! If you are interested in reading a thorough report on NOTROJ.COM, James H. Coombes has written an excellent text file on the matter named NOTROJ.TXT.
TIRED	T	Another scramble the FAT trojan by Dorn W. Stickle.
TSRMAP	T	This program does what it's supposed to do: give a map outlining the location (in RAM) of all TSR programs, but it also erases the boot sector of drive C:.

PACKDIR	T	This utility is supposed to "pack" (sort and optimize) the files on a [hard] disk, but apparently it scrambles FAT tables.
PCLOCK	T	This program reputedly destroys FAT tables! Be careful!
PCW271xx.ARC	T	A modified version of the popular PC-WRITE word processor (v. 2.71) has now scrambled at least 10 FAT tables that I know of. If you want to download version 2.71 of PC-WRITE be very careful! The bogus version can be identified by its size; it uses 98,274 bytes whereas the good version uses 98,644. For reference, version 2.7 of PC-WRITE occupies 98,242 bytes.
QUIKRBBS.COM	T	This Trojan horse claims that it can load RBBS-PC's message file into memory 200% faster than normal. What it really does is copy RBBS-PC.DEF into an ASCII file named HISCORES.DAT.
QUIKREF	T	Little is known about this trojan, other than it scrambles FATS.
RCKVIDEO	T	This is another trojan that does what it's supposed to do, then wipes out hard disks. After showing some simple animation of a rock star ("Madonna," I think), the program erases every file it can lay it's hands on. After about a minute of this, it will create 3 ascii files that say "You are stupid to download a video about rock stars," or something of the like.

SCRNSAVE.COM	C	I know nothing about this program, but a user of mine reports that it erases HDs.
SECRET.BAS	T	BEWARE!! This may be posted with a note saying it doesn't seem to work, and would someone please try it. If you do try it, however, it will format your disks.
SEX-SNOW.ARC	T	This trojan deletes all of the files in your directory and creates a gloating message using those file names. Ugly.
SIDEWAYS.COM	T	Be careful with this trojan; there is a perfectly legitimate version of SIDEWAYS.EXE circulating. Both the trojan and the good SIDEWAYS advertise that they can print sideways, but SIDEWAYS.COM will trash a [hard] disk's boot sector instead. The trojan .COM file is about 3 KB, whereas the legitimate EXE file is about 30 KB large.
STAR.EXE	T	Beware RBBS-PC SysOps! This file puts some stars on the screen while copying RBBS-PC.DEF to another name that can be downloaded later!
STRIPES.EXE	T	Similar to STAR.EXE, this one draws an American flag (nice touch), while it's busy copying your RBBS-PC.DEF to another file (STRIPES.BQS) so Bozo can log in later, download STRIPES.BQS, and steal all your passwords. Nice, huh?!
TOPDOS	T	This is a simple high level [hard] disk formatter. Do not confuse this with the pirated TOPDOS.COM.

VDIR.COM	T	This is a disk killer that Jerry Pournelle wrote about in *BYTE* Magazine. I have never seen it, but two users of mine have.
VISIWORD.ARC	C	A user of mine called this trojan in complaining that it destroyed his hard disk. Other than that, I know nothing about this program.

HACKED PROGRAMS

Name	Size	Category	Notes
ARC.COM		H	Someone keeps running SPACEMAKER or a similar EXE squeezer on SEA, Inc.'s ARC archive program, then uploading the resulting COM file to BBSs without the author's permission. SEA will *not* support the COM version, for they definitely do not allow modifying ARC.EXE in their license agreement.
AUTOMAXX.ARC		C	This DOS menu-making program comes with documentation that Marshall Magee, author of the popular AUTOMENU program, contends is plagiarized. Marshall believes that the AUTOMAXX documentation uses exact phrases from his documentation, and if this is the case, AUTOMAXX is clearly illegal. However, as I understand it, the courts are currently deliberating on the case, so AUTOMAXX is not currently illegal as of today. For more information, please contact Marshall Magee at (404) 446-6611.

DOG102A.COM *	H	Apparently this is a renamed early version of DP102A.ARC, a disk optimizer. One person has reports that it trashes hard disks that use DOS 3.1 (2KB clusters).
LIST60	H	Vern Buerg's LIST 5.1, patched to read 6.0. Mr. Buerg has released a legitimate version 6.0 of LIST. Every legitimate version will have a letter in the filename (e.g. LIST60H.ARC)
LIST799	H	Vern Buerg's LIST 5.1, patched to read 7.99.
QMDM110.ARC	H	This is version 1.09 of Qmodem patched to read 1.10. There have been rumors of a worm in 1.10, but I have seen no evidence of it. Other versions are OK.

PIRATED PROGRAMS

Note: In the following sections the additional letters have been added to the category code to aid in further identifying the program:

U=utility

G=game

M=miscellaneous

P=patch (a modification usually involving DOS DEBUG)

T=text

Name	Size	Category	Notes
1DIR.COM		PU	"The ONE Dir": DOS shell.
21C.EXE		PG	Blackjack, copyright by IBM

ACUPAINT.ARC	148221	PM	PC Paint
ALLEYCAT.COM		PU	"Alley Cat" - CGA
ALTEREGO.ARC	45????	PG	Alter Ego game from Activision
ARCHON.COM		PG	Electronic Art's Archon.
ARTOFWAR		PG	Ancient Art of War by Broderbund
AUTODEX		PU	AUTODEX, file manager
AXX.EXE		PU	Also AUTODEX
B1-BOMB		PG	Avalon Hill's B1 Bomber
BATTLE		PG	Battle Zone
BBCHESS		PG	Blues Box Chess
BC-QUEST		PG	BC's Quest for Tires
BIGMAC.ARC		PU	Borland's Superkey
BORDERZO.ARC	205824	PG	Infocom's Borderzone
BORROWED.ARC		PG	Borrowed Time
BRUCELEE		PG	Bruce Lee
BUCK		PG	Buck Rogers on Planet Zoom
BURGER		PG	Burgertime
BUSHIDO		PG	Karate Game by a manufacturer in Canada.
BUZZBAIT		PG	Buzzard Bait
CALL2ARM		PG	Call to Arms
CENTIPED		PG	Be careful with this one. At least two other legitimate, PD copies of Centipede are in circulation. The pirated one is supposedly PUBLIC DOMAIN BY ATARI. Yeah, right.

CMASTER.ARC	PG	Chess Master 2000 by Electronic Arts
COMMANDR.ARC	PG	Norton Commander
COSMIC	PG	Cosmic Crusaders
COPYRITE	PU	Quaid Software's COPYWRITE
COPYWRIT	PU	Quaid Software's COPYWRITE
COSMIC	PG	Cosmic Crusaders a
CROSFIRE.COM	PG	Crossfire
CRUSH-CC.ARC	PG	Crush, Crumble & Chomp
DAMBUST.ARC	PG	Dambusters by Accolade cracked
DEB88.EXE	PM	DeSmet 'C' debugger
DECATH	PG	Microsoft's Decathalon
DEFENDER	PG	Defender, by Atari
DIGDUG.COM	PG	Dig Dug, by Atari
DISKEX	PU	Quaid's Disk Explorer
DOSHELP.EXE	PU	This is really Central Point Software's PC-tools. One special note: poorly written documentation usually accompanies this file. In the documentation ERIC HSU asks for a monetary contribution to his BBS. Well, It seems that this was a poor attempt to damage ERIC HSU's reputation; Eric is a legitimate SysOp in the Houston area
DOSMENU.ARC 208240	PUI	NTECH'S DOSMENU—Opening screen says "PC DOS MENU SYSTEM 5.0."—(C) is on the bottom of the screen

DOSSHELL	PU	Autodex
DRL	PG	Avalon Hill's "Dnieper River Line"
DIPLOMCY	PG	Avalon Hill's "Computer Diplomacy" game
EGADIAG	PU	Quadram EGA (Quad EGA+) diagnostics
EINSTIME	PU	BM internal utility
EXPLORER.COM	PU	Quaid Disk Explorer
EVOLUTIO	PG	Evolution
F15	PG	F-15 Strike Eagle
FIGHTER.ARC	PG	Sublogic's JET
FILEEASE	PU	A File manager
FILEMGR	PU	Filemanager by Lotus Development Corporation
FILEMAN.COM1 ????	PU	Filemanager
FINDIT	PU	IBM internal 'locate a file' utility
FSDEBUG	PU	IBM's Full Screen Debug program..
GOLDCUP	PG	Gold Cup championship soccer
GOLF21.ARC	PG	Golf's Best version 2.1
GREMLINS.COM	PG	Gremlins
HARDHAT.COM	PG	Hard Hat Mack
HIGHORBT	PG	High Orbit (like Star Wars)
HOOP.COM	PG	One-on-1 by Electronic Arts
ID	PU	Persyst Ram disk software
IBM21	PG	21c

IKARI.ARC	210944	PG	Ikari Warriors—CGA/EGA, joystick required
IPLTIME.COM		PU	IBM Internal Clock utility
JBIRD		PG	Jbirds—Q-bert Game
JEOPARDY195	???	PG	Jeopardy, the game show.
JET		PG	Jet
JETDRIVE.ARC		PU	Jet Drive—copies files quickly
JOUST		PG	Joust. There is a 6K, PD version
KEYWORKS.ARC		PU	Keyworks macro program, usually version 2.0
KOBAYASH.ARC		PG	Star Trek—The Kobayashi Alternative
KONG		PG	Donkey Kong
LIGHTNIN		PU	Can be either the cache or spell checker
MACE+		PU	Paul Mace's MACE+ utilities
MACROS		PU	Superkey—sometimes Prokey
MEDMAG.COM		PU	Quaid Software's Media Magician
MINER49R.ARC		PG	Miner '49er
MISSLEC		PG	Missile command
MONTYS.COM		PG	Montezuma's Revenge
MOONBUGS		PG	Moon Bugs
MS		PU	IBM utility
MTS		PU	IBM Multitasker like Double-Dos
MULE		PG	M.U.L.E—player is on alien planet

MULTASK	PU	MTS
MURDRBY#	PG	Murder by Numbers by Electronic Arts
MUSICCON	PM	Music Construction Set, also by EA
NFL.ARC	PG	Xor's NFL challenge
NGHTSTLK	PG	Night Stalker
NICE	PM	NicePrint - printer controller
NODISK-A.COM	PU	Central Point software's Nokey
NORTON.COM	PU	Peter Norton's Utilities
ANORTON.ARC	PU	Peter Norton's Advanced Utilities
NOVATRON	PU	Tron light cycles
ONE-ON-1	PG	One-on-1 basketball game
PATHMIND	PU	Pathminder, Dos Shell
PC-POOL	PG	Pool
PC-TOOLS	PU	Central Point Software's PC-tools
PCBOSS	PU	DOS shell
PCED	PU	Pro CED, DOS command line editor
EIIPUI	BM	Personal Editor II
PINCONST	PG	Pinball Construction Set by EA
POOL.ARC	PG	PC-POOL
POPALARM.COM	PU	Part of POP DOS
POPDOS.ARC	PU	TSR DOS utilities
PRIME	PU	Columbia Data Co. hard disk utility
PROKEY	PU	Prokey macros program

PROMPRPH	PG	Star Trek—The Promethian Prophecy
PSHIFT	PU	Memory Shift
PSRD.ARC	PU	IBM utility (redirects PrtSc)
QDOS	PU	Quick DOS
QUCKDOS	PU	Quick DOS
QIX	PG	Qix
RACTER	PG	Racter
RASTER-B	PG	Raster Blaster
RE.ARC	PG	Romantic Encounters at the Dome
RIGHTW	PU	Right Writer (writing style checker)
ROBOTRON	PG	Robotron, hacked to read PUBLIC DOMAIN BY ATARI. Do pirates have any imagination?
ROGUE.EXE	PG	Game very similar to the PD: HACK.EXE
ROMANTIC	PG	Romantic Encounters at the Dome
SEADRAG.ARC	PG	Sea Dragon
SEE	PM	DeSmet editor
SFX	PU	Autodex
SKYRUNER	PG	Sky Runner, $14.95 game
SM.COM	PU	Realia's Spacemaker utility. EXE>.COM
SMAPPUI	BM	Internal utility, with the copyright notice and real author's name replaced by "Dorn W. Stickle"

SNIPER		PG	Sniper—arcade action type game
SOLOFLT.ARC		PG	Solo Flight (by SSI?) cracked
SPYHUNT		PG	Bally's Spy Hunter
STARFLIT.ARC	0????	PG	Electronic Art's Star Flight
STARGATE.EXE	57???	PG	Hacked to say "PUBLIC DOMAIN BY ATARI," but don't you believe it! Be careful not to confuse this arcade game with the public domain STARGATE MERCHANT game, which is a little 12 KB BASIC program by G. E. Wolfworth.
STRIPKR		PG	Strip Poker by Artworx
SUBCMDR.ARC		PG	Gato cracked: SUBCMDR.EXE & overlays
SUPERCAD		PM	Easy CAD
SUPERCAD.LQR	242660	PM	Easy CAD
SUPERKEY		PM	Superkey
TEMPOFAP		PG	Temple of Apshai
THEQUEST.BAS/EXE		PG	The Quest
TIRES.EXE		PG	BC's Quest for Tires
TREASURE		PG	Pirate's Treasure
TROJAN.ARC	304128	PG	Trojan—CGA/EGA, (C) 1987, like D&D
TWIN.ARC	22784	PU	Central Point's Copy II PC
TWINCOPY.ARC	22784	PU	Copy II PC
ULTIII	111616	PG	Origin's Ultima 3
ULTIMA2.ARC	84992	PG	Origin's Ultima 2

UTILITY	PU	Norton's Utilities Arced and with the file names changed. When run, however, the program display the copyright notice of Peter Norton. Many other pirated utilities could also go under the name UTILITY
VOYAGERI	PG	Avalon-Hill Game
VS	PU	Also INTECH'S DOSMENU
WCKARATE	PG	World Championship Karate by Epyx
WG-BBALL	PG	World's Greatest Baseball Game by SSI
WGAMES	PG	World Games by Epyx
WORSTR	PU	Word Star
XDIR	PU	Pre-release version of DOS FILE TRACKER
XTREE	PU	DOS shell
XTREE+	PU	Xtree Plus
ZAXXON	PG	Hacked to say "PUBLIC DOMAIN BY SEGA." (sound familiar?)

MISCELLANEOUS

Name	Size	Category	Notes
COPYWRIT	2???	MP	Although the real COPYWRITE is going around Bulletin Boards like fire, there is another illegal file under the same name. The former takes around 40 KB ARC-ed, whereas this takes about 2 KB. What I'm referring to is an archive of 1-3 files that ex-

plains how to remove the serial numbers from copywrite. Now it's allright to "unprotect" a program for backup purposes, but removing serial numbers can only lead to piracy.

LOCKPICK	MT	This is a text file, usually with a .TXT extension, that casually explains how to pick locks. This is not illegal, but it's definitely in poor taste. It could be used as evidence against a burglar, though.
MONEY.ARC	MT	This text file claims that with minimal effort *you* can become a millionaire. This text file, as some of you may know, is simply another chain (pyramid) letter that is of course illegal. A pyramid writer sends a letter to four people requesting money. Then, according to the pyramid writer's plan, those four will send letters to four more asking for money for themselves and the original writer. Unfortunately when the chain breaks people lose money. What one person gains someone else must lose. That's why this type of letter is illegal.
MONOPOLY	MG	This program may or may not infringe upon Parker Brothers' patent of the famous boardgame. One of my users claims that the court sides with Parker Brothers. Don Gibson, the author of monopoly, says that he and Parker Bros. have settled out of court and Monopoly is 100% legal. I don't know what to think. If Monopoly *is* illegal, however, then so is PCOTHELO.ARC (Othello) and a few other boardgames that are circulating on BBSs. Someone,

		please, let me know what the status on Monopoly is. Until proven otherwise, Monopoly is LEGAL.
MOVBASIC	**MU**	This highly illegal file breaks IBM's SBASICA or copyright on BASIC and BASICA. It SBASIC creates new files called SBASIC or SBASICA that run "IBM BASIC" on an IBM clone. C'mon, don't you think that these clones don't run IBM BASICA for a good reason? The clones don't support BASICA because it's illegal! This file comes with Alloy's PC-Slave card. Alloy has a license agreement, and users of the PC-Slave are allowed to create copies of IBM BASIC for themselves. NO ONE ELSE IS. Stop complaining that this file is legal, people; this is one of the more blatant cases of piracy that I've seen.
XTALK	**MP**	Like Copywrite, there is a patch circulating BBSs to remove the serial numbers from Crosstalk.

Part II

Applications

5

Notes on the Shareware Revolution

by Jim Button

There has never before been anything quite like the computer disk. Not only is it copyable, it is perfectly copyable. And it's easily and cheaply done.

Perfectly Copyable

Compare it to a photograph. No matter how you make a copy of a photograph, the copy isn't quite the same quality as the original. Copy the copy, then copy that copy, and you can visually see the degradation in quality.

Compare it to a tape recording. Same thing. Each copy loses something through the copying process. A good ear can hear the loss in quality from one generation to the next. After just a few generations, no one will want the copy.

The copied computer disk, on the other hand, retains all the qualities of its master, or father. Every "bit" is faithfully reproduced. Nothing is lost. The copied programs and files behave exactly like their parents. It's impossible to tell a tenth generation, or even a twentieth or thirtieth generation from the original.

Easily Copyable

With a computer disk, everyone who would want a copy can easily obtain one.

Compare that with a photograph. Copy machines are expensive. Not everyone who would want a copy of the photograph has access to a copy machine. Furthermore, few copy machines have full color capability.

Compare it to a tape recording. Most tape recorders lack dual tape capability. To get a copy of the tape, you may need to find a friend with decent recording equipment.

Almost every personal computer, on the other hand, has a floppy disk drive. Every floppy disk drive can both read and write. Each has the inherent capability to perfectly reproduce the media that it uses.

Unnatural Acts

With computers it's not only easy to copy, it's natural to do it. So natural, in fact, that to prevent copying, the software manufacturer has to perform unnatural acts on the disk. It is, in other words, unnatural not to copy computer software.

Perfectly copyable and easily copyable—these are the two features that made software piracy such a popular and widespread phenomenon. And this gave software manufacturers fits. A whole industry was built up around performing unnatural acts to computer disks—making them uncopyable. Every major software vendor fell into line. It was commonly believed that software without copy protection was doomed to produce little or no revenue for its manufacturer.

What a radical idea it was then, in 1982, for a software author to encourage copying of his programs. More than radical, it was revolutionary. When Andrew Fluegelman and Jim Button encouraged users to copy their programs and share them with others, the rest of the software industry was outraged. Many industry leaders pooh poohed the idea. Most of them tried to ignore it—they buried their heads in the sand and hoped that the idea would go away. Surely it wouldn't work! After a short time, they thought, these young radicals will go broke from such a scheme.

But they didn't go broke. They prospered. Shareware was an idea whose time had come. Users revelled in the luxury of trying out programs for as long as necessary before purchase. They reacted with enthusiasm at being treated with honesty and respect.

If You Can't Beat Them, Join Them

In 1985 and 1986, almost every major software manufacturer dropped copy protection. The weight of public opinion and the pressure of competition forced them to it. While Shareware authors cannot take all the credit for this revolution, they can surely take some of it. Shareware was a major factor in educating the public to the silliness of copy protection and the penalties that it imposes on the software purchaser. The naturalness and beauty of freely copyable software stands out in stark contrast to the handcuffs of copy protection.

In recent months, the impact of the Shareware revolution has been further felt. Increasingly, software manufacturers are improving the quality of their "demo" software—removing more and more of the crippling. They are also trying harder to utilize the same distribution channels that have been so successful for the Shareware authors—computer clubs and software clubs—to distribute their demonstration disks.

Shareware has become a share war, and the common folk are the ultimate winners.

It Runs on Faith

Why wasn't the Shareware distribution method discovered earlier in microcomputer history? Apple, TRS-80, Northstar, and other personal computers had been popular for years. Why did Shareware wait until 1982?

A software author makes a huge investment of time, talent, and thought in his product. His program is his brain-child, his baby. He would like to make some money from it. He surely doesn't want to see it gleefully stolen by software pirates.

Even if Shareware was considered, it wasn't attempted because it required a great exercise of faith in the honesty of the American public and in the quality of the product.

Andrew Fluegelman originally said, "Only the good products will survive." Unlike traditional software marketing, which can bring success to a mediocre product through lavish advertising and promotional campaigns, the Shareware product relies solely upon its own virtues to elicit a sale. If users don't like the program, they simply won't pay for it. And they won't share it with others. It will die unceremoniously.

The Advantages of Shareware for the Users

Most of what you pay for when you buy software is slick advertising and promotional campaigns. But Shareware is almost 100 percent "user promoted." This is the reason that Shareware programs typically sell for less than half (and sometimes as much as 1/10) the price of their commercial counterparts.

Shareware offers the luxury of being able to try out the software before buying it. You try it out at your own pace, on your own equipment, on your own data, and in the peace and quiet of your own home or workplace. It has rightly been said that Shareware offers the ultimate money back guarantee—if you don't like it, don't even pay for it.

The Advantages of Shareware for Authors

The Shareware approach allows the program author to test the water before entering. For only a few hundred dollars, he can put his program into the Shareware distribution channels. Of the successful Shareware companies, not one has ever had to borrow or seek venture capital.

The business can be started as a hobby in your spare time. Success, if it comes, will be slow enough at first to allow you to adapt and fund the growth with the incoming revenues. The jump to full time business can wait until the flow of income is adequate to sustain you.

Where is Shareware Going?

At the time of this writing, there are at least four Shareware companies with annual sales of 1 million dollars or more. These four are:

- ButtonWare (PC-File, PC-Dial, PC-Calc, PC-Type, etc.)

- Quicksoft (PC-Write)

- Datastorm Technologies (ProComm)

- Magee Enterprises (Automenu)

These companies have all recently been successful in entering their products into the traditional dealer marketing channels.

Two of them are relative newcomers to the Shareware pack. They have experienced a rise to stardom in the past year or two. This shows that the window of opportunity is not closed. All that other companies need to join them is:

- the right product

- expertly coded

- nicely documented

- carefully supported

- skillfully marketed

All four of the above companies, and many other Shareware authors, have recently joined together to form an organization called Association of Shareware Professionals. The stated purpose of the association is:

- to inform users about Shareware programs and about Shareware as a method of distributing and marketing software.

- to encourage broader distribution of Shareware through user groups and disk dealers who agree to identify and explain the nature of Shareware.

- to assist members in marketing their software.

- to foster a high degree of professionalism among Shareware authors by setting programming, marketing and support standards for ASP members to follow.

- to provide a forum through which ASP members may communicate, share ideas, and learn from each other.

Meetings of the association are conducted "continuously," via an on-line dialog on CompuServe.

In its first two months of existence, the association has attracted more than 50 of the top Shareware authors in the U.S. and Canada. It is believed that membership could exceed 1000 within the next year or so. The association invites interested Shareware authors everywhere to join. Further information and an application for membership can be obtained by writing to:

> Association for Shareware Professionals
> Membership Committee
> P.O. Box 5786
> Bellevue, WA 98006

Shareware is alive and well. It is widely viewed as a major new force in the software industry. In its five year history, it has proven to be popular with users and profitable for authors and software dealers. It is a revolution that has succeeded.

6

Accounting

There are many accounting programs available in public domain and Shareware. Some are basic checkbook managers. Others are complex double-entry systems. There are even Lotus worksheets designed to perform accounting functions. Picking a good accounting system can be difficult. Each of us may look for a different feature or set of features. There may be no single product that completely meets our needs. We didn't look at all the systems available, but we did find a couple of good products. Jerry Medlin's accounting packages are excellent Shareware products that can fit into a business accounting environment, and Money Counts offers Shareware checkbook management that is versatile, cost effective, and easy to use.

CheckMate 1.7 and CheckMate-G/L 1.7
Custom Technologies
Shareware $29.95 (CheckMate)
                   $39.95 (CheckMate G/L)

CheckMate and CheckMate G/L are nice, easy to use personal finance programs. The manuals are straightforward and contain a very good background on general bookkeeping and business concepts. A person new to electronic accounting will find CheckMate and CheckMate G/L easy to comprehend. The system features pull down menus and on-screen, context sensitive help, and enough capacity for any home or small business needs. At $29.95 and $39.95 respectively for

CheckMate and CheckMate GL, the prices are very affordable ($59.95 for a "bundle"—$10 savings).

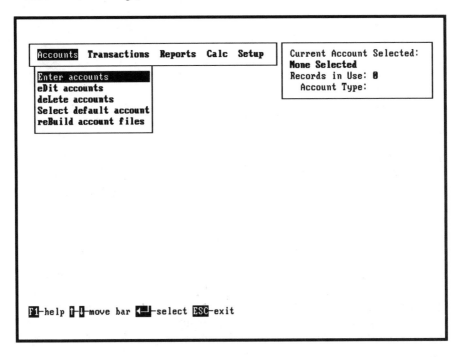

CheckMate Features:

- Pull-down menu system
- Up to eight accounts simultaneously (total number of accounts is limited only by disk space)
- Checking and Savings accounts
- Up to 32,767 transactions may be active per account
- Prints reports in standard format or in Borland Intl's Traveling SideKick (tm) format
- Reports and Checks may be printed in PICA, ELITE or CONDENSED print
- Transactions may be edited or printed and search criteria may be specified on any field in the transaction.
- Check printer supports continuous feed *and* standard checks
- Predefined transactions can be entered via keyboard macros
- Includes a financial calculator for the calculation of loans, regular, and compounding deposit accounts

- Reconciliation function helps reconcile your accounts and prints a report of outstanding transactions
- Includes extensive, context sensitive, on-line help
- Supports printing addresses on checks for use with windowed envelopes
- Mouse support added with Version 1.7

Reports available with CheckMate include check printing, transaction reports (check register) with all kinds of searching and filtering abilities on one or multiple fields, on-screen or disk reports, account reports, etc. All reports can be short (one line per item) or long (several lines where necessary). Reconciliation reports are also available.

You can use CheckMate with CheckMate G/L and assign each check to appropriate G/L accounts at periodic intervals. This means that you can use CheckMate as a simple, easy method of keeping a checkbook, then quickly and conveniently incorporate the transactions into your G/L.

CheckMate uses a full-screen editing format with WordStar compatible commands. You can pop up a menu of up to 50 pre-defined checks and fill in any part of the pre-defined checks on the fly during check entry. CheckMate automatically uses the last date entered and updates check numbers for you.

CheckMate G/L

- Pull-down menu system
- Supports up to 256 accounts simultaneously.
- Integrates with CheckMate
- Powerful search and filter routines for data files and reports
- Quick look reports (generate balance sheet and P/L statements on screen—instant, brief reports)
- Predefined balance sheet P/L (monthly and year-to-date)
- Custom report command language allowing complete control over report formats
- Fully editable journal entries allowing pen and ink corrections, no reverse entries prior to posting
- 50 predefined journal transactions with multiple split to accounts called up with a keystroke
- Pop-up chart of accounts
- Pop-up accountant's calculator with rolling tape
- Extensive context sensitive on-line help
- Mouse support

For someone who doesn't know how bookkeeping works, the menus could be misleading. However, they are well conceived and work well once a user is familiar with the system. While the help is immediately available, the manuals are a must when learning to use these products.

CheckMate G/L has the same basic look and feel as CheckMate. Both are easy to use and are designed to make accounting easier.

—Gregory Salcedo

CheckMate and CheckMate G/L
Custom Technologies
P.O. Box 62118
Colorado Springs, CO 80962
(800) 541-6234 (orders only)
(719) 260-0402 (support only)

Shareware: $29.95 (CheckMate) $39.95 (CheckMate G/L); $59.95 for bundle
pack

Category: Checking and Accounting

System Requirements: Requires IBM PC or compatible with 256K RAM
and two floppy disks. Hard drive and color monitor optional.

Recommended use: personal accounting

Major Pros: fast, easy-to-learn, and menu driven; ideal for beginners; pre-de
fined options; pop-up options; full-screen editing; search and filter features

Major Cons: no A/R or A/P or other support modules so far available; menus
could be confusing; context sensitive help could be more extensive

Sources: popular BBSs and commercial services, or directly from the author

---

CONTRARIAN 1.0

DANLEN Corporation
Shareware—$25.00

If you really like to think and win at investments, Contrarian could be the package for you. Contrarian's philosophy is simple, but as it points out, its not always easy to execute unless you have grasped it completely—BUY LOW-SELL HIGH!

The principle is to be aware of the emotions of the market and be in tune with your own investment strategy. The idea is to play upon the emotions of the marketplace without letting your own emotion get in the way of good strategy.

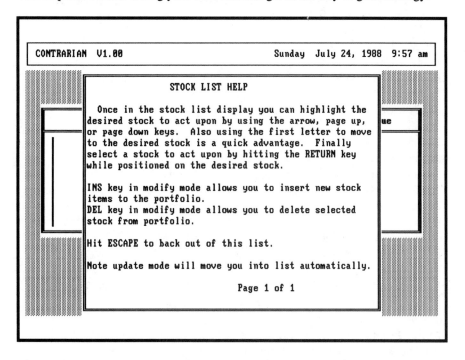

```
CONTRARIAN  V1.00                      Sunday  July 24, 1988  9:57 am

                          STOCK LIST HELP

        Once in the stock list display you can highlight the
       desired stock to act upon by using the arrow, page up,   ue
       or page down keys.  Also using the first letter to move
       to the desired stock is a quick advantage.  Finally
       select a stock to act upon by hitting the RETURN key
       while positioned on the desired stock.

       INS key in modify mode allows you to insert new stock
       items to the portfolio.
       DEL key in modify mode allows you to delete selected
       stock from portfolio.

       Hit ESCAPE to back out of this list.

       Note update mode will move you into list automatically.

                          Page 1 of 1
```

Contrarian quotes John Paul Getty: "If you want to make money, really big money, do what nobody else is doing. Buy when everyone else is selling and hold until everyone else is buying." In the marketplace this principle has come to be known as "Contrarian Strategy." It's very powerful, simple to follow, and based on common sense in the face of emotion. Contrarian's system consists of a portfolio tracking system that includes a stock history and strategy components that aid in you discerning the best "contrarian" moves to make.

Contrarian utilizes beautiful pull down menus and color to provide a very easy-to-use portfolio entry section. If you don't have color, the pull down menus are well arranged on the screen and the screen does not have the "cluttered" look some pull down systems seem doomed to display. What I especially like about this product is that it allows for a very diverse portfolio. If you don't want to "think" a strategy, Contrarian is not for you. This product is not a "point-n-shoot," hold your hand product. Contrarian introduces you to a different way of thinking, one that can be translated far beyond the trading world and one that is extremely effective if implemented correctly. I like the way Contrarian puts the emotion of the market into a perspective that can be translated into an executable investment strategy.

CONTRARIAN 1.0
DANLEN Corporation
166 Maple North
PO Box 1660
Manteca, CA 95336   BBS (209) 823-6133

Shareware: $25.00

Category: Investment Software

System Requirements: IBM PC, PC/XT, PC/AT, PC/Jr, PC Portable, or a 100% compatible computer with minimum of 256Kb of memory; minimum one double-sided disk drive (one 360 Kb floppy drive and a high-density 1.2 Mb floppy disk drive and a hard disk are recommended); 80-column monochrome or color display for running the Portfolio Management Module; PC or MS-DOS 2.1 or later version (DOS 3.1 or greater is recommended)

Recommended Use: Portfolio Management (need an intermediate knowledge of investment strategy; not recommended for beginners)

Major Pros: excellent, professional investment package; good strategy, nice documentation, great screen presentation

Major Cons: needs a tutorial, sample files; documentation presents a good overview but actual examples would help a user learn strategies faster

Sources: popular BBSs and commercial services, or directly from author

---

To use Contrarian, you simply enter your portfolio into the portfolio management system. You describe the investment, how much you own, at what price you bought, etc. You next establish a BUY/SELL band (Danleen recommends novice investors accept Contrarian's defaults to start with) and any history associated with your investment. Contrarian then monitors and recommends various strategies as you enter in data about your investment and assess market conditions relative to your portfolio.

The documentation is very well put together and may be worth the cost of the product all by itself; moreover, the manual also references other readings that would benefit all investors.

CAUTION—If your system does not have an in-board clock, you *must* set your date and time with DOS each time you use CONTRARIAN. Because CON-TRARIAN makes static and dynamic data files which are date/time stamped, the correct date and time *must* be associated with these files for CONTRARIAN to operate successfully.

—Gregory Salcedo

Money Counts ver. 3.86
Parsons Technology
Shareware—$12

Money Counts (MC) is a personal accounting program that provides the basic necessities for managing your personal finances. The program uses color where available, and is entirely menu driven. This product is so easy to use that you may not even need the 80 page manual that comes with it. The structure for setting up the accounts is straightforward—the program asks for an account number, then, at the bottom of the screen, gives you a list of ranges for different account types. For example, 050-099 are reserved for checking accounts. In addition, the program asks for the account name, actual starting balance, and optionally, budget amounts for 12 months. The account types allowed are cash, checking accounts, savings, assets, credit cards, liability, income, and expense.

After establishing a chart of accounts, you can begin to add data through the data-entry portion of the program. Data entry allows you to specify the type of transaction as well as how the transaction should be applied. Forget your accounts? MC has a pop-up window which shows you all of the account numbers and names. The program also supports splitting transactions over several accounts. Incidentally, during any input operation, MC gives you the option of calling up a pop-up calculator. The results of your calculations will automatically be entered in the value field you're working with. Unfortunately, transaction entries cannot be mixed. You can't enter deposits and checks within the same input screen, for example, which we found a bit cumbersome. The program does maintain a real-time account balance at the bottom right portion of the input screen, so that you know the status of the account as you are entering data.

The reports module will give reports on your financial status using a variety of options. These options include actual account balances by month, budgeted account balances by month, actual versus budgeted, actual versus prior month, account analysis in which it will list all transactions affecting an account, transaction analysis in which all transactions involving a particular party are listed, transaction register, chart of accounts, and general ledger—where all transactions for all accounts are listed by month. A graph module is also included for viewing data in a hi-resolution (640x200) bar graph. The graph module gives you a variety of options to view your data, such as actual versus budgeted, etc.

Money Counts ver. 3.86
Parsons Technology
3925 Surrey Drive NE
Cedar Rapids, IA 52402
319-373-0917

Shareware:$12

Category: Accounting

System Requirements: 128k of available memory; IBM PC, XT, AT or any close compatible; color recommended but it will work with composite or monochrome displays

Recommended use: personal accounting

Major Pros: fast, easy-to-learn, and menu driven; ideal for beginners

Major Cons: limited to general ledger only

Sources: popular BBBs and commercial services, or directly from the author

---

This program provides the necessities for maintaining your personal accounting. Its interface is good, but may not compete with some of the better commercially available programs. Money Counts is great for book-keeping novices because the program is self-explanatory and friendly to use. Even if you end up using a commercially available package, you may consider this as an introduction to how personal accounting programs work, and what they require in terms of maintenance and the types of information needed to set them up. And the price makes this one of the best values in its class. For $12, how can you go wrong?

Medlin Accounting Shareware

PC-GL, PC-AR, PC-AP, PC-PR

Jerry Medlin

Shareware—$35 per module

Jerry Medlin's accounting series is best characterized by the word simplicity. Whether you find simplicity in an accounting package an asset or a liability depends on your approach to accounting. Another word that applies to these packages is consistency. The interface from module to module is always the same, and requires no complex setup or learning curve.

On the other hand, it is absolutely essential that you know your accounting system. Medlin's programs will not make your accounting work if it isn't organized (no accounting program that I know will—that gets into some future area of artificial intelligence [Doctor Books—the intelligent auditor program?]). But you will have to know your debits from your credits to work with these packages.

All four modules are very fast. Since they keep all transactions in RAM, they do not suffer from disk access delays. On the other hand, saving on-going transactions is a good idea. Transactions are not posted until you specifically post them. This means that you can go back over old transactions to make adjustments without having to fiddle with the books, but only before posting. After posting, adjusting entries will be required. Although you can set your own accounting period, Medlin's Accounting requires that you close the books at the end of one period to begin the next. Some people prefer open books, and this method will not appeal to them. But most businesses run on specific accounting periods, so this shouldn't pose a problem under most situations.

One limitation on the length of a period is that a whole period is kept in RAM until closed. This means that you have room for a maximum of 4000 transactions per period and up to 800 items on the chart of accounts.

Another feature that may appeal to some and not to others is that the modules (with the exception of Accounts Payable) do not automatically integrate to the General Ledger. Medlin defends this position by stating that you can cause more confusion and potential error by automatically posting to the G/L, and that it is easy to obtain a summary value from the Accounts Receivable and the Payroll, and place a simple entry manually in the G/L to handle it. This point of view is shared by some of Medlin's users whom we contacted. Reports can be previewed on the screen, then sent to the printer. Only one report, the end of period audit trail, must be printed. The others need be printed only if desired. Also, when each period closes, the program creates a history file on disk for that period. This file allows you to view and print historical information, and can save a lot of time during end-of-year audits. A yearly trial balance report can be printed from the history files.

Basic General Features

Fast, easy, flexible entry system; consistent menu-driven interface (all transactions for each module take place on a single screen); reports printed at any time; use numeric keypad for data entry; short, but effective documentation.

PC-GL Features

Comes with standard chart of accounts; consistent account coding; instant entry verification; flexible modifications to chart of accounts and to un-posted data; view chart of accounts during data entry; print chart of accounts, transaction listing, G/L, income statement, balance sheet, account summary, year end update.

PC-AR Features

Sums sales by sales code; aging (30, 60, 90 days); individualized late charges; customer codes can be numeric or alpha; sorts statements and mailing labels by zip code; prints statement only for customers with ending balances; automatic posting of fixed amounts for each customer; flexibility of data entry and modification; print mailing labels, charges and payments, A/R ledger, statements, sales summary, customer activity report, customer listing; apply charges and payments.

PC-AP Features

Checks posted to PC-GL for cash basis; Invoices posted to PC-GL for accrual basis; automatic sorting of vendors; invoices sorted by due date; easy selection of invoices to pay; check listing in check number order; up to 1500 vendors and invoices per period; export vendor data to ASCII file, print mailing labels, checks for selected invoices, check listings, invoice listings, vendor activity report, vendor listing.

PC-PR Features

Federal tax tables included; Employees sorted alphabetically; up to five deductions per check; deductions input from keyboard or as percentage of gross; annual limits for each deduction; deductions can be percentage of Federal tax; non-taxable income allowed; zero employee balances; export employee data; print employee listing; payroll check listing; payroll ledger.

One large bank we spoke with said that they use PC-AP for fixed fees (such as parking), but don't find the product flexible or powerful enough for other uses within the bank. They like it for situations where the amounts don't change from month to month.

Other users have made a virtue of the program's simplicity, and report success stories at getting the program up and running in record time. They contrast these stories with horror stories of commercial accounting systems that took hours of setup and weeks or months of learning. Although Medlin's Accounting systems can't be everything to everybody, some of his users swear by the program. They may use a spreadsheet for some calculations (like various deductions not easily calculated in the Payroll module) and then enter the results manually. In all, this is a product that is worth looking at. Medlin believes in his product and supports it actively, and his customers seem satisfied with what they have. For those who want to tinker and modify, source code is also available in Turbo Pascal.

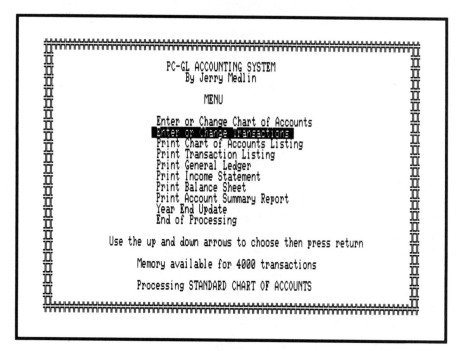

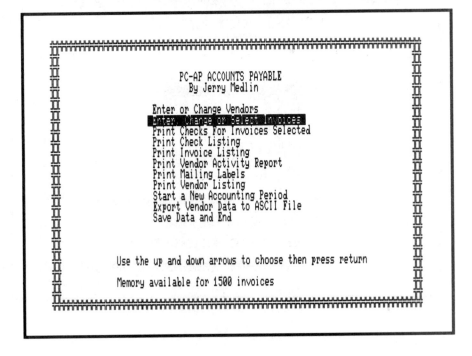

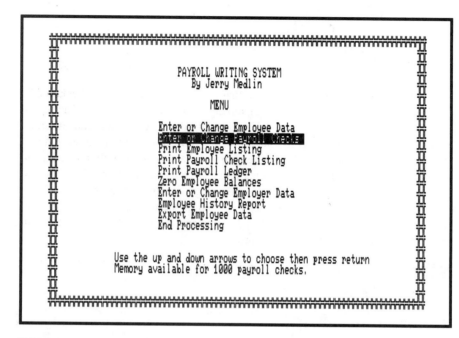

Medlin Accounting Shareware
Jerry Medlin
P.O. Box 357
Napa, CA 94559

Shareware: $35 each module; Turbo Pascal Source Code—$95 each module

Category: Accounting

System Requirements: IBM PC, XT, AT, or compatible; 256K; one disk
drive; 80 column printer (96 column printer required for Payroll)

Recommended use: small to medium business accounting

Major Pros: fast; simple to learn and to use; cost effective for those who can
use it

Major Cons: size limits; missing many features popular in commercial sys
tems; not fully integrated

Sources: popular BBSs and commercial services, or directly from the author.

FastBucks Ver. 3.18

Software Expressions
Shareware—$30

FastBucks is a home finance package that can be used to manage checkbooks, budgeting, financial planning, and organizing your financial records. The registered version of this product comes with a spiral bound manual and diskette. Sample data is also included so that you can try out some of the features without the fear of losing your own data. The entire package is completely menu driven and is designed for the non-accounting and novice computer user. The program supports up to 25 checking, savings, and charge accounts, and one cash sheet. Though transaction editing is possible, it requires the user to do editing from a different screen than data entry. A minor drawback, but it can be annoying if you make a mistake during the data entry process.

FastBucks Ver. 3.18
Software Expressions
Dennis C. Lozen
PO BOX 301002
Houston, TX 77230-1002

Shareware: $30

System Requirements: IBM PC,XT, or AT, or compatible, with 128K of RAM, DOS 2.0, or greater, two floppy disk drives, a monochrome or color monitor, and a 80 column printer (132 column or a printer that can print in compressed mode is recommended).

Recommended use: Home accounting and finances

Summary: An easy-to-use, fast, menu driven, home financial and accounting package designed for the computer and accounting novice in mind

Major Pros: Fast, easy-to-use, menu driven. Good features that perform reliably. Workswell with floppy disks

Major cons: Minor inconveniences in the editing features. No telephone support to registered users

Sources: BBSs, commercial systems, or directly from the author

---

Another minor inconvenience requires you to enter a transaction number in order to edit a transaction. If you don't know the transaction number, then you must list the account from another screen, then return to the edit screen to complete process. Once a transaction is edited, however, FastBucks automatically updates the account balance. The system uses a recursive budget model that is pretty easy to use, even if you have never done a home budget before. You can also display your expenses in a bar graph for the last year. A very handy feature that is also included is a financial calculation section. In this section, you can calculate item depreciation, savings, and loan information. In fact, you can even print out (to your screen or printer) a complete loan amortization. This kind of capability allows you to try "what-if" scenarios about costs and savings.

FastBucks is easy to install and use. The manual comes with step-by-step installation instructions. It also includes special configuration options to match your system environment. Presently, FastBucks supports about 32 different printers. If your printer is not directly supported, a special user configuration screen is provided to allow you enter your printer's control codes.

Another nice feature is the size of data files that FastBucks creates. Six years of activity only requires about 87K of disk space. This makes the program well suited for floppy disk users. Overall, the program works reliably, and quickly. Except for a few minor inconveniences, it provides good performance and features for the money while offering an easy-to-use environment for the novice. The program is user supported, so no support phone is available to answer questions. You can, however, write the author for support.

Finance Manager II G/L Ver. 1.2d

Hooper International
P.O. Box 62219
Colorado Springs, CO 80962
(719) 528-8989
Shareware—$40

This menu-driven accounting system packs the kind of power and tremendous features you would expect to find in packages at 3 or 4 times the price. The General Ledger module of Finance Manager II is the only one that is considered a Shareware product and has been user supported since 1984. However, several other commercial modules are available at low prices for registered users of the G/L. In fact, registered users can evaluate these commercial modules for only $3 each before purchase, but they are not Shareware products. These additional built in modules interface with each other almost flawlessly. The modules available are:

Accounts Reconciliation (for GL) ($15), Financial Utilities ($20), Accounts Receivable ($30), Accounts Payable ($30), and Payroll ($35).

Finance Manager is a menu-driven, double-entry bookkeeping system designed for both personal or small business use. To best utilize the system, you must be familiar with double-entry bookkeeping (debits and credits). To assist the beginning bookkeeper, Hooper has included sample accounts to help; during setup and to increase a novice user's understanding of the Finance Manager System.

An experienced bookkeeper will be up and running with this system in a matter of minutes. Novices will find themselves gently guided into an easy to use PC program and pleasantly presented bookkeeping system.

You can customize screens, reports and graphs to your own needs, and all are attractively presented. You simply can't miss with this package. Even though the G/L is used as a come-on for the rest of the package, it is worth it. For under $175 you can have a full blown accounting system that rivals larger, more sophisticated setups. We would recommend this package for home, and small to medium size businesses or departments.

```
AUG-2-88                   YOUR PERSONAL FINANCES          ESC to Exit
10:23pm                      HOME Demo Accounts




              ┌──────────────────────────────────────────┐
              │    FINANCE MANAGER II MASTER MENU          │
              ├──────────────────────────────────────────┤
              │                                            │
              │    ESC   End/Restart Program               │
              │    F1    System Utilities Menu             │
              │    F2    GENERAL LEDGER                     │
              │    F3    Accounts Payable                   │
              │    F4    Accounts Receivable               │
              │    F5    Payroll                            │
              │    F6    To be announced                    │
              │    F7    Financial Utilities               │
              │    F8    Order Form                         │
              │                                            │
              │                                            │
              │    ENTER YOUR SELECTION:                    │
              │                                            │
              └──────────────────────────────────────────┘



Version 1.2d                                    Free Memory 436K
```

The General Ledger keeps track of assets, liabilities, net worth, income, and expenses. Finance Manager also provides some trend line analysis, and graphic displays of account information are provided to supplement a wide range of standard business reports. The program is transaction based and transactions can be viewed and edited in detail, as well as summary entry. The program monitors functions such as bank balances, credit cards, loans, etc. Budgeting and budget tracking are incorporated into Finance Manager II.

We would like to see some export functions to allow data sharing with other programs. This feature is present in many other systems, and is necessary if you need to work with accounting data in spreadsheets, word processors, and databases. In fact, this system is would also benefit from an import function that would be able to take input from other programs and departments, avoiding extra data entry tasks.

Finance Manager II G/L 1.2d
Hooper International
P.O. Box 62219
Colorado Springs, CO 80962
(719) 528-8989

Shareware: $40 (printed manual $10 extra)

System Requirements: PC or compatible; 256K memory; at least 2 floppy-drives; DOS 2.0 or higher—Hard disk, 640K, and Hercules Graphics or EGA optional for increased performance and display.

Recommended use: Personal and Small Business Accounting

Summary: Fine introduction to the Finance Manager II accounting system; useable G/L module

Major Pros: Fast, easy-to-use, menu driven.; printer configuration works very well; reports are easy and very thorough

Major Cons: All modules are not Shareware; really not for home use (for serious bookkeeper)

Sources: BBSs, commercial systems, or directly from the author

---

Additional Features:

- Stores up to 1999 accounts
- Tracks monthly budget for income and expense accounts
- Maintains multiple sets of books (e.g. home and work)
- Provides three subtotal levels
- Reconciles checking accounts or other accounts
- Allows up to 32,000 transactions per year (3,800 with floppy disks)
- Sorts transactions by date order or by input order

With registration of the G/L, you receive: the most current version of product, free phone support for one year, a quarterly newsletter, $5 to $10 upgrades on new modules, disk and on-disk manual (printed manual is $10 extra).

Although the Shareware G/L program is the only part of this program that is treated as Shareware, the entire system is priced right for Shareware. We prefer Jerry Medlin's approach in offering all his modules as Shareware, but agree that Finance Manager II is a very worthwhile product.

—Gregory Salcedo

PFROI 3.2c
Techserve,Inc
Shareware—$20

Techserve, Inc. of Bellevue, WA offers one of the most comprehensive and de-lightful-to-use personal investment packages around, Shareware or otherwise.

PFROI is a personal portfolio manager that can serve the beginning as well as the experienced PC user/investor. PFROI stands for Portfolio Return On Investment. The program features clear, easy to understand screens, reports, and suggestions on how to track your personal portfolio. PFROI gives you true return on investment before and after taxes. The system is easy to customize to work with your own particular equipment configuration right down to the ability to switch from 4.77 MHz to a speed more suitable for faster machines.

PFROI's main use is in the charting and trading of various investments and ac-counts. Techserve offers an upgraded version of PFROI in the form of a commer-cial program called CAPTOOL ($79). This program adds expanded communica-tions and automatic data gathering capabilities. Techserve also markets BOND-

PRO ($30) and STOCKPRO ($30) which are included in CAPTOOL and are also available separately. These products can be combined to handle any type of security or client need and provide excellent portfolio analysis. People who have the Shareware product, PFROI, can get CAPTOOL for $59.

```
          Transactions : DEMOPF    Symbol : ALL***   siGn=On
 Esc Arws Pg ^Pg Ins Del ^Y   Alt + Sort  Print taX Rates Mask Dup saVe Arc Help
 Mo/Dy/Yr TAC Symbol-L#      Description      Quantity        Amount     Est. Tax
 == == ==  === ====== ==  ================== ============ ============  ========
 06/18/87 DV+ XON   -   Exxon                              340.00         95
 06/29/87 BUY USCRX - 1 USAA Cornerstone     162.1622    -3000.00
 06/30/87 DV+ TAN   -   Tandy Corp                          50.00         14
 06/30/87 DV+ MER   -   Merrill Lynch                       75.00         21
 06/30/87 IN- *BRKR -   Q2 Brkr mrgn int                   -11.23         -3
 07/02/87 BUY FMAGX - 1 Fidelity Magellan    35.3982     -2000.00
 07/15/87 BUY ASTA  - 1 AST Research 013 7/8    200       -2857.40
 08/13/87 SP+ XON   -   Exxon 2/1 split         400
 08/18/87 SLL DEC   - 1 Digital ($ to brkr a   -100       16825.00      3353
 89/01/87 DV+ F     -   Ford                               253.85         71
 09/10/87 DV+ XON   -   Exxon                              340.00         95
 09/15/87 SLL XON   - 4 Exxon 049              -100        5025.00       753
 09/16/87 BUY TCOR  - 2 Tandon Corp. 03        1200       -3696.00
 09/21/87 SLL F     - 2 Ford ($ to brkr acct   -100       10200.00      1309
 09/30/87 DV+ TAN   -   Tandy Corp                          50.00         14
 09/30/87 DV+ MER   -   Merrill Lynch                       75.00         21
 09/30/87 BUY TNOTE1- 1 2yr T-Note 8.5%         100      -10000.00
 09/30/87 IN+ *BRKR -   Brkr Q3 int                         93.12         26
 - / /            -
```

Shareware, Please Copy & Share

We like the author's thinking in this area. He reasons that if the user found out about CAPTOOL from Shareware, then he didn't have to spend money on advertising, and he passes the savings back to the consumer. This is a nice use of Shareware, not only because the Shareware product serves to help sell the commercial one, but because the Shareware product itself is more than adequate for many people's needs.

PFROI Features:

- Easy data input format.
- Computation of true return on investment (IRR method) on portfolio and securities before and after taxes.
- Reports including capital gains, dividend & interest reports for tax preparation and detailed open lot report for tax planning.

- Tax lot assignment methods including FIFO, average cost and specific assignment. Tax rates are user•configurable and estimated taxes are computed.
- Valuation graphics (CGA & Hercules supported).
- PFROI supports a number of security types (stocks, bonds, mutual funds, cds, depreciable assets, options, etc.) with many transaction types including reinvestment of dividends, interest and capital gains.
- Output is user selectable to a printer, text file, or screen.
- On registration you receive a disk containing the following enhancements:
  - Merge utility to merge multiple portfolios
  - Commission tracking
  - Portfolio security Beta calculation
  - Forecast income calculation
  - Price importing from text file
  - Telecommunications for price downloading from Dow Jones, CompuServe, GEnie, and Warner systems
  - Return on investment by security report
  - Additional open lot reporting detail
  - Beefed up manual (about 100 pages vs. about 45 in the distributed version). An up-to-date printed manual is only available with CAP-TOOL.

For foreign investors, PFROI handles international date conventions, currency formats, and decimal placement. A French version is also available.

This product performs a wide range of useful services for the moderate investor, but for those of you who require more sophistication, Techserve also markets a "pro" version called, not surprisingly, PFPRO. PFPRO's price, $495 ($695 after 12/88), may be more than you wish to lay out. However, if you do find yourself wanting or needing more investment features, PFPRO looks to be an excellent "upgrade." I recommend that you try the Shareware products first and then decide if you require the more involved commercial product.

--Gregory Salcedo

PFROI 3.2c
Techserve, Inc.
POB 70056
Bellevue, WA 98007,
1-800-826-8082 or 206-747-5598

Shareware: $20

System Requirements: AT-compatible or higher computer with a minimum of 256K RAM, more is recommended. (PFPRO requires a minimum of 512K)

Recommended use: Managing a Portfolio

Summary: An easy-to-use portfolio management package with powerful upgrade path

Major Pros: Easy to use; communications for price downloading, tax planning; reports

Major cons: none

Sources: BBSs, commercial systems, or directly from the author.

7

Databases

We use databases to file everything from stamp collections to our national debt. There are people handling lemonade stands with databases, and others handling billion dollar asset accounts—all on PCs. Some of the most successful and powerful programs produced for PCs have been databases. And one of the first Shareware products was a database as well. What follows is a very basic discussion of databases. If you already know about databases, skip to the applications. If you are new to computers and/or databases, read on.

Databases divide information into various categories. If you think of a database as a collection of organized information, you might call a phone book, card file, or lawyer's filing cabinet a database.

The information in a database is divided into files, records, and fields. If you think of an ordinary card catalog as a database, then the catalog itself would be like the entire file. Each card, on which there was a set of information per person, would be a record. And each entry (name, address, phone number, etc.) would be a field.

Databases allow us to sort information in various ways, to select certain information that shares common elements (like all people who live in New York and have the last name Smith), and also to produce reports formatted to be readable and often containing totals and sub-totals to make the data more meaningful. Databases do all this much faster than we could by hand.

Database Terms

A *Field* is a single unit of information in a database. A name, dollar amount, or zip code may be a field. A field is the smallest unit of information in a database.

A *Record* is a collection of fields. In a database, each record will contain the same fields, though the information contained in those fields will vary. For instance, in a mailing list database, one record may contain the name and address of John Q. Public, and another record would contain the name and address of Jane Doe.

A *File* is the collection of records in a database. The file is, at the same time, the file on disk and the collection of records. Most databases save information on a record-by-record basis, so whenever you add or change a record, it is saved to the disk file.

Some databases use one or more *Key fields* to help order and identify records. The key field is handled in a special way to speed up database operations. Some applications require a key field; in others it is optional.

An *Index* is a special file created by a database to help speed up operations. In some programs, you can create an index using certain fields. Indexes are used to speed up operations like searching and sorting.

Flat File refers to a database that manages only one file. A mailing list or check-book is a good example. For a contrast, see *Relational*.

The definition of a *Relational Database* can get quite complicated, depending on who is defining it. However, for our purposes, a relational database is one that can share data between two or more files. The extent of this ability to share determines how relational it is. Some relational databases can display and print fields from more than one file at the same time. Others can actually perform calculations based on fields from different files.

File Express ver. 4.15

Expressware
Shareware—$49.00

File Express is a flat file database program. Its major purpose is to create mailing databases. But to limit the description thus would be to short-change the program. In fact, File Express does everything a non-relational database should do, and does it well.

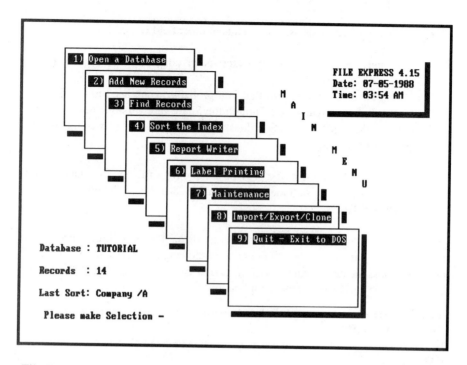

File Express is pretty well stocked with features. For example you can:

- generate reports that have subtotals, totals, multiplication, division, and subtraction on any numeric field

- sort records on up to 10 fields, with each separate field sorted in its own descending or ascending order

- search for or sort specific information within a record, regardless of case

- search for certain records on a global basis and replace any or all of the information found in them

- search for duplicate records within the records of a file

- search for duplicate information in two files

- merge up to 10 different files into one new file

- create automatic entry fields, like the automatic time stamping of a record during entry

- create calculated fields using constants or other field values

- print mailing labels up to five across in condensed or regular mode

The program is so straightforward that you probably won't need to use the 300 page manual that accompanies it. Though the Shareware version does not come with an index, the registered version does. Even so, the manual is complete and easy enough for a beginner.

To create a database you must first provide a name for a file, the field names, and their types. This process is all menu driven and is ideal for beginners and convenient for advanced users.

After you define a file, you can begin to enter data. The only limitations in this area are: a file can only have 120 fields; the field lengths can't be larger than 250 characters; and the maximum number of records can't exceed 16,000,000 records. This should be sufficient for most applications.

File Express ver. 4.15
Expressware
P.O. Box 230
Redmond, WA 98073
Phone (206) 788-0932

Shareware: $49

Category: Database

System Requirements: 320k of available memory recommended; IBM PC, XT, AT or any close compatible; color recommended, but it will work with composite or monochrome displays

Recommended Use: managing mailing databases

Major Pros: easy to learn and use; very powerful sort and extraction features

Major Cons: limited record lengths, fields and file lengths

Sources: popular BBSs and commercial services, or directly from the author

---

Creating reports and labels is easy. Again, the program guides you through a series of menus, prompting you for the information required in the report or label.

Enhanced label-generation features are included, such as the ability to print in condensed mode as mentioned above. When you are finished, File Express saves the layout for later use.

The program really shines in its ability to sort and extract data. It does these operations with extreme ease and flexibility. With this new version expect to see a dramatic increase in speed. Even if you have never used a database program before, you can work with this one. There are no equations to enter. All you do is answer the program's questions on how you want your data organized, and it does the rest. This, combined with the enhanced label generation features, makes File Express the ideal program for handling small to medium sized address files.

Though this program is missing some database features, its straightforward approach to filing, ease-of-use, and unique approach has to make it one of the best filing programs available in Shareware.

FLOWMAIL 3.0

Flowsoft Custom Programming
Billy Anderson
875 Franklin Road # 1635
Marietta, GA 30067
(404) 428-4028

Flowmail is not technically Shareware anymore. The author has informed us that the current version, 4.2, is a commercial program selling for $129. However, he also informs us that he will still honor the $50 price to upgrade from the Shareware version to the commercial one. For that reason, we have elected to include Flowmail 3.0 in this book. We feel that the Shareware version is a very good program, and that, for $50 more, you can get a commercial program with major enhancements at less than half the price. Such a deal!

Reprinted by permission of PDN Newsletter. This review is based on the <u>registered</u> version.

Mailing list managers seem to abound on the various bulletin boards and data services I frequent. So, when I set out to add some depth to the mailing list section of PDN's program listing I was surprised to find most of them were fairly weak and lacking in the quality for which I try to find. I must have rejected eight to ten mailing label programs when I came across FLOWMAIL 3.0. I already had a label program that specializes in small, highly repetitive labels and one that was well suited for small or personal mailing list but I wanted to find something with some teeth in it.

FLOWMAIL appears to be just the tiger I was looking for. The SHAREWARE version has about two-thirds of its features disabled but even that one-third runs circles around programs such as dBASE III+. First, let's look at what one gets with the SHAREWARE version.

To start, FLOWMAIL can handle up to 10 million names. Very few individuals have a need for this much power but I know there are numerous small businesses that can easily build up a mailing list of ten thousand plus. That size would be child's play for this program.

Data entry is very painless. The full-screen format is well laid out and includes such features as adjustable parameters whereby you can establish fields that carry over the entry of one record into the next record being added. Thus, if every name your adding lives in Muskogie, Oklahoma you only need to type it once and it will be carried over to the next entry until you type in another name such as Tallahassee, Florida. Obviously, this can save a lot of wear and tear on the finger tips. If that isn't good enough there's also an "overlay template" feature where you can add certain data to the blank template form and each time you hit page-down all of the template entries are added to the new entry.

Other fields along with the standard address information include print codes which I discuss later, two separate date fields, a money field and a carrier route field which will also be covered later.

All mailing label programs sort records. Some by last name, some by zip code, and some by user defined fields such as states. FLOWMAIL can sort by company name, an individuals last name, street address, state, zip code, phone number, either of the two date fields, money, data line or in bulk mail format. I'm sure an experienced dBase programmer could get dBase III+ to do a bulk mail sort but he would have spent a lot of time writing and debugging code to do it.

FLOWMAIL'S printing features are even more impressive. One can specify label to print within a range of record numbers, dates, money, data lines or print codes. The print codes are single letter codes assigned by the user. One can use a "C" for an active customer, "P" for prospect, "L" for lost customer, "E" for employee or anything else you might choose. Printing can then be set by any individual print codes or combination.

FLOWMAIL will print one, three, or four labels across. It will also do Rolex cards, 3 x 5 cards, and envelopes. When printing in bulk mail format labels will show if they are part of a five digit or three digit zip code series, and state and mixed state sort. A bulk mail report is also available listing the distribution of names to help with bagging and preparation of postal forms.

The above is a brief overview of the active features in the SHAREWARE version of this program. Those who register receive a fully operational version that includes the following features:

- Sorting capabilities to the carrier route level

- Import and export files

- Duplicate purges

- Deleted names retained in separate file

- Check and adjust proper state abbreviations

- Prints sack labels for postal mail bags

- Merge files

- Convert files to Upper or Lower case

- Global updates

- Totals for money and record counts

- Mail merge in quote/comma and Word Perfect format and more. . .

Like most things in this world, FLOWMAIL is not perfect. The documentation states that indexing might be a little slow for the first twenty records and should speed up from there. The first twenty records were extremely slow at indexing and, as promised, things did speed up but I still found there to be a three to four second delay while the last record is indexed and a fresh screen is written. I hope I don't come across as being too picky, but it is a minor situation that does exist.

I also had a problem with the printer installation. Both the documentation and the installation screen request you enter the decimal printer codes for a few different commands. This should not cause most people problems unless they are like me and have an inexpensive printer who's manual only lists the hexadecimal codes. For me, this involved locating a program that converted hexadecimal to decimal, which wasn't that big of a deal, but I bet there's a whole bunch of people who have no idea of the difference between these two numbering systems, let alone what a hexadecimal number represents. I might recommend a paragraph be added to the documentation addressing this situation and offering recommendations where a less experienced user might get help if their printer manual (if they have one) does not contain decimal listings for specific commands.

I found FLOWMAIL 3.0 to be very impressive. Obviously, one wouldn't need this much punch to handle a thirty name Christmas list but if it's an industrial strength mailing list program you're looking for I would highly recommend you take a look at this one.

—Tim Mullen

Instant Recall
Precept
Shareware—$69.00

Instant Recall is another one of those Shareware programs that eventually went commercial. Although the Shareware version can still be obtained from various sources, the program is now licensed to Broderbund Software.

```
══↓↓ InstantRecall ↓↓═══════════════════════════════════↑↑ Application ↑↑══
Find  Narrow  Reject  Cut  Ditto  Paste  Jump  Save  Window  Kill  Help  ──>esc
                                                                    14 of 35 Found
To-Do List

Communications:
* Call Barbara about the sales presentation
* Write Bob about media package

Pick Up:
* File folders
* New phone directory

Action Items:
* Sales forecast due 10/5
* Assign documentation task
  ───────────
Comments:
Here's a record which keeps your To-Do List.  You can get to it any time, just
by switching to Instant Recall and FINDing To-Do.

Press the grey plus key at the right of your keyboard to get the next record,
OR press ctrl-E to exit Instant Recall.
─────────────────────────────────────────────────────────────────────────────
created: 3/12/86   modified:           reminder:                    Ins   more
```

Instant Recall is a free-form text base that can work in the background as a TSR (Terminate and Stay Resident) utility. It works like a text editor and a database at the same time. Each "record" can be up to 60 lines of free-form text. No fields are used. Each word in every record is indexed, and you can almost instantly find an occurrence of any word, phrase, or combination of words and phrases.

The *Find* feature is the best part of this program. You can use several Boolean operators like *AND* and *OR*, stacking queries up to seven levels. For instance, you could *Find* Bill Jones (which would find Bill and Jones), or *Find* (Bill or Bonnie) Jones, which would find Bill Jones or Bonnie Jones. You can also find records that were created on or around a particular date (Find created > 1/1/88), or between dates (Find created >1/1/88 and <12/31/88). Also find records by the date they were last modified. You can also flag a record to come up on a particular date. Use this feature to remind you of appointments, birthdays, or any other future event.

Instant Recall version 1.64F
Precept
(415) 647-2879

MemoryMate
Broderbund Software
(415) 492-3500

Shareware: $69

Category: Free-form Database (TSR)

System Requirements: 256k of available memory recommended; IBM PC, XT, AT or any close compatible; DOS 2.0 or higher.

Recommended Use: Free-form information storage and retrieval; multitudes of uses including todo lists, notes, addresses and phone numbers, etc.

Major Pros: easy-to-use memory resident operation text editing functions com bines with powerful search facilities cut, copy, and paste

Major Cons: unregistered version limited to 80K file size

Sources: popular BBSs and commercial services, or directly from the author

---

With Instant Recall, you can enter any text and find it again when you need it. Write those random notes, phone numbers and addresses, reminders, to do lists, etc. Use tag words to find records again. For instance, I use the word TODO for my to do list. I simply type Control-F then "todo" to find that record.

When you use the find command, Instant Recall finds all records that match the criteria. A prompt at the top of the screen lets you know how many records have been found, and which one you are currently viewing in the form *3 of 15 Found*. You can use the Narrow command to further refine the search, or use the Reject command to remove specific records from the current group. You can also cut and paste information from one record to another, import or export ASCII data, and print selected records out to the printer. The Window command lets you see the application which resides under Instant Recall when you are using it in memory resident mode. Instant Recall uses about 70K as a TSR.

The Shareware version of Instant Recall is limited to an 80K file, but the registered version (MemoryMate) is capable of virtually unlimited sizes.

Instant Recall is an excellent product. However, Precept has licensed it to Broderbund Software, and it is now marketed as MemoryMate. MemoryMate has many improvements added, and Broderbund will sell the commercial product for $69.95 (the same price as the Shareware price, so it amounts to the same thing).

I've been using MemoryMate now for many months and it has completely replaced my notepads and phone directories. I even take notes from phone interviews directly in MemoryMate. I highly recommend Instant Recall or Memory-Mate. They are both winners.

LAB'L ver. 1.41

MAE SOFT
Public Domain (Some donation would be appreciated by the author)

LAB'L is a free-form database system designed for maintaining address lists and generating mailing labels. The program allows you to create labels from two to 12 inches in length and from ten to 50 columns wide. It also supports several printers and will print one, two, or three labels across the page on a standard 8 1/2" printer.

Since LAB'L has no set fields, i.e. name, address, etc., you have the flexibility to create a custom mailing file exactly to your needs. To create a new file, you simply tell LAB'L how many lines you require in the file, and how many columns across. You can also use more lines than you need for the labels and use the remainder for notes, phone numbers, etc.

One feature that is most notable is the built-in buffer for storing often used lines. You can put lines into and take them out of any label. You can also store any extended ASCII character like double line, or double line corner. This is useful if you wish to put a fancy trim on your labels. LAB'L also stores the last deleted label in the buffer. This allows you to undelete the label, or move the label to a different position in the file.

Since LAB'L is written in BASIC and uses random access files, you are limited to about 32,767 records per file. The sort routine will only sort 2,000 records, so anything beyond that is pointless, unless your needs don't require sorting. Another drawback is the sorting speed—for 2,000 records, it takes about 4 1/2 minutes. Also, the sort routine only sorts based on a line in a given record, not on a position in a given line of a record. This means that if you want to sort your file in zip-code order, for example, you must place the zip code on a separate line of each record. You can also import and export ASCII data files.

LAB'L
MAE SOFT
Rt. 3 BOX 620
Rockwell, N.C. 28138
704-279-4433
704-279-2295

Public Domain: (However some donation would be appreciated)

Category: Specialized database

System Requirements: 256k of available memory recommended, IBM PC, XT, AT or any close compatible, color recommended but it will work with composite or monochrome displays. A hard disk is highly recommended, but not required. An EPSON or IBM compatible printer for printing labels, and a modem for the phone dialer

Recommended use: Maintaining small address files

Major Pros: Easy to learn and use. Powerful editing features with easy-to-use menu driven interface

Major Cons: You can only sort 2,000 records. Slow sort speed. You can only sort by line not by a position in a line

Sources: Popular BBSs and commercial services, or directly from the author

---

If you have a modem, LAB'L has built-in phone dialer which will dial any number in your file. Also included is a pop-up directory of area codes by state.

LAB'L has a very easy-to-use menu interface and excellent editing features. The program allows you to customize its configuration depending on your needs. Though the manual is brief, it does explain each feature adequately.

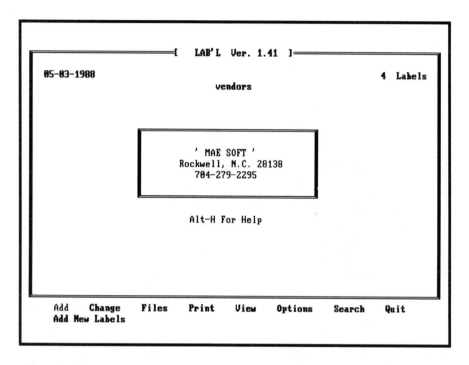

Though this program has some drawbacks, it does provide a quick and easy method of maintaining small address files where the formatting of the labels does not have to be precise. For larger jobs, see FILE EXPRESS.

PC File+ ver. 2.0

Buttonware
Shareware—$69.95

PC File+ is a flat file, data base program that has limited relational file capabilities. It is probably one of the most popular database programs in shareware today.

The program is completely menu driven and contains over 187 pop-up help screens which can be moved around using the directional keys. In addition, these help screens can be activated through a teach mode which brings up the help screen just before a menu action executes which allows the the user to review what the selection will do or what the various options mean. The program also has macro keys which can be customized for each application.

To create a database, you must first define the fields that will be in the file. There are two methods of doing this. The first method is called the fast method, when you type in all the names and the lengths of the fields you wish to use, and PCF defines an entry/edit screen for you. The second method is called paint. In this mode you are presented with a blank screen in which you place your field names along with brackets ([ ]) to show the length of the field. You can define up to 70 fields per database, but the screen size is limited to 21 lines by 80 columns. Fields will take any type of data in them—numbers, letters and special characters. However, you can create an edit mask for a field that restricts what is entered into it. In addition, you can define a field as containing a constant value, an automatic value which automatically enters a value into a field (like the date and time for the operator), or a calculation that performs a calculation among fields in a record of the database, or performs a calculation based on a field from another data base by looking up its value. This is the only relational file capabilities that PC File+ has. Most fields are limited in length to 200 characters, however, there is one exemption which is called a super field. A super field, is a field that can vary in length, and it is entirely dependent on the number of fields you have defined in your database. For example, if you have 10 fields defined, then the maximum length is 945 characters. If you have one field defined, then the maximum length would be 1665 characters. In order to define a super field, you must have less than 21 fields defined in your data base and the super field must be the last field defined on your input screen. Super fields are especially useful for creating free form text in a record, like a comments field. Since the text wraps to the next line when it reaches the end of a line, entry of text is very much like using a text editor.

Once your data base is created, entering data is fairly easy. You can move around the input form using the keypad directional keys, as well as make corrections with the backspace, insert, and delete keys. Two other handy keystroke combinations are provided during data entry. The first key combination allows you to duplicate the entire last record entered onto the next new record. The second keystroke combination will memorize an entry of a particular field which allows you to repeat that entry in the field as needed on subsequent entries.

PC File+ also has various ways for you to search the data you have entered. First, the program will ask whether you want a simple or complex search. A simple search allows you to enter the information you want to find in the field you want the program to look in. The second search, called the complex search, allows you to enter a search criteria using conditional and logical formulas. Within each search type—simple or complex, there are four different ways to tell PC File to look at the data. The first method is called *scan across,* which tells PC File to look for every occurrence of the data you told it to search for in a given field in every record. The second method, *generic*, will search for all occurrences of fields that begin with the data you told it to search for. For example, if you enter *mit*, the program will also find all records that begin with *mit*, like mitten, mitsy, etc. The third type, *soundex*, looks for data in a given field that sounds like the data you are searching for. For example, a search for the name Rawlins in a name data base, will also find Rollins, and Rawlings. The fourth type is called *wildcard*, which will find information based on characters in a certain fixed position within a field.

Once you find the information you are looking for, you may either modify or delete the record, or you can enter a browse mode that lets you look at the record and the next records that follow in a columnar format. Once in browse mode you can scroll either forward or backward.

Setting up an application environment can be done easily. The program allows you to set up to five levels of password protection in the file and editing functions. To make life easier for the user, PC File allows you to create macro keys which can do a sequence of events like sort a file by zip code and print mailing labels, in one keystroke.

The report capabilities of PC File give you the ability to create just about any type of report you would want from your data base. To create a report is similar to creating an input screen. You are given an option of creating a simple report such as a simple listing, or a complex report such as an invoice, which you paint on your screen. The command language provides such features as the ability to look up a value from another data base, conditional page breaks, etc.

The sort utility provides the option of sorting the file with up to 10 levels of sort conditions, and a mixture of ascending and descending order parameters. In addition, you can sort by *soundex*, which means you can sort your file by how the records sound, and sort on calculated fields.

Other features included are a built in mini-wordprocessor called the letter writing feature, which is used for creating letters and correspondence, and by using the data from your data base, you can create personalized form letters. PC-Label is also included with the package for creating mailing labels with your data. You can also import and export your data to a variety of file formats such as DBASE, Word Perfect, Word Star, Word, ASCII, Peachtext, and others.

In this most recent version, some significant enhancements have been added to the product which include:

- The ability to graph your data in a variety of formats and the ability to display plotted averages, weighted averages, and least-square regression analysis lines with your graph.

- Window fields which allow you to create fields that are wider than the screen. The window scrolls across the field as needed.

- Calculator hot key allows you to calculate at any time. Field names can be used in hot-key calculations.

- 8087 or 80287 math-chip support when it is available in your machine.

- PC File now provides network support.

PC FILE+ Version 2.0
ButtonWare, Inc.
P.O. Box 96058
Bellevue, WA 98009-4469
(206) 454-0479
(800) JBUTTON (order line)

Shareware: $69.95

Category: Database

System Requirements: 416k of available memory, IBM PC, XT, AT or any close compatible, color recommended but it will work with composite or monochrome displays (graphs will not work in monochrome).

Recommended use: Flat file database operations that are not application intensive. Beginners tool to learn more about database setup and operation.

Major Pros: Easy to use menu interface with plenty of help screens to guide the novice user. Versatility in handling most flat file database operations.

Major Cons: Lacks the power to create true relational database systems or applications for end users.

Sources: Popular BBSs and commercial services, or directly from the author.

The limitations of the program in the area of data base design and input screens are numerous. Since the files are fixed length, the program will reserve the total amount of disk space needed for every record, regardless if any data is entered into a field or not. Field names cannot be any larger than twelve characters, and cannot have any spaces or special characters like *()*, *<>* ,+, or - in them. This is very annoying since the field name has to be used as the input prompt, i.e. first name must be defined as *first_name*. Though the program will allow 70 fields in the database, its ridiculous for the author of this program to think that anyone could fit 70 fields with labels on a screen size which is limited to 21 rows by 80 columns. Similarly, the author claims that 71 databases can be open at one time. This gives the appearance that program is truly relational, but in reality it means that you can look up 70 fields in 70 different databases and use one field from the data base you are using.

In conclusion, this program may be one of the best database programs available in Shareware, and it is certainly the best supported. It contains many features and a certain amount of good organization. But compared to high-end commercial products, it rates below average. In any case, this product would be good for beginners who have no experience with database programs because it is easy to use with its help screens and menu driven interface. Also, the well-documented manual features a good index and good examples. For various purposes that take it slightly beyond a simple flat file database, PC File+ may be very useful, however we would not recommend this product for developing true relational data processing systems.

Wampum ver. 3.2B

Ward Mundy
Shareware—$25 per PC; $75 per network (plus $5 shipping & handling)

WAMPUM stands for Wards Automated Menu Package Using Microcomputers. The program attempts to provide some of the basic features of the dBASE III through its menu interface. The features of this program include:

- Creation and use of dBASE III-compatible databases.

- Complete multi-user network support using any dBASE file—however in our Shareware version, that capability is limited to a file size of 100 records. You must send in your $75 (plus $5 shipping and handling) to get the full working network version.

- Field types that can be Characters, Numeric, Date, Logical and Memo.

- Creation and use of up to 7 indexes per database file.

- Add, edit, delete, and undelete records in a database file.

- Display, list and print records from a database file.

- Creation and use of dBASE reports and labels via Nantuckets CLIPPER Report and Label Generator which is included in the package.

- WAMPUM mail-merge form letter files.

- Use of a keyed relational field to a second database during output functions such as reports and labels.

- Copy utility that allows copying to and from ASCII and dBASE III files.

- Calculated fields.

- Files can be rebuilt if they become damaged.

- Boolean searches with on-screen selection assistance.

- Global search and replace of up to 10 data elements in one pass.

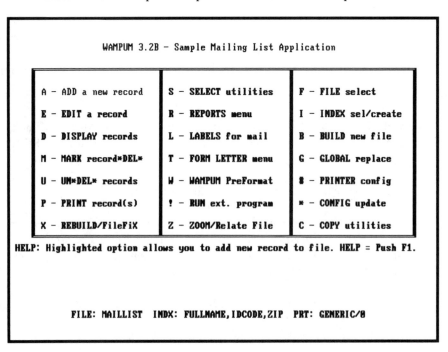

```
            WAMPUM 3.2B - Sample Mailing List Application


   ┌──────────────────────┬──────────────────────┬──────────────────────┐
   │ A - ADD a new record │ S - SELECT utilities │ F - FILE select      │
   │                      │                      │                      │
   │ E - EDIT a record    │ R - REPORTS menu     │ I - INDEX sel/create │
   │                      │                      │                      │
   │ D - DISPLAY records  │ L - LABELS for mail  │ B - BUILD new file   │
   │                      │                      │                      │
   │ M - MARK record*DEL* │ T - FORM LETTER menu │ G - GLOBAL replace   │
   │                      │                      │                      │
   │ U - UN*DEL* records  │ W - WAMPUM PreFormat │ # - PRINTER config   │
   │                      │                      │                      │
   │ P - PRINT record(s)  │ ! - RUN ext. program │ * - CONFIG update    │
   │                      │                      │                      │
   │ X - REBUILD/FileFiX  │ Z - ZOOM/Relate File │ C - COPY utilities   │
   └──────────────────────┴──────────────────────┴──────────────────────┘

 HELP: Highlighted option allows you to add new record to file. HELP = Push F1.



       FILE: MAILLIST  INDX: FULLNAME,IDCODE,ZIP  PRT: GENERIC/8
```

In this new release, some significant enhancements have been made to the product. Most notably, is the increase in performance from version 3.1. In addition, registered users of the product can now choose between three different versions of the product: one supporting Clipper indexes, another supporting dBase indexes, and a third supporting FoxBASE indexes. All three still support single user and network applications with automatic file and record locking. The Shareware version, which is the version that is reviewed here, uses Clipper indexes.

Along with the good, there always seems to be some bad: The price of the network version has increased by $25 from the previous version, and the author is now charging a shipping and handling fee of $5 as well (it is still a good deal for those that need the program, however).

On a more disturbing note, the author has "time-stamped" the Shareware version to stop working in two years. Though the author explains that you can set your system clock back to re-enable the program he makes one frightening note in his documentation. We quote "If a version has expired, however, it does mean that you should continue to use it with extreme caution and AT YOUR OWN RISK!" He then goes on to explain that his experience in the Shareware market has been that programs are more likely to be corrupted once their age reaches the two year mark. He then talks about trojans and virus programs infiltrating the market. From all of this, one can presume that the author has placed some kind of time bomb in his product. We found this all very unsettling, even though the author may have very good intentions and we fully support his right to be paid by people who use the product for two years! Lastly, the author still does not provide a telephone number for technical support.

The program offers two modes of operation—developer and end-user mode. In end-user mode, the menu of operation is essentially the same as the developer mode menu, except that some of the functions like the "copy utilities" have been removed. In addition, the end user is locked into manipulating data in one file, and he or she can not change the file selection unless you want him to. WAMPUM decides which file is the default by reading a configuration file.

The program comes with a sample mailing list application as the original default configuration. Creating a file with WAMPUM is like creating a file in dBASE—you are prompted to enter field names, their types, lengths, and the number of decimal places in a dBASE-like format. The major difference lies in how the two products behave. In dBASE III, when you enter a date field type, for example, dBASE automatically fills in a field length of 8 and skips the rest of the prompts, and asks you for the next field name. WAMPUM will allow you to enter arbitrary lengths and other garbage in the remaining fields, and then return an error message after the last prompted entry.

Entering data into the file is much the same as entering data while using dBASE. There are some minor directional key differences such as the use of the PgUp and PgDn keys, but these are only minor inconveniences. In this version, the developer has complete control over how the data entry screen will look and perform for the end user.

Creating an index of a file is optional, but in order to retrieve a record you will have to know the relative record number. If you do decide to index the file on a particular field, you will be prompted for a key value any time you wish to edit or display records in the file. You can switch between the two methods though, through one of the menu commands. This method of entering key values to display or edit records is very cumbersome, since most people may not know what a key value is. The only option is to use the search utility and specify a boolean search for a range a records, find the record you are looking for, and then return to the edit function. WAMPUM comes with a "Record Selection Assistant" to help you with the boolean searches.

The report and label functions of the program are handled externally by Nantucket's CLIPPER Report and Label generators which come bundled with the product. The WAMPUM mail merge form letters are supposed to fill the gap where dBASE leaves off—specifically, dBASE does not have a convenient method for creating form letters, and then mail-merging data into the letter. WAMPUM gets around this by actually creating a form letter in a database file. You enter the data or letter one line (record) at a time in a standard dBASE-like form field 136 characters in length. In order to edit your form letter, you must purchase a form letter editor from the author at a cost of $20. We're not particularly fond of this feature and think that using an ASCII editor or word processor is much easier.

Though this product has some weaknesses, it is very useful for manipulating dBase files. Due to its design it is not suited for extremely complex applications, but for basic flat file applications requiring compatibility with dBase, it may be just the ticket The manual provides a good index and is clearly written. Its recommended that you purchase the soft-bound manual from the author. The documentation is 180 pages long!

Wampum Ver. 3.2B
Ward Mundy
4160 Club Dr.
Atlanta, GA 30319

Shareware: $25.00 (single user) $75 (network version) add $20 if you want a
soft-bound manual (both versions) plus $5.00 shipping and handling (both
versions)

Category: Database

System Requirements: 640k of available memory recommended, IBM PC,
XT, AT or any close compatible, color recommended but it will work with
composite or monochrome displays. A hard disk is highly recommended,
but not required (in most versions)

Recommended use: Flat file data base applications

Major Pros: Easy to learn and use. DBase file compatibility. On-line help
available

Major Cons: Shareware version time-stamped. No phone number provided for
technical support

Sources: Popular BBSs and commercial services, or directly from the author

PC Tickle ver. 1.0

ButtonWare
Shareware—$29.95 (plus $5.00 for shipping)

Taking a different approach to database management, ButtonWare's PC Tickle allows you to create reminder lists, checkbook managers, and other applications
with some simple ASCII editing. The basic premise behind this product is that
you must create and maintain an ASCII file of dates and things to do, or variables. The program will automatically scan for dates on lines, and if a date
matches the current system date, then that item will display in a printed or screen-
displayed schedule for that day.

In addition to its general functions as a reminder file, PC Tickle also can be used with variables. It will total all variables individually and also provide a grand total. The program includes sample checkbook and expense management programs.

Dates can be written with wild cards. For example, a line in the file containing a date written as *07/**/87* would display any day in July of 1987. A date written ***/**/87* would display all during 1987. A format like *(WED) **/**/87* would display each Wednesday of 1987.

Variables are formatted as *$$VARIABLE*, and each tickle file can contain up to 50 different variable categories.

An unusual manual is contained on disk. It can be printed out, but it can also be viewed on screen via a system of menus and bookmarks. You choose what section of the manual you wish to read, and the program displays that section a screen at a time. Unfortunately, the manual is not available as an ASCII document, so you must use the routines provided to read or print it.

PC Tickle 1.0
ButtonWare, Inc.
P.O. Box 96058
Bellevue, WA 98009-4469
(206) 454-0479
(800) JBUTTON (order line)

Shareware: $29.95 plus $5 shipping and handling

Category: Database

System Requirements: PC or compatible; DOS 2.0 or later; 40K of RAM to run TICKLE, 175K to run TICKLED (the editor); at least one 360K drive; 80 column display; optional printer

Recommended Use: keeping schedules and other date ordered material

Major Pros: keeping logs and to do lists; versatility of applications through the use of variables and simple math

Major Cons: somewhat dependent on user to keep information current; few data entry shortcuts

Sources: popular BBSs and commercial services, or directly from the author

---

PC Tickle is a clever program. It's boundaries depend on the user's ability to keep the text file of dates and other data current. The program comes with a pretty fair basic text editor, *TICKLED.COM*, but keeping the file up to date is probably more work than it's worth. The slogan for PC Tickle is, "The program that never forgets!" Unfortunately, most of us do. If you forget to update PC Tickle, it won't have a chance to remember. One criterion for the program, as explained in the manual, is to be organized. I guess I figure that the more organized I am, the less I need a program like PC Tickle. There are some excellent commercial products that do many of the same things this program does, but better.

We've included PC Tickle here because it's unique, and we're sure that some readers will be saying to themselves, "That's for me!" Also, it's ButtonWare, and that means that support and quality will be high.

Note: For another product with excellent database features, see Homebase in the Desktop Manager chapter.

Applications Generator System (AGS) ver. 2.0

Other Database Ideas
RL Coppedge, CDP
Shareware—$50 (recommended registration fee)

AGS is an applications generator for dBase III+ (or a work-a-like). The product is designed to eliminate about 90% of a programming job by automatically creating menus, forms and reports based your specifications. AGS is actually a protected dBase application that runs as a "front-end" to dBase during the creation process. The resulting dBase code is a set a values that is piped into the AGS run-time system.

AGS has some unique features. The system allows you to export data for form-letter processing in several popular word processing formats. In addition, the system allows you to maintain a library of filters which can be recalled during most operations that require your data to be filtered (i.e. searching all accounts over 30 days). The author also promises that a file transfer module will be added in future releases to aid in entering data from remote locations.

Several things are really lacking in AGS. For example, there is no "paint" facility to create custom forms or menus. All menus and forms follow a predefined layout in AGS which stifles creativity. In addition, if there are certain menu items which are not used in an application, it simply blanks out the unused menu items. So, what you end up with is a menu that could be numbered 1,2,3,5,9 with gaping holes in the middle. Also, there is no relational file handling. In other words, you can not relate information from one application to another.

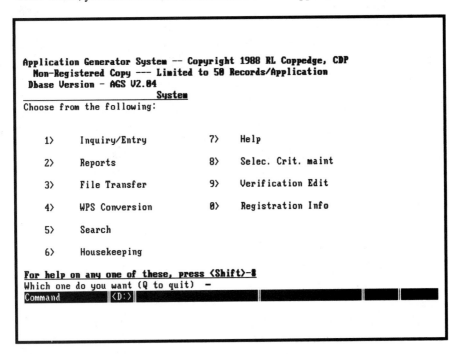

This Shareware version only allows you to enter 50 records into your application. You'll also find the manual incomplete and not suited for a novice.

For creating simple flat-file applications where looks aren't important, this may be the tool for you, though this program does not really stack up against some of the commercial products available, except in price.

```
┌────────────────────────────────────────────────────────────────┐
│                                                                │
│ Application Generator systems (AGS) ver. 2.0                   │
│ RL Coppedge, CDP                                               │
│ 446 Richmond Pk. E 402A                                        │
│ Richmond Hts, OH 44143                                        │
│                                                                │
│ Shareware: $39.00                                              │
│                                                                │
│ Category: Application tool                                     │
│                                                                │
│ System Requirements: 640k of available memory, IBM PC, XT, AT or any │
│     close compatible, color recommended but it will work with composite or │
│     monochrome displays, a hard disk, dBase III+ (or work-a-like) │
│                                                                │
│ Recommended use: Simple flat-file application generation       │
│                                                                │
│ Major Pros: Easy to use.  Unique export features built-in.  Forms and menus │
│     are built automatically for you                           │
│                                                                │
│ Major Cons: Shareware version limited to 50 records per application.  No paint │
│     facility for menus and forms.  The manual is incomplete and technical │
│                                                                │
│ Sources: Popular BBSs and commercial services, or directly from the author │
└────────────────────────────────────────────────────────────────┘
```

Easy Project Version 2.5

Parcell Software
Shareware - $39.00

Easy Project or EP is a versatile Project Manager and scheduling tool. With it, you can plan, control, and track a variety of projects. EP features include:

- Up to 20 user defined phases per project.
- Unlimited number of resources per project.
- Up to 1000 user defined tasks with up to 100 subordinate tasks per task, per project.
- Multiple resource assignments per task.
- Automatic Scheduling.
- Gantt charts showing planned vs. actual dates with variable scales.
- A variety of reports, including work plans, status reports and earned value accrual reporting.
- Context sensitive help screens.

- dBase III file compatibility.

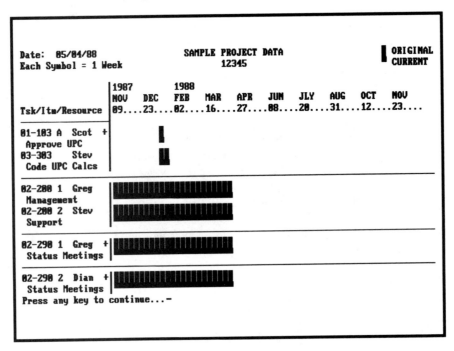

The guide and sample data is sufficient to get the novice started. It points out the key features of the software and how to use it. It also explains how to install the software in different computer environments. By registering the product, you receive a printed user manual and the latest version of the program. We didn't have the user manual while working with the product -- only the Shareware guide.

The program is easy to use and it makes excellent use of color, if you have it available on your system. The user interface is consistent, and it also includes an excellent help facility that rivals some of the best commercial programs. The program does slow down a bit when generating the automatic schedules and there is no tickler generation for resources that are behind schedule. These minor drawbacks should only affect those of you who want to manage really large projects.

To enter your project, you first perform a project setup—beginning by assigning a project number. If you forget the numbers that you have assigned to other projects, simply press the "F1" key and you will see a list of projects already entered. Now you simply fill out a project description, enter the project's phases and their descriptions, and indicate whether you wish GANTT information shown in days or weeks. Next, you must enter the resources that you will use for the project, regardless of which phase they will be used in, and the costs associated with each. These resources can be categorized as people, machines, vendors, etc. and the cost options allow you to define in units or as flat one-time costs for the entire project. In addition, the resource function allows you to tag special notes to each resource record, to further describe and identify the resource. Finally, you enter the tasks associated with the project by phase and assign the resources required to perform the task. Tasks may have sub-tasks to help you group smaller, less defined steps required for a task. These sub-tasks would be necessary for the completion of a task, but would not require a task definition of their own. I found the Automatic Schedule Generator an excellent way of letting Easy Project show me how the project might be approached. After the ASG has been used, you can go in and customize the resulting project by editing the specific tasks that may require your attention and assessment.

Easy Project Version 2.5
Parcell Software
P.O. Box 165
Geneva, Il 60134

Shareware: $39.00

Category: Project Manager

System Requirements: 256k of available memory recommended, IBM PC, XT, AT or any close compatible, color recommended but it will work with composite or monochrome displays. A hard disk is highly recommended, but not required.

Recommended use: Managing small to medium sized projects

Major Pros: Easy to learn and use. Powerful editing features with an easy-to-use menu driven interface, and excellent on-line help.

Major Cons: Lacks tickler generation.

Sources: Popular BBS's and commercial services, or directly from the author.

Another key feature is the file compatibility with dBase III. I easily imported the sample projects into a series of Paradox tables and was able to perform all sorts of management reports that would supplement Easy Project very nicely. I also brought the Paradox tables into Quattro and quickly produced graphs that could be presented in any project meeting to greatly enhance project communication and status. It isn't necessary to convert Easy Project to a database and then to a spreadsheet. Any program that can read dBASE file format can instantly make use of Easy Project Data.

In short, this is a first class project manager with good help facilities and features that are ideally suited for small to medium size projects. If you've never worked with a project manager before, then you may want to look at this one.

Avatar I Expert System 2.01

Essence AI-AMC Publishing
P.O. Box 1420
Beaverton, OR 97015-1420
(503) 644-2438
Shareware—$35

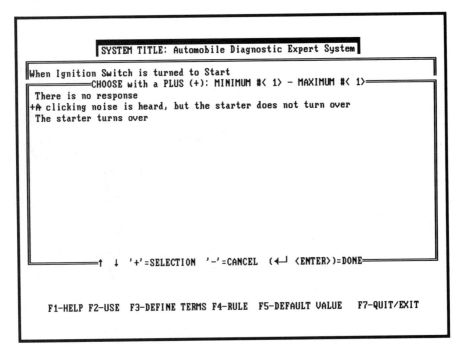

Avatar is an inference engine Expert System Shell that allows you to create and distribute your own Expert Systems royalty free. I reviewed the Shareware product, Avatar I, though there are commercial products with greater capacities, numbered Avatar II and Avatar III. I was quite impressed. Expert Systems are a very misunderstood art, and products like this can help the novice and the not-so-novice gain a better understanding of how these type of systems can be built.

The Essence AI-AMC Publishing people have got a great little system that, at the very minimum, teaches you a lot about how an expert system is built. The manual is fairly well written and takes a step by step approach to building an expert system. I would recommend some reading on PROLOG if you really want to get into some of the concepts, but the manual is more than adequate to get started.

I would have liked to see more of a tutorial with the public domain product. I think this would entice more people to want to move up a level. If users could understand the concepts and capabilities a bit more quickly, I'm sure it would whet their appetite for the more involved and capable versions of the Avatar series.

Avatar is built around a PROLOG concept. The heart of its system is an inference engine. This engine is the part of the expert system that actually puts your knowledge and rules about that knowledge to work. The engine employs a backward chaining technique with a forward chaining capability.

An expert system works by examining a list of possible conclusions for a problem, analyzing the conclusions by validating whether they are true or false and then arriving at the proper "answer" that meets the goals you have imbedded in the system. Avatar builds a system by breaking up information you enter into several categories:

> **GOALS**: The conclusions or answers that your system will try to prove and validate.

> **RULES**: A list of statements that will prove and lead the system to one or more conclusions. These rules are recorded in an *IF: and THEN:* format.

> **ATTRIBUTE-VALUE pairs**: The part of the system that users of the expert system will employ to communicate their answers.

You create the expert system by:

> 1) Creating GOALS the system will arrive at. GOALS are divided into TERMINAL (CONCLUSIVE) or CONNECTING (leading to other GOALS). Example:

```
SHAPES ARE
    equal sided
    curved
    straight
    etc.
```

Each GOAL must be contained in at least one of the RULES in the *THEN:* part of the rule contained in the system. In this way, the system will be able to find your GOAL (answer) by examining and validating the rules of the system.

2) You must create an ATTRIBUTE-VALUE set. The system will use this group of information in its validation process. The A-V statements are either a) set in the *THEN* part of the rules, or b) set by asking the user what values the attributes should take when you run the system. Example:

```
Length,4"
Width, 4"
etc.
```

Explanations for the A-V groups and their queries take the form of paragraphs.

3) Create the RULE set the system will use at RUN time.

```
IF the SHAPE is
    equal sided
    the angles are 90 degrees
THEN
    the SHAPE is a SQUARE.
```

As you add or change elements in the system they are immediately available since the inference engine is an interpreter. Avatar recommends that you start by by entering broad goals and refine your system "as you go." The next step would be to break down sections (RULES and A-V groups) into more detail, perfecting your Expert System on the way.

Avatar is available in a series of products that range from its entry level public domain product to its high end Level III product that includes the user defined customized reports. All levels of Avatar are distributed with a royalty-free provision.

Avatar I Expert System 2.01
Essence AI-AMC Publishing
P.O. Box 1420
Beaverton, OR 97015-1420
(503) 644-2438

Shareware: $35

Category: Expert System
   Avatar I—Level I 50 Rule Set (Public Domain)

   Avatar I—10,000 Rule Set, RunTime system, no royalty requirement. Ex
   panded Documentation and Tutorial. ($35.00)

   Avatar II—Same as Avatar I and in addition has the ability to access DOS to
   run external programs. Also included are variables with character entry and a
   feature that allows you to import data from other files. ($55.00)

   Avatar III—Same as Avatar II but in addition allows for variables and match
   functions along with a report generator that allows for customized report
   output following a system run. ($115.00)

Recommended Use: Introduction to Expert Systems/Inference Engines

Requirements: IBM PC or compatible; 256K Minimum 512K-640K recom
   mended; Mono or Color (user defined); Single Floppy operation;
   Recommended: Dual Floppy or Hard drive.

Major Pros: good learning tool, easy upgrades to more sophisticated versions,
   good value for the money

Major Cons: despite being a good learning tool and having good documenta
   tion, the tutorial and examples could be beefed up

Sources: Popular BBSs and commercial services, or directly from the author

—Gregory Salcedo

Fund Director (unknown version)

Kent A. Guske
Public Domain ($20 contribution requested)

Fund Director is a complete fund-raising application system for charitable groups and organizations. It is designed to help the fund director in record keeping, forecasting, producing progress reports, and other statistical functions for an annual or capital fund drive.

```
M E N U

1.  Enter Prospects and Amounts.
2.  Enter Pledge or Amount Paid.
3.  Correct Prospect Information.
4.  Give Goal Forecast.
5.  Suggest Giving Levels.
6.  List Top Prospects.
7.  Evaluate Goal Progress.
8.  Suggest Report Meeting Targets.
9.  List, Report, or Print Mailing Labels.
10. Begin a New Year.

Choose a Number ( - ). Hit Enter.
```

Features include the ability to add or change prospects, enter pledges and amounts paid, provide goal forecasts, suggest giving levels, evaluate goal progress, and suggest report meeting targets. Fund Director will provide printed reports on the top prospects, a master listing of the pledgers (alphabetically if desired), a solicitor's report, and mailing labels for mailing solicitations.

The program is menu driven and is easy to learn and use. Fund Director is written in BASICA and requires BASICA to run. Because of this, the application is extremely slow. It appears that Fund Director does not maintain an index of the data, since a search requires it to read every record sequentially. Also, producing a report requires the program to make several passes of the data file.

The editing features are extremely primitive—to edit a line you must type in the line number to change and retype the whole line rather than correcting just the portion that needs to be corrected.

The manual provides good information for the novice fund director about how to manage a fund drive and it gives detailed information on how to use the program.

Fund Director (unknown version)
Kent A. Guske
107 Willow
Sylvester, GA 31791

Public Domain: ($20 contribution requested)

Category: Fund raising

System Requirements: 64k of available memory recommended, IBM PC, XT, AT or any close compatible, BASICA or any BASIC interpreter equivalent. A printer for printing labels and reports

Recommended use: Managing annual fund raisers

Major Pros: Easy to learn and use. Comprehensive features for managing a fund drive. A good primer is included in the manual for the novice fund director

Major Cons: The application is extremely slow and it has primitive editing capabilities

Sources: Popular BBSs and commercial services, or directly from the author

---

Overall, the program is quite comprehensive and it works—though at a snail's pace. It's too bad the author decided to write the application in BASICA. If it were written in dBase (the manual makes mention that the author is a dBase programmer) and compiled using a product like Clipper or DBIII Compiler, it would be faster and easier to use. However, the BASICA source code makes it easy for a novice to change the code to match his organization's specialized needs.

8

Desk Managers

Desk Managers are those wonderful memory resident programs that provide tools for instant access. The genre was popularized by Borland's Sidekick, and people have been improving on the idea ever since. There are quite a few Shareware Desk Managers in circulation. Homebase and Right Hand Man are two of the best.

Terms

A *TSR* (Terminate and Stay Resident) application is a program that, once run, remains in memory until you need to use it. Generally, a TSR can run at any time, even when you are running another application.

The *Hot Key* is the key combination used to activate a TSR. Some TSRs allow you to define the hot key, thereby avoiding conflict with your other applications.

DESKTEAM 1.05

ALTERNATIVE DECISION SOFTWARE, INC.
P.O. BOX 1807
WILLIAMSVILLE, N.Y. 14221
(716) 688-6673
Shareware—$25

Reprinted by permission of PDN Newsletter.

DESKTEAM is an excellent example of the quality that can be found in SHAREWARE today. DESKTEAM is a memory resident desktop utility that provides you with a calculator, calendar, note pad, phone dialer, alarm clock, DOS commands, and typewriter. Just tapping a couple of keys on your keyboard and all these tools are at your disposal without having to exit an operating program.

Not all users want to load up their system's memory with an assortment of TSR (terminate and stay resident) utilities. DESKTEAM is loaded into memory with the command *Deskteam /m*. Omitting the */m* will access DESKTEAM from your disk drive. Assuming DESKTEAM is directed to load into memory, you will briefly see Alternative Decision's SHAREWARE notice telling you DESKTEAM is active and resident and asking for regular users to register. This notice disappears and DESKTEAM stays hidden until you summon it by typing *<Alt> M*.

When you call up DESKTEAM, a small window appears in the upper right hand corner of your screen. Inside the window are the primary DESKTEAM commands:

F1	Exit
F2	Alarm Clock
F3	Calculator
F4	Calendar
F5	DOS Commands
F6	Notepad
F7	Phone Dialer
F8	Printer
F9	Typewriter
F10	Setup

Tapping any of the listed function keys calls up that particular function. *F1* allows you to back out of DESKTEAM or, if your in a hurry, you merely hit *<ESC>* and you will return to your interrupted program.

While working inside any of the DESKTEAM functions, you can call for help through the *F2* function key or, if you find the window is blocking a particular piece of information you need, *F3* will move the window to the opposite side of the screen.

Each of DESKTEAM's features can prove to be extremely helpful. The *alarm clock* is capable of alerting you with an individualized message that it is time to do a certain task. It can also set the system time and date, display the time on your monitor or execute a system command (DOS, Batch, Program) when the alarm is activated.

The *calculator* is a full function calculator with a tape display on screen. It is also capable of reading numbers directly off your screen and copying results back to another program.

The *calendar* not only displays a calendar for the current month but it also allows you to move back through previous months or years as well as ahead to future dates. Included with the calendar is a separate calendar notepad that allows you to make notes concerning certain dates. When the calendar is in a certain month, relevant notes will be listed below.

DOS Commands can also be executed from DESKTEAM without having to exit a program. The commands available include *ERASE, CHKDSK, PRINT, CHDIR, RENAME, COPY, TYPE* and *DIR*. Again, all this can be done simply by tapping *<Alt> M* without having to leave a running program.

The *NOTEPAD* feature of DESKTEAM allows you to enter a note on your computer at any time and recall or print that note at any time you choose.

The *phone dialer* is just that. Using a phone list made up by the user, DESK-TEAM will dial a number using any Hayes compatible modem. It should be noted that this is not an abbreviated communication program but rather a utility that allows you to dial numbers quickly and easily.

If you've ever had to change printing functions by sending commands to your printer you should find the *print control* portion of DESKTEAM helpful. Not only will this allow you to switch between several printers but it also permits you to send commands to a printer that will change the printing features. DESKTEAM comes with a files that include Epson and Okidata commands and it also allows you to tailor commands that might apply to another brand of printer.

If you've ever had to do just one envelope on your printer or had to type a brief note you know how nice it would be to be able to type directly to your printer as if it were a typewriter. DESKTEAM permits this with its *typewriter* utility. *F9* brings up a ruled window where you can change margins, set tabs and send form-feeds. Type a line, hit return and your text jumps to your printer.

DESKTEAM doesn't make you live with a certain list of default settings. For those with color displays, DESKTEAM has a wide variety of foreground and background colors one can choose from. You can also permanently adjust printer and modem settings. Once these adjustments are made they can be saved and DESKTEAM will use these settings every time it starts.

SUMMARY: This is no piece of back-room programming. A lot of thought, time and effort went in to produce this quality piece of software. Alternative Decisions asks $25 to become a registered user, and considering that you could spend three to four times that much on a similar retail product, any regular user of DESKTEAM should have no problems registering.

It was no accident that I chose DESKTEAM to appear in this sample issue of PDN. This is a prime example of the quality work currently appearing in the SHAREWARE market. I did test the major features of DESKTEAM and could not find any bugs. I believe it would be safe to predict that this problem-free operation would also extend to its more complicated minor features. It's for this reason I believe DESKTEAM qualifies for an *excellent* rating.

—Tim Mullen

Homebase ver. 2.0 production

Brown Bag Software
Shareware—See box

Homebase is a memory resident utility program (TSR) that works in the same fashion as Sidekick, from Borland International. Though the program may work in the same fashion, and have similar features, Homebase definitely takes memory residency to its limit.

Homebase comes loaded with features. These features include a terminal communications program, database management system, calendar/appointment system, text editor, name and address Rolodex with an auto-dialer, cut and paste from any screen to another, and of course, a calculator.

Homebase comes on two disks. Included on one of them is a program that installs the necessary files on your hard disk or floppy disk, depending on the type of system configuration you have and how you want Homebase to behave. For example, Homebase takes up about 170k if it is fully loaded as a permanent memory resident program.

You have an option of making Homebase "swappable" though, which means that Homebase will load a kernel of about 80k which will stay resident, and when you call up Homebase it will swap out any application from memory to disk, and then load itself from disk to memory. This option is great if you have expanded memory to use as a virtual disk. It takes about a second to make the swap. If you configure Homebase to swap from a hard disk however, it takes about 3 to 5 seconds to complete the operation. Therefore, it's not recommended to set Homebase in this mode, unless you absolutely need the memory.

After you install Homebase on your computer, you can activate it at any time by hitting *Alt-Shift-H*. Homebase will pop-up and present a menu of options. You can also hot-key to the function you want directly rather than going through the main menu. For example, if you want the calendar, you can type in *Alt-Shift-C*. This will take you directly to the calendar without having to go through Homebase's main menu.

The text editor in Homebase is quite good. To best sum up its features, you could call it a WordStar clone. This program incorporates all of the basic WordStar editing features including a mail-merge option. The size of the text window can also be changed on the fly. This program even allows you to sort lists alphabetically within the editor, which WordStar doesn't (but which Sidekick's editor does do).

The database system is both a free-form and template-style database system. The free-form database is called Notebase. After you create a Notebase, you enter data as if you were using the text editor. In fact, all of the editor commands are exactly the same. After you enter your note, the program prompts you for a key value. You can have several key values associated with one note. The built-in search feature allows you to search these key indexes for information.

The other type of file you can create is a more formal template-type database files. To create a template you must run an external program, but the data entry and file manipulation are all performed through Homebase. The program comes with several examples showing how to use these template files, such as a name and address file, a messages file, etc. You can even build auto-dialing functions into a template file, and also include little help prompts at the top of the screen.

Homebase comes with a report generator for creating mailing labels, Rolodex cards, or reports from your template files.

DOS service acts as a DOS manager or "front-end" to DOS. It has such features as displaying DOS directories in scrollable windows, erasing, renaming, copying and moving files between directories or disks, and editing or viewing text files with an editor. You can sort the files in the directory windows in just about any format you choose. This utility is very similar to Norton Commander, Commando, and PowerMenu's Disk Manager (see Menus).

Quick Term acts as a quick and dirty telecommunications program and auto-dialer. Though the terminal program is not as sophisticated as the others reviewed in this book, it does provide background ASCII file transfers. In other words, while you're working in your Lotus spreadsheet, Homebase can be sitting in the background capturing MCI mail or a stock report. Unfortunately, it does not support background Xmodem file transfers, but Xmodem transfers are possible using Homebase in foreground processing. Although the terminal program lacks sophistication, its convenience as a TSR makes it great for those quick telecommunications jobs like impromptu calls to the neighborhood BBS.

Cut and paste allows you to cut and paste from one screen to another. For example, you can cut a paragraph from a word processing document and paste it into a memo field in a dBASE file. This program makes cutting and pasting the easy two-step operation it should be. The cut is not destructive, so you don't have to worry about damaging the text that's being cut. Unfortunately, the cut and paste only works with text. If it could cut and paste graphics as well as it does with words, this program might make the IBM a serious contender to the Macintosh desktop.

The Calendar/Appointment system includes a to-do list, time and expense diary, alarms, and daily appointments. You can also maintain multiple calendars, like one for business and one for personal use. The calendar can be displayed in a daily, weekly, or monthly format. In addition, the program rolls the daily to-do list to the next day if you didn't get all of your tasks completed. The only thing the calendar/appointment system doesn't have is some special mark for a day having an appointment in it. This makes it difficult to look quickly at a week and see which days are free and which ones have appointments. But it's fairly easy to page through each day, so this is only a minor inconvenience.

The calculator provides enough power for even the most sophisticated computer user. The program gives you the ability to use up to 26 memory variables (which can also be used in calculations). In addition, it has a paper tape function which can be turned on or off. It has other unique features: you can place the calculator into add mode and enter numbers without pressing the plus key, or you can cut a column of numbers from a word processor and paste them into to the calculator for addition. The calculator does not provide for functions like tangent, cosine, sine, etc. It does provide the four basic math functions, and exponential, and can handle hexidecimal to decimal conversions.

This program is a superior product. It's so full of features that you may not need any other memory-resident programs in your computer. Despite some little quirks and minor drawbacks, we highly recommend it.

Homebase ver. 2.0
Brown Bag Software
2155 South Bascom Ave., Suite 114
Campbell, Ca. 95008
(408) 559-4545

Shareware: price varies with support options; ranges from $29.95 to $89.95

Category: Utility

System Requirements: 256k of available memory; IBM PC, XT, AT or any close compatible; color recommended, but it will work with composite or monochrome displays; any Hayes-compatible modem (optional)

Recommended Use: memory resident utility

Major Pros: flexible, easy-to-use utilities that provide all the desktop functions you could possibly want

Major Cons: memory hungry when fully resident; calculator has limited functions

Sources: popular BBSs and commercial services, or directly from the author

---

Right Hand Man ver. 3.3

Red E Products, Inc.
Shareware—$25

Right Hand Man (RHM) is a memory-resident productivity tool that provides an Appointment Calendar, ASCII Chart, Black Book, Calculator, DOS Services, Text Editor, Guarded Notepad, Card Index, regular Notepad, Transfer Window, and Typewriter. All of these features are modular, and can be added or deleted depending on your needs.

Because the program is memory resident, you can have access to RHM while working with your application programs.

The Appointment Calendar allows you to display a calendar for any month. Appointments can be created for any day of the year, and alarms can be set for any time of the day. The display showing the month at a glance shows which days have appointments by highlighting the date. This is a very convenient way of seeing which days are free.

The ASCII chart gives you a scrollable menu of all the ASCII characters, and what their decimal and hexidecimal values are, while the card index permits you to create up to 1000 electronic index cards for names, addresses, phone numbers, and comments (which can be 256 characters in length). Index cards can have multiple indexes with forward and backward searches using any of the entry fields. Wild cards are permissible. If you have a modem, you can use the call option, which will call the number entered in a card's phone number field.

The Black Book is a private index of names and addresses. It works the same way as the card index does, except that it requests a password every time you invoke an index. The program uses the password to encrypt or decrypt what is added, written to, or read from the card index file. All of the features of the card index are available in this module as well.

The Calculator feature provides an algebraic calculator with up to 16 digit accuracy. It can add, subtract, multiply, and divide. You can also use memory functions, logical functions of *AND*, *OR*, *XOR*, bit shifts left and right, reciprocal, percent, and number base change.

DOS functions provided in RHM are similar to DOS commands. When you activate the module, DOS prompt is presented. You can run any DOS command, including other programs that are "well behaved"—in other words, programs that do not bypass normal operating system calls. In addition, RHM provides some enhancements to the *DOS COPY*, *DIR*, *REN*, and *TYPE* commands which make them more versatile. For example, using the *RHMCOPY* command will make RHM ask for verification before each file is copied.

The File Editor allows the editing of text files that do not exceed 64k. The editor takes advantage of the function keys and directional keys for editing text. The features provided are fairly plain vanilla, and the commands are easy to learn and use. The commands or structure are not similar to WordStar or any other word processor, however.

Right Hand Man ver. 3.3
Red E Products, Inc.
P.O. Box 640267
Kenner, LA 70064

Shareware: $25

Category: Utility

System Requirements: 256k of available memory; IBM PC, XT, AT or any close compatible; color recommended, but it will work with composite or monochrome displays; any Hayes-compatible modem (optional)

Recommended Use: desktop management

Major Pros: modules can be added or deleted depending on your needs; basic design makes it easy to learn

Major Cons: design is uninspired

Sources: popular BBSs and commercial services, or directly from the author

---

The Notepad is used for keeping personal notes and for on-the-fly text editing. The Notepad also uses the editor, and operates almost in the same way. You can create multiple Notepads if you wish. A Guarded Notepad uses a password to en-crypt and decrypt notes, but is otherwise similar to the Black Book mentioned earlier.

The Transfer Window is used in conjunction with the cut and paste feature of the program. You can cut a portion of text from any screen and paste it into any ap-plication. The Transfer Window gives you the ability to use the full screen editor to edit text that has been cut from another source. In addition, you can send the text in the buffer to output devices like the printer and modem.

The Typewriter allows you to send text directly to the printer, line by line. It is useful for doing quick jobs like addressing an envelope, or typing out a quick note.

This product does not have the flair of Homebase, but it gets the job done. If you find working around menus to do DOS services is a chore, then the direct DOS of this program may be the answer. It also provides a great deal of configurability which can mean great savings in time and memory. Its approach to utility is basic, yet efficient, and that's why we recommend this program.

9

Editors

Editors are generally used by programmers and people who want to edit from DOS or from within a program (like Procomm or a DOS shell that allows you to call a text editor directly). Editors produce ASCII documents with no formatting. They are called full-screen editors if they allow you to place information virtually anywhere on the screen. Some editors are called line oriented because they operate on text a line at a time. Many editors have complex functions specially designed to help programmers. Others are used for very basic tasks such as editing an ASCII document or a batch file.

Terms

Editor usually refers to a program designed to edit and compose text. Editors are often used by programmers when writing computer programs as they often contain features useful for that work. Word processors are more useful for general writing tasks.

ASCII stands for American Standard for Coded Information Interchange. What it is: a standard set of computer codes to represent letters and graphic symbols. ASCII is recognized by many different types of computers, and can be reliably used to transfer text-only messages.

Cut and paste—remove text from a document (cut) and place it (paste) somewhere else. This could be another location within the same document or a different document all together.

A *Macro* is a set of commands which are triggered from a single keystroke or command; conceptually similar to DOS batch files, but generally occur within applications.

Window—refers to the viewing area of a document. Some programs support several windows which allow you to view several documents at the same time on your computer screen. Windows usually can be resized to accommodate your viewing preferences.

C— a computer language.

PASCAL—a computer language.

DOS shell—two possible interpretations exist. A program that replaces the DOS commands (like Commando, Directory Scanner, Tshell, etc.) is sometimes called a shell program. The actual DOS shell is a partition taken out of memory to run a second *COMMAND.COM*. Many programs that allow exiting to DOS from within a application use a DOS shell. Some care needs to be taken when running a DOS shell. Particularly, do not run BASIC, and do not attempt to run TSR within a shell (see TSR). To return to the program that called the shell, you always type *EXIT* at the DOS prompt. If you type *EXIT* and nothing happens, you were probably not in a DOS shell.

Pick buffers—a slang term describing an area in memory used to hold text during cut and paste operations.

Line editor—an editor that acts on a line of text at a time rather than a whole screen. Example: DOS Edit program.

Screen editor—an editor that allows you to change a whole screen full of lines by simply moving around the screen with the directional keys (or mouse in some cases), and making your changes.

Blackbeard ver. 4.2.4

Blackbeard
Shareware—$20

Blackbeard is primarily a text editor designed to assist programmers in editing and creating source code, but with some useful word processing features added. The program allows you to configure the system to your liking. You can set various editing options and keystroke macros—you can customize the program to perform repetitive commands with a single keystroke.

The automatic indenting feature allows for easy entry of structured language source code like C or Pascal. Also included is a versatile cut and paste feature that allows column cut and paste operations. The program supports up to 10 windows which can be individually sized. Each window can show the same file or different files, and you can move easily from window to window with a single keystroke.

One feature we liked very much in the intelligent paging. For example, by hitting the PgDn key three times in rapid succession, the program will take you to the third page without viewing the pages in between.

Pop-up menus make it easy to learn and to use, and it supports mice with standard mouse drivers. The program also includes a text reformatting program which uses straightforward reformatting commands to polish output. You can also draw lines and boxes with this editor using the IBM extended graphic characters. Blackbeard can be installed as a memory resident program. Although it will take up approximately 150k of memory, some users may find this feature very useful.

The overall performance of this editor is outstanding. The ability to use a mouse, ease of learning, ease of use, configurability, and overall feel make this program an excellent general-purpose editor. It definitely competes with some of the commercial editors that cost much more. We highly recommend it.

Blackbeard ver. 4.2.4
Blackbeard
1198 East Baseline #113
San Bernardino, CA 92410

Shareware: $20

Category: Editor

System Requirements: 256k of available memory recommended, IBMPC, XT, AT or any close compatible, color recommended but it will work with composite or monochrome displays

Recommended Use: Programming editor

Major Pros: Easy to learn and use. Very powerful features including mouse support

Major Cons: Memory hungry when fully resident. The manual is rather skimpy

Sources: Popular BBSs and commercial services, or directly from the author

New York Edit ver. 1.2

Magma Software systems
Shareware—$39.95

New York Edit is a programming text editor. Its primary purpose is to provide an optimum environment for writing source code. The program's main feature is its powerful macro language—used to define your own commands within the editor. The macro language is very similar to the C programming language.

Other features include the ability to remap your keyboard, the capability to show up to 12 windows simultaneously with a different file shown in each window, regular expression pattern matching, column block operations, keyboard macros, a DOS shell, and pick buffers.

The macro language can best be described as a C language look-alike. Conditions, expressions, and branches can be specified. The real advantage of this macro language is that it gives you the true power of creating your working environment, which means you can become more productive. There is a learn mode provided that will remember the keystrokes typed and convert them into the macro language. The resulting code file can then be compiled and optionally called up anytime the file is loaded into the editor.

The keyboard remapping feature allows the keys to be redefined to one of 256 possible values. An example of how this might be useful would be the reassignment of a function key to a two-key combination.

The windowing feature allows up to 12 documents to be displayed at the same time. Each window can be resized up to the size of the whole screen if needed.

The search operations of this program are very powerful and incorporate UNIX-like metacommands which give more flexibility in wild card searches of text.

Up to 10 pick buffers can be specified with the program. Special commands allow you to append to buffers, and even write the buffers to disk.

This program offers a lot of power. If you are a C programmer, you'll especially like this product, since a lot of the major features either mimic or gear themselves to the C language. The command structure of the program is difficult to learn because there is no command reference sheet included in the manual. You have to search through the whole manual to find commands. Perhaps if a pop-up menu of commands were available it would make learning them easier. The manual itself is big, complete, and technical. No index is provided. Because of this, beginners are recommended to work with QEDIT first, before trying out NYE. If you're fluent with programming editors and have dabbled a bit with C, then you'll be able to jump in with both feet and love every minute of it!

The New York Text Editor
Magma Software Systems
15 Bodwell Terrace
Millburn, NJ 07041
201-912-0192

Shareware: $39.95

Category: Text editor

System Requirements: 192k of available memory: IBMPC, XT, AT or any
close compatible: color recommended, but it will work with composite or
monochrome displays

Recommended Use: advanced programming source code development in C

Major Pros: powerful macro language and the ability to customize the working
environment to your needs; extended search capabilities

Major Cons: may be difficult to learn for first-time users because the manual is
complicated and not well organized

Sources: popular BBSs and commercial services, or directly from the author

---

QEDIT ver 2.0
SemWare
Shareware—$39

QEDIT or "the quick editor" is a text editor primarily designed for programmers.
Though you can use this product as a text editor for short documents or letters,
its features are geared to creating or maintaining program source code. The program is very fast and uses about 36k of memory for itself, and the rest of the
available memory in your computer for editing your documents. In other words,
you can edit files as large as the memory in your computer permits. With
QEDIT you can edit multiple files at the same time, and again the number of
files is determined by the amount of available memory. While editing multiple
files, you can display up to eight files at the same time on the screen, using the
windows feature. The program provides for scratch buffers so that you can cut
and paste within and between documents. You can also cut and paste directly be-

tween documents. A DOS shell is also provided so that you can exit to DOS and return to where you left off in the program.

QEDIT is completely configurable depending on your environment and needs. You can redefine all of the special keys on the keyboard (Ctrl, the function keys, Alt, Home, PgUp, etc.). In addition, you can configure the different aspects of the screen display with 127 different color combinations. Most of the command keys mimic the Wordstar-Turbo Pascal editor. For example, ^KS is used to save a file. You'll especially like the display QEDIT provides. The ability to configure the cursor line (the line that the cursor presently resides on) to a different color than the rest of the screen, makes it very easy to see what line you are currently editing. There is also a command that allows you to draw graphic boxes around text using box commands. Most editors require that you use the alt-numeric pad combination to generate the extended graphic character set of the IBM.

In this new version, the following enhancements have been added from version 1.35D:

- Character as well as line blocks.

- Working word-wrap and paragraph reformat commands.

- Deleted lines and blocks are saved and may be recovered.

- Keyboard macros.

- Multiple commands per key in the key definition file.

- User-configurable helpscreen.

- Load multiple files from the DOS command line or via the *edit_file* command inside the editor. Either multiple filenames or wild cards may be used.

- Directory lister/file picker option.

The manual provides the only reference, so if your are new to programming editors, you may have trouble getting used to it.

This product is a good programming editor. It's fast, takes up a small amount of memory space, and provides good features within an environment that a programmer will have little trouble adapting to. We recommend it.

SemWare
c/o Sammy Mitchell
730 Elk Cove Ct.
Kennesaw, GA 30144

Shareware: $39

Category: text editor

System Requirements: 96k of available memory, IBM PC, XT, AT or any close compatible, color recommended but it will work with composite or monochrome displays

Recommended use: creating programming source code

Major Pros: Fast basic programming editor with good features and custom configurable

Major Cons: No on-line help

Sources: Popular BBSs and commercial services, or directly from the author

Note: Many programmers use notepads found in TSRs like Homebase and Right Hand Man (see Desk Managers). There is even a TSR editor (called TSREDIT) which is a simple editor whose main feature is memory residency. Others use the editors that are built into their compilers for convenience. Many other programmers use PC-Write for its easy handling of ASCII files, automatic symbol pair marking, and other features useful to programmers (see Word Processing).

WED Text Editor Version 3.13

Mason Washington
Washington Computer Corp.
P.O. Box 16504
Alexandria, VA 22302
Shareware—$20

Reprinted by permission of PDN Newsletter.

The WED Text editor is a full function text editor that is geared toward a program developer's text editing needs.

WED comes with an installation program which allows the user to permanently set the options of the WED text editor. Included, among other things, are screen attributes, the cursor type, auto indent, macro definitions, tab expansion, and color graphics adaptor snow removal.

The WED editor itself accepts a file name on the command line for ease of use but prompts for a file name if one is not given. After a file has been given for editing, WED loads the file into memory. You are then presented with a screen that has a line showing valid editor commands, a status line, and 22 lines of the file which you are editing. WED begins in a pseudo-command mode. Any cursor keys which are pressed will change the current cursor position within the file, and any non-cursor motion keys are taken as input.

While in the command mode, any data key strokes overlay the current file contents. This gives the "what you see is what you get" affect. If you type a word it will overlay the current contents of the file a the current file contents. If you type past the end of the file, the file end will automatically be extended. Also from this mode you can use special editing keys such as the *delete* key, the + key on the keypad (which inserts a single space at the current cursor position), and the - key on the keypad (which deletes a single character at the current cursor position).

All commands in WED are entered from command mode by pressing ALT-<char>. Some of the commands which are included are as follows:

- ALT-I (insert) which allows insertion of new data lines or data within a line.

- ALT-E (erase) which allows deletion of data by moving the cursor with the cursor motion keys.

- ALT-P (pointer) which allows the user to set up to 8 markers.

- ALT-G (goto) which allows the user to move the cursor to the top of the file, the bottom of the file, to any specific line (by line number), or to any pointer which has been set.

- ALT-C (copy) which allows the user to do a block copy from or to the top of the file, the bottom of the file, or any pointer which has been set.

- ALT-M (move) which allows the user to do a block move from or to the top of the file, the bottom of the file, or any pointer which has been set.

- ALT-Z (zap) which allows the user to do a block delete from or to the top of the file, the bottom of the file, or any pointer which has been set.

- ALT-L (locate) which allows the user to search for words or phrases (which can include control codes such as tabs).

- ALT-R (replace) Which allows the user to replace words or phrases.

- ALT-Q (quit) which allows the user to exit the current file with saving the file, or abandoning the file.

- ALT-W (write) which allows the user to write part or all of the file to another file.

- ALT-A (append) which allows the user to insert an entire file into the current file at the current cursor position.

- ALT-F (format) which allows the user to indent or unindent a block of code.

- ALT-O (other) which allows the user to jump between two files being edited.

- ALT-B (bridge) which allows the user to copy data from the "other" file when two files are being edited.

- ALT-D (DOS) which is a DOS gateway.

- ALT-U (user) which allows the user to execute DOS-level commands like assemblers or linkers.

- ALT-T (text) which toggles the editor into and out of text or graphics modes.

- ALT-S (setup) which allows the user to change setup options.

- ALT-N (next) which toggles between two top lines that show the user all of the commands which are available.

I have been using WED version 2.11 for about two months and really like the feel and options of the WED editor. However, since I use a text editor about six hours a day, the few bugs which were in WED version 2.11 kept me looking for another editor to use on a daily basis. I was just about to give up the search of user-supported software and get my boss to buy a text editor for me when Tim Mullen asked me to review the new version of WED.

After using WED 3.11 for about one day, I sent in the registration fee to the author. All of the bugs that were in the previous version have been fixed as well as adding several new features.

Some outstanding features of the editor are the following:

1. The ability to edit two files at once. The two files can either be edited on a split screen or on a switched screen where only one of the files is shown at a time. This ability was in the previous version of WED, but some bugs (which have been fixed) kept me from using this feature on a daily basis. This allows me to edit an assembler routine on half of a screen and edit the program variables on the other half of the screen. No more notes on what variables need to be added to a program or compiling to see what variables were forgotten. Now I can just press ALT-O and define the variables as they are needed.

2. The bridge command which allows you to copy a block of data from one file to another. I find this is very useful for copying routines from other programs which have been already been written.

3. The macro keys, which allow multiple editor commands to be executed with a single key stroke.

4. The ability to enter graphics characters from the keyboard without using the ALT key and the numeric keypad. This makes it much easier to enter screen definitions and layouts.

5. The ability to define more than two pointers in a file. I have never used all eight pointers but have found that I often use four pointers.

The things that I think could be changed or improved are as follows:

1. The cursor is not reset upon exit if WEB version 3.11 is used on a monochrome monitor.

2. There is no cursor on an EGA monitor which is in 43 line mode. This is a fairly new feature, so it is not surprising that it is not included in most software.

3. If you ALT-W (write) a portion of a file to the printer (i.e. PRN) you get a *DEVICE FULL* message which doesn't really cause any problems but which could be fixed.

4. It would be nice if the ALT-H (help) function would work after a command key was pressed to give context sensitive help (i.e. ALT-M, ALT-H could give help on the move command).

5. It would be nice if more macro keys were available, instead of just F-1 through F-10.

I have used WED version 3.11 for a solid week as I write this review and am very happy with the editor. The editor provides all the functions I need to write programs efficiently. It is very well tested and bug free. The editor is easy to learn and easy to use, and I would recommend it to any programmer or person doing text editing.

—John P. Loper

Shareware Goes Formal

by Bob Wallace

Bob Wallace is one of the original Shareware authors: His marketing ideas and commitment to quality support have earned him a solid place in the shareware community and his product PC-Write, has stayed among the Shareware sales leaders—while continuing to evolve and to support its many users' needs

Bob has taken a very personal look at his approach to Shareware, and we think you'll find it interesting—and maybe a little inspiring, too.

Thoughts from Bob Wallace

I really enjoy programming and working with people. I discovered programming when I was twelve and immediately knew it would be my career. My first major programming project, in high school, matched fellow students for a computer date dance. I forgot to make the program remove couples from the list after matching them, and delivered 384 matches to one very compatible sophomore!

That was 21 years ago. I've been programming ever since. In 1982 I was working at Microsoft on their Pascal compiler, and still concentrating on the programming side of the software business. But I wanted more control over my programs, over what features to include and how to market them. So my first decision was to start my own software company.

My second decision was to design a word processor. I wanted to do something that many people could use, and something I could do a good job on. More people use word processing programs on their personal computer than any other type of software. And I knew a lot about text editors from writing programs, and also knew about typesetting and publishing from doing a computer club newsletter.

Most of all, I wanted to help people be creative. I considered painting or drawing software, but computers are still too primitive and coarse for most visual artists. My wife Megan, Quicksoft's VP of Operations, is a painter, and still finds personal computer graphics too fuzzy for her work.

In early 1983 I declared myself in business as Quicksoft, began writing what is now PC-Write, and started to think about marketing. Up to that point, I felt "marketing" was a dirty word; something Madison Avenue types did to make people buy junk. But I discovered marketing is just connecting people and products—first designing products to meet people's real needs and then letting them know your product exists and really does meet their needs.

I knew people would like my word processor. At the time, the market leader was WordStar, and may users said it was slow, awkward, and unfriendly. But how do you convince people your word processor is better because it's fast and friendly? Especially if you have no money for ads? I had $20,000 saved up to start Quicksoft, plus $7,000 available on my credit cards.

About then I discovered PC-Talk, PC-File, and the concept of "user supported software." I had the answer. People could try PC-Write and discover for themselves if they liked it better. Lots of people could use my software. Hopefully, enough would also pay for it to keep Quicksoft afloat.

At the time, user supported software typically had a front screen that simply asked users of the software for a "contribution" of $35 or so. I decided on a more formal, even commercial approach; after all, I was starting a company, not making a few dollars to pay for my computer.

First, I coined the term "shareware" for this approach. Next, I called the payment a "registration fee" instead of a "contribution," and asked enough to support a viable business (then $75, now $89). Finally, I made a list of all the extra things I would give PC-Write users who registered, and described these registration bene-fits on the front screen. After all, users already had the software, and I wanted to give them more than a feeling of honesty and support (although those are important reasons to register as well).

The list includes the current software, printed manual, technical support, and free updates. I added something else: the right to earn money be sharing copies of PC-Write. If someone gives a copy of their PC-Write diskette to another person and that second person registers, we send the first person a $25 commission. Letting people share your software was unusual; paying them to do it was un-heard of. But I wanted to let people know I was serious about encouraging copy-ing, and I wanted them to overcome some of the shyness and inertia about doing it. A few people might think it was a pyramid scheme or something, but most people realize it's just a straight sale's commission. As it turns out, we pay commission on about one fifth of our registrations.

PC-Write version 1.0 was launched at the IBM PC Faire in San Francisco, on Thursday, August 25, 1983. I finished the program on Tuesday night, and spent Wednesday at the show duplicating diskettes. Then, the following February, our first review was published in PC Magazine. The reviewer liked PC-Write, and we received enough orders to support a second person, Megan. We were in busi-ness. By the end of 1984 there were four of us.

As I write this in mid-1987, we have 20 employees and have done 13 releases of PC-Write. I still do much of the programming, but we have another programmer and five more technical support staff. I've learned the joys and frustrations of managing people. Putting together a group of people to develop, publish, sell, and support a software product is as challenging as writing the software in the first place. We may not be the number one independent microcomputer software company. But we are number 86 (based on 1986 sales of about $1.5 million). We're earning a reasonable living, and are still growing.

Quicksoft's mission is to help people create documents. With our present re-sources, that means producing word processing software for IBM PC-type com-puters.

Word processing programs are highly interactive and subjective. They have to "feel right" as well as provide the necessary features. People use data base and spreadsheet programs in a more logical, analytical way; they think, enter com-mands, think, enter commands, and so on. People use a word processor almost like a video game; creating a document is a continuous flowing process of typing and editing.

Software, particularly word processing, is one of the few creative tools which evolves over time to meet new requirements and environments. Writers who were happy with their word processor software just a few years ago, now rightly expect a newer version with state-of-the-art features. One of the hidden benefits of registering a shareware package is keeping the company around to evolve the product.

Software is so complicated; people need to try a package first and make sure it's suitable before buying it. Several times I've paid a few hundred dollars for a product, only to find it doesn't meet my needs. That's another benefit of shareware registration: keeping the shareware method itself viable.

By the way, I don't worry about the people who use PC-Write and don't register. The people I worry about are those who *do* register. I want them to get the best software, documentation, phone support, and whatever else they need to create their documents efficiently and enjoyably.

10

Games and Entertainment

For some of us, just downloading and de-ARCing another mystery file from the local bulletin board is fun. But there are those times that you want to involve yourself in something entirely unimportant. That's where games and other entertainment products come in.

People have been playing games on computers almost as long as there have been computers. It should come as no surprise that there are plenty of games around.

Unfortunately, creating a first-class game often involves some of the most challenging aspects of programming—graphics and animation. For that reason, really excellent games do not abound in the public-domain or from Shareware sources. There are exceptions, but as a rule, games found on BBS or in PD and Shareware catalogs do not contain the same complexity or sophistication as the best of the commercial games do. Still, they can be fun and imaginative, so they are certainly worth checking out. Also, there are some adventure games (for those who like a challenge) from ButtonWare that range from beginner level to totally dedicated adventurers only.

There are lots of arcade games. We've looked at a few below, but there are many, many more. There are derivatives of many commercial games like Frogger and Q-bert, Breakout, and, of course, Pac-Man. There are also some original concepts (see Beast below).

Another area of gaming takes place while on-line on a BBS. We've briefly touched on that area of entertainment as well. Another type of game is the Star Trek derivative. Star Trek games started on mainframes and have been popular with computer users ever since. Several variations on the theme are available everywhere.

There are also traditional game translations like Monopoly (a fine adaptation of the board game) and many card games like blackjack, solitaire, and poker. If that kind of game appeals to you, check out the various sources; there are lots of examples of traditional games.

Into the Mystic Dungeons

DND

R. O. Software
4757 W. Park Boulevard, Suite 106–107
Plano, TX 75023
Shareware—$25

DND (Dungeons 'n Dragons) is a role playing game that uses graphics sparingly and imagination with abandon. This kind of game appeals to some (who usually become addicted), and does not appeal at all to others (who think the addicts crazy). You probably already know which one you are. If you are the former, you want to read on. If the latter, turn the page and look at something else.

DND is a pretty sophisticated game. Once loaded, it becomes an environment in which you operate, much as dBASE becomes a database environment. It has the basic elements of a role playing game—various numeric attributes like Strength, Wisdom, etc. plus the inevitable Hit Points.

DND is full of strange enemies and objects, magic spells and objects, gold, and other items. You gain insight into the meaning of the game as you proceed. You also gain experience levels if you survive. It helps to find some good weapons and armor, however, or you won't survive long.

DND makes very rudimentary use of graphics and is equally at home on a color or monochrome system. For the adventurous, DND can provide hours of entertainment. Try it if you like this sort of thing. Don't expect much in the way of graphics (an ASCII graphic map is about all you get)—but the game is in the imagination anyway, right?

Hack

Hack is like DND. It is a version of the popular role playing game Rogue that has migrated from mainframes to all kinds of systems. Hack has many of the same qualities as DND, so they can almost be considered variants of each other. The operating environment is a little different, but otherwise there's a lot of similarity. Anyone liking DND should like Hack, and vice versa.

3DEMON

PC Research, Inc.
Shareware—3D
8 Village Lane
Colts Neck, NJ 07722
Shareware—$10

Maybe 3Demon belongs in the arcade section because it is really like a three dimensional version of Pac-Man, but we've included it here because the perspective it gives you is a lot like that of a role playing game. The main difference between 3Demon and Pac-Man is that you only see your present location within a 3D maze. You see dots on the floor that you pick up automatically as you pass, and you see the three dimensional hallways and turns. But you don't see the whole maze at once. You also can see a smaller representation of the maze which shows you the approximate location of the enemy ghosts. If you find your way to a power point, just as in Pac-Man, you gain the ability to eat the ghosts. The rest of the time you're fair game.

3Demon is a fine game, with good sound effects and good programming. But if you don't like Pac-Man games, you probably won't like this (unless you find the unique perspective improves the game sufficiently). Works in color or monochrome modes.

Getting a Little Action

Hostages

Texasoft, Inc.

An amusing little arcade game in which you must try to shoot through walls that imprison unfortunate hostages. Simple graphics on monochrome or color screen. You attempt to shoot through moving doorways that allow your shots to reach the walls. You are given a limited number of shots, and various other dangers threaten you. In the version we saw, there was no documentation, so you're pretty much on your own. Good for 15 minutes or so of mindless entertainment.

Beast

I don't completely understand this game, but you are a small cursor, and you are in a maze being chased by large H's. What makes the game interesting is that you can move the walls of the maze. The goal seems to be to entrap the H's within a prison of walls. After a while, if the H's can't move, they disappear. This is a pretty interesting game of speed and strategy, since you must move quickly to form a trap, then lure the H's into the trap without being blind-sided. H's naturally home in on cursors, so time is important. On the other hand, H's do not seem to be overly intelligent, so it isn't too hard to outwit them.

Other options include eggs which hatch more H's, hatching speed, super Beasts (H's), explosive blocks, and more. You can choose from among 26 levels of difficulty, each of which contains different combinations of options. Good on color or monochrome systems. Speed setting allows use on PC, AT, or PCjr. Can be slightly addicting.

Pango

Sheng Chung LIU
Public Domain

Pango is a very good professional game. In Pango, you must guide your character using keyboard or joystick through a maze while avoiding the killer bees that are chasing you. If you can kick one of the blocks into a bee, you squash the bee against another block or against the wall. The graphics in this game are excellent and so is the programming and game control. There is some amount of strategy necessary, but there's also plenty of action.

This game does not adjust speed, so it plays very fast on AT class machines. Otherwise, it is a fine arcade game.

Heart

A Pac-Man type game that works well on color or monochrome systems, from keyboard or with a joystick. One drawback: using the numeric keypad to control the game on an AT is awkward because your character (Ace) moves in a direction until you press a different direction key, and on the AT the game runs very fast. This makes turning corners difficult, especially with enemy characters close on your heels.

Another Pac-Man type game is Pac-Gal. This one is a bit noisy, and not too well behaved on an AT. It only displays in monochrome, even on a color system. It is a good implementation of the arcade program, however, and the speed can be set on PCs.

Willy the Worm
Alan Farmer
2743 McElroy Drive
Charlottesville, VA 22903
Shareware—$10

Willy the Worm is a sort of Donkey Kong derivative, a game in which you must guide your character, Willy, up a series of ladders and over some jumps while avoiding dangers. If Willy reaches the top, he gets to ring a bell, his favorite activity.

Although the game is fairly simple, it does feature user-definable screens (using a separate program, *EDWILLY.COM*), and has become fairly popular. It may not appeal to everyone, but it does have a following, and many people like the basic challenge of this sort of game.

Janitor Joe

Kevin Bales
Public Domain

Janitor Joe, sometimes seen as *JUMPJOE.EXE*, is a fairly elementary climbing and jumping game. What makes it remarkable, as Nelson Ford states in his article later in the book, is that this game was written by a 15 year old programmer back in 1984. What are you doing now, Kevin?

There are five levels of jumping, climbing, and gathering keys while avoiding robots gone mad. Finish the five levels and there's an intermission. Then they start over, but with madder robots. It's a true arcade game. The graphics are so-so, and the game mechanics are fair. But it can be fun if you like that sort of game. Requires color screen. Joystick optional.

Spacewar 1.72

Bill Seiler
317 Lockewood Lane
Scotts Valley, CA 95066
Shareware—$20 ($30 for source code)

Back in the seventies, there were two spacewar games—one at MIT and one at Stanford University. These games pre-dated all but the most early Pong games, but were as sophisticated as many games in existence today. Spacewar is a version of that original game on the PC.

Bill Seiler actually programmed his first version of Spacewar on a PDP11/24 with 8K of core memory, an analog vector scope for a display, and variable resistors connecting analog to digital converters for input. Later, he wrote a version for the Commodore PET. He has written several versions since, including a special Hercules graphic board version, a version for standard IBM color cards, and one for the AT&T compatible machines.

Spacewar involves two ships in combat in a universe that expands out one side of the screen and back into another. As in various Asteroid games, Spacewar takes place in a gravity-less condition, so a little propulsion goes a long way.

The object is to shoot the other player's ship with short range phasers and long range torpedos until his shields are depleted and he blows up. Using the keyboard, each player can turn and accelerate, fire, and enter hyperspace (at a cost of considerable fuel), or use a cloaking device to become invisible (also at a cost of fuel). Phasers can shoot incoming torpedos. Good strategy will use the screen wrap-around to fire down into a corner at an angle that will end up coming out on the other side of the screen and hit the enemy.

Various options include having a planet, or a gravity hole, and a left or right robot enemy. A separate version of the game is designed for a monochrome graphics board in 720 x 348 mode.

What makes this game work is the intriguing feeling of free-fall that you get when you try to control the ship, and the sense of competition that the game can inspire. It's a classic game, and done well.

Striker

Derek Williams
10503 Doering Lane
Austin, TX 78750
Shareware—$10

Striker is another arcade game of a particular genre. In this game, you fly a helicopter over hilly terrain and through various tunnels while avoiding enemy fire and enemy rockets, etc. There are five missions—to pick up spies, return the spies, pick up cargo, rescue people, and finally, destroy a missile factory.

We've seen several commercial games like this one, and some coin-operated arcade games as well. The action scrolls across the screen horizontally while you control the speed of your helicopter and its altitude. You can shoot bullets or drop bombs to destroy enemies and to gain fuel (by shooting fuel cannisters—ok, it doesn't have to make sense, does it?).

The game works well, and the graphics are pretty good. It works well from the keyboard or with a joystick. It's another real arcade game, so if you don't like arcade games, you may as well skip this one.

Flightmare

Peter Adams
882 Hagemann Dr.
Livermore, CA 94550
Shareware—(The author requests any contribution between $5 and $50).

Flightmare is a clever game in two parts. The first part isn't much, but involves engaging a small bi-plane with a group of marauding motorcyclists. Once you engage, the "real game" begins. In the real game, you must line up your plane with each motorcycle and shoot it. The trick is that you must line up in three dimensions using a split screen and two sides of the keyboard at once. The graphics are pretty good.

This game offers a different sort of challenge. It isn't easy to get used to the coordination of the game, and on an AT class machine, the game is too fast. The game is hard enough on a standard PC.

The unique quality of this game makes it a good bet for some amusement, and its rather odd theme makes it stand out as well. Oh, and Peter has played an amusing joke on us. When you try to leave the game, the usual Esc and Ctrl-C or Ctrl-Break keys do not work. Finally, in desperation, you try the warm boot sequence, Ctrl-Alt-Del, and, for Pete's sake, you end up back in DOS. Very clever, Peter.

NYET

David Howorth
Compuserve ID 71600,521
Public Domain

I couldn't resist this one. It's based on a game from the Soviet Union (the first one to make it here that I know of). The original game is called Tetris, and was programmed by A. Pajitov and V. Gerasimaov. There is a commercial version of the game, but this PD one is a pretty good adaptation.

The object of the game is to rotate and drop falling shapes, attempting to make as many as possible fit into the available space. If you can make them form a solid row of squares horizontally, one line disappears, giving you more room. You automatically move to the next level of difficulty for each 10 lines you can make disappear.

The game is tougher than it sounds, and has ten levels of difficulty. Even at level zero, it is challenging. You can move shapes and rotate them, finally dropping them into the space you've chosen. If you don't work fast, however, the falling shapes will find their own place. You can pause the game, and there is a command that allows you to preview the next shape (although you lose some penalty points in exchange).

This is a different sort of action game, and one that takes a quick geometrical mind. It's fun, and it's addicting.

EGA Games

EGAroids

This game is great with an EGA monitor. It is the basic Asteroids game in which you guide your spaceship in free-fall while trying to blast careening bits of rock which split into smaller, faster moving pieces of rock until you blast even those into oblivion. The graphics are excellent and the animation is very smooth.

For those who haven't seen Asteroids-type games, the rocks begin very large, and move on a fixed path across the screen, wrapping to the other side rather than bouncing back when they reach an edge. That's what makes the game so interesting. Objects disappear out one side, and reappear on the other side.

You control your ship by turning with cursor keys, then giving short blasts of rocket power. Remember, any power you give the ship sets it in motion, and without gravity, nothing stops it except a counter force (or destruction from a flying rock). Every once in a while, an enemy spacecraft shows up and shoots at you. You must try to shoot them before they get you, while avoiding the asteroids. As a last resort, you can enter hyperspace which makes you safe for a moment, then replaces you elsewhere on the screen. Hyperspace is not to be used lightly.

When you get all the flying rocks off one level, you proceed to another, more difficult one. (Except for the graphic quality, this description will fit most Asteroids-type games).

Adventures of Captain Comic

Michael A. Denio
1420 West Glen Avenue, #202
Peoria, IL 61614   309-693-2719
Shareware—donation appreciated

The Adventures of Captain Comic is an entertaining EGA graphic game that puts you in control of the intrepid Captain Comic. The Captain must explore a scrolling world that is well populated with unfriendly nuisances. His weapon is one or more cans of Blastola Cola, and he is protected (somewhat) by his shield. Other objects (like a magic wand, keys, and a special corkscrew) can be found throughout the world of Tambi. Basically, Comic must obtain the three treasures stolen from the planet Omsoc. His quest will take him through various realms on Tambi.

You play this game using the keypad to move right and left on a scrolling screen. The Spacebar causes Comic to jump, and the Ins key shoots the Blastola Cola fireballs. Alt key opens doors (if you have a door key), and the Caps Lock key invokes the magic wand (if you have it). Game play is easy, but the game itself becomes more and more difficult as you play.

Although this game is fairly simple, it is entertaining and the graphics are excellent. Considering that it is a Shareware game, it is very well done, and worth some contribution if you find it enjoyable. Denio seems somewhat dubious about the game's ability to make money, and sets no actual price on it. However, he does appreciate contributions and any suggestions for future games or updates to this one.

EGA SORRY 1.04

Joseph Glockner
141 Circle Dr.
Denison, TX 75020
Public Domain

The Parker Bros. board game, *Sorry!*, has been a popular family board game for many years. EGA Sorry is an excellent adaptation of this game that will make all automatic moves for you and gives easy to follow directions for moves which require a choice. The game displays an excellent game board with color coded game pieces. Up to four players can play the game, or you can play a solitaire game, playing each player. Since the computer takes care of almost all operations, including moving the pieces, it's easy to sit back and enjoy the game.

Board games are good prospects for computer simulations, but they usually lack the social aspect that has made board games popular. Still, this is an excellent programming job, and can provide some genuine enjoyment. If you love *Sorry!*, but can't find anyone to play with, this game will really make your day. Requires 384K memory and EGA system.

EGA TREK

Nels Anderson
92 Bishop Drive
Framingham, MA 01701

There have been several versions of the venerable Star Trek game (loosely based on the TV series), but this one has the nicest graphics to date. Requiring an EGA card and monitor, EGA Trek features fine color graphics throughout the game. Otherwise, the game is pretty much the same as other versions, and involves moving through a 64 quadrant universe vanquishing enemy Klingons, docking at friendly space stations, and exploring planets for dilithium crystals.

This game moves quickly and is highly enjoyable as can be seen by the longevity and widespread distribution of various Star Trek versions.

Playing On-Line

Trade Wars and Other Doors Games

Trade Wars is intergalactic trading game played through the Doors feature of an RBBS. It is an entertaining game in which many different users can participate. If you come across another player's ship, you can attack it with your escort fighters. If you win, you can plunder his goods. There is an all-pervasive enemy called the Cabal which you want to avoid until you are very strong.

The central idea of Trade Wars is to buy low, sell high. You have only so many moves you can make in any 24-hour period, so you must make the most of your opportunities. If you can get enough credits, you can build a world of your own and have it produce goods for you to trade. This is an advantage, since you don't have to pay for those goods. But building a planet and setting it in production is expensive, and you'll have to leave some fighters behind to defend the planet from marauders.

Trade Wars can be a lot of fun if you find a local board that supports Doors.

Other Doors games: Chess (play multiple matches against other BBS users), several adventure-type games, a version of ReverSi, and more.

Play it Again, Neil

Pianoman Ver. 4.x

To register:

> Support Group Inc.
> P.O. Box 1577
> Baltimore, MD 21203
> (301) 889-7893
> (800) USA-GROUP

To write the author with comments:

> Neil Rubenking
> 300 Page Street
> San Francisco, CA 94102
> CompuServe 72267,1531
> GEnie NRUBENKING
> Shareware—$25

As I write this, another computer is playing me some of my favorite Scott Joplin. The sound is a bit strident (what do you expect for the dime store speaker in the IBM machine?), but the tune marches along in self-involved good humor. Doesn't it know it is operating in an environment normally reserved for uninspired beeps? Doesn't it realize that it isn't supposed to work that way?

Apparently not. Pianoman is a Turbo Pascal program that turns your PC into an electronic piano (organ?) and recording device using the keyboard to play the notes. You can create tunes by recording while playing, then edit them with Pianoman's editor. You can even create self-running songs, songs that run as SuperKey macros, source code for Turbo Pascal or Basic music, and even polyphonic tunes that combine several single line tunes into one piece.

The recorder is remarkably accurate, and records every note and rest into memory where it can later be edited, combined with other tunes, or just played back for fun. The editor contains a pretty unusual looking music display. Each note or rest is displayed as a note value, octave value, staccato value, and duration. Any of these qualities can be changed. You can also change the tempo, key, or overall octave of an entire piece or marked block.

Although it might give a trained musician nightmares when compared to traditional notation (which conveys a lot of information more readily), Pianoman's notation system is effective, and some remarkable music can be created using this system. Evidence is easy to obtain as Pianoman comes with a plethora of tunes in various forms.

After you've edited to your heart's content, you can use the Player Piano utility to create Turbo Pascal or Basic routines, self-running *COM* files, or even SuperKey macros of your tunes. Or you can take some single parts and combine them into a polyphonic piece. Although the IBM is not a polyphonic device, Rubenking has fooled the system into playing the notes so fast that the effect is remarkably like polyphony.

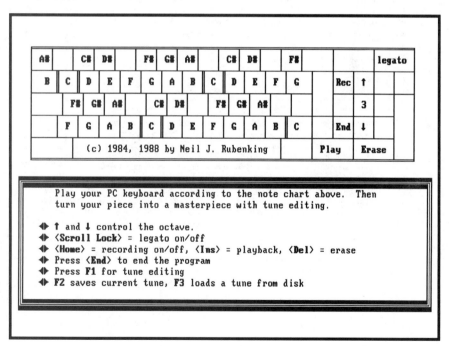

In any case, playing Pianoman songs would make most audiophiles get up and leave the room—the IBM speaker being a noise maker more than an audio device—but for enjoyable tinkering with music on a system not designed for it, this program is a masterpiece.

Up to this point, everything we said about Pianoman is true of former versions. When we talked with Neil about upgrading the product, he informed us that he wasn't sure he would. We're happy to say that he did. With version 4.x, Neil has added some nice refinements. The program has a slightly more polished look (not that it was suffering in that department before), and better documentation. In addition, a new file format saves about 20% over the old format. The Player Piano utility will convert between all supported formats (.*COM* files, SuperKey macros, older *MUS* files, the new .*MUZ* files, *SPKR* files (see below), and polyphonic formats).

										♭ ♯
E 3	D 3	C♯ 3	D 3	F 3	G 3	F 3	E 3	F 3	A 3	10
5 100	5 100	5 100	5 100	1 400	5 100	5 100	5 100	5 100	1 400	
A♯ 3	A 3	G♯ 3	A 3	E 4	D 4	C♯ 4	D 4	E 4	D 4	20 E
5 100	5 100	5 100	5 100	5 100	5 100	5 100	5 100	5 100	5 100	s
C♯ 4	D 4	F 4	D 4	F 4	C 4	D 4	E 4	D 4	C 4	30 c
5 100	5 100	1 400	5 200	5 100	5 10	5 10	5 200	5 200	5 200	t
D 4	C 4	D 4	E 4	D 4	C 4	D 4	C 4	D 4	E 4	40 o
5 100	5 10	5 10	5 200	5 200	5 200	5 100	5 10	5 10	5 200	E
D 4	C 4	B 3	A 3	E 3	D 3	C♯ 3	D 3	F 3	G 3	50 x
5 200	5 200	5 200	1 400	5 100	5 100	5 100	5 100	1 400	5 100	i
F 3	E 3	F 3	A 3	A♯ 3	A 3	G♯ 3	A 3	E 4	D 4	60 t
5 100	5 100	5 100	1 400	5 100	5 100	5 100	5 100	5 100	5 100	

BLOCK EDITING	⌐Begin block	⌐Copy block	⌐File save block
? more help "X" =	⌐End block	⌐Delete block	⌐Retrieve File
F1 detail ⟨Alt⟩X	⌐Un-mark block	⌐Move block	⌐Play block

SPKR V1.01

Christopher J. Dunford
10057-2 Windstream Drive
Columbia, MD 21044
(301) 992-9371
CompuServe 76703,2002
Public Domain

SPKR V1.01 is a new device driver that is being distributed with Pianoman. It is written by Chris Dunford, and it lets you play tunes in the background while DOS continues to work. In fact, the SPKR.SYS program is called from your *CONFIG.SYS* (instructions are included), and from then on, SPK is treated as a device just like your printer port PRN, console CON, or your serial port, for instance, COM1. Install short tunes in your batch files. Using SPKR, they can continue to run without interrupting the user.

And, I don't know if I've mellowed, or if Pianoman has, but the "music" from the speaker on my Compaq Deskpro 386 sounds pretty good. Maybe Compaq uses a better kind of speaker than the AT I used when I first used Pianoman.

Namegram 1. & 2. plus

Neil Rubenking
Shareware—various

Have you ever toyed with making anagrams? Well, toy no longer. Namegram is a program that will make more anagrams than you'll know what to do with. Thinking of creating a pseudonym? Use Namegram to find something "pseudable" (but, *pardonnez moi,* this is the Game chapter)!

The only drawback inherent in the program is that it can make so many anagrams that you actually get tired of looking before you've seen them all. Also, if you don't print directly to a printer, it outputs everything to an ASCII file.

Not even a large fraction of the resulting anagrams convey any meaning. This is closer to the monkeys and typewriters model where the source is compared with a set of word lists, then words are combined from matches within the word list. For instance, on the words Rusel DeMaria, there were 705 matching words found, but over 300,000 bytes worth of anagrams created from those words. Out of those anagrams, few were very meaningful, and even fewer were more than a little amusing. Still, sometimes you get lucky. One I liked was MARAUDERS LIE.

Another was MEASURED LIAR. Also, MEASURED LIRA. Can you guess who produced A SORROWING LEAN LAND? (*Hint:* The initials = RWR.)

This is a very entertaining program. It figures that it was written by someone named Rubenking.

Other Programs from Neil

As a sort of corollary to the Namegram program, there are also the Namesmal program (which searches fewer words), the Foneword program which converts phone numbers into anagrams (and possibly into words), and Wordfone which will convert word phone numbers back to digits.

Another unique program takes text files and reorganizes them. This one is called Break Down, and it follows the monkeys at typewriters scenario down another path. This one takes all the words in a text file and does some sneaky reorganization of them, then outputs the results to another file. In Rubenking's own words, "Break Down is a moderately sophisticated database program with almost no 'serious' uses. However, there are all kinds of non-serious uses for it." He goes on to describe some fanciful ways to use Break Down, like re-writing some of the President's speeches or seeing what Lewis Carrol would have said if he had been a Zen Master (using Break Down's merge capabilities). Perhaps we could see what the President would say if he were a Zen master.

Review by Samuel Raider.

An Interesting Strategem

Sleuth Vers. 1.1

Eric N. Miller
1433 North Fuller Avenue #5
Los Angeles, CA 90046
Shareware—$10

Sleuth combines elements of the board game Clue, a graphic arcade game, and a typical adventure game. You must solve a murder by finding the murder weapon, finding the scene of the murder, checking the suspects' alibis against each other, and finally, gathering the suspects in the murder room and accusing the perpetrator. If you are clumsy or take too long, the murderer will get suspicious of you and end your investigation—permanently.

Sleuth is an amusing and entertaining game—at least for a few rounds. It lacks the competitive and social aspects of Clue, and probably will tend to seem repetitive after a while. It does randomize the victim, murder room, and weapon, but the choices are limited and the game does not have a lot of depth. Still, it can be played quickly, and provides an enjoyable diversion. Also, it can be challenging to gather all the clues before the murderer gets you. Another nice touch—you can personalize the game by entering in seven character names of your own choosing to replace the generic names normally used by the game.

Adventure Games

Adventure games are a genre in themselves. For starters, try ButtonWare offerings. In addition to the ButtonWare adventures, there are a whole series of Eamon adventures. These are all PD text-only adventures and are very popular with adventure game lovers.

Adventure Game Toolkit
Shareware—$20

We are big believers in creative thinking—hence a book like this which is a paean to creative thinkers of all kinds. Therefore, we love to see something that encourages imagination and creativity. Adventure games are typically seen as swords and sorcery type plots, or wild flights of fancy. But an adventure game can be anything its author wants it to be, and therefore, need not be limited to fantasy. An adventure game could be used as a tutorial for a complex procedure at work, or an elaborate electronic greeting. There is virtually no limit to what you can do with an adventure game. But to do anything, you have to be a programmer—right?

Wrong.

The Adventure Game Toolkit is an adventure game system that allows you to create, edit and play your own text adventure games without any programming experience. AGS replaces (and expands upon) the former Generic Adventure Game System (GAGS).

There are two levels of development available. The first (which is similar to the GAGS system, but faster and with several other advantages) requires no programming at all. This "standard" system handles all basic game play options. You use a text editor or word processor to create the descriptions of rooms, objects, and characters. Many parameters can be used to define the characteristics of game elements.

Since the data files are easy-to-read ASCII files, any editor can be used to change or create a game, and, once created, you can compile the game into a fast running, encrypted code. Then, using the *RUN.EXE* program, you can run the game you create. Of course, you keep the ASCII source files for later modifications. The play of the game created is much like the Infocom text adventure games. The player types in commands like "push button" or "go south" at a command line prompt. There are sufficient action verbs built in to the system, and you can add more if you wish.

You can control color in the games, changing the text, background, and highlight colors at any point in the game, though it will work on monochrome systems without difficulty. You can even change the display on a color system to monochrome (great effect as punishment for a player who makes a wrong move!).

The parser (the part of the game that interprets user inputs) is very sophisticated. It allows you to enter multiple commands like "USE THE WRENCH TO PUT THE LUG NUTS ON THE CAR, TIGHTEN THE NUTS, THEN DRIVE AWAY" or "PICK UP THE KNIFE, CUT OPEN THE WATERMELON, AND REMOVE THE LARGE RUBY." The parser will ignore many unnecessary words, or will return a message indicating that it doesn't understand the entry. The games developed with the standard system can be quite complex, and can include special events or magic words that cause unusual occurrences. The quality of the game depends on you and your creative thoughts and writing.

At least one sample game generally accompanies the system and demonstrates its capabilities. You'll probably find the sample game only moderately entertaining, since it contains only a small number of creatures and rooms to explore. However several very sophisticated games have been programmed using just the standard option.

AGT even includes a macro system for automating the creation of templates for specific parts of the data file which describes a game. For instance, use the macro utility and pressing Alt-1 would create a template for a standard AGT room. Alt-2 creates an object (noun), etc.

The "professional" level of game generation uses the same basic modules, but can be used to create much more sophisticated and complex games, rivaling those from commercial adventure game manufacturers. A "meta-language" is included for professional level development. This language allows you to program all kinds of special commands with corresponding conditions and results. Here's a simple example of some special code that would test whether a torch had been lit for 75 or 100 turns. If more than 75 turns, a message is displayed. If 100 turns, the lit torch is swapped with an unlit torch and the message informs the player that the torch has gone out. The torch is object 210; The unlit torch is object 211. Message 21 reads "Your torch is flickering and growing weaker." Message 22 reads "The torch finally goes out!" The torch counter is counter 2.

Adventure Game Toolkit
David R. Malmberg
Mark J. Welch

Distributed by:
Softworks
43064 Via Moraga
Mission San Jose, CA 94539
(415) 659-0533

Shareware: $20 (Some restrictions on distribution of games for profit may
    apply)

Category: Generic adventure game generator

System Requirements: 256k of available memory, IBM PC, XT, AT or any
    close compatible, color recommended but it will work with composite or
    monochrome displays; DOS 2.x

Recommended use: Creating text adventure games

Major Pros: Easy to use creation editors. Produces a good playing text
    adventure game—with or without programming

Major Cons: Creation and edit editors could be combined into one module

Sources: Popular BBSs and commercial services, or directly from the authors

---

```
Present 210
CouterGT 2 75
PrintMessage 21
CounterEquals 2 100
PrintMessage 22
TurnCounterOFF 2
SwapLocations 210 211
```

There are many other aspects of the system that allow developers to create very complex effects. And there are some games, both compiled and uncompiled, that you can use as resources and examples. Moreover, the manual (which we saw on disk, but which will be in printed form by the time this book comes out) is full of examples, suggestions, secrets and hints of good adventure game writing.

If you've ever wondered what it was like to create your own adventure games, but didn't have the programming knowledge to do it, then this product is for you. The process is easy to understand with this product, and though you may not produce a commercial quality adventure game, you'll have hours of fun creating it. If you do know some programming, or want to tackle a fairly easy programming language, the professional level of development will allow you to create the electronic novel of your dreams. Future versions of AGS should include the ability to use graphics and other enhancements.

Other Kinds of Entertainment

The Haiku Generator
Public Domain
Charles Frankle

> a dappled firefly sleeps;
> a twilight wildflower
> over the lingering sound

The Haiku Generator is for fun. It's not exactly the monkeys and typewriter model, but it isn't exactly predictably brilliant either. It does, however, produce some enjoyable haikus generated from a special data file. You can alter the data file, but you must do so very carefully to preserve the number of words as well as the appropriate part of speech.

This program can be found as HAIKU.ARC on various BBSs. If you are ever stuck for a thought provoking statement, you might like to try this program. Simply type "haiku" and follow directions.

A winter meadow;
under the little sunset
the sound has passed

Taipan2

Tony Adler
Public Domain

Taipan was a game I used to play on the Apple II machines. This public domain version of it is faithful to the original game in which you must play a sea-going merchant who sails from port to port buying low and selling high. Set in the 19th century world of opium and silk traders operating out of Hong Kong, Manila, and other Far Eastern ports, this game also owes some of its flavor to James Clavell's novel, Taipan. The operation of this game is simple, and just a bit crude at times, but there is an addicting quality to it. The goal is to become a Master Taipan worth over $1,000,000. To do so, you must contend with pirates, confiscation of your cargo, and a few other variables. You can store cargo in special warehouses, or store money in the Hong Kong bank. You can also borrow money at high interest rates. And if you want to stay out of trouble, you may want to pay off the master pirate Li Yuen who can be either a protector or a destroyer.

This game is pretty much a complete version of the original commercial game, but we aren't aware if the commercial game is still available, or if it was ever made for the PC. Still, the legality of this program may be suspect. On the other hand, it is fun to play, despite some small programming glitches (like having to have the Caps Lock key down).

BLACKJACK TUTOR

Stephen A. Jacob
Honolulu, HI
Shareware—$25

Requires: IBM or compatible PC with minimum configuration. Runs on both color and monochrome systems.

This review reprinted by permission of PDN Newsletter.

I bet you thought everyone in Hawaii spent their days lounging around a sun-soaked beach. Obviously, someone in our fiftieth state was able to drag himself away from bikini watching long enough to dash off a few lines of programming code. Fortunately for us, Stephen Jacob did more than slap together a program, and if you ever plan to visit a casino then you may want to spend some time with his BLACKJACK TUTOR.

Blackjack programs are not too hard to find. Both commercial and Public Domain versions can be found pretty easily. But not too many attempt to do what Mr. Jacob does with his program. If you looking for just a game BLACKJACK TUTOR will do the job but you'll be using very little of its full potential. This program is meant to be used to ready yourself for the real thing.

To start with BLACKJACK TUTOR does a nice job with the basics. The program opens with a deck of cards being spread across the screen. This is attractive but if you're in a hurry to get your bets down, one simply hits any key and you advance to the actual program. BLACKJACK TUTOR gives you the option of working with up to four decks. The screens are easy on the eye and the cards are drawn quickly. You pick the size of your initial bankroll (should real life be so easy) and your total winnings (in my case, losses) are recorded and displayed between each hand. From here on we start to get into new territory.

Mr. Jacob tells you in his documentation that BLACKJACK TUTOR is not meant to teach you all there is to know about blackjack. Its primary objective is to give you a flexible tool with which you can practice various betting and card counting strategies. He recommends you peddle yourself down to a local bookstore and pick up one of the numerous blackjack books on the market. Novices can use BLACKJACK TUTOR to first experiment with different betting systems and how they might actually work in a casino setting. If needed, there is also a "Best Bet" help screen that recommends certain plays (Hit, Stand, Double, Split).

I was somewhat surprised to learn that different blackjack rules apply to different cities. To allow for this, Mr. Jacob has built several data files that allows one to focus on the Las Vegas Strip, Downtown Las Vegas, Reno, Northern Nevada or Atlantic city. If you lean toward the more exotic casinos Mr. Jacob has provided a utility that allows you to build your set of rules and card counting standards.

There's more, too. BLACKJACK TUTOR also contains a graphing program that allows you to graph your progress. Should there be areas where you need some work (i.e. splitting hands) there are commands that will load the deck to provide more potential splits.

Obviously, Mr. Jacob knows a little bit about blackjack. Maybe that's why he's able to write his programming code in Honolulu while I bang on my word processor in Cincinnati.

—Tim Mullen

AT-Slowdown

Better Software Co.
10 W. Wilburn Ave.
Greenville, SC 29611
Shareware—$5

AT-Slowdown is a TSR utility that many game players may find useful. It will slow down the speed of fast machines like the IBM AT. It works directly with the system clock, and so will only work with IBM ATs and very close compatibles. It allows you to select the amount of slowing from the command line when you run the program. If you have tried to play games that didn't automatically compensate for faster clocks, you may find this program very helpful.

11

Graphics

Graphics are used in so many ways—for drawing, painting, graphs, slide shows and presentations, for CAD (Computer Aided Design) applications, and desktop publishing systems. We've located several graphics programs that meet different needs. We can't promise that any of these programs will meet all your graphic needs, or even that all of them put together will meet your needs. But there are some good programs here, especially to create drawings and color pictures, slide shows, and graphs.

If you use a database or spreadsheet then look at Draftsman, a program that can create a variety of business graphs from outside data. For a simple paint program that doesn't use a mouse, try PC-Art. For a more versatile system, try PC-Key-Draw, a program that combines features of several types of packages—drawing, painting and CAD. There are also some specialized programs like Map Maker and Molecular Modeling.

Graphics Terms
—with thanks to Edward Kidera

> B-spline—B-spline is a mathematical technique that produces a smooth curve over a series of points providing a convenient method of producing complex curves.

bitmapped—graphic images are saved as a series of individual bits or pixels. One bit per pixel provides black and white only, ie. on or off. Two bits per pixel provide four colors, while 8 bits per pixel provides 256 colors. Paint programs save graphics as a bitmap. Scanners and video digitizers are bitmapped devices.

CADD—Computer Aided Design and Drafting. CADD programs are primarily object oriented.

draw programs—store the graphic image as objects, ie. points, lines, circles, etc.

fatbits—to provide pixel level editing the individual pixels are enlarged or fattened on the screen for easier viewing and manipulation.

fill—areas on the screen can be filled with solid colors, mixed colors or complex patterns. Paint programs generally allow significant more flexibility in filling areas.

fillets —a rounded interior corner is called a fillet, while a rounded exterior corner is called a round.

font—text character's style and size. A font is one size for a given typeface.

grid—grid provides reference positions to aid drawing. Using a grid is like drawing on graph paper.

layer—layers allow a drawing to be separated into various components. Think of using layers as drawing on separate clear sheets. One layer is the top layer that is being drawn on, but the other layers can be seen as part of the drawing. Layers are found primarily in object oriented programs.

mirror—process of producing mirror image duplicate of object or portion of screen.

object oriented—graphic images are saved as separate objects. Draw and CADD programs are object oriented.

paint programs - provide pixel level control of the screen.

pixel—Each individual dot on the computer screen is called a pixel. The GCA 640X200 mode has 640 pixels across the screen and 200 pixels down the screen for a total of 128,000 pixels that can be controlled at 1 bit per pixel.

slide show—A series of computer screens can be arranged and shown in much the same way as 35mm slides are shown on a slide projector. Computer slide shows add the ability for many special effects including animation.

vector graphics—CAD programs store drawings as individual points and lines. A line is defined by its x and y coordinate and a direction.

zoom—drawing scale size can be adjusted for editing or viewing. Zooming effectively moves the view closer to or farther away from the drawing to reveal more or less detail.

210

Curve Digitizer ver. 3.0

West Coast Consultants
Shareware—$89

Curve Digitizer is a two dimensional computer aided drawing program. It comes with a variety of features, such as the ability to draw curves, arcs, circles, squares, and lines. You may print the finished drawing to one of the supported plotters, or to a disk file for use with the Slideshow utility provided with the system. Slideshow can display, onto your screen or your printer, up to ten different slides. You'll find the program very easy to use. There are six menus of functions each accessible through function keys F1-F6. A unique audible tone is emitted for each menu selected. In fact, the entire program uses sound effects as feedback for each command. For the beginning user, this has some benefit, but for the more advanced user, these sound effects could drive you up a wall. We were not able to determine whether the sound effects could be disabled. The manual that is provided with the shareware product is skimpy—providing only an overview of each command and how to configure the application. As with many shareware products, registering will supply you with a 300 page manual giving much more detail on the programs more advanced features. We hope to get a look at the registered version for the next update to this book. Though this product may not be suitable for use by an expert craftsman because of its simplistic user interface, it does provide a medium for creating two dimensional drawings and outputting them to a plotter or printer.

Curve Digitizer ver. 3.0
West Coast Consultants
11272 Pabellon Circle
San Diego, CA 92124
(619) 565-1266

Shareware: $89 (plus $2 shipping and handling)
Category: CAD; Graphics
System Requirements: 256k of available memory required, IBM PC, XT, AT or any close compatible
Recommended use: Generic graphic utility
Major Pros: Easy to learn and use. Good user interface
Major Cons: Manual is skimpy. Sound feedback is annoying
Sources: Popular BBSs and commercial services, or directly from the author

---

Draftsman 1.0

Hire Education
Shareware—$25

Draftsman (AKA *DRAWMAN.EXE*) is a package for creating color graphs using data entered from keyboard or data files extracted from spreadsheets and other sources. The program allows several graphic options, including overlayed graphs and other specific modifications. Draftsman is a fairly complex program, and isn't made any simpler by its extremely non-standard user interface.

Throughout the program, you use function keys to do things that ordinarily would be performed by cursor keys, or you find yourself pressing F2 to go on instead of Return. These features make working with the product somewhat irritating. On the other hand, Draftsman does offer a considerable amount of power to create the graphs that most spreadsheets can't. You can modify and enhance the color values of bar, pie, exploded pie, scatter, and line graphs; overlay several graphs together; output to files, to printers, and to plotters; add titles, legends, footnotes; etc. For better screen displays, you can set the aspect ratio to match your monitor. Also, the program comes with a complete manual and context sensitive help.

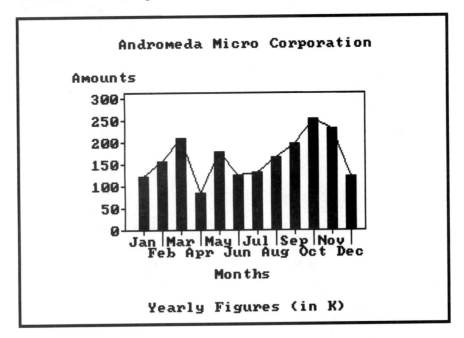

The most useful feature of the program is its ability to import data from DIF files (as created by most spreadsheets) or comma-delimited files. You can also enter data directly into the program, a prospect that would be more welcome with a more standardized set of key commands. When you finish creating graphs, you can create slide shows for presentation. People who like to make attractive, presentable graphs, either free-form or from existing data sets, should look at Draftsman.

```
          4.2  BAR CHART SPECIFICATIONS                  Free: 32290

    Title:    Andromeda Micro Corporation
    Footnote: Yearly Figures (in K)
    X-label:  Months
    Y-label:  Amounts                    (one or two lines)


    Bar format [stack, cluster]:         (if more than one y column)
    Bar color(s):                        (one color for each y column)
                    [ 1  2  4  6]
                        ▮      ▮
                    (add 100 for dot shading, 200 for line shading)
    Enclose chart in box [y,n]:  y
    Horizontal reference value:          (y value, or leave blank)
    Baseline value:                      (y value, or leave blank)
    ------------------------------------------------------------------
    Data file # [1,2,3]: 1      Y column(s):        [blank, or 1-5]
    Minimum column width [8-100]: 8
    Chart size [blank or 1-320]:    and position:    [x,y from 0-319]
      (size and position will normally be left blank or filled with the
      maximum value: size = 320, position = 0,0)

    TYPE:  F1 (Help!)  F2 (Entry complete, Proceed)  F3 (Return to previous menu)
```

Draftsman 1.0

Hire Education
3631 Jenifer NW
Washington, DC 20015

Shareware: $25

Category: Graphics

System Requirements: IBM PC or compatible; DOS 1.1 or higher; 128K
    (160 recommended); color graphics card (monochrome graphics monitor OK)

Recommended Use: for creating impressive graphs and slide shows from data

Major Pros: offers more sophisticated graphing options than most spreadsheets
    do; multiple graphs on one screen

Major Cons: non-standard user interface

Finger Paint Version 2.0

Poisson Technology
Shareware—$20

When we first saw Finger Paint, we were impressed with its range of features. Like an increasing number of products, this one supports EGA graphics (640 x 350 pixels), and is certainly a pleasure to use in that mode. It will also work in CGA (640 x 200) or in Hercules monochrome (720 x 348) modes.

Finger Paint is quite reminiscent of the Macintosh MacPaint style program, though it doesn't use pull down menus. It uses hierarchical menus in the style of Lotus 1-2-3. However, it does feature a palette of options which can also be chosen from menus or using keyboard shortcuts. The program works fairly well from the keyboard, but, as with many drawing and paint programs, it is more suited to a mouse. Especially when moving the cursor from one place to another, the mouse is superior.

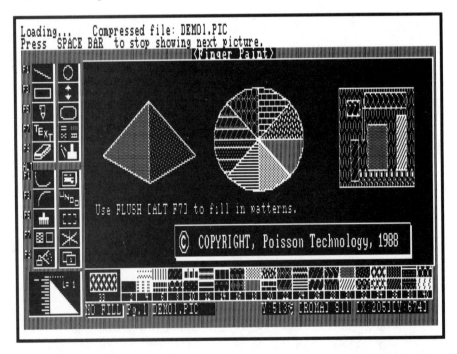

Basic features include various shape formations, fill patters (like the Mac), brush shapes and air brush effects. There is also a zoom mode that lets you see a small part of the image blown up to full screen size where you can edit it pixel by pixel. Additional options allow you to create specialized formations like splines and blines (curves off the end of a line). You can cut and paste images or parts of images, load and save files compressed PIC format images, print to any of several supported printers, and use any of 6 built-in fonts in up to 81 different sizes.

But the ordinary features are not the only ones included. In addition, this program supports two simultaneous "pages" of graphics. You can, in effect, be working on two drawings at once, flipping back and forth, and even cutting and pasting one to another. There is a transparent paste mode that lets you overlay one image over another.

This dual page format lends itself to another side benefit of the program—movies. You can, with some effort, create a series of pictures that are displayed in smooth animation by flipping the pages. Although the process is not effortless, the result is effective.

Finger Paint 2.0
Poisson Technology
816 Gregory Ct.
Fremont, CA 94539

Shareware: $20

Category: Graphics/Paint

System Requirements: IBM PC or compatible; DOS 2.0 or higher; 320K;
   graphics card and monitor; Compatible graphics printer and mouse optional

Recommended Use:for graphic development and simple movies

Major Pros: easy to learn; strong on standard paint features, two simultaneous
   images with cut/paste between, good curve options for paint program

Major Cons: No compatibility with other file types, somewhat slow to use
   from keyboard

Sources: popular BBSs and commercial services, or directly from the author

---

The program is relatively easy to learn and to use—depending on what input method you employ. Finger Paint will currently print hardcopy to HP LaserJet, EPSON, and IBM dot matrix printers. However, one unfortunate omission of this product is support of some of the common graphic file types. In fact, although this product uses the PIC extension used by Lotus graphics, it does not create a standard paint file that can by used by any other program. Nor does it read in files from other sources (as far as we can tell). If the authors of this program could add file conversions to and from some of the popular formats, Finger Paint would be a real winner!

Image-3D Version 1.8

The Quest Company
Shareware—$25

Image-3D is a three dimensional, wire-frame modeling program that allows you to create, edit, and view three dimensional objects or pictures. The program has easy-to-use menus for choosing commands to view or design pictures. Image-3D also allows you to scale, move, rotate, or tip your image anyway you choose.

The program comes with a reference manual describing each command available, as well as some sample files showing various capabilities of the system.

Image3-D Version 1.8
The Quest Company
3117 W. Holland Ave.
Fresno, CA 93722   209/222-5301

Shareware: $25.00

Category: CAD/CAM

System Requirements: 512k of available memory, IBM PC, XT, AT or any close compatible, CGA or EGA required (depending on version) two floppy disk drives or a hard disk recommended

Recommended use: Designing three dimensional wire frame graphics

Major Pros: Easy to use interface, good features, inexpensive

Major Cons: No mouse support, no built-in printing facility

Sources: Popular BBSs and commercial services, or directly from the author

---

All of your design work is done with the arrow keys on the keyboard—no mouse support is available. However, for the novice designer this drawback is minor.

Also, there is no printing facility built into the program. In order to print your design, you must use a memory resident screen printing utility. The author suggests several that are available in public domain or Shareware.

Though the CGA version was tested for this review, there is a Shareware EGA version available, providing full color support to your design needs. When you register the product, the author will send you version 3.0 which has additional capabilities such as drawing circles and ovals, and the creation of object libraries which allow you to paste objects from the library into your design, and full CGA and EGA support.

Though this product does not rival commercial products available, it is a quick and easy to use system for designing three dimensional images and pictures. For those of you who have wanted to tinker with doing this kind of design, but didn't want to spend a lot of money to do it, this product is definitely worth a look.

PC-Art 3.1

Paul Michael Stone
Shareware—$25

Since we first looked at PC-Art, it has evolved into an increasingly well-conceived paint program. Although PC-Art is still not the most powerful program for drawing and painting on a PC, it does have the advantages of being easy to learn, and not requiring any extra equipment (although it will work with a joystick or a mouse). It works adequately from the numeric cursor pad, and allows you to draw lines, circles, and boxes, freehand draw, spray paint, and fill with various colors. You can set patterns and the color palette from simple menus, and also set foreground and background colors. Now you can even edit patterns using a zoomed screen and up to four colors. Text can be added as well, using various fonts and sizes provided. You can Zoom a portion of the screen for pixel by pixel editing.

The command structure has changed as well. Function keys still open mini-menus from which you choose the current type of operation, color, font size, etc. Then F10 closes the menu. In many cases you have to press a key to initiate or complete an action. For instance, to draw a circle you would press F1 to get a menu containing the drawing, painting, spray paint, line drawing, and shape options. Next, move the cursor to the circle icon and press F10 to complete.

Now use the cursor keys to establish the circle's size, and finally press C for circle. This method of using the first letter to finalize an action extends to other options, such as P for paint, S for spray paint, etc. It takes a little getting used to, but eventually it becomes automatic. Since PC-Art isn't a very large program, it can be learned in one sitting.

You can save entire files, portions of files (called snapshots), and keep several files in image libraries. You can retrieve snapshots into current work, position them, and even produce multiple images, since the current snapshot is kept in a buffer.

Although this isn't an extensive program, and lacks any on-screen help (even a command list would be useful), it does what it does well, and could provide color graphics if you don't want to learn a more complex package or you don't want to get a mouse.

PC-Art Ver. 3.1
Paul Michael Stone
201 Heyden Dr.
Eureka, MO 63025

Shareware: $25

Category: Graphics

System Requirements: IBM PC or compatible; DOS 2.0 or higher; 256K; color graphics card and monitor; IBM or Epson compatible graphics printer and joystick optional

Recommended Use: for simple CGA art

Major Pros: simple to learn; graphics libraries

Major Cons: limited by comparison with other products on the market

Sources: popular BBSs and commercial services, or directly from the author

---

PC-Key-Draw 3.51

PC-Key-Draw is that rare program that attempts to be all things to all people. In fact, PC-Key-Draw is such a versatile and feature-laden product that it is nearly impossible to give a full list of its abilities here.

After one look at the new tutorial, you can see the potential power of the Hyper-Draw feature. You can use a joystick, mouse, or the keyboard to point at specific portions of a screen. Pressing enter or clicking a button will take you to an associated screen. We weren't able to learn all the secrets of the HyperDraw system because, as of our deadline on the book, HyperDraw was so new that there was no documentation on it yet. However, the tutorial convinced us that it represents a major step in the evolution of this fine graphics program.

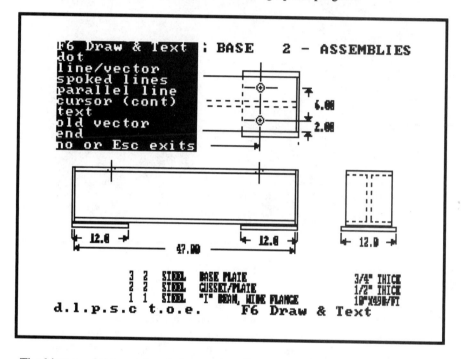

The history of this product is interesting. The author, Edward Kidera, is a mechanical ocean equipment engineer. This specialty produced in him a need for engineering features. On the other hand, Kidera is surrounded by artists—his mother, sister (an architect), and wife (a graphic design artist). So Kidera has been motivated by the desire to fulfill the needs of many different graphic environments.

We're not prepared to say that he succeeds in all these attempts—not being all those things ourselves—but we can see immediately that PC-Key-Draw combines in one package features that are ordinarily found in two, three, or even four separate programs. He has the paint features of a paint program, the drawing and measurement features of a drafting program, many of the control features of a

CAD program, and the animation and slide show of a presentation graphics system.

PC-Key-Draw features a system of pop-up menus, making it all the easier to learn, and various short cut keys for more experienced users.

The high points: it creates many standard and non-standard shapes (circles, ellipses, polygons, rose curves, arcs, pie shapes, fillets, sine curves, b-spline curves, etc.); it has CAD, drafting, and paint features; it works well from keyboard but supports Microsoft Mouse and Mouse Systems Mouse; it can rotate, mirror, smear, replicate, zoom, revolve, tilt, slide, shrink and grow, and even edit pixels on objects; it can select from several palettes in color, and several patterns; it uses high resolution monochrome mode for sharper images; it can work with fonts and text in various ways, create a BASICA subroutine from a graphic; it can save as vector symbols, save partial images; includes a sophisticated macro language and animated slide show software; and it also has an undo feature. In addition, PC-Key-Draw can calculate areas and centers of objects and measure distances.

In version 3.51, PC-Key-Draw has entered a new phase of its development. In addition to several speed improvements, nested macros, and a lot of refinements throughout the system, the product has added an interactive tutorial which will get new users started expediently. The tutorial uses PC-Key-Draw's major enhancement—HyperDraw. HyperDraw adds certain database and hypertext-like abilities to this product. The author likens it to HyperCard on the Macintosh.

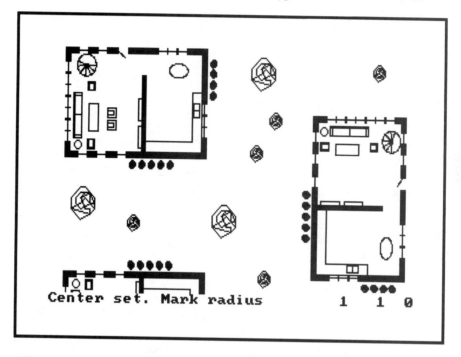

There isn't much that isn't included. However, PC-Key-Draw does not yet support EGA or VGA modes (although it will work with EGA and VGA cards in CGA mode). It doesn't yet support plotters (although Kidera states that he uses the program to create color slides). And there are several input devices that Kidera plans to eventually incorporate. Support for the HP LaserJet printer is now available on registration.

The Shareware distributed version (*PCKEYDRW.ARC*) is a complete system. A separate library disk with extra fonts and pictures and the slideshow program is also available as Shareware, but, since Kidera himself does not upload the programs to BBS, we can't be sure under what name(s) it can be found. The library disk and the most recent version (3.51) of PC-Key-Draw are both available from PD and Shareware catalogs. (see Part III, Sources). Three additional library disks are available to registered users with additional fonts and patterns, etc. There are a few other enhancements available only to registered users, including a complete printed manual—highly recommended considering the depth and complexity of this program.

PC-Key-Draw 3.51
Edward H. Kidera IV
OEDWARE
P.O. Box 595
Columbia, MD 21045-0595
(301) 997-9333

Shareware: $100

Category: All-in-one Graphics

System Requirements: IBM PC/XT/AT/jr/Portable or compatible with 256K memory (320 preferred); one floppy drive and standard color card (CGA). A second disk drive or hard disk is preferred; can access up to 1.5 megabytes in a RAM disk if available; mouse optional; does not work with Hercules card at present

Recommended Use: Drafting, drawing, painting, CAD, animation, HyperDraw and presentations

Major Pros: all-in-one graphics package; tremendous flexibility in manipulating images; various measurement options; macros; runtime for presentations; HyperDraw hypertext/database features

Major Cons: somewhat complex for casual users; needs to support more hardware

Sources: popular BBSs and commercial services, or directly from the author

Although PC-Key-Draw goes as far as it can to make life easy for the user, it is not really a beginner's program, unless that beginner is prepared to invest time and effort learning to use the package. To make full use of its many features, including its macro programming, requires the investment of a considerable amount of time. On the other hand, the rewards of mastering this program may be incalculable. We highly recommend this program for those who want it all. We know of nothing else like it .

Present Vers. 5.1

Fernando Pertuz
Shareware—$40

Present makes creating PC slide shows almost effortless. It uses Basic Bsave compatible images (which most graphics packages for the PC will produce) or screen images captured with the enclosed PD program, Camera. To create a slide show, you string images together with a selection of display times (from Flash to 128 seconds) and dissolves (like sweep, fade, close, open, expand, shrink, etc.).

You initially create a presentation with the PREPARE program. Creating a slide show is as easy as selecting from a list of images on disk (up to a hundred), listing them in order of appearance, and selecting the display length and dissolve type.

The PREPARE program allows you to move or delete images after you have placed them in the queue. You can also view any picture file by selecting it with the cursor keys and typing the letter L. In this way, you can always see what you're working with.

There's not much more to it—creating the slide show is that easy. When you execute the show with the PRESENT command, you have several options. On a single screen system, you can instruct the program to run the show automatically, or you can run it in Manual mode (which means a keypress for each new screen, plus key to move forward, minus key to move back).

With two screens you can actually use the monochrome screen as a controller for the slide show. You can display a pointer on screen (with a joystick), change the order of slides, back up, skip files, change dissolves, etc. We found Present's performance to be excellent. All dissolves and image changes were fast and smooth, and worked with our EGA card without special emulations.

There are a few features we would welcome in this program. For one, a conditional branch based on keyboard input; also, some animation capabilities and the ability to manipulate partial images on screen. With these features added, Present could become a versatile package with the ease of use to make it a winner in any market.

PRESENT Vers. 5.1
Fernando Pertuz
SML Services, Inc.
6095 River Chase Cir., NW
Atlanta, GA 30328

Shareware: $40

Category: Graphics; Presentation

System Requirements: IBM PC/XT/AT/jr/Portable or compatible; DOS 1.1 or higher; one drive; color display; second monochrome display and joystick(s) optional

Recommended Use: user directed or automatic slide shows

Major Pros: fast performer, with smooth dissolves; very easy to use; comes with Camera for taking screen shots; basic Bsave compatible; unique control using two monitors (joystick optional)

Major Cons: no conditional branching based on keyboard input; no animation

Sources: popular BBSs and commercial services, or directly from the author

Graphic File Conversions

There are a variety of different, non-compatible file types for graphics. Because of this, there are many programs designed to help you view, convert, and/or print files from different types. The ultimate graphic file program is Optiks from Keith Graham, but there are several other programs that may interest you, depending on your circumstances.

OPTIKS ver. 2.08
Keith P. Graham
Shareware—$79.95

OPTIKS is a graphics utility for displaying, editing, printing, and resaving your graphics in a variety of formats including:

- LOTUS PIC and Postscript files

- BLOAD/BSAVE format files

- APPLE MACPAINT files

- PC Paintbrush

- EFS Image files

- Datacopy Corp. uncompressed WIPS files

- RLE (Run Length Encoded) files from Compuserve

- Dr. Halo II CUT files

- FONTASY load block or BASIC PUT/GET files

- Microsoft Paint

- RICOH IS30 Pixel Image Generation files

- Show files in RAS format

- Aldus-Microsoft TIFF files

- GEM paint files

- IBM Image Support Facility 2 v1.00

- DEGAS Atari ST files

- PFS First Publisher .ART files

- Mouse Systems Paint v1.5 format files

- PC Paint v2.00 and PC Paint +

- Compuserve GIF (Graphics Interchange Format)

And this program doesn't stop there. In addition to these features, you can place text on your picture with a wide choice of fonts, overlay other pictures or graphics, merge graphic files, and resize or manipulate any picture as you choose. OPTIKS also supports CANON, JLASER, and PRINCETON scanners for input and can print to a variety of dot matrix and laser printers. You can also print to a disk file or to a LaserMaster Corp. CAPCard.

All these features are bundled together into a nice Lotus 1-2-3 menu interface. If you know how to use 1-2-3 then you know how to use this product. The product also supports a mouse if you have one.

OPTIKS comes with a brief manual that introduces you to some of the basic features of the product. Though the manual is not entirely adequate, it does explain the basic operation of the program.

We weren't able to test all the file formats included in this program. Of the ones that were tested, however, the program worked properly. If you work with graphics, desktop publishers, or paint programs, you'll want to have this program in your library. We predict that this program will evolve into a classic "must have" program for graphics compatibility.

OPTIKS
Keith Graham
(914) 359-3560
PC-Rockland BBS (914) 353-2176

Shareware: $79.95

Category: Graphics

System Requirements: 256k of available memory required, IBM PC, XT, AT or any close compatible.

Recommended use: Generic graphic utility.

Major Pros: Easy to learn and use. Wide variety of file formats available.

Major Cons: Manual is skimpy. No on-line help for commands.

Sources: Popular BBSs and commercial services, or directly from the author.

ALLMAC

Frank Schweiger
10083 Heytesbury Ln.
Snady, UT 84092
Shareware—$5

ALLMAC is a MacPaint viewer/editor that will display MacPaint type graphics in various CGA and EGA modes. It will also print to several different printers. With this program, you can load a MacPaint file and view it in several different ways. A full screen view allows you to scroll the image. A reduced "photographic" view allows you to manipulate the amount of white and black in the image. You can also print the image or even perform limited editing on the image in a blown up mode (similar to Fat Bits in MacPaint) where each pixel is made large and you can change its state from black to white or vice versa. This program is very easy to use and has features missing from other MacPaint file viewers.

MACEGA

Kyle R. Roberson
Public Domain

This program should be found under the filename MACEGA10.ARC and contains the files MACEGA.DOC and MACEGA.EXE. This public domain program will display MacPaint type pictures and scroll them smoothly across the screen in EGA mode. Owners of the Vega Deluxe EGA card receive the added benefit that the program will automatically switch to 640x480 mode.

MAC2

Bob Berry
Mel Kurth
Public Domain

Another simple, but nicely done MacPaint file viewer, this one automatically produces a list of files with a .MAC extension. Select with arrow keys and press Enter to view. Other options include automatic scrolling and "colorizing" in EGA (which basically places a transparent color over a slightly reduced version of the image). Found as MAC20.ARC which contains the file MAC2.COM.

CVTMAC

John Bridges
Copyright Microtex Industries, Inc.
Public Domain

This program is supposed to convert MacPaint files to PCPaint Plus format.

PIC2MAC Version 1.10

Bill and Laurie Fleisher
4680 Carriock Ave.
Grand Rapids, MI 49508
(616) 531-2776
Shareware—donations accepted

This file is supposed to convert PCPaint Plus files to Macintosh format.

FASTGIF v2.0

James C. Beebe
2170 Dow Drive
Akron, OH 44313
CompuServe ID 74746,2444
Shareware—$19.95

FastGIF is a program that displays GIF files (CompuServe's Graphics Interchange Format) on a PC with EGA or VGA graphics capability. The program is, as its name implies, very fast, and it will display GIF images in a variety of modes. Using a special user-defined command file, you can create slide shows of GIF files that FastGIF will then display.

There are a variety of other helpful features, including help, various directory sorting options, and very complete documentation. The author mentions the wide range of GIF files suitable for viewing that are available on CompuServe's PICS forum.

GIFEGA
Public Domain

Another GIF file viewer, this one is much simpler than FastGif, but works well without any frills.

STRIPGIF
GEnie mail address R.EPPS
Public Domain

StripGIF is a small program that is designed to remove incompatible information from GIF files that were created on a Macintosh. In our experience, both FastGIF and GIFEGA would display Mac GIF files, though not always preserving detail or color (from Mac II files). We noticed no difference when using StripGIF on those files, but include the file here in case it can help someone else.

12

Learning

Chemical ver. 2.0

Larry Puhl
Public Domain (source code $20)

Have you ever wondered what it would be like to mix TNT with Nitroglycerine?
Well, here's your chance. CHEMICAL is a molecular modeling program that allows you to create three dimensional pictures of chemicals. To assemble a chemical, you first select the desired atoms from a Periodic Table. Then, you bond the
atoms to make your chemical. A graphic representation of the chemical is
displayed as the chemical is being constructed. Once the chemical is constructed
(or even during the construction phase), you can view the chemical from all different directions. If you wish, you can create hybrids or ionize an atom before bond-
ing. In addition, atoms can be bonded into groups. These groups can then be
bonded with other groups to form very large chemicals.

A companion program, CHEMVIEW, is also included with the distribution ARC
file. It allows you to view 3-dimensional animation of the models generated with
CHEMICAL. CHEMVIEW was not reviewed because it would not work properly
with a NEC multisync card installed on the review system.

Though this program does not provide a course in chemistry, it does provide brief
introductions to some of the concepts used in the program. Also included is a set

of example chemical files which can be loaded, viewed, and manipulated as you require. The documentation also gives several lessons on the construction of the very simple, to the very complex chemicals.

The program works well, and makes excellent use of color. There is basic error trapping for certain no-no's in chemistry—i.e., creating a hybrid of hydrogen. However, combining chemicals with chaotic abandon will bomb the program (in real life, it would probably create sludge)—so you do have to follow some rules of chemistry to use this product.

This product is ideally suited for the high school chemistry student to maybe a freshman or sophomore college chemistry student. The program has the potential of enhancing a student's studies by making abstract concepts tangible through visualization. And something that is tangible will be remembered better than something that is simply memorized and forgotten after the final exam.

Chemical ver. 2.0
Larry Puhl
6 Plum Court
Sleepy Hollow, IL 60118

Public Domain: (source code $20)

Category: Educational

System Requirements: 640k of available memory required, IBM PC, XT, AT or any close compatible, CGA or EGA required; EGA is recommended

Recommended use: Educational aid to applying chemistry concepts

Major Pros: Easy to learn and use; makes excellent use of color; fast operation

Major Cons: Viewing program does not work with all hardware configurations

Sources: Popular BBSs and commercial services, or directly from the author

---

Decide

Public Domain

I'm not sure where I found this program, but it's called DECIDE.EXE and I "DECIDEd" to put it in the learning section of the book. I didn't know where else to put it, and this section seemed as good as any. You can use DECIDE.EXE to learn about your decision making process.

Everyone has, at one time or another, flipped a coin to make a decision. You may not have liked the result, so you made it the best of two out of three, three out of five, and so on. Yes, making decisions can be pretty hard sometimes.

There are some very sophisticated decision support programs available in the commercial market, some of them using special artificial intelligence techniques. This program is not one of those, but it might be a good way to help you identify the factors that are influencing a decision as well as help prioritize the options and considerations.

Decide can help you make decisions based on several alternatives, choosing a course of action from various alternatives, or making a yes or no decision. In each case, you must identify and enter the various considerations. The program then prompts you to weigh each alternative on a scale, using different combinations of alternatives as the baseline value. When you are finished, the program does some mathematics in the background and comes up with a listing of suggestions based on their percentage of meeting your goals.

This is a program that could actually help you make decisions, but, like other decision support products, it is only going to reflect what you put into it. On any given day, you may alter you feelings or arbitrarily enter a different set of considerations or values. So the answer you get is really a reflection of the information you already possess. I think of this program as more fun than serious, and use it in that spirit.

Decide (take two)

It doesn't happen often, but there are two public domain programs that have exactly the same name. Another program called DECIDE.EXE (but downloaded from a file called DECISION.ARC) is available. This one is very different. It's called the Executive Decision Maker, and it simply displays a list of six possible answers—*DEFINITELY, NEVER, WHY NOT, ASK AGAIN, FORGET IT*, and

POSSIBLE. You ask the questions (silently or out loud—your choice), then press a key. Some random sounds are played while a red square alternates quickly between the options. After a second or so, the square lands on one of the options. That's your answer. This is sort of the computer's answer to the Magic Eight Ball (if you remember that). Definitely in the same category as flipping a coin.

One warning: There doesn't seem to be a command for exiting the program, but pressing Control-Break and then Enter should do it.

Eldorado Type

William Burke
Eldorado Springware
2675 Upham CT
Wheatridge, CO 80215
Shareware—$10

Eldorado Type (found as ELTYPE.ARC) is a very simple program designed to help you improve typing skills. I like this program because it doesn't attempt to be more than it is, but it allows you to select any ASCII file as the practice file. This means that you can practice on files that are typical of the work you do, or create lessons of any kind with an ASCII editor.

All this program does is display a text file, one line at a time, on screen. You must type exactly what appears on the screen, including shifted characters. If you make a mistake, it is highlighted and a beep sounds. At the bottom of the screen is a running display of your speed and accuracy, plus the number of keystrokes entered and the number or mistakes made.

The practice file that accompanies this program is a lesson in Shareware ethics, which is a clever way this Shareware author has found to make his point. Unfortunately, the author has allowed a few typos in his document, something that can be disturbing during typing practice. Otherwise, this is a useful program.

HELPDOS

Help Technologies
Shareware—$20

HELPDOS is the ultimate DOS utility for people new to DOS. By placing the HELPDOS files in a directory on the current DOS Path, help is always available for any DOS command. The Shareware version of HELPDOS works with DOS 2.0, but versions are available with registration for DOS 3.0, 3.1, and 3.2.

For help with a specific DOS command, you type *HELP* and the command name. For example, for help with the *ERASE* command, type *HELP ERASE*. A screen or more of material about the *ERASE* command is displayed. These screens explain in detail how to use the *ERASE* command. In addition, a menu of function key commands is available to get more help, to browse through a list of subjects, to print the contents of the current help subject, or to return to the DOS command line (leaving the help message displayed).

You can even customize the colors, default directory, etc., using the *HELPSET* program supplied. Or define and write your own help files (useful for explaining specific batch file operations or other system specific jobs).

HELPDOS is absolutely the best beginner's DOS assistant we've seen. It is a complete, sophisticated product. The files require about 320K of disk space, but for beginners, this could be space well used. Even for intermediate users, there's lots to learn from *HELPDOS*.

HELPDOS
Help Technologies
25 Pope Road
P.O. Box 399
La Honda, CA 94020
(415) 856-2322

Shareware: $20

Category: DOS Help

System Requirements: IBM PC or compatible; DOS 2.0 or later; could be run on floppy disks, but hard disk recommended

Recommended Use: beginning DOS users

Major Pros: has command line help as well as menu selection of specific screens; help information prints out user created help messages

Sources: popular BBSs and commercial services, or directly from the author

---

KIDS WORD PROCESSOR

Sidney D. Nolte
13858 Peyton Drive
Dallas, TX 75240
Shareware—$10 SPECIAL REQUIREMENTS: COLOR GRAPHICS ADAPTER

This review is reprinted by permission of the PDN Newsletter.

One of the advantages of owning a PC is the ability to allow our children to gain familiarity with a computer. To many parent's dismay this familiarity goes little farther than the world of Pac Man and Donkey Kong.

Recalling my own childhood, I seriously doubt I would have become very excited by a feature-heavy, professional word processing, spreadsheet or database program. Even numerous adults become bogged down in these, and in some cases, totally frustrated trying to wade their way though some of the more complicated programs currently on the commercial market.

With this in mind, Sidney Nolte has developed a colorful, uncomplicated word processing program designed to appeal especially to children. Learning need not be painful, and in fact can be fun. With a program such as this, children can ease their way into real computing and see how a word processor can simplify written communication.

In the documentation, Mr. Nolte points out how this program will help kids separate the problem of putting ideas together on a page, from the motor skills needed to write properly on paper. Who cannot recall a teacher admonishing those in class about poor penmanship or sloppy papers? On the computer, the DEL key takes care of any mistakes and, as Mr. Nolte points out, "...writing is reduced to the mental activity it should be."

When starting **KIDS WORD PROCESSOR** one is greeted with a large-lettered (40 column mode) opening screen. Letters of the alphabet appear on the screen one at a time to the A-B-C tune. This can be played out or, if you prefer, hitting the space bar will take you to the main menu. The main menu gives a child six options (*HELP*, *WRITE*, *LIBRARY*, *PRINT*, *DELETE* and *QUIT*) and beside each option is an icon that conveys what that function does. The cursor is shown as a color bar and determines which option will be activated. The arrow keys move the cursor to the desired option and hitting the <ENTER> key activates the command.

Each option provides a secondary menu that lists all old files currently on the disk. From here, a child either recalls an existing file on which to work or creates a new one. Several demo files are included with the disk to help with initial training. At any point, pressing <ESC> will return you to the main menu.

One really nice feature about this program is the choice of letter sizes available to the user. Younger children can use large, oversized letters when creating their text. Those who are a little older or perhaps more experienced can adjust to smaller letters simply by tapping the F3 function key.

A *HELP* function is also available just like on the big programs. Typing F1 brings up a help screen that offers instructions on moving the cursor, inserting or deleting text and changing screen colors.

The print function is very straight forward. When you choose a story to print, it is directed to your printer. The documentation claims it will be printed in big letters but I assume this is on an Epson-compatible printer. My extra-cheap dot matrix printer just printed straight text but it is far from being an Epson compatible, and the program most likely performs as promised.

In general, there seems to be a shortage of quality educational software available in public domain or SHAREWARE. It's fortunate that Mr. Nolte took the time to write this program. If you are looking for a way to pry your kids off the games and sway them towards more useful computer time then this could be a good addition to your software library.

—Tim Mullen

Language Teacher 2.0

Cindy & Andrew Bartorillo
Micro Tutor Products
1819 Millstream Drive
Frederick, MD 21701
(301) 694-7108 (modem)
Shareware—$10 per module

If you want to learn Spanish, French, German, or Italian, you may want to look at these programs. We looked at the Spanish programs, and have found them to be excellent. For instance, the Spanish Teacher #1 program contains over 700 vocabulary items and almost 1500 verb conjugations. Testing includes: noun vocabulary drill (multiple choice or fill in), verb vocabulary drill, miscellaneous word drills, random word drills, phrase translations, and verb conjugations. You can view diagnostic information about your progress, print the various drills, and even edit the vocabulary and phrase files. Function keys are used to input special characters like accented characters or those with tildes. This means that you don't get a watered down approach, but a complete test in the language.

Though the program is excellent, we did find some places in the Spanish version where the answers were somewhat rigid. For instance, the word *cena* is translated as *supper*, but the word *dinner* was unacceptable. In conventional American English, *dinner* is an adequate translation of *cena*. These situations were rare however, and we recommend these programs to people who want to learn languages.

Learn-C (PonzoTUTOR)

P.J. Ponzo
Dept. of Applied Math
University of Waterloo
Ontario, N2L 3G1
Canada
Public Domain

If you are a beginning programmer and would like to learn C, you should look at this program. Learn-C is a wonderful introduction to C programming, and a wonderful example of programming itself. It makes extensive use of built-in ANSI codes for graphics.

This series of lessons is imaginative and humorous, and makes excellent use of graphic effects as teaching tools. For instance, when a sample of code is displayed, sections of it will be highlighted on subsequent screens with explanations of each individual highlighted section. A small graphic PC logo frequently displays comments. For instance, when the first small program has been presented, the tutorial explains that it can't be run yet. The little PC image displays "...alas..." on the screen.

Explanations are clear and simple. This program is a pleasure to use, even if you don't want to learn C. It is the kind of approach that more programs could use, though it obviously required some work, particularly due to the extensive use of ANSI codes. The author states that he wrote this tutorial as he was learning the program, that it is free, and carries a money-back guarantee that all statements are correct. Of course, this is another way of saying that there may be inaccuracies in the lessons. We think that most of the lessons are accurate however, and recommend this product. You can't beat the price.

QHELP and QHCOMPIL

Mark VanKekerix
2035 J Apt. 6
Lincoln, NE 68510
(402) 475-0601
Shareware—donation appreciated

If you have ever wished you could create a context-sensitive help system for an application or system on your PC, QHELP and QHCOMPIL might be just what you are seeking. QHELP is a memory resident pop-up driver for help files generated with QHCOMPIL.

You can create any system of help, and when the user of an application presses the appropriate hot key, up pops help in the form of an index of topics. If the cursor is on or next to one of the keywords listed in the help file, a help screen directly related to the word on the screen will pop up.

You create your own help system, complete with colors and hot key assignment, using QHCOMPIL. Creating a help file isn't as simple as whistling Dixie, but this program takes much of the drudgery out of the process. You still have to create keywords, related keywords, and descriptions; but the program takes care of most everything else. You write the necessary information using any text editor or word processor that creates ASCII files. You will also need to create a default screen (which is generally the index of keywords that can take the user to any definition screen). When the entire help file is written, you can compile it into a QHELP file. You can also designate other keywords that occur within a specific definition as references. These keywords will be highlighted within the help description, and selecting a highlighted related keyword will take the user to that word's description.

This is a sophisticated product that allows you to create multiple pages of help descriptions. Built-in commands take users to the index screen, or allows them to select a different help file to view.

There are some limitations to this system, but they are should not inconvenience most users. The biggest limitation is that the pop-up help windows will only display in text mode. Most application software runs in text mode, so this will not be a problem for most users. Also, any single help system can contain no more than 500 keywords, 10 fifteen line "pages" per description, and no more than 100 reference words per keyword description.

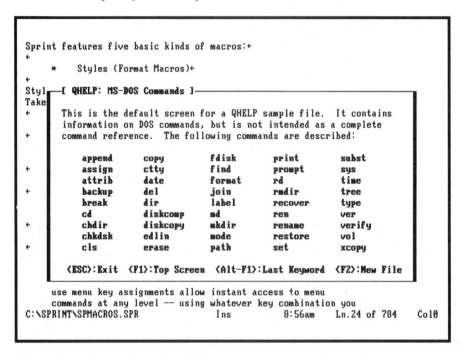

The QHCOMPIL program itself is menu driven and easy to use. Once the appropriate text file has been created, QHCOMPIL will allow you to define header information like color and hot key, then compile (or uncompile) a help file. You can change the header information on an existing help file (without uncompiling it), or create a header for a new help file, then compile it.

A sample help system is included with QHELP, and you can uncompile it using QHCOMPIL's uncompile option to see what a help file should look like.

This product is based on Borland's Turbo C help system, and the author acknowledges the debt. But his implementation of this system is excellent and could add value to many applications. Also, you can distribute QHELP with your own help files for free, unless you are charging money for the program it accompanies, in which case a license fee is requested. Since QHELP uses only about 37K bytes, it is small enough to fit on most systems.

13

DOS Shells
and
Menu
Programs

Many people don't know—and don't need to know—how to use DOS. After all, computers are meant to be used for practical purposes—purposes well served by the cornucopia of applications available. Most computer users don't wish to spend any more time and effort than necessary to learn to massage DOS data.

Like any interface, DOS has its strengths and its weaknesses. Some people prefer to run programs by choosing from a list instead of typing the file name, and DOS is definitely command line oriented. Others want additional information that DOS does not readily provide. They may not know how to work at the DOS level, but only how to run a particular application—a word processor or database program, for instance. For those people, there are menus and DOS shells.

Menu programs allow a user to select available applications from a list instead of typing DOS paths and file names. Each item, or choice, in a menu environment is associated with a DOS command, or a list of valid DOS commands. Menu data is generally created and maintained by the user or MIS director. Batch commands are stored with the menu program to change directories quickly (if necessary) and to run appropriate files. Usually, after quitting an application, the user returns automatically to the menu. Menus are excellent for computer systems that are used by many non-technical users, or where job stability is not high. Of course, many technically proficient users prefer a menu system for additional ease and convenience.

A DOS shell program can be similar to a menu program, but it incorporates DOS functions as a built-in aspect of the shell. A DOS shell is designed to replace DOS as much as possible. Shells generally add a great deal of utility and visual appeal by placing system and directory information on screen while offering many DOS commands as simple menu entries. For example, a shell might include file copy and delete commands as well as sophisticated methods for changing directories and selecting files to run. One shell, DOSamatic, even allows you to run more than one program at a time.

Each program mentioned in this section is great. There is no way to say one is considerably better than another. They are all fine applications. It seems that authors love to create menus and shells, and to add all kinds of features to them. Because these are all Shareware offerings, we recommend that you try several before you decide which is best for you. Frankly, they are all so good, that we have a hard time deciding which to use.

Automenu 4.01
Magee Enterprises
Shareware—$50

Automenu has been around for several years, and has undergone multiple updates. It is one of the most successful Shareware products, in use in many Fortune 500 companies all around the country. The most recent version is Version 4.01.

Each menu can have up to 8 pages, each with 8 menu choices. Linking menus provides virtually unlimited menu choices and flexibility. For instance, all DOS functions and commands could be placed in a DOS Menu, itself called from a Main Menu.

Automenu is very simple in operation. Press a number key (1-8), or function key (F1-F8) to activate a menu selection, or use the space bar or mouse to move to the selection desired and press Enter (or mouse button). Pressing PgUp and PgDn, F9 and F10, or the right and left arrow keys will scroll through menu pages. The screen displays time and date, plus free system RAM, and the current state of the toggle keys (*NUM*, *CTRL*, *ALT*, *SHIFT*, *CAPS*, and *SCROLL* display if on). Also displayed is the menu page you are currently viewing, i.e. MENU 2 of 8.

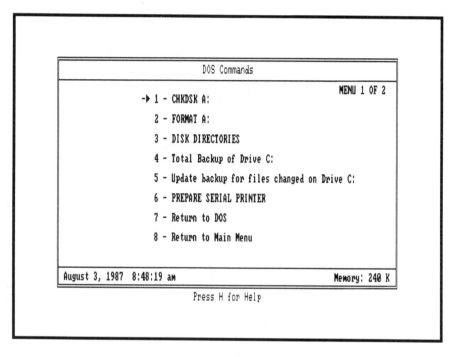

For security, Automenu offers password protection on individual menu choices, and file encryption on a Menu Definition file (which prevents unauthorized users from reading the passwords you have set). In addition, there is no way to drop out of Automenu to DOS unless a specific menu choice allows it (or a program called by Automenu allows exit to the DOS shell).

Automenu features several types of DOS commands. Using simple punctuation inside the AUTOMENU.MDF file, the user controls the way the menu system works. The syntax is similar to that of a batch file, but with some differences. For example, an asterisk precedes the title of a menu item. A minus sign precedes a single DOS command (associated with a menu item). Other commands allow issuing a batch of commands while Automenu remains in memory (for instant return to the menu without disk access), issuing commands without keeping Automenu in memory, issuing a single DOS command, then pausing for a keyboard input before returning to the menu, ad hoc DOS command execution (from direct keyboard entry), etc.

Automenu allows command line input on command execution. In other words, when you load a program that takes additional parameters, Automenu can pause and allow the input from keyboard, or from a selection of pre-defined choices. Automenu can also be set to execute specific commands at pre-set times (useful, for instance, if you use a telecommunication program to automatically call, send or retrieve data at night).

To make the program even easier to use, you can define specific help messages for any menu item, or create special text output lines to run with batch commands and offer further assistance with the current operations. An example of a text output line would be to create a message like ":Insert Disk in Drive A, then press any key." The message would be displayed during batch execution.

Automenu 4.01
Magee Enterprises
P.O. Box 1587
Norcross, GA 30091
(404) 446-6611

Shareware: $50

Category: Menus

System Requirements: 32K of available memory; IBM PC, XT, AT or
    compatible; DOS 2.0 or later; one disk drive or more; compatible with
    networks like Novell, 3COM, and Alloy

Recommended Use: hard disk menu program, create interlinking floppy
    menus, turn-key systems

Major Pros: wide variety of options and uses, including timed execution,
    menu-driven parameter passing, memory resident operation, switch between
    monitors, customize configurations, screen blanking, linked menus, etc.

Major Cons: menu setup requires some understanding of DOS commands;
    could be easier

Sources: popular BBSs and commercial services, or directly from the author

---

Previously, the most difficult aspect of maintaining an Automenu system was creating and editing the Menu Definition file (AUTOMENU.MDF) that runs it. Now a special file (AUTOMAKE.EXE) automates the process of batch file creation and includes on-line help for the specific symbols used in Automenu. I use a menu selection to call the Automake program directly from my menu.

When you select a menu item, Automenu writes and executes a temporary batch file based on the DOS commands associated with it (as defined in the Menu Definition file).

AUTOCUST is the customization program for Automenu. Use AUTOCUST to change colors, select automatic screen blackout options, set mouse options (Automenu also works with some voice recognition systems), and several other options.

Automenu has proven reliable and effective in a great many systems over the years. It is one of the most successful Shareware products being used by corporations and small businesses, and on private computers nationwide.

Commando

Sandi & Shane Stump
Box 13719
College Station, TX 77841
Shareware—$30

Several programs in this chapter feature excellent DOS shells, and each approaches the idea in a different way. This is true of Commando. As much as we like some of the other products, we like Commando, too.

First of all, Commando has a popback feature using *ALT-=* as the hot key. This means that you can re-enter Commando instantly from within many applications. It also means that Commando requires at least some of the available memory when it is active. Although this is a fine feature, it is too bad it can't be turned off (as Automenu can be left or not left in memory by command options).

Commando features a colorful, informative display. While it normally doesn't show the visual tree feature of Directory Scanner and Tshell (below), it does show a lot of other information on the screen. Along with three columns of files, the program displays: the current directory; the current selection mask (i.e. *.* or *.EXE, etc.) by which the files are selected and displayed; the current volume, its size and free space; a set of statistics on the current directory including number of files, bytes used, number of tagged files and the bytes they represent; and the date, day of week, and time.

```
┌─────────────────────────────────────────────────────────────┐
│                                                               │
│ ┌─────────────────────────────────────┬─────────────────────┐│
│ │FILES IN C:\123                      │FILE: *.*            ││
│ ├─────────────────────────────────────┼─────────────────────┤│
│ │123     .CNF   123     .CNF  123     .DYN │VOLUME:           │
│ │123     .EXE   123     .HLP  123     .SET │SIZE :  21178368  │
│ │BLOCK1  .FNT   BLOCK2  .FNT  BOLD    .FNT │FREE :   4149248  │
│ │COPYHARD.COM   DBF2    .XLT  DBF3    .XLT ├─────────────────┤│
│ │DEMO    .WKS   DIF     .XLT  DMEGATXT.DRV │DIRECTORY STATS   │
│ │FORUM   .FNT   FUNCTION.WKS  GS      .COM │  FILES       56  │
│ │G_HOTKEY.EXE   INSTALL .DVC  INSTALL .EXE │  BYTES  1516679  │
│ │INSTALL .LBR   INSTALL .SCR  ITALIC1 .FNT │TAGGED            │
│ │ITALIC2 .FNT   JZZLOTUS.XLT  LOTUS   .COM │  FILES        0  │
│ │LOTUS   .FNT   MANUAL  .GS   MULTI   .WKS │  BYTES        0  │
│ │NEWPRO  .WKS   OILPRICE.WKS  OLD     .SET │TODAY'S INFO:     │
│ │PGRAPH  .CNF   PGRAPH  .EXE  PGRAPH  .HLP │  DATE:  8-03-87  │
│ │REMOVE  .EXE   ROMAN1  .FNT  ROMAN2  .FNT │  DAY :  MONDAY   │
│ │SCRIPT1 .FNT   SCRIPT2 .FNT  SIBM025 .DRV │  TIME:    8:51   │
│ ├─────────────────────────────────────────┴─────────────────┤│
│ │▓ATTRIB▓ COPY DELETE DIRECTORY DISK EDIT PRINT RENAME SPACE UTILITY││
│ │ATTRIB is used to change or set a file(s) attributes.       ││
│ ├───────────────────────────────────────────────────────────┤│
│ │C>                                                          ││
│ └───────────────────────────────────────────────────────────┘│
│                                                               │
└───────────────────────────────────────────────────────────────┘
```

There are also two lines of commands, one accessed via the Spacebar and Backspace keys; the other accessed via function keys. The Spacebar commands perform various DOS tasks such as changing a file's attribute, copy, delete, directory create and remove, various disk commands (including disk copy and format), edit a file (current or new—there is even a disk sector editor for the technically inclined), print files, rename, and a command to find the remaining space on another drive. The Utilities command will even abort a program, set new date and time, and squeeze/unsqueeze files.

Most of these Spacebar commands use pop-up menus to query the user. The Copy command, for example, actually contains several options—copy, move, or backup (archive) files. Another list of options appears when you select one of the first three. In the case of the Copy command, they would read: Copy Current Files, Copy Tagged Files, and Copy Untagged Files.

This menu structure covers just about any option you could want. The only drawback to it is that you must use cursor keys to choose an option. You can't just select, by letter or number, the option you want. The process would move much more smoothly with one-key selections within menus.

At any rate, the second line of commands uses the function keys. F1 allows you to change directory, selection pattern, re-read the current disk, or re-log the entire disk. F2 lets you change the sorting of files; F3 lets you perform commands in a DOS shell; F4 executes a highlighted program; F5 marks files using wild-card parameters you set (+ or - tag and untag individual files); F6 lists a file a page or a line at a time. Unfortunately, you can't go in reverse when viewing a file. F7 finds a file on the current directory, or on any disk drive. This is a slight improvement over the Directory Scanner find feature because it can search another disk. F9 toggles the file display between a short, three column display of file names only, and the long form with file size, date and time of creation, and attribute. Finally, F10 quits Commando or returns to the application that was in use when Commando was called with the ALT-= hot key.

We mentioned that Commando doesn't normally use the visual tree, but when you change directories, the tree is displayed for you to scroll up or down, then select the new directory to display.

So with all these features, how does Commando stack up against other programs of its type? That depends. It has many fine features, it is fast, and it is very easy to use. Although it lacks on-screen help, it does come with an excellent manual, and most commands are intuitive and easy to use.

On the other hand, we sometimes found working with Commando awkward, and the lack of a true DOS command line access makes the program feel cramped. With Directory Scanner, you can access DOS easily and for as long as you want. With Commando, the best you can do is to enter a DOS shell or exit the program. And Commando almost always requires you to select from one of its many menus. Sometimes that gets to be a chore.

One of our favorite features is the editor. While it has only two built-in commands (delete line and quit), and it is limited to 29K files, it allows you to create a new file when you call it, something none of the other shell programs we've seen can do. It is good for programming and for creating ad hoc batch files. It lacks word wrap, so it isn't much good for word processing tasks.

Commando presents a great variety of options and features. There's no doubt that it is a very useful program. Many people will prefer it to the other programs in this chapter. We prefer Directory Scanner for its unlimited DOS command line access, but others may wish to use DOS less. For those who can use the hot key return to Commando, it is clearly superior. People who regularly perform disk patches will probably love the Patch Editor.

Commando 1.0
Sandi & Shane Stump
Box 13719
College Station, TX 77841

Shareware: $30

Category: DOS Shell +

System Requirements: IBM PC or compatible; 192K; DOS 2.0 or higher
(3.0 or higher for at least one function)

Recommended Use: Replace DOS

Major Pros: hot key return from application; create ad hoc files with built-in editor; patch editor; powerful, intuitive set of features; attractive, informative display; shows total of tagged files; won't allow TSR to be run from within Commando—prevents memory conflicts; no special setup

Major Cons: Limited DOS access; some awkwardness in working with menus; no control over memory residency of program

Sources: popular BBSs and commercial services, or directly from the author

---

Directory Scanner ver. 3.2

LCDR Nat Martino
Shareware—$15

This program is amazing. It takes the same approach as Commando (above) and PowerMenu's Disk Manager, but it goes much farther. This is quite a complex program that many will find replaces DOS. For those who like to use DOS, Directory Scanner can be a handy helper. It may easily become your favorite program from this book. Now that we've given it such a build-up, you're probably wondering what it does.

Everything.

Well, not exactly, but it does display a graphic tree of your directory structure (like Tshell, later in this chapter) along with up to four columns of file listings. You can move easily from directory to directory, point to and run a *BAT*, *EXE*, or *COM* file, List or Edit a text file using your own favorite list or editing program (specified in a configuration screen), tag specific files for moving, copying, printing, or sorting (including tag or untag all files), and display in any color and even in EGA 43 line mode. You can even change the default DOS color so that when you return to the DOS prompt you get any color you choose, not the bland white on black that you usually see.

You can also create macros, use the context-sensitive help screens to learn the program, create, rename, and delete directories, run DOS commands directly, and more. One of my favorite features is the Find feature. Press F and then enter a file name or wild card designation, and the program searches the directory tree, displaying the found files in the file columns. You can then operate on the located files in various ways or press F2 to continue searching.

Perhaps the best feature of Directory Scanner is that it lets you access DOS whenever you want. Pressing C places you on the normal DOS command line. Until you press Return at the prompt without a command, you stay in DOS. This is not a second DOS shell. It is DOS, and Directory Scanner seems to be completely gone. But when you hit Return at an empty line, it's back again instantly. This removes some of the awkwardness of other shells where the DOS command access is limited or slow. It makes Directory Scanner work even for those who prefer to be in DOS most of the time. (Directory Scanner is actually residing in memory, and requires about 86K RAM in this mode, although the amount may vary from one system to another.)

Using the TAB key and a first letter will move to the first directory whose name begins with that letter. In a previous version of this program, no such feature existed for moving to file names, but that has been changed. Now, pressing TAB TAB and a letter moves to the first file name that begins with that letter.

Earlier versions of this program had built-in system limits that might have restricted some users. The present version, however, has pretty hefty limits. You can have up to 26 hard disk drives defined, up to 150 directories per drive, and up to 300 files per directory. The maximum size of a directory path name is 39 characters. These limits should not inconvenience most users.

Finally, since the program has so many features, why not add a screen blanking feature to protect the monitors of people who use it in place of DOS?

Installing Directory Scanner is much easier now than it was in earlier versions. A command must be executed (probably in the *AUTOEXEC.BAT* file) that sets an environment variable (*SET DS=C:\DS*). That's about it. Earlier versions required modifications to the *CONFIG.SYS* file and rebooting. The new method is superior. In addition, Directory Scanner likes to work with Dpath (see Utilities) so that all of its associated files can be used. To do so effectively, Martino suggests adding DPATH to the *AUTOEXEC.BAT* file. The documentation gives details on how this works.

```
    Drive = C        8:52 pm                        C:\DS
  c:\                              ▶ds      .exe◀  ds_ovrly.exe   logi    .def
    ├─ $&sense                       ds_bkup .exe   ds_prog .def   logi    .mnu
    ├─ 123                           ds_drv_c.log   ds_read .me    ms_mouse.bat
    ├─ arc                           ds_drv_d.log   ds_singl.lic   ms_mouse.def
    ├─ cap                           ds_globl.log   ds_site .lic   ms_mouse.mnu
    ├─ carmen                        ds_help .exe   ds_users.man   ms_mouse.txt
    ├─ cpi.net                       ds_init .exe   inf     .fil   read    .me
    ├─ demo                          ds_mouse.msc
    ├─ dos
    ├─ ds
    ├─ genai
    ├─ graph
    ├─ instant
    ├─ mace
    ├─ magic
    │    └─ data
    ├─ mailsys
    │    └─ incoming
    ├─ master
    ├─ menu

  Total: 33,462,272│ Help=? Name ↑ │ Files: 22 Used: 395,264            Tagged: 0
  Used:  30,107,648│ Free Core 492k│ ──name──  ──size── ──date── ─time─ atr
  Free:   3,354,624│ Drive 90% Full│ ds     .exe    2,021   1 Jul 88 12:00p
```

Directory Scanner has no built-in text file lister or editor, but it allows you to specify a program to use. Therefore, you can use your own favorite lister (like LIST.COM) and editor. There are even two modes available for running them. In one, Directory Scanner remains in memory. In the other mode, most of the program is removed (freeing about 83K).

Directory Scanner can be located as *DS320.ARC* and is a fairly hefty 168K. But it's worth the download and the fiddling with *AUTOEXEC*. It's a superlative program. Try it.

```
┌──────────────────────────────────────────────────────────────┐
│ Directory  Scanner  Version  3.20                              │
│ LCDR Nat Martino                                               │
│ 501 W. Vineyard Ave., #514                                     │
│ Oxnard, CA 93030                                               │
│ (805) 485-6340                                                 │
│                                                                │
│ Shareware: $15                                                 │
│                                                                │
│ Category: DOS Shell +                                          │
│                                                                │
│ Recommended Use: replace DOS                                   │
│                                                                │
│ Major Pros: many excellent features that streamline working   │
│    with DOS; excellent help                                    │
│                                                                │
│ Major Cons: no screen blanking                                 │
│                                                                │
│ Sources: popular BBSs and commercial services, or directly     │
│    from the author                                             │
└──────────────────────────────────────────────────────────────┘
```

Easy Access Menu System

TengWare Ent.
Shareware—$20

There really are more menu systems around than fleas on a dog, but each approaches the subject of hard-disk menuing from a different perspective, and each has a personality all its own. TengWare's Easy Access Menu System is just such a critter. It's easy to use, and easy to configure. It offers simple menu definition: You define the drive, directory, and program name, along with a few other parameters and a menu title. That's all it takes. It does require that you know what program is called and where it resides, but this is pretty typical.

Easy Access Menu System has excellent features to support different users with different levels of access to the program. Each user can be defined by name and password. Their privileges are also defined on an individual level. Access to the configuraion, the menus, user setup, the usage report, access codes, and DOS can all be granted on a restricted basis for each user. A master code is also available for menu system administrators.

Easy Access Menu System version 4.2a
TengWare Ent.
2225 N. Arden
Santa Ana, CA 92706
Compuserve 71541,1317
GEnie J.Tengwall1

Shareware: $20

Category: menu and calendar

System Requirements: IBM PC, XT, AT, or compatible

Recommended Use: hard disk file and application management

Major Pros: easy installation and easy setup; multiple user support with passwords;logs application usage; screen blanking; calendar and reminder system; good help

Major Cons: no timed execution; imposes limits on command line parameters

Sources: popular BBSs and commercial services, or directly from the author

This program can keep a log of all activities by user. Therefore, if the administrator wants to see who has been running which programs, and for how long, he can do so at a glance. The password driven sign is an option that is set in the main configuration section of the program, and can be bypassed.

This program also includes a simple, but usable calendar/reminder mode. The calendar displays three months at a time (you can scroll forward or backward a month or a year at a time), and it allows you to enter reminders that can occur on any date you choose, or can occur monthly, quarterly, semiannually, annually, or until cleared from the reminder list. Unfortunately, there isn't a weekly option, which I think would be very useful. Finally, you can enter how many days in advance you want to be notified of your appointments.

Help is always available when you press F9. The screens are well documented, and the commands are simple. Interestingly, when you exit to DOS, you always end up in the root directory, no matter where the menu program resides.

This program is likely to be most useful in situations where many people use the same machine at different times and access to specific programs (as well as monitoring program use) must be monitored. The security measures taken by this menu system are not foolproof, but they should prove difficult for novices and average users to bypass.

Hard Disk Menu (HDM III) Ver. 1.35

Jim Haas
Shareware—$15

Hard Disk Menu is a menu system designed to run up to 10000 batch-like command sets in a single menu. Commands are divided into one hundred menu files (at the most), each with up to ten "pages" of ten commands each. HDM is especially useful where access to DOS must be restricted. Once the menu is installed, there is no obvious way to break out of the menu environment into DOS, though Ctrl-Break does return to DOS. Also, there is an Exit command that executes the DOS shell, but its use can be restricted with password protection (as can all HDM features). You can even lock the screen and the keyboard using a password so that casual passers-by can't have access to it. Without the password, the only way to get back into the computer seems to be rebooting.

The menu screen displays time and date at the top of the screen, a main title, then ten menu item titles (up to 49 characters) along the left screen, and an index of the ten pages along the right (though these positions can be reversed). You can pick any menu item by its number or scroll to it using cursor keys or the space bar and then pressing the Enter key. Change to another page by pressing the appropriate function key (F1-F10). Any inappropriate keystroke is greeted with a rather rude sound (something reminiscent of an arcade game).

HDM is designed to run from the *AUTOEXEC.BAT* file. Key features include: auto-display of any page or menu selection, or auto-load of any application when starting up the program, and up to ten definable variables, each with up to ten possible sub-arguments. Variables and arguments may be included in procedures written for HDM. It can also run DOS commands, batch files, or programs using the menu's internal Run command or Exit to enter the DOS shell; all HDM commands can be password controlled. More versions of HDM can be chained if 100 menu entries are insufficient. User can be queried for input. On-line help is available. A phone dialer is included, as well as a screen save option.

Procedures are written within the program using the Add or Change commands. Each menu item contains a simple procedure which uses various reserved characters and basic DOS commands. For example a procedure to run Lotus 1-2-3 might read *C:~ cd \lotus~ 123~*. The tilde *(~)* represents a carriage return. A question mark represents a user prompted input. For instance, to allow the user to set criteria for a disk directory command, the menu procedure would read *DIR {?Enter the search criteria}~PAUSE~*. This procedure would wait for user input (*C:\123*.wk?*, for example), then display the resulting list and wait for a keyboard input before returning to HDM.

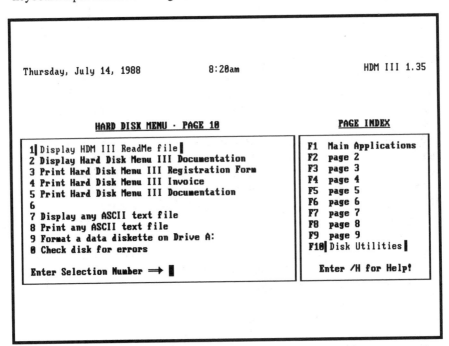

```
Thursday, July 14, 1988          8:20am              HDM III 1.35



               HARD DISK MENU · PAGE 10              PAGE INDEX

    1 Display HDM III ReadMe file        F1  Main Applications
    2 Display Hard Disk Menu III Documentation    F2  page 2
    3 Print Hard Disk Menu III Registration Form  F3  page 3
    4 Print Hard Disk Menu III Invoice            F4  page 4
    5 Print Hard Disk Menu III Documentation      F5  page 5
    6                                    F6  page 6
    7 Display any ASCII text file        F7  page 7
    8 Print any ASCII text file          F8  page 8
    9 Format a data diskette on Drive A:  F9  page 9
    0 Check disk for errors             F10 Disk Utilities

    Enter Selection Number  ⟹          Enter /H for Help!
```

HDM programming can be fairly complex for the non-programmer, and nearly impossible for those who don't understand DOS. On the other hand, it only requires one person to set up and maintain the menu. Once created, it should be easy for anyone to use. A new feature with release III is the Auto-Build feature which will build a simple action string for you by asking you the drive, directory, and program name of the menu item you wish to define. Also, the manual is full of action string examples, so anyone who really wished to learn the syntax and methodology of this menu programming language should have no great difficulty. However, this language will not be popular with people who do not like "computerese."

Jim Hass also markets a geneology program called EZ-TREE, which you can use to maintain family trees. This is a slick, menu driven system that makes creating and maintaining a family tree a breeze.

Hard Disk Menu III Ver. 1.35
Jim Hass
P.O. Box 447
Richfield, OH 44286-0447
(216) 842-8491

Shareware: $15

Category: Menus

System Requirements: no specific requirements documented

Recommended Use: hard disk file and application management

Major Pros: attractive display; low Shareware price; versatile programming for specific menu item configurations; multiple menus; phone dialer

Major Cons: advanced capabilities still require a thorough knowledge of DOS; may be overly complex for some casual users

Sources: popular BBSs and commercial services, or directly from the author

Magic Menus

Custom Technologies
Shareware—$29.95 plus $3 shipping

Magic Menus somehow finds a way to add something to the lexicon of menu program features. It has many of the options available in other menus and shells, including:

- Up to 100 definable applications in 10 user-defined menus

- Five levels of password protection

- Screen blackout

- Context sensitive help

- Many user configurable options

The user interface makes use of pull-down menus and keyboard shortcuts for many menu items. New applications and other options are automatically added to the appropriate menu. When defining applications and other commands, there are various options for inserting parameters and other user prompts. There is even an option for displaying a text file of explanation with each menu option. In this way, you could use the text file to explain an operation or application to the user before he or she actually begins to work with it.

A special menu contains many DOS command options, and you can get instant file listings and other information as well as a scrolling tape calculator and DOS shell command. One of the most unusual features of this program is the Boot Options menu which allows you to pre-define several *AUTOEXEC.BAT* and *CONFIG.SYS* configurations. When you select a pre-configured *AUTOEXEC* or *CONFIG*, the program creates the appropriate file, then reboots the computer. This might be handy for people who must use different configurations for their systems, and it certainly qualifies as an option that other programs don't offer. You can create up to ten different boot options, each with a separate *CONFIG.SYS* and *AUTOEXEC.BAT*. There are some limitations. For instance, you are limited to 10 lines of about 46 characters each. This should not be a problem for most uses, but some AUTOEXECs can require more or longer lines.

There are some work-arounds for the limits in the AUTOEXEC using other batch files, but they are somewhat complex. The manual explains some of the ways around the limitations. Still, in most cases, this multiple boot option setup could be very useful.

Magic Menus normally reserves about 160K RAM while an application is running, but a special option allows you to run larger applications while Magic Menu retains as little as 3K RAM.

There are many printer configuration options in Magic Menus, and these might be useful, especially for people who are using multiple printers.

Most menu systems that I've seen tend to be pretty slick and easy to use. Therefore, it is hard to decide which one to prefer. The choice is very much an individual one. But that's the beauty of Shareware. You can try them all, and finally settle on the one you like best. Certainly Magic Menus has an identity all its own, and it's worth a try.

Magic Menus
Custom Technologies
P.O. Box 62118
Colorado Springs, CO 80962
(800) 541-6234 (orders only)
(719) 260-0402 (technical support)

Shareware: $29.95 plus $3 shipping

Category: Menus and Shells

System Requirements: IBM or close compatible; DOS 2.x or better (3.x or better for maximum memory option); 2565K RAM; hard disk recommended

Recommended Use: hard disk file and application management

Major Pros: unusual options including multiple boot option selections, parameter passing for application selection; built-in DOS functions; easy interface; context sensitive help screens

Major Cons: no major drawbacks, but value of program is subjective as thereare many other fine programs in competition

Sources: popular BBSs and commercial services, or directly from the author

Overview Too 2.20

Magee Enterprises
Shareware—Call for current price information.

The most recent hard disk organizer to come to our attention is Overview Too (OV.EXE). This program contains many of the same functions as programs like Commando and Directory Scanner, but like each program in this section, it approaches its job from its own perspective.

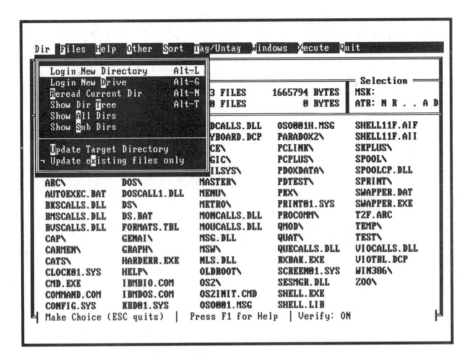

The program displays a line of menus at the top of the screen, then informaton about the current disk and directory below that. Next it displays four rows of file names. The top line menus allow you to perform simple DOS functions (like copy, delete, change directory, etc.) as well as more complex ones (move, view files, etc.) In addition, the program makes simple work of setting file attributes, sorting directories, and tagging files for later operations (including tagging by name or wildcard). You can run any executable file under the cursor as well and display the directory tree with a single command. Though the menus are easy to use, many of the menu options have Alt key equivalents for faster operations.

Two features of this program are remarkable. One is the windowing feature which allows up to 6 windows, each with its own directory listing. The other very useful feature is the ability to show all files from all subdirectories within a single listing! As you scroll through such a full list, the path description changes as you move from one subdirectory to another. This allows you to perform operations on all files in a directory and all its subdirectories at the same time. To limit the display, you can set various file listing attributes so that the program would only display files with a particular archive bit, or with other criteria.

Overview Too also has a find-file feature that is a delight to use. You simply type an = and then begin typing letters. Each letter you type further refines the find parameter and the cursor moves instantly to the next match. Overview Too features indexed and context-sensitive help, and excellent documentation. Also excellent are the ten user-definable function keys which allow you to predefine macro strings of commands and assign them to the ten Alt-function keys.

Overview Too 2.20
Magee Enterprises
P.O. Box 1587
Norcross, GA 30091   (404) 446-6611

Shareware: $15 (registration only) $20 with disk (quantity discounts available)

Category: Hard Disk Management

System Requirements: IBM PC, XT, AT, PS/2, or close compatible; DOS
  2.0 or better;; hard disk recommended (program uses about 95K RAM);
  DESQview aware, can use LIM expanded memory

Recommended Use: hard disk file and application management

Major Pros: multiple windows; display files from all subdirectories; userdefined
  function keys; command line macros; sophisticated tagging and
  sortingfeatures; Point-and-Go with definable options for non-executable files

Major Cons: no obvious way to go 'up' a directory from a file listing
  (otherthan using the change directory feature)

Sources: popular BBS's and commercial services, or directly from the author

---

Various other features include command line macros which can facilitate DOS command execution, and Point-and-Go features which allow you to pre-select an action based on a file's extension. For instance, you can set the program to run your word processor every time you Point-and-Go on a file with the .DOC extension. There are many other possible actions that can be pre-defined for the Point-and-Go feature.

Overview uses about 95K of RAM, but it can use EMS (expanded) memory if you have it. In addition, registered users can request optimized versions of the program for 80286 and 80386 machines.

All in all, this is a classy program which seems to be at the forefront of technology. Overview Too adds yet another excellent utility to this genre, and one that offers some unique power features and some great options, and at a price that is almost negligible considering the professionalism of the product.

Powermenu 3.00c

Brown Bag Software
Shareware—price varies (see box)

Like Brown Bag Software's other programs, Powermenu is a class act. It operates a little differently from Automenu and some of the other menu programs, in that it uses a series of pop-up windows to display menus. For instance, you might have a menu selection titled Utilities which might, itself, call another menu (called Utilities) which would pop up in front of the main menu. Thus, although the main menu can only accommodate ten entries, each of those entries can call other menus, each of which can be calling still more menus. To put it another way, where other menu programs have menu pages, PowerMenu has menu pop-ups. Any main menu item can call other menus up to four deep. The higher mathematics of this system provide several hundred different menu choices.

PowerMenu can be loaded from any directory or disk (if the Menu program is in a directory on the DOS Path), and it can work with programs on other drives. It features password protection of menu entries (including sub-menus), default parameter passing or on-the-fly parameters, configurable color screens, movable windows, access to DOS command line, on screen help, and various utilities for maintaining the database (which is kept in dBASE III format).

Also, defining individual menu selections is itself menu driven. The program automatically handles the manipulation of DOS during menu definition (as opposed to programs like Automenu and HDM which require some command line definitions). PowerMenu includes screen blanking at user definable intervals, selection of most menu items and commands using the first letter of the item or the item number.

As further evidence of PowerMenu's ease of use, its installation routines are among the most painless I've seen. Typing *MINSTALL X:* installs the menu on drive X: (whatever drive you want). It sets up a subdirectory called *\menu* and copies the files over to it. If you want, the installation program then searches your disk for common programs like Lotus 1-2-3, Microsoft Word, AutoCAD, and others. If it finds any of these programs, it automatically sets up menu entries for them. Not only is this a great "Gee Whiz" product, but it really helps streamline the installation process (although it can take a few minutes). The only drawback is that when the installation finds a valid file, it stops searching for more files in that genre. Therefore, if you have more than one word processor, it will find and set up one, but no others.

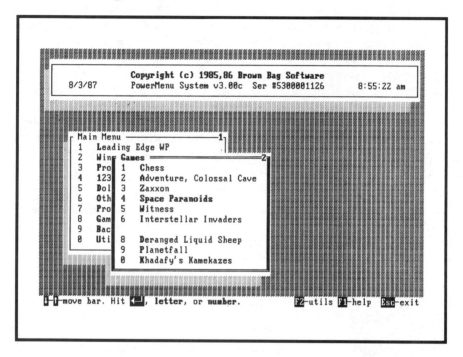

PowerMenu utilities include: a DOS shell; a very interesting screen that shows all programs currently in memory, their size, and their starting memory address; and some other utilities like current printer status, a graph of free RAM vs. Total RAM, etc. The memory map mentioned above is one of my favorite features. It shows the space taken by DOS and the device drivers, any memory resident programs currently loaded, and, of course, the PowerMenu programs currently residing in memory. It's an unusual view of your computer's contents, and can also be useful for checking to see what TSR (Terminate and Stay Resident) programs are currently loaded. A Disk Manager program (like Commando, above) is included in the program and accessed through the Utilities command (F2). This program allows you to view and sort files, run selected files, and perform other file-based functions like copy, move, delete, and set attributes. You can mark multiple files for file operations, and a window at the top of the screen shows you how many files are marked as well as their combined size. A single command will clear all marked files. You can also change drives or manipulate directories with erase, rename, make, open, and close commands. For file copy and move operations, a simple point and press feature allows the selection of the destination drive, and then further refinement of the destination directory.

Disk Manager even lets you open a sub-directory listing that extends the main file listing. If you are showing the root directory, simply move the cursor to a sub-directory, then press (D)irectory-(O)pen. The root file listing remains, but the subdirectory listing is inserted into it. Although this can result in some very long listings, it allows you to see information from different parts of a disk concurrently. A unique user-defined help feature allows definable help screens to be kept in an ASCII file up to 400 lines long and 54 columns wide. Each selection in a menu can be associated by name with a specific Shift-Function Key number (i.e. Shift-F1), and called from within PowerMenu. PowerMenu may be the most complete menu program of all. It incorporates features found in several other programs while making the user interface as simple as possible. It is lacking some features found in other programs, so it may not be everyone's choice, but it certainly should do the job for most people.

PowerMenu 3.0
Brown Bag Software, Inc.
2155 South Bascom Ave., Suite 114
San Jose, CA 95008
(800) 523-0764
(800) 323-5335 (in California)
(408) 559-4545 (overseas)

Shareware: price varies with support options; from $29.95 to $89.95

Category: Menus and Shells

System Requirements: IBM PC, XT, AT, or compatible; 1 floppy and 1 hard disk; 256K; DOS 2.1 or higher; optional color monitor

Recommended Use: hard disk file and application management

Major Pros: easy installation and easy setup; no knowledge of DOS necessary; fully configurable; screen blanking; point and shoot directory manager; user-definable help screens; lots of extra utilities

Major Cons: no timed execution; password protection on menu items but not on DOS access; no side by side directories in file manager (but extended directory listing partially makes up for it)

262

When you send in your Shareware money to Brown Bag, you get a shrink-wrapped edition of PowerMenu with a professionally bound manual. In addition, you get an operating speed-up utility called Doctor DOS. Doctor DOS works in the background of DOS (as a device driver) to speed up screen handling and certain application DOS I/O. When using Doctor DOS, you will notice a dramatic speedup of certain activities (like DOS DIR) and some programs including database managers and word processors (programs that use DOS for screen handling I/O).

Menu and shell programs are among the most common Shareware products; therefore no attempt has been made to cover all the good ones. There are many. However, we'd like to mention a few other programs that we have liked.

Still River Shell 2.36

Bill White and Bob Dye
Shareware—$39 (abridged manual version $15)

The Still River Shell is a useful product that can quickly replace the DOS command line. You can delete, copy, move, and locate files. You can run DOS commands directly with a command stack of up to 20 commands (with editable command line). Like TSH (below), Still River Shell can show a graphic directory tree, but not as an integral part of the system. Both are a fine programs and both could certainly be used in many of the same ways as other products in this section. Each adds a few wrinkles of its own. Still River Shell adds saved command lists, command stack, and a useful replacement for the DOS command line (with command-line editing), etc. There is also an excellent file-view feature with text search ability.

In addition, the newest version of Still River Shell supports tagging of files, one-key directory switching, up to 40 user-defined commands, and more. One unique aspect of this program's file tagging function is its ability to pass files on to the command line one at a time. For instance, you could tag several files, then call your word processor or editor, and each file would be sent to the word processor or editor in succession. This is an excellent product, and one which performs a wide variety of functions with a minimum of fuss. However, despite its simplicity, the manual for Still River Shell is a respectable 150+ pages long and clearly explains all the uses of the program. With all the menus and shells available, it is hard to stand out in the crowd. Still River Shell stands out, if for no other reason, that it, like Automenu, is one of the original programs dating back many years, and its longevity is an indication of the commitment of its authors, and of its staying power as a product.

```
AFORMAT .BAT A        87  07-08-88  10:07p | Still River Shell 2.36
FORM-N  .BAT A         8  05-10-88  03:27p |
FILL    .C   A     10368  02-15-87  01:27p | Drive - C:  OS2
CDTO    .COM A       574  10-07-87  10:56p |
CMOVE6  .COM A      9216  09-27-86  06:22a |   32010240   (bytes allocated)
DIRNOTES.COM A      1704  05-19-87  08:07a |    1452032   (bytes free)
FILL    .COM A      7760  02-15-87  01:28p |         95   (% allocated)
IL      .COM A     27240  10-04-87  02:56p |
DIRN-TES.DAT A      1863  07-12-88  11:52a |
AFORMAT .DOC A      3763  05-11-88  01:12a | Directory - \TEST\
CDTO    .DOC A      1050  10-07-87  11:02p |
COPYTREE.DOC A     15988  08-29-86  10:22a |
FILL    .DOC A     21377  01-04-88  05:06p | Set - C:\TEST\*.*
FILL1   .DOC A      4352  12-10-86  07:38a |
IL      .DOC A     22136  06-27-88  02:24p |
INFO    .DOC A      2674  06-27-87  02:42p |         23   (files)
CT      .EXE A     20264  08-29-86  10:48a |          0   (directories)
FILL1   .EXE A     43301  01-04-88  03:12p |     235520   (bytes allocated)
ST      .EXE A     11538  08-29-86  09:33a |         89   (% used)
READ    .ME  A       422  06-27-88  02:27p |
FILL    .PIF A       369  01-04-88  05:12p | Free memory - 469K
```

Copy Delete Find List Move Other Prv Sort taG Tree View Xdos [Fn]

return to previous list   <ESC> to exit

Still River Shell 3.26

Bill White and Bob Dye
P.O. Box 57
Still River, MA 01467
(617) 456-3699

Shareware: $39 (abridged manual version $15)

Category: DOS Shells

System Requirements: IBM PC, XT, AT, or compatible; DOS 2.1 or higher; optional color monitor; program requires 94K to run

Recommended Use: hard disk file and application management

Major Pros: major DOS enhancement through editable command line and command stacking; sequential passing of tagged files to command line or application; user-defined command sets; simple to setup and use; good, stable application

Major Cons: requires 94K when running, but otherwise, none

264

TSH (Tshell 1.1)

BTM Software, Inc.
P.O. Box 49365
Austin, TX 78765
(512) 459-6026

The version mentioned here is a Shareware version only. Although this is a crippled version, it works well. For a registration fee of $37.50, you can get Version 2.0. Version 2.0 adds some nice features. We have included this program here because it is a unique and enjoyable product.

TSH is a shell program that shows the directory tree of the current disk (current directory and up to six sub-directories) in graphic form. By moving along the shell, you display up to 14 files at a time. You can run a *COM*, *EXE*, or *BAT* file from the file listing. You can also copy, erase, move, protect, rename, type, sort, or find files. The screen also displays time and date, total memory, memory used, memory available, disk capacity, used and free amounts of disk space, and statistics on the current directory (size, number of files, number of sub-directories). This is an excellent product, and its visual shell makes a hard disk structure easy to grasp.

DOSamatic

Marin Pacific Software
1001 Bridgeway, Suite 514
Sausalito, CA 94965
$39.00

As far as we know DOSamatic is not being actively supported or developed at this time. We tried to reach Marin Pacific Software several times, left messages on a machine, but never received an answer. Nonetheless, DOSamatic belongs in this book, if you're willing to wing it alone. In addition to being a fine shell program like the others mentioned here, DOSamatic offers the ability to run up to seven concurrent applications (true multitasking).

Like all DOS multitasking, there are some limitations to DOSamatic's abilities, but it does work with major applications like Lotus 1-2-3 and others. Determining whether it works with any specific programs of your choosing is probably a matter of guesswork and experimentation. Programs that are "well behaved" in DOS will very likely work. Other programs may or may not.

DOSamatic displays the usual system and file statistics, and includes the ability to run multiple programs from a directory listing. Although we are in doubt as to the future of DOSamatic, versions of it are available, and they will work with some software. The message on the machine claims that if you are a registered user, they will call you back. We are registered (as Rusel DeMaria), but in approximately 2 months we have received no calls.

14

Nelson Ford's Five-Year Summary

The following excerpt is from Nelson Ford's January 1987 newsletter and is reprinted by permission. This is an excellent summary of Ford's five years of hard work evaluating Shareware for his catalog. From his unique perspective, this document is an intriguing look at products and Shareware authors who stand out after five years.

Not every product mentioned in Ford's article is reviewed in this book. Still, you may wish to take his recommendation that they are all excellent products, and look for them wherever you look for Shareware.

THE PUBLIC (SOFTWARE) LIBRARY
January 1987 Newsletter
Copyright 1987 Nelson Ford
P.O. Box 35705, Houston, TX 77235-5705
(713) 721-5205

Note: This file may not be copied for others nor put onto a BBS without the expressed written permission of the copyright holder.

The Best of 1982–1986

For five years, we have been collecting, comparing, and cataloging public-domain and shareware software for PCs and compatibles. Because we constantly go back and compare new programs to old ones and only keep the best, only the best programs have survived into the current library listing. Therefore, every program in the library can be considered the "Best of 1982-1986" for its particular features and style of operation, so we would like to honor and thank all of the 1,000+ programmers who have programs in our library, as well as those whose programs have come and gone.

In selecting programs for special recognition, it doesn't seem fair to single out one program just because it may appeal to a broader base of users. For example, Procomm is a more popular program than Autosig, but Autosig is only useful for those who use CompuServe. However, in terms of program features and performance, neither program could be said to be "better" than the other.

On the other hand, it does seem fair to acknowledge the programs that, because of their greater popularity, have had a greater impact on the computer users of the world.

One PD programmer advises: "I've too much experience with [selecting the best] among scientists. In the end, the choice is as much politics as anything else and if you choose 5 among 100, you'll make 95 people unhappy rather than 5 people happy."

Heeding this advice, we will not attempt to list the "best" programs, but we would like to mention the more significant programs—and programmers—of the last five years.

ANDREW FLUEGELMAN started the shareware concept five years ago with PC-Talk. Because the BASIC source code came on the same disk, dozens of people added their own enhancements to PC-Talk. These hacked versions of PC-Talk were left in the dust when other programmers wrote their own programs from scratch with more features than could be simply patched into PC-Talk. The best known general purpose comm program is PROCOMM. Not as well known, but just about as good is GT-PowerComm.

JIM BUTTON, the nom-de-programming of a former IBM employee, was the first to adopt Fluegelman's shareware concept. Button's program, PC-File, was solid, if not flashy, and easy to learn, if not particularly easy to use, database program that filled a huge need of companies—an easy way to manage simple lists of data. Over the years, Button continued to add whistles and bells so that the current version has become a very sophisticated "flat file manager" while still being easy to learn and easier to use. Button was also one of the first ones to adopt "incentives" to register by leaving out parts of the documentation from the shareware disk.

BOB WALLACE is perhaps the most visible and possibly the most successful author of shareware programs. His PC Write serves as a glowing example of the possibility of achieving success via shareware. As popular as PCW has been as shareware, it's hard to imagine that it could have succeeded in the big-bucks, cut-throat world of more conventional software marketing that has swallowed up many other excellent word processing programs. Still, it's to Bob Wallace's credit that he has kept faith in the shareware concept while others have been withholding features, "shortsheeting" documentation or "going commercial." PC Write continues to be one of the very few shareware programs that clings to the original concept as espoused by Fluegelman five years ago (if you don't count Wallace's licensing Brown Bag Software to distribute the program commercially under a different name).

VERNON BUERG and CHRISTOPHER DUNFORD have long stood far above the crowd in their contributions of software to the public domain. To list all of the outstanding utilities that these two have written would require another couple of pages. (We have often been tempted to rename this newsletter "The Vernon Buerg Report.") Their best?—for Vern, it must be LIST, the ultimate utility for viewing disk files. For Chris, his CED utility should be considered an essential part of every system, but his BURNOUT is also the definitive screen-blanking utility.

The comments above were all pretty safe. These people and programs have all stood the test of time. The proudest programmer around would not begrudge our giving credit to these people. The following is a little riskier in terms of possibly alienating those who don't get mentioned, but these are some people and programs that stand out in my mind for their programming excellence (in no particular order):

John Friend is not listed in the group above only because his PC-Outline is relatively recent (1985, I believe). It's a pleasure to see a shareware program that is widely acknowledged to be better than any of its commercial competitors, though the pleasure was dampened some when Friend also sold out to Brown Bag Software who promptly raised the price a substantial chunk. (For the present, BBS is at least leaving Outline as shareware.)

Jerry Medlin's PC-GL continues to be a shining example to others for efficiency and ease of use. PC-GL practices what we preach: allow entering, searching and editing of data on the same screen without having to go back and forth through a bunch of menus (a la PC-File).

Neil Rubenking worked magic to give a multiple voice to a one-voice machine with his Pianoman programs and music files.

PC-DeskTeam beat out Sidekick when we did a comparative review in 1985. It is another program that has remained true to the original shareware concept with all the program and documentation being on the disk and offering a very reasonable price ($25) to register.

Richard Wilson and Barry Simon, while relatively new to the PD scene, have already become major contributors with programs like CTRL-ALT and STACKEY. What a team—Richard writes feature-filled utilities with super-tight code resulting in 5k COM files, then Barry writes 150k documentation files to go with them. Where is that InfoWorld writer who said a while back that public-domain software is undocumented?

JANITOR JOE, an excellent arcade game from 1984, still impresses us for having been written by a 15-year-old.

CHESS88 has been around since 1982. We know only that the name of the author listed in the program is Don Berg. The graphics are excellent and the program is undefeated by other upstart PD/shareware chess programs over the years.

Genealogy programs have been surprisingly popular, and we've heard more good things about the Family History System, though the others are quite good too. All the other programs in the *HOME/MISC.* section deserve credit for their originality (which is why they are classified as "miscellaneous"). WORLD, in particular, is a very popular, educational and entertaining program—well conceived and well written.

ARC, by Systems Enhancements Associates, certainly deserves credit for becoming a success in the face of numerous detractors (including us) who didn't want to change from the LU "standard."

Marshall Magee also deserves credit for making a success of Automenu in what is a *very* crowded field, DOS menu programs.

We are also proud of the other shareware authors whose programs have proven to be better than many, if not all, of their commercial competitors. Among these are Edward Kidera's PC-Key-Draw, David Black's EZ-Forms, Kim Kokkonnen's Mark & Release (to remove memory-resident utilities), Skip Gilbrech's KBFIX, and many others.

To these and all the others who, over the last five years, have made our computers more useful and easier, more efficient and even more fun to use, we say a heartfelt "Thank you."

15

Shareware in Paradox

Paradox is a powerful commercial database and application development program. Because of its flexibility and growing popularity, some excellent Shareware applications have become available. These are add-ons to the Paradox application environment, not stand-alone products. Paradox users will find these programs very useful and very interesting from a PAL (Paradox Application Language) programming point of view.

As we go to press, some of these products are not ready. However, by the time this edition is out these Paradox add-ins will be available.

In addition, ANSA supports a 24-hour bulletin-board service for Paradox. The number is:

(415) 595-0432

Some interesting products can be found, including the latest information about Paradox. Some files to include: *EXTAB.ARC*, *DO.SC*, *BASEBALL.ARC*.

The utilities in this chapter can also be found in this BBS.

Documentor

Gregory B. Salcedo
Shareware—$25

A handy utility tool for developers. Validity checks on tables, and documentation of reports created in Paradox (# of pages, field, set up strings, layout, etc) can be printed out.

Editor2

Gregory B. Salcedo
ParaDocs
16553 162nd Place SE
Renton, WA 98058
(206) 277-0265
Shareware—$45

Editor2 is an editor for Paradox (vers. 1.1 or 2.0). What makes it unique is that it is written entirely in PAL script and operates as a TSR within Paradox. It adds several features to the Paradox environment that would not ordinarily be there. For one thing, it allows you to edit, save, and re-edit Miniscripts at any time (even copy them into your PAL scripts). Also, it works within the Report and Form generators as well as the PAL editor.

Editor2 is a relatively simple program, but it contains many of the features that are most notably lacking in the Paradox editor. For instance, it allows you to create instant ASCII graphic boxes and lines. It also allows you to cut and paste single lines or blocks, search and replace, save (to file or printer) without exiting the editor, report, or form generator, and edit miniscripts as mentioned above. Best of all, it can be called up using the Alt-F1 hot key.

One pleasant side effect of the program occurs when you save a report to a file. The resulting file preserves an ASCII representation of all report bands, headers, footers, etc. It is excellent for proto-typing and archiving report formats.

PAL Bar Menu Utility

Gregory Salcedo
Shareware—$20

Another program from Gregory Salcedo helps PAL programmers make impressive pop-up and bar-line menus with almost no effort. By following the templates provided in this utility, anyone can add sparkle and pizzazz to a PAL application.

Bar menus can have context-sensitive help, and pop-ups can be set to display progressively on screen. Pop-up menus are displayed on screen intelligently according to placement of menus.

16

Spreadsheets
and
Helpful Utilities

Spreadsheets are so common and so useful that several good ones are in the Shareware world. One of the original Shareware spreadsheets is PC Calc, but others have appeared that do an excellent job of competing with Lotus 1-2-3, the undisputed benchmark by which spreadsheets are measured.

Spreadsheets are generally complex products, and judging which is best is often a matter of personal taste. Some people, particularly those who must process large amounts of data, look for speed above all. It just doesn't do to wait for several minutes or several hours every time you change a value.

Other people look for programming power (like Lotus' macros) or a full set of math and business functions.

Still others look for convenience and a smooth user interface. A bad interface can slow down data entry and make any job much more laborious.

In this chapter we'll look at some fine Shareware spreadsheets and a couple of unique utilities. We will not attempt to review the many fine worksheets that are available for Lotus 1-2-3. There are so many of them, and they are adapted for so many purposes, that we have chosen not to include them specifically in this book at this time. Every source in the Sources section of this book has listings of 1-2-3 worksheets and templates. If this is something that you want, let us know, and we'll include some close looks at these products in an update.

Spreadsheet Basics

For those who are not familiar with spreadsheets, they are used to perform magic with numbers. A spreadsheet can automatically calculate figures based on formulas that you enter.

A spreadsheet is a matrix of *cells*. Each cell is formed by the intersection of a *column* and a *row*. Suppose you have a matrix where the columns are designated by letters and the rows are designated by numbers. The first cell, therefore, would be A1 (writing column/row).

You can enter *numbers*, *text*, or *formulas* in a spreadsheet cell. When you enter a formula, you often will refer to the value in another cell. For instance, if you want to multiply the value in cell C17 by the value in cell E22, you would enter C17 * E22 in another cell, say E23. To add a row or column of cells, you can designate ranges, i.e. *@SUM(B12..B20)* would total all the values from cells B12 through B20.

Some spreadsheets use *macros*. Macros are sets of commands that are run all at once. A single keystroke sets the macro in motion. In essence, a spreadsheet macro is spreadsheet programming

As Easy As ver. 2.08
TRIUS, Inc.
Shareware—$30

The name As Easy As implies a lot, and the program does a pretty good job of living up to its expectations. As Easy As is a $30 Shareware spreadsheet that comes close to cloning Lotus 1-2-3. It loads worksheets in both 1A and 2.0x formats, and will output worksheets compatible with 1-2-3 version 1A.

Some Lotus imitators have got the look and feel right, but leave out the macro capability. This isn't so with As Easy As. It has macros and many built-in functions. It can also create the same graphs as Lotus 1-2-3, plus a couple more.

What it doesn't have (at the time of this writing, anyway) is a manual or a phone number, though there is some built-in help.

Since As Easy As is virtually the same as Lotus 1-2-3, a good book on that product would be very helpful, but there are some differences. People very familiar with 1-2-3 will find themselves right at home, but may become confused from time to time when looking for a command or function and not finding it. The clone is not perfect.

For instance, default settings, which in 1-2-3 are found under Globals, must be defined on the DOS command line that calls the program. If you want the default directory to be *C:\EASY*, you must run As Easy As with the following command:

```
ASEASY /DIR=C:\EASY
```

Unfortunately, the program always defaults to the B: drive for the directory unless otherwise stated.

As Easy As Ver 2.8
TRIUS, Inc.
15 Atkinson St.
Lynn, MA 01905

Shareware: $30

Category: Spreadsheet

Recommended Use: almost anything Lotus 1-2-3 is used for; also handy for converting 2.0x worksheets to 1A

Major Pros: really captures the essentials of Lotus 1-2-3; pop-up menus; on-screen, indexed help

Major Cons: no manual; no phone support; a few incompatibilities and differences with Lotus 1-2-3

Sources: popular BBSs and commercial services, or directly from the author

---

Also, even though As Easy As can use Lotus worksheets, macro compatibility is not 100 percent. Therefore, we suggest that you test important macros before relying on As Easy As. Although some macros we tried worked, others produced odd, scrambled results.

Although the spreadsheet size is large (1024 x 256, and as far as we can tell without documentation), the program does not support expanded memory, so it is limited to conventional memory. This should not pose any problems under normal circumstances, but people used to Lotus version 2.0 or higher may not be able to do all the same things.

We've spent a good deal of space on the fact that As Easy As is not a 100 percent knockoff of 1-2-3, but we don't mean to belittle the program's main accomplishment. For a fraction of the price, you can get a spreadsheet that is, indeed, easier than Lotus 1-2-3. Where Lotus has the traditional top line menu opened with the slash key, As Easy As has added colorful pop-up windows to represent the command line. This feature can be defeated for those who prefer the standard Lotus look, but the addition of the pop-ups makes reading the current command line much easier.

For those who would like a good, inexpensive 1-2-3 clone, this is a pretty good bet. If you test any existing worksheets first, you should have no trouble, and a little trial and error will expose any differences between the programs. In all, As Easy As is a remarkable product, and for $30 it is a fine bargain.

InstaCalc ver. 2.01
FormalSoft
Shareware—$49.95 plus $5 shipping & handling

InstaCalc is a two-dimensional version of FormalWare's QubeCalc program (see below). It features a 256 column by 256 row TSR spreadsheet. The default program uses 128K RAM (about 80 for the program and 48 for the data), but registered users get a utility called *INSTAMEM* that allows them to configure the memory usage of the program more precisely.

Aside from the lack of 3D processing, InstaCalc has all the fine features of QubeCalc, including macros; many built-in statistical, mathematical, and business functions; range and formatting functions; and (for registered users) interactive help screens.

InstaCalc is a small spreadsheet, but its ability to stay in memory and work within other applications makes it especially useful. Like QubeCalc, its automatic recalculation can be limited to a block of cells, speeding up the process on large worksheets. Another very useful feature allows pasting InstaCalc graphs directly into an application.

Another kudo goes to FormalSoft for providing a program to remove InstaCalc from memory.

New features added beginning with InstaCalc 2.0 include range names, spreadsheet linking, import/export of Lotus Release 2, DIF, dBASE II and III, title locking, additional functions (including conditionals), sorting of rows and columns, starting the program with a filename (from the command line), improved directory path support, and more.

As a spreadsheet alone, InstaCalc is not the biggest or the most powerful, but it is full of features, and its memory resident status is a big plus. For the price, it is a great deal.

INSTACALC Version 2.01
FormalSoft
P.O. Box 1913
Sandy, UT 84091-1913
(801) 565-0971

Shareware: $49.95 plus $5 shipping & handling

Category: Spreadsheet

System Requirements: IBM PC/XT/AT or compatible; DOS 2.0 or higher (uses up to 640K for spreadsheet); CGA compatible graphics equipment necessary to display graphs

Recommended Use: simple PSR spreadsheet

Major Pros: convenience of memory-resident spreadsheets

Major Cons: some may find it lacking in features or too small for big jobs

Sources: popular BBSs and commercial services, or directly from the author

---

Qubecalc Ver. 3.01

FormalSoft
Shareware—$69.95 plus $5 shipping and handling

Qubecalc is a three-dimensional spreadsheet. This means that, in addition to rows and columns, there are virtual pages where data can be contained. Moreover, it means that the same data can be viewed from vastly different perspectives.

A 3D spreadsheet makes it possible to contain several separate, but related worksheets in one structure. For instance, in a traditional spreadsheet, a company might keep complete monthly books in twelve similar worksheets, then consolidate those books into a consolidation worksheet.

Using a 3D spreadsheet, each monthly worksheet can become a page in the structure. By rotating the cube that makes up the 3D "image" of the spreadsheet, you can view the data from very different perspectives—effectively changing columns to rows, rows to pages, etc. Also, consolidation can be performed by simple formulas totaling cell ranges in appropriate perspectives.

If this seems confusing, it can be. But the process can yield very useful results.

Qubecalc comes with an example file, *EXAMPLE.QUB*. As a practical example, this small WorkQube (a QubeCalc worksheet) contains expense figures and totals for 1983-1986. In any cube there are six sides. QubeCalc labels these sides Faces A through F, and by selecting the /WorkCube Perspective commands, you can view any one of the faces.
Face A looks as follows:

	Jan 83	Apr 83	Jul 83	Oct 83	1983
Rent (83)	$300.00	$310.00	$320.00	$330.00	$1,260.00
Util (83)	$50.00	$51.00	$52.00	$53.00	$206.00
Auto (83)	$150.00	$152.50	$155.00	$157.50	$615.00
Food (83)	$250.00	$252.00	$254.00	256.00	1,012.00
Tot (83)	$750.00	$765.50	$781.00	$796.50	3,093.00

Viewing Face B, however, shows all figures for one month at a time for each of the years 1983-1986 and monthly totals for the four expense categories. Face C shows a summary of yearly values for one of the expense categories. Which month will show in Face B or which expense category will show in Face C, depends on where the cursor was when you switched perspectives. If the cursor was in the row containing Rent information when you switched from B to C, then Face C displays quarterly figures and their totals for Rent for each of the four years. To see figures for other expense categories, you use the PgUp and PgDn keys, because, in addition to the six sides of the cube, QubeCalc can organize data into up to 64 pages (64 rows by 64 columns by 64 pages). From the perspective of Face C, the expense categories are all in different pages. Face B organizes each monthly summary in a different page, and so on.

```
[C]C4;7: NUMBER (9)        Dir: C:\CUBE                    File: example
310
Y Z   A      B      C      D      E      F      G      H
X 1
  2              Rent (83)Rent (84)Rent (85)Rent (86)Rent
  3       Rent (Jan) $300.00 $340.00 $380.00 $420.00 $1440.00
  4       Rent (Apr) $310.00 $350.00 $390.00 $430.00 $1480.00
  5       Rent (Jul) $320.00 $360.00 $400.00 $440.00 $1520.00
  6       Rent (Oct) $330.00 $370.00 $410.00 $450.00 $1560.00
  7       Rent (Tot) $1260.00 $1420.00 $1580.00 $1740.00 $6000.00
  8
  9
 10
 11
 12
 13
 14
 15
 16
 17
 18
 19
 20
1)HELP 2)EDIT 3)BLOCK 4)ABS 5)GOTO 6)FIND 7)STAT 8)MACRO 9)CALC 0)GRAPH
 340416 Bytes           AutoCalc ON:A1;1..BL64;64
```

Interestingly, Face F shows the same information as Face C, but with columns and rows reversed. Faces D and E don't really show very intelligible results.

We found that it takes some powerful visualization to imagine what is going on in the six-sided cube of data, but once a structure is established, working with it is easy. QubeCalc uses the familiar slash key to open the main menus, and has a structure similar to, but not mimicking, Lotus 1-2-3. The spreadsheet, by comparison with many spreadsheets on the market, is not large, but then it does things a little differently. As mentioned, QubeCalc allows up to 64 x 64 x 64 cells, or 262,144 cells.

QubeCalc handles numbers, text, and formulas in much the same way as Lotus 1-2-3 does. In version 2.02 there are about 44 special functions for statistics, math, business, etc., and formulas can be up to 70 characters long with unlimited nesting of operations.

Another useful feature is the ability to define a range of cells for recalculation. QubeCalc does a remarkable job of handling data that is inter-related in three dimensions, but to do so it pays some price in speed. However, by defining a block of cells for automatic recalculation, you avoid having to recalculate the whole WorkQube while retaining the convenience of automatic recalculation. QubeCalc also has macros, CGA compatible bar and line charts, variable data fill, etc. Also note that data fill and graphics can take place in any of the six directions. Also, blocks of cells can be defined in three dimensions. When referring to a cell, you enter the row, column, and page. For instance, *[A]A7;4* refers to Face A, column A, row 7, page 4. If you rotate the view to Face B, then the designation of that cell changes to *[B]C8;3*. Confused? It isn't so bad after you work with it for a while, but it does take some getting used to.

QubeCalc can also be used as a simple two dimensional spreadsheet. Note that the former Shareware price was $49.95 plus $5 shipping, and that it has gone up. New features beginning with version 3.0 include block names, spreadsheet linking, import and export of Lotus Release 2 (as well as 1), DIF, dBASE II and III formats, additional functions, title locking, new formats, block sorting, moving by screen, enhanced directory listing capabilities, copying to multiple pages, loading a file from the command line, /M macro prompts, and more.

QUBECALC   Version   3.01
FormalSoft
P.O. Box 1913
Sandy, UT 84091-1913
(801) 565-0971

Shareware: $69.95 plus $5 shipping and handling

Category: Spreadsheet

System Requirements: IBM PC/XT/AT or compatible; DOS 2.0 or higher
(uses up to 640K for spreadsheet); CGA compatible graphics equipment
necessary to display graphs

Recommended Use: integrated spreadsheet designs, especially those that
would ordinarily require consolidations

Major Pros: see data in unexpected ways by executing simple commands;
powerful functions; powerful macros (not 100% Lotus compatible, but similar)

Major Cons: lack of examples/tutorial on 3D spreadsheet design

---

The potential of this program is immense, but unleashing its power takes a pretty sophisticated approach to spreadsheet design or a good head for 3D visualization. There is really no ordinary equivalent for this kind of spreadsheet (although a stack of ledgers would simulate it in a static form).

PC CALC ver. 3.0

ButtonWare
Shareware—$59.95 plus $5 shipping and handling

PC Calc is the original Shareware spreadsheet. It still performs well enough to be recommended. Even though it does not emulate Lotus 1-2-3, some people may find its user interface convenient. Among its many features are: easy data entry, sorting of columns and rows, cell formats, program configurations, keystroke macros, simple bar graph format for numbers, show/hide cells (choice of screen, printer, or both), conditional functions, imports DIF, ASCII (comma delimited), or HDR (PC File) programs, LOOKUP command for table lookups, and several math and business functions.

It's easy to enter data using the Smart Cursor (which remembers the last direction you moved, and automatically moves that way when you enter a value and press Return). Also, the program allows labels, numbers, and formulas to be entered without special characters (unless a number begins a label). You don't have to differentiate between these types of entries as you do in most spreadsheets. The program automatically reads B4 + C8 as a formula, 1234 as a number, and "This is a test" as a label. To enter 1987 as a label, you would have to enter it as '1987.

When replicating ranges of numbers and formulas, the program asks whether it should adjust entries for absolute or relative references. Answering (Y)es adjusts for relative references. In formulas with several values, you can answer (A)ll to force all values to relative references.

PC Calc also includes some customization features to allow users to modify defaults and various aspects of the user interface. Sample data on PC Calc file formats is provided in the manual, along with a sample Basic program that shows how to access information in a PC Calc file from Basic.

PC Calc is not going to replace Lotus 1-2-3, but it is a good, solid spreadsheet program well suited for beginners and for people with light duties. It's not recommended for bigger jobs, but definitely applicable to small to medium chores.

PC Calc 3.0
ButtonWare, Inc.
P.O. Box 96058
Bellevue, WA 98009-4469
(206) 454-0479
(800) JBUTTON (order line)

Shareware: $59.95 plus $5 shipping and handling

Category: Spreadsheet

System Requirements: PC or compatible; DOS 2.0 or later; 256K; at least one 360K drive; any monitor; optional printer

Recommended Use: relatively simple manipulation of numeric data; can be used with PC File data

Major Pros: easy to use and to learn; performs basic functions well; includes several extras useful for light or medium duty

Major Cons: lacks more powerful features of other spreadsheets, including some of the more powerful functions; limited size (64 columns by 256 rows) not for the space hungry; macros limited to smart keys

Sources: popular BBSs and commercial services, or directly from the author

---

Goalseeker

Brown Bag Software
Shareware—price varies (see box)

Goalseeker is a Brown Bag utility that adds a much needed feature to several spreadsheet programs. It operates as a TSR (Terminate and Stay Resident) program that you load prior to loading your spreadsheet programs. Goalseeker supports Lotus 1-2-3, SuperCalc4, Multiplan, and VP Planner. It also supports a math co-processor, if present.

Goal seeking involves the use of dependent and independent variables. A dependent variable is one whose value depends on some other value. Suppose you have a simple spreadsheet model that looks something like this:

```
Item Cost    $23.45          Price:$40.00
Fixed Costs  $5.43
Commission   $4.00           Profit:$7.12
```

Commissions are set at 10 percent. You see that at $40.00 per item, you are only making a little over $7 profit. You want to make at least $18. Using Goalseeker, you position the cursor on the Profit cell, press the hot keys (Alt-Spacebar), select (G)oal, and enter 18. Now you move the cursor to the Price cell, press the hot keys, select (S)olution, and press Return. In a flash, the new value ($52.0888) appears in the Price cell. In this case, the dependent variable is Profit and the independent variable is Price. To further understand the principle, the dependent variable does not change. It is your goal. The independent variable changes (independently).

In the example above, Goalseeker finds the answer quickly. Figuring the answer manually would take longer because you would have to take into account the effect of the commissions on the profit. Even though this is a simple example, it shows a practical use of goal seeking. Other more complicated models can also be solved, including mathematical problems, break-even analyses, and other places where unknown target values must be calculated.

Goalseeker even allows you to set several different goal seeking operations to run sequentially. Multi-Goal procedures can even execute macros as part of the goal seeking process. Very complex operations are possible using macros and Multi-Goal techniques.

A special Review option allows you to see the computations the computer used to arrive at its answer. It shows you each iteration of the test values and their differences from the target goal. Also, there is a set of user definable options that you can use to tailor Goalseeker to your needs.

Goalseeker includes a program called *REMOVE.EXE* that will remove it from memory. This is something that all TSR programs should include in one form or another. It is important to be able to free memory without rebooting.

If you use spreadsheets a lot, you will love Goalseeker. Chances are, you run into situations where solutions are hard to find. Goalseeker may be the answer. Few commercial spreadsheets include goal seeking, but now it is easy to add it to at least four that do not. Goalseeker is highly recommended. It works.

Goal Seeker Vers. 3.4
Brown Bag Software, Inc.
2155 South Bascom Ave., Suite 114
Campbell, CA 95008
(800) 523-0764
(800) 323-5335 (in California)
(408) 559-4545 (overseas)

Shareware: price varies with support options; ranges from $29.95 to $69.95

Category: Spreadsheet Utilities

System Requirements: IBM PC, XT, AT, or compatible; a compatible spreadsheet; 40K (in addition to what your spreadsheet uses); DOS 2.0 or higher; optional color monitor; requires 80 column mode; optionally 8087 or 80287 math co-processor support

Recommended Use: perform automated What-If analysis (goal seeking) on various spreadsheets (see review)

Major Pros: performs fast and easy goal seeking on spreadsheet data; stays memory resident, always available; works very fast; user configurable; adds a major function missing from most commercial spreadsheets

Major Cons: multiple goal seeking awkward and complex

Sources: popular BBSs and commercial services, or directly from the author

SolveIt! ver. 2.5

Pine Grove Software
Shareware—$50

SolveIt! is a financial calculator program that can be memory resident or a stand-alone utility. It comes with 31 different routines ranging from finance and loan calculations, to general business and real estate equations. A set of equations is also included for handling various types of depreciations. Also included is a DOS directory function to examine any directory on any disk.

SolveIt! operates the same way in either memory resident or stand-alone mode. When the program is memory resident, however, it takes up a whopping 168K of memory. The program uses pop-up menus with scrolling bars or one-letter picks to make menu selections. As you scroll through each menu choice, a one line description is presented at the bottom of the screen for each menu selection. Of the equations that are included in the package, most are pretty standard financial routines.

Two equations that you'll really enjoy are Present Value of an Amount and Affordable House Price. Suppose your ex-wife owes you $40,000. She's agreed to pay you off in two years at 10% interest. One day she calls you up and offers you $30,000 now, in cash, so she can be rid of you and the debt. Is it a good deal? With Present Value of an Amount, you can determine whether its better take a lesser amount (according to the program, anything more that $32,000 would be a great deal!). Now that you're divorced, you want to buy a new home. What can you afford? The Affordable House Price equation will tell you exactly what you can spend on that new house.

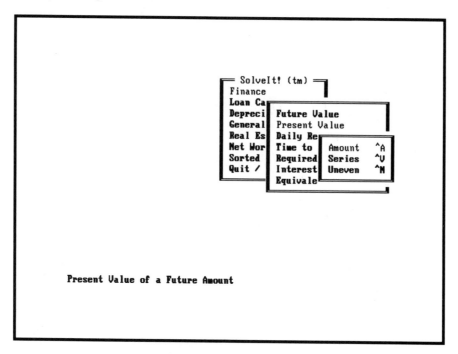

Though the manual that's included with the Shareware version of the product is for version 1.0, it does explain each routine sufficiently. By registering the product, you'll get the latest version along with a printed manual. If you have color in your system, you can configure SolveIt! to be any color you choose. The only thing really lacking is the ability to print the tables generated in nicely formatted reports rather than taking screen dumps of each screen.

SolveIt! is an excellent financial tool for anyone, including those of us that are not financial wizards. It's well conceived, innovative, and easy to learn and use. Recommended.

SolveIt!
Pine Grove Software
120 W. 97th St. Suite 6L
New York, N.Y. 10025

Shareware: $50

Category: Financial Calculator

System Requirements: 640k of available memory recommended for memory resident mode, IBM PC, XT, AT, or any close compatible, color recommended but it will work with composite or monochrome displays

Recommended use: Financial calculator

Major Pros: Easy to learn and use; good financial routines as well as a few innovative ones

Major Cons: No print facility for printing reports; memory resident option is memory hungry (168K)

Sources: Popular BBSs and commercial services, or directly from the author

---

@Last

Alan Wassyng Consulting Ltd.
Shareware—$28 (US)

No product is perfect, and, despite its phenomenal success, Lotus 1-2-3 is missing some useful functions. This product adds one such function and uses only about 20K memory.

@Last is a Shareware add-in product for Lotus 1-2-3 release 2 or 2.01 that adds search and replace functions. This is a welcome addition to the Lotus 1-2-3 system, and @Last includes quite a few useful options.

The program comes with accessory files that will help install the product on floppy or hard disks as well as reset the LOTUS.SET to include or remove the add-in drivers automatically. The inclusion of these support files as well as a sample worksheet and thorough on-disk manual make this a well-conceived product. The manual makes use of the sample worksheet to illustrate some of the possibilities of using @Last.

Once invoked, @Last lets you search cells in a designated range for specific contents. You can search four kinds of cells—formula, label, value, and error. Use these options respectively to search for formulas, text strings, numbers (integer or real), or error conditions in a cell. Text searches include limited wildcard capabilities. @Last will even find information in hidden cells, and will display the location of the cell on the screen.

@Last
Alan Wassyng Consulting Ltd.
20 Darby Way
Thornhill, Ontario L3T 5V1
Canada
(416) 731-4053

Shareware: $28 (US)

Category: Spreadsheet Utilities

System Requirements: IBM PC, XT, AT, PS/2 or compatible;Lotus 1-2-3
    Rel. 2 or 2.01; 20K (in addition to what your spreadsheet uses); DOS 2.0 or
    higher

Recommended Use: Range specific search and replace in 1-2-3

Major Pros: Add-in product works within 1-2-3; multiple options for search
    and modify cells

Major Cons: No major disadvantages

Sources: popular BBSs and commercial services, or directly from the author

---

You can also use a search/replace function which @Last calls Modify. This works just as you would expect it to. It first finds a match within the designated range, then replaces it with information you provide. You can even search for one type of cell (say number) and replace the information in the cell—at the same time changing it to another kind (say label). @Last will prompt you before making modifications, and will warn you if you are attempting to modify a protected cell.

You can also set the direction of a search, global search/modify, and even verification on or off. Searches can be case sensitive or not.

Most Lotus 1-2-3 users will welcome this product. It's amazing no one has thought of it before.

Word Plan
DEA Software
Shareware—$49.95

Word Plan might have as easily been reviewed in the Word Processor chapter, but its strength lies in its use with spreadsheets (Lotus 1.0 and 1A). It is a text editor with a sophisticated formatting language, but it is designed for a particular purpose—to read and manipulate text and spreadsheet data in a live link. By live link, we mean that data in a Word Plan document changes along with referenced data in a Lotus worksheet.

To use Word Plan, you intermix programming commands, output text, spreadsheet cell references, and formulas. By mixing well, you end up with a document that is nicely formatted and responsive to changes in related spreadsheet data.

Suppose you publish a price list, and you keep the main list in a worksheet. You want to extract parts of the price list to send out in letters to potential customers. You might have a form letter created in Word Plan that included specific price and product information. Using Word Plan's built-in programming, you can specify some *IF* conditionals to determine the composition of the product information for different customer groupings. Now, suppose you change all your prices. No problem. Since Word Plan reads its data from specific cells, the letters will print out with the new prices.

You can also perform several math and business functions on spreadsheet data. These functions are built into Word Plan. Another built-in function allows format definitions for cells and cell ranges. An example of an annual report for the fictional ACME Credit Union comes with the product. It includes text with imbedded cell references and a complete financial statement.

Although a Word Plan document with all its formatting commands, programming language, and cell references is far from being a WYSIWIG (what you see is what you get) text editor, its basic text editing is powerful. The editor includes pull-down command menus and full screen editing with word wrap, incremental undo command, and a lot of other features. It is based around Borland's Turbo Pascal Toolkit word processor, and is functionally similar to word processors like Galaxy and Free Word. But, in addition, Word Plan includes its unique and considerable programming power.

You can direct output to printer, screen, or file for a polished, formatted document. All commands are prefixed with backslashes.

Limitations in the current version require that all files reside in the current directory and the program is not presently rated to work with Lotus 2.x or Symphony.

Word Plan Vers. A.00.00
DEA Software
P.O. Box 968
Fremont, CA 94537

Shareware: $49.95

Category: Spreadsheet Utility; Word Processing

System Requirements: IBM PC, XT, AT, or compatible; 128K
(recommended 256K+); Lotus 1-2-3 worksheets

Recommended Use: for creating formatted documents with live spreadsheet
data included

Major Pros: has no competition; powerful text editing and formatting features;
powerful script language; unique live linking to Lotus 1-2-3 worksheet data;
powerful built-in business functions

Major Cons: not completely WYSIWYG (but how could it be?); complete
usage requires some programming; not for novices

Sources: popular BBSs and commercial services, or directly from the author

---

Word Plan is recommended for people who use Lotus 1-2-3 Version 1.0 and 1A and who wish to use spreadsheet data with word processing. For many, Word Plan's word processing features alone would be sufficient, but with its powerful programming and live cell referencing, it stands alone among word processors and spreadsheet utilities.

17

Telecommunications

Telecommunications is what a lot of this book is about. If you have not already done so, please take a look at Part I and Part III of this book for more information about telecommunications in general. Also, if a term is unfamiliar in the product reviews that follow, the *Glossary* is packed with definitions.

Because it is so much a part of the distribution process for public-domain and Shareware programs, telecommunications is one area in which these authors clearly excel. The popularity of PC Talk, the original Shareware product (with PC File), was so immense that other programmers didn't attempt to compete for some time after its introduction. But now the telecommunications competition has heated up. There are several products so sophisticated that they certainly are among the best telecommunications products available anywhere. Procomm, for one, is an undisputed success from a marketing as well as a programming standpoint.

We thought about reviewing PC Talk in this book, if only because it was so popular for so long, but we have heard that an upgraded version of PC Talk is about to be released as a commercial product. To avoid confusion, we will only present the following three telecommunications powerhouses.

Procomm 2.4x

Datastorm Technologies, Inc.
Shareware—$50

Procomm is a telecommunication program that anyone can use. The program combines some very advanced features with an ease of learning suitable for beginners. Some noteworthy features include the ability to emulate a number of popular terminals, a 100 number dialing directory, automatic redial facilities with a dialing queue for connecting to hard-to-reach numbers (like popular BBSs, etc.), and several file transfer protocols such as Xmodem, Ymodem, Telink, and Kermit. A sophisticated command language can provide control of automatic logon and unattended operation, while keyboard macros provide a measure of convenience without programming. Forward and backward scrolling while on-line offers access to information that may have scrolled off the screen. Printer and disk logging for capturing incoming text is also provided.

If you are experienced with other telecommunication programs, then you will find this program easy to learn. It is completely menu driven, has on-line help a keystroke away, and comes with a complete manual of all of its features. The manual lacks a tutorial, however, which may make it more difficult for first-time users of communication packages

The program can be downloaded from popular BBSs, and is usually found contained in two *.ARC* files which must be unpacked. One *.ARC* file contains the documentation, while the other holds the program. The first time you run the program, it creates several new files on your disk, so make sure to use this program on a disk with free space, or copy it to a hard disk. The documentation takes approximately one hour to print on a standard dot-matrix printer, but it's an hour well spent as you'll require documentation if you intend to use the program's more advanced features.

Procomm's over-all performance is very good. It presents options in the form of pop-up windows with optional sound effects that can help you identify the current status of the program even if you aren't watching the screen. The placement of some of the windows could be improved. For example, the pop-up window for adding a new directory number to the dialing directory completely blocks the view of the current list. Unless you remember what the next available number is, you have to abort the procedure and start again, or guess. The file transfer menu is also poorly positioned. Perhaps future versions of the program will allow the user to move the menus around the screen.

Aside from the window placement, the program works beautifully. I particularly like the ease of forward and backward screen scrolling and the use of the *PgUp* and *PgDn* keys for invoking the upload and downloading functions. The program makes excellent use of color, and you can change the color defaults of the screens the way you can in Qmodem or GT-Powercomm. Procomm also provides a DOS shell which allows you to exit the program and run other programs while keeping Procomm asleep in memory. As with other DOS shell programs, memory-hungry programs (like Paradox, for instance) can destroy the shell in an instant.

Procomm Version 2.42
Datastorm Technologies, Inc.
P.O. Box 1471
Columbia, MO 65205
BBS: (314) 474-8477

Shareware: $50

Category: Telecommunications

System Requirements: 192k of available memory, IBM PC, XT, AT or any
    close compatible; color recommended, but it will work with composite or
    monochrome displays; any Hayes-compatible modem

Recommended Use: advanced telecommunications for home or business

Major Pros: the ability to emulate a variety of different terminals; a dialing
    directory of 100 numbers plus a dialing queue for hard-to-reach numbers;
    several popular file transfer protocols; command files (scripts) to control
    automatic logon and unattended operations; DOS shell that allows you to
    execute DOS commands or other programs while you are still on-line.

Major Cons: may be difficult to learn for first-time users because the manual
    lacks a telecommunications tutorial; few example scripts are provided so
    learning the command language is difficult

Sources: popular BBSs and commercial services, or directly from the author

---

The command language is similar to programming in dBASE or some other high-level language. There are enough commands to do some pretty sophisticated things, like calling up a system at a particular time of day, downloading some files, and logging off. The manual lacks any real example scripts, so learning the command language may require a lot of trial-and-error attempts to get everything running smoothly. Some common logon scripts are provided with the software, and others may be available from BBS.

This program rivals many of the commercial programs that cost several hundred dollars. The author promotes a $25 registration option (which allows you to legally use the program) to a $50 "The Works!" package which includes registration, a copy of the program on diskette, and a printed bound manual. Even at $50, the program is a steal.

In summary, Procomm is a flexible, easy-to-use telecommunication package that provides a host of features rivalling many of the commercial telecommunication packages costing much more. This product is an excellent performer.

Qmodem ver. 3.1a

The Forbin Project
Shareware—$30

Qmodem is a general-use telecommunication package. It has some very advanced features while providing a slick windowed environment for easy execution and learning. This program is similar to Procomm reviewed earlier. The program's list of features are impressive as with Procomm. Some of these features include: the ability to emulate TTY, VT100, ANSI, and TVI 952 terminals, and ANSI color graphics support. You can have unlimited telephone directories of 200 numbers each—plus it records the password for each entry, the activity, and the number of file transfers. A circular redialing queue. Keyboard macros. Several file transfer protocols which include xmodem, ymodem, zmodem, Kermit, Sealink, windowed xmodem. Printer and disk logging for capturing incoming text. A sophisticated command language that provides control of automatic logon and unattended file transfers. On screen real-time clock. Split screen capabilities complete with a keyboard buffer during TTY operations.

As with Procomm and GT-Powercomm, this program lacks a tutorial for beginning users. The manual is small compared to its list of features, but it is complete. The installation of Qmodem requires running a separate installation program. The program prompts you through a variety of menus that cover everything from the color of the screens and the placement of the dialog windows to the exact modem commands that your modem needs. Fortunately, the modem commands are already set for a Hayes compatible modem. Incidently, Qmodem was the only telecommunication package found that allowed so much customization ability. The ability to move the windows around the screen (though not while actually using the program), was a big help.

The program also supports external protocol drivers for its file transfers. Unlike the other packages tested, this program allows you to add or delete any external drivers from the system. One protocol that was included with this package as well as GT-Powercomm was the Zmodem protocol which is the fastest seen so far. Zmodem was developed by Omen Technology. Ymodem which is included as an internal driver is the proprietary protocol of the Forbin Project. It transfers files in 1k blocks. Also included is an external ymodem variant known as ymodem batch which allows multiple file transfers. In order to have host mode operation, you must run an external script which reconfigures Qmodem for host mode operation. The biggest advantage to the external script host is the ability to custom configure your host application needs. The command language is very similar to Procomm. It is a high level dBASE type language that supports a number of very powerful commands for creating scripts to handle automated logon, and unattended file transfers.

Qmodem ver. SST 3.1a
The Forbin Project, Inc.
4945 Colfax Avenue South
Minneapolis, MN 55409

Shareware: $30

System requirements: IBM PC/XT/AT or close compatible with at least 256K of memory, color graphics or monochrome monitor, a serial port and any modem

Recommended use: Advanced telecommunications for the home or power user

Major Pros: Unlimited telephone directories of up to 200 numbers each; several popular file transfer protocols supported; supports multitasking software such as TopView, DESQview, Taskview; circular redialing queue; command files to control automatic logon and unattended file transfer operations; DOS shell for running external programs or executing DOS commands while Qmodem stays in memory; EGA support

Major Cons: No printed manual included in registration fee; no variety in terminal emulations

Sources: Popular BBSs and commercial services, or directly from the author

---

In this newer version the script language has been even more enhanced The manual lacks any example scripts, so you will have to experiment. There are several public domain scripts available from other users that can be easily modified for your particular needs. A DOS shell is also provided which allows you to execute DOS commands or run other programs while remaining online. Qmodem supports three multitasking environments, TopView from IBM, DESQview from Quarterdeck Systems, and TaskView from Sunny Hill Software.

This program competes very well with commercial programs available that cost hundreds of dollars. The initial registration is $30 ($40 if you want the newest version on diskette). For registering you do not get a printed bound manual which is unusual. Most companies will send you their most recent version, and a manual. Perhaps in future versions, this policy may change.

In summary, Qmodem is a comprehensive and powerful program that is fully loaded with features. It will provide all the communication needs of the power user, yet it is simple enough for a beginner to operate. This package is the certainly one of the best Shareware communication packages available. Recommended.

GT Powercomm 12.1

P& M Software Co.
Shareware—$40

GT Powercomm is a general-use telecommunication package that can meet anyone's communication needs. The package contains advanced features while providing an easy-to-learn "windowed" environment for beginners. This program is very similar in operation to Procomm, which is reviewed earlier in this chapter. The program's list of features is as impressive as Procomm's. Some of these features include: the ability to emulate an ANSI and VT100 type terminal; ANSI graphics support without the need of a separate, external ANSI driver; multiple telephone directories, with 999 entries each (plus it records the password for each entry, and records and tracks activities for each entry such as date and time last called, number of file transfers, etc.); circular redialing queue; keyboard macros; several file transfer protocols such as Xmodem, Ymodem, Zmodem, Kermit, Telink, and its own proprietary protocol called 1k Telink; printer and disk logging for capturing incoming text; a sophisticated command language that provides control of automatic logon and unattended operation; advanced call progress detection with modems that have extended result codes such as the US Robotics 2400 courier modem; on screen real-time clock; a sophisticated Host mode operation that provides security, and unattended file transfers, and a message system.

GT-Powercomm ver 12.10
P & M Software Co.
9350 Country Creek #30
Houston, TX 77036
Voice: 713-778-9471
BBS: 713-772-2090

Shareware : $40

Category: Telecommunications

System Requirements: Exact amount of memory needed is unknown—192k
is assumed; IBM PC, XT, AT or close compatible; color recommended but it
will work with composite or monochrome displays; any Hayes compatible
modem, but takes advantage of US Robotics extended result codes

Recommended Use: advanced telecommunications for home or business

Major Pros: multiple telephone directories of up to 999 entries each; several
popular file transfer protocol; circular redialing queue; can use COM3 and
COM4 (Everex standard); command files (scripts) to control automatic logon
and unattended file transfer operation; DOS shell that allows you to run
external programs or execute DOS commands while you are still on-line;
advanced Host mode operation that includes a basic messaging system, user
bulletins, and other features normally found in separate message based
systems like RBBS and FIDO; non-host version of the program is included
for those with limited disk space

Major Cons: no variety in terminal emulations; no example scripts are
provided so learning the command language is difficult; setting up the host
mode operation may be difficult for first time users; the package contains
many files which require a lot of disk space

Sources: popular BBSs and commercial services, or directly from the author

The program is easy to learn because of its windowed environment and adequate
manual. As with Procomm, the manual lacks a tutorial which may make it
difficult for first-time users. Depending upon how you obtained the program, set
up usually requires unarcing several files and printing the documentation. The
main documentation is not lengthy, and printing time is about 1/2 hour on a dot
matrix printer. There are also several smaller documentation files included which

cover the host mode operation in greater detail and the external protocol drivers included with the program.

I liked the overall performance of GT-Powercomm. As with Procomm, and Qmodem, this program is easy to use because of its windowed environment and sound effects to help you identify the current status of the program when not watching the screen. This program also makes use of the *Pg Up* and *Pg Dn* keys for starting file transfers. The placement of the dialog windows is better than Procomm's. Unlike Procomm, GT Powercomm supports external protocol drivers for its file transfers, but its advantage is limited since you can't add on additional drivers as they become available, as you can with Qmodem. You can, however, update your drivers without updating the program.

A DOS shell is also provided for running external programs or DOS commands while you keep GT-Powercomm in memory. GT also provides a proprietary file transfer protocol called 1k Telink. This protocol is an off-shoot of a popular file transfer protocol found on FIDO BBSs. It allows you to download files by using wild card type delimiters (i.e. *.exe), and it transfers in 1k block lengths. Surprisingly, the protocol is actually slower than Ymodem in single file transfers. But because it has batch downloading capabilities, it is faster in multiple file transfers since the operator doesn't need to stop and type each file name of the file being received.

The host mode operation is very sophisticated and provides many of the features found in dedicated messaging systems, including a message area, user bulletins, ability to run external programs remotely, and uploading and downloading capabilities. You may find the host mode a bit tricky to set up if you are new to messaging systems. The documentation is barely adequate and the author assumes you understand how a messaging system works. Aside from the initial set up, the operation is relatively simple and can provide you with a nice messaging system for your home or business all in one complete package.

The GT-Powercomm package also includes a version of the program that does not have the host mode operation. The advantage is that the non-host version uses less disk space and can be operated comfortably from a floppy disk. The command language is very similar to Procomm's. It is a high level dBASE type language that supports a number of powerful commands for creating automated logon and unattended file transfer procedure scripts. The manual lacks example scripts, so you have to experiment.

This program competes very well with other commercial programs that cost hundreds of dollars. The initial registration of this program costs $40, which includes a free upgrade to the current version. After that, future upgrades cost $10.

GT-Powercomm is powerful program that is fully loaded with features. It provides all communication needs for both the business and the home user. This product is an excellent performer.

Invisible Link

Robert Best and Garland Wong
Shareware—$20

Background communications. I've heard it over and over again, but have rarely seen it. Yes, I have seen it, but not often enough, and with some disclaimers. The Invisible Link works. It remains in memory controlling an upload or download while you continue to work. So nice!

```
                    INVISIBLE LINK HELP SCREEN



ALT - RIGHT-SHIFT> Invoke Invisible Link
ALT - X > Exit Invisible Link But Leave On-Line
ALT - Q > Exit And Hang Up Phone (Drop DTR)
ALT - C > Clear The Screen
ALT - P > Change The Baud Rate
ALT - H > Hang Up The Phone
PAGE UP > Start a Upload
PAGE DOWN > Start a Download
ALT - D > Dial a Number Using a Directory
ALT - M > Manually Input a Number to Dial
ALT - R > Change Redial Delay Count (Seconds)
ALT - LEFT-SHIFT> Terminate Backgroud Dial or Enter File Transfer Status Screen
Valid Baud Rates - 0 = 300, 1 = 1200, 2 = 2400, 4 = 4800, 9 = 9600




                    PRESS ANY KEY TO CONTINUE
```

The Invisible Link
Robert Best and Garland Wong
C/O Garland Wong
8663 Via Mallorca #86
La Jolla, CA 92037

Shareware : $20

Category: Background Telecommunications

System Requirements: IBM PC, XT, AT, or 100% compatible; DOS 2.0 or
   later; 26K RAM; modem

Recommended Use: advanced telecommunications for home or business

Major Pros: works in the background

Major Cons: user interface could be more intuitive and nice, but at the cost of
   memory.

Sources: popular BBSs and commercial services, or directly from the author

You simply load the program, begin your communication session, and then begin your upload or download. The Invisible Link takes over and manages the file
transfer sending you back to DOS (or your application) where you belong. When
the file is finished, IL beeps you and sends a message to the screen.

You can also define a dialing directory, designate up to ten files to up/download,
and even use IL along with your favorite communications program. So if you really like the interface of Procomm or Qmodem, or whatever, you can still use it
for dialing and other chores, but use IL when you want to be free to keep working.

Pressing Alt-Right Shift invokes the program, but during a file transfer, pressing
Alt-Left Shift displays a running status screen of the transfer. You can also
change baud rate and other settings on line.

This program could be glitzier if it had more menus, pop-up windows, and the
like, but the main thing is it works very well. It gets bogged down during I/O
intensive operations like formatting disks or intensive file copying, but can handle a good deal of interruption without violating the integrity of the transfer. This
program is much needed and very welcome. And it's steal at $20.

Privacy 1.1

George Fontaine
Andromeda Micro Corporation
181 Aconi Lani Street
Pukalani, HI 96768
Shareware—$15

Privacy was written by George Fontaine. Because he is one of the authors of this book, we wouldn't feel right reviewing it. But we would like to describe what it does.

Privacy is a file encryption program that allows you to send your text file messages to services like BBS and E-Mail in encoded form. Most E-Mail and local BBS message sections require ASCII file transfers, and most encrypted files are binary files, unable to be transferred that way. Privacy therefore fills a gap by allowing a user to encrypt a message, send it to a public board, and have it be read only by the intended recipient.

Although most BBS and all E-Mail services maintain confidentiality in private messages, there are always people who can read these messages. Sysops and their friends may have access to your messages. And some people may have a secretary or other employee download their messages from time to time. If the messages must be kept private, Privacy is a good alternative.

Privacy can take whole phrases as the encryption key, so you can use something familiar like, "Call me Ishmael," or "Remember the Force, Luke." Also, you can encrypt an already encrypted file for double encryption requiring two keys to decrypt. Privacy does not alter the original file in any way, but creates a special coded output file.

If you feel that Privacy could be useful, it is available from major services or from our RHS RBBS.

18

Turbo Pascal Programs and Utilities

Turbo Pascal has become a favorite programming tool of many business people. It is easy to learn, and produces fast, executable, and easily modifiable code. Furthermore, it is extremely well supported by its developer, Borland International, and by a host of third party programmers. Third party support includes many Shareware and public-domain authors.

We asked Don Miner, librarian of the Turbo User's Group, to make some recommendations. Here are his suggestions:

FontEdit

Version 1.01 delves into the the hows and whys of your Epson, IBM Proprinter, or compatible printer. It enables you to create and edit font characters, print them, and even save in a file for later use. With FontEdit, you can create custom graphic characters, create extra-large characters, and even print sideways. This is done in object code format.

Sprites

Sprites is intended for those who have ever wondered where Pac-Man came from, or where those asteroids go after you've blasted them with your laser weapon. The Designer and Composer programs will delight young and old alike. Create your sprites with Designer, and use Composer to control their action on the screen. This is done in object code format. Demo source programs are included to show how to use these graphics from Pascal.

NewFont

This is an excellent Turbo Pascal graphic font design tool. It includes complete documentation and a pre-compiled library of functions and procedures for designing special graphics fonts on the PC. This is done in object code format, but source code is available directly from the author. Requires a PC with at least 256K and a color graphics adapter.

PToolwin

This is a suite of Turbo Pascal procedures for easing the manipulation of text windows in the IBM PC environment. The routines perform a number of duties, including border support and the opening and closing of a window while saving data covered by the window.

TCalc

Version 1.0 is an easy-to-use spreadsheet that supports 256 rows by 26 columns. The screen display consists of 7 columns by 21 rows and supports vertical and horizontal scrolling. Full documentation is included on the disk. This is done in object code format; requires a PC with at least 256K.

TPaint

TPaint will turn the screen on your IBM PC or compatible into an artist's canvas! TPaint is a painting program that will enable you to paint electronic portraits that you can display in Turbo Pascal programs. Includes several example paintings and a utility that will convert paintings made by other programs into

.PIC files used by TPaint. The ideal way to improve those artistic talents! This is done in object code format; requires a PC with at least 256K, a color graphics adapter, and a mouse.

T-Ref

T-Ref is not a demo program. It is a fully operable package, born out of more than just a need for a detailed cross referencing program. It had to be one that would provide "intelligent" flexibility and selectivity. T-Ref is actually two programs combined into a single package. First, it is a source lister for Borland's Turbo Pascal programs. T-Ref's sophistication for listing the source files goes far beyond just printing the source code. Along with the source listing, you can specify a line-by-line printout of the lexical levels and block levels, the active procedure or function of that line, and the line numbers along with the listing.

The second part of T-Ref is the Cross Reference List, which was specifically designed to cross reference Borland's Turbo Pascal programs. It will give a complete cross reference of all identifiers declared within a program or a partial listing (on requested basic types). The listing gives each identifier's name, its type, the code line declared on, all lines referencing the names, and the scope (the procedure or function name and level within which the identifier was declared).

World

This program is a map projecting the world. It allows the user to make selections using a particular latitude and longitude. Other selections that can be made are Europe, USA, US capital cities, other major cities, national capitals, and for the weather buffs, provisions are made to allow the tracking of hurricanes. A Mercator projection is displayed with a pointer which becomes an expanded view with a keystoke. (With a little work, this program could have tremendous possibilities. Imagine calling up the city of your choice, expanding the view to locate the address or find the street you are looking for (*D.MINER TUG* librarian).

Another program Don recommends is TheDrw24.

For more information, or to inquire about membership in the Turbo User Group, contact them at:

TUG
PO Box 1510
Poulsbo, WA 98370
USA

Shareware as an Enigma
by Mark Barnes

Mark Barnes edits the Shareware Magazine, *(formerly PC Sig Magazine) a periodical devoted to public-domain and Shareware information. As we did with other contributors to this book, we simply asked that Mark provide us with some insight into his world. We hope you enjoy his unique viewpoint on the public-domain and user-supported market.*

As a copywriter in an advertising agency, I was called upon more than once to push a lot of water uphill. Selling products with no socially redeeming value is one thing. Selling products where the marketing strategy comes from another planet is a copywriter's nightmare. When I accepted the job as editor of PC-SIG Magazine I had never heard of Shareware, Freeware, user-supported or public-domain software. PC-SIG being the world's largest distributor of this type of software, it was to my interest to find out about this type of software and its marketing.

It took them a week to convince me that shareware was a valuable marketing tool, that it actually worked, and that it was not some cruel joke they were playing on a former copywriter. I may not have been a business-school candidate, but I did know human nature. I was, at the time, completely convinced that giving people software for almost nothing and then asking them, if they liked it, to send a voluntary registration fee to the originator of that software was the type of marketing (if successful) that would put Harvard Business School out of business.

This scheme is the literary equivalent of having an author sell his book to a reader at a fraction of the retail price. After reading the book and enjoying it, the reader sits down and sends a check for the full retail price to the author. In return, the author tells him how he wrote the novel and will offer assistance if the buyer can't understand certain chapters. Further, the reader is encouraged to share the book with friends. Talk about a license to steal.

If you were selling programs that were of little more worth than the price of a blank floppy disk, this type of marketing would make sense. However, when you are selling software which is on a par with, and often better than, its commercial

310

equal—for hundreds of dollars less—somebody's ladder is missing a few steps. Yet it works in spite of a basic advertising principle: "Sell the sizzle, not the steak."

As I got to know the authors and listened to my readers, it became clear that in this type of high-tech merchandising the selling of the steak rather than the sizzle was brilliant. It was also appreciated by the end-users, who for years have fallen victim to committing to high-priced software based on the advertising and the packaging. And then, only to find the software was not anywhere close to what they were looking for or needed.

While a large thorn in the side of major commercial software houses, whose marketability is based on bell-and-whistle packaging, Shareware is just now beginning to reach its commercial potential. As it has expanded rapidly among individual users, the acceptance in the business community is just now beginning to bear fruit. There is a fear beating in every corporate heart that you get what you pay for and if these programs are so inexpensive; can I take that risk? The real question they should be asking themselves is: Can I afford not to take that risk?

If we put this in a one-to-one format, it is easier to understand why corporations cannot afford not to invest in Shareware software. I have talked to authors that have taken technical support questions from registered users at 3 a.m.; believing that it was their obligation to the registered users who tried the software and sent in their checks. Take a long look at most commercially-packaged software and tell me where it gives you the actual programmer's name and home telephone.

Although some of the giants of Shareware now support a large technical staff, a person or corporation would be hard-pressed to find one author who, when needed, would not offer personal service.

With any product, buyers must know what they want, and they must shop around. The advantage to Shareware is the inexpensive review cost—the cost of getting an actual hands-on feel of the program. After almost a year of editing PC-SIG Magazine, dealing with authors and customers. . . I still can't figure out why the damn concept is so successful, but I'm really happy it is!

Turbojocks Turbo Toolkit 4.0

TechnoJock Software
P.O. Box 820927
Houston, TX 77282-0927
(713) 293-2760
Shareware—$29.95

Here, despite the whimsical name, is shareware at its best: an innovative product, a superb manual, quick mail-order service, and a reasonable price.

TTT is a collection of procedures and functions for Turbo Pascal Version 4.0. It provides powerful single-line commands that may be inserted into TP code to produce windows, boxes, menus, data input screens, mouse input, and much more.

The full Toolkit consists of ten Units, each for a certain class of procedure. WinTTT.TPU, for instance, has 22 commands for formatting the screen. KeyTTT.TPU has ten commands for mouse or keyboard input. FastTTT.TPU has 17 commands for writing to the screen.

Here is a command example from Unit WinTTT:

```
GrowMkWin(10,5,70,16,15,0,2);
```

This creates a window for text on the screen, and saves the screen contents that are overlaid by the window. The numeric variables in this example mean that the window will "grow" from the centerline of the screen outward, stopping with its top left corner at column 10 and row 5 and its bottom right corner at column 70, row 16. The foreground of the window will be white (15), and the background will be black (0). The boundary of the window will be a double line (2). The block of screen covered by the window will be saved in memory, then restored when the command "RmWin" is given.

That's a lot of action from a single command. Here is another from the Unit FastTTT:

```
WriteCenter(10,14,4,'SMUG NOTES');
```

This command will center the string "SMUG NOTES" on row 10, with the characters in yellow (14) and a red (4) background. This is a lot simpler for the programmer than the generic TP equivalent:

```
TextColor(14);
TextBackground(4);
GotoXY(45,10);
Write('SMUG NOTES');
TextColor(15);
TextBackground(0);
```

PullTTT contains a procedure for creating very sophisticated pull-down menus with a minimum of code. IOTTT includes a system for user input and editing of screen fields. DirTTT contains a procedure for displaying a Sidekick-like directory, allowing the user to scroll through the files and select one.

There are so many more grand programming shortcuts in TTT that I can't begin to cover them here. Two of the Units contain assembler language for speed, and all are written in Turbo Pascal before compilation. The distribution disk includes the assembler (.ASM) files, the object code (.OBJ) files, the Pascal (.PAS) files, and the Unit (.TPU) files already compiled and debugged.

The User's Manual is 125 pages, beautifully laid out and set in big type on 8-1/2 x 11 pages, and spiral bound (it lies flat!). After an introduction with general instructions on the use of Units in TP 4.0, a full page is devoted to each of the 90 procedures, with the purpose of each, the declaration form and an explanation of each variable, the Units used, remarks, cross-references to related procedures, and an example.

There are two indexes in the manual; one alphabetical and one organized by Units. My manual was printed on March 8, 1988 and the disk was released Feb. 1, 1988.

If you're programming in Turbo Pascal, you absolutely *must* have TTT!

—Robert K. Barcus

Review reprinted from SMUG (Spokane Microcomputer User Group) Newsletter:

SMUG, Inc.
P.O. Box 1753
Spokane, WA 99210

19

Utilities

Utilities are often small but very useful products. They may improve on DOS commands or they may perform new functions. They often perform with little fuss what it takes an expert to do with DOS. Sometimes they look like "Gee Whiz" products (flashy, but without substance), but one person's Gee Whiz may be another's productivity enhancement.

There are thousands of PD and Shareware utilities. Finding, testing, and reporting on all of them is a monumental task. We've tried to include a sampling of good utilities in this chapter. You'll find that using these utilities is mostly a matter of replacing old DOS habits with new ones. For instance, I love *HDIR*, but I still find myself using the good old *DIR* command over and over. Why? Because I forget. Many of these utilities make life easier, but you have to remember to use them (and place them on the DOS Path).

Some products, particularly ButtonWare and Brown Bag software products often include useful utilities with the shrink-wrapped registered versions of their Shareware products. We've noted some of those utilities with individual applications elsewhere in the book.

One utility I use almost constantly is List. List ranks at the top of my favorites. It's great for displaying Shareware documentation on screen. If you get any of these programs, be sure to find and download List.

Utilities Basics

Often in this chapter, you will see samples of the command syntax for a particular program. There are certain conventions used in this syntax. For instance, suppose you are running a program called *DOTHIS.EXE*:

```
DOTHIS [D:] <filename> [/S} {/Q]
```

Everything in square brackets *[ ]* is optional. This means that you may omit these options if you need to. In the example, *[D:}* means the disk drive designator is optional and so are the command line switches */S* and */Q*. The filename is not optional. Required components of the command are often placed in the greater/less than signs <...>. You will find these conventions fairly consistent throughout the public-domain and Shareware world.

We have done our best to include the basic terminology of DOS and computers in the Glossary at the end of this book. Many terms in the Utilities chapter may be unfamiliar to you. If you don't recognize a term, it may be in the Glossary. If it is not, let us know and we'll be sure to add it in the next version. There are simply so many terms, we weren't always sure what needed to be defined and what didn't.

Aformat

Tom Doerner
Public Domain

Aformat is a simple set of batch files that allow you to format floppy disks without interruption on a two-floppy system. This is not a fast formatter. In fact, it uses the DOS FORMAT command, so it works exactly like normal formatting, but it alternates between the A: and the B: drives, and doesn't require that you press Y between formats.

Since this system uses the DOS FORMAT command, it will format any kind of DOS disk—360K, 1.2 M, or 3.5 inch drive. If you are doing something like formatting a 360 diskette on a 1.2 M drive, you may have to make a minor modification to one of the batch files.

There's nothing spectacular about this idea, but it works well, and doesn't have any of the potential instabilities or incompatibilities that can occur in formatters that are written from scratch.

Anadisk 1.2

Sydex
153 North Murphy Ave.
Sunnyvale, CA 94086
(408) 739-4866
Shareware—$15

Anadisk can perform all kinds of technical miracles on a floppy disk. It can scan the entire disk, reporting any problems it encounters. It also tells you what kind of disk it is and how the data was recorded on it. Other features of the program allow you to perform sector level modifications to disks, repair damaged disks, and sector copy floppy disks.

This product is mostly aimed at people with technical knowledge. In particular, the sector and file options are not for the novice. The disk repair is self-running and could be used by anyone, as can the disk-copy facility.

This is a slick, colorful program that almost makes sector-level editing fun. The on-disk manual is pretty well done, and the full manual that is provided to registered users is supposed to be very complete. We didn't see it, however, so you'll have to judge for yourself.

Sydex also has some other programs on the market including Teledisk (which can compress an entire floppy disk for sending over telecommunications lines), SIMCGA (which simulates a CGA adapter on a monochrome system), 22NICE (reads, writes, formats various CP/M disks), and COPYQM (which will perform fast bulk copies of floppy disks on multiple drives by reading one entire floppy into memory and then formatting and copying to only the tracks needed).

Apath

Apath is a handy public-domain utility that allows you to add a value to your DOS PATH statement without retyping the whole thing. For instance, if your path already reads *C:\DOS;\UTILS;\MENU*, you could add a directory to the path by typing, *APATH \TEMP*. The new path would read *\TEMP;C:\DOS;\UTILS;\MENU*. (See also DPATH, CHGPATH, and NEW-PATH)

ARCHIVE ver. 2.7c

Colossus Systems
Public Domain

ARCHIVE is a public-domain backup utility. It allows you to back up selected directories or files from an easy-to-use menu interface. You can also select certain files and directories in the same fashion. The program works on any computer, but it only reads and writes to 360k floppies. This may be a disadvantage for owners of AT computers who want to take advantage of the higher capacity disks to save on the total number of disks needed to do a complete backup. The program also has a little trouble reading back 360k floppies used in a backup in the higher capacity drive, but it will work. The program is fast, but does not provide any file compression when doing a backup like other commercial programs do. The program does provide a large amount of flexibility in selecting files and directories, and even provides a tally of how many disks will be required in the backup and of how many files have been selected. Forget to format your disks before you start the back up? No problem. Archive will format the disks, as an option, as it does the back up. Unfortunately, the formatting is not done at the same time as the back up, so it does slow things down. Despite these inconveniences, ARCHIVE is a good program and well worth a look. You might consider this program for daily backups of a directory or certain files you're working with.

Archive Utilities

ARCF 1.06

Vernon Buerg
139 Whiteoak Circle
Petaluma, CA 94952
BBS # (707) 778-8944
Public Domain

ARCF is used to find text strings within the files in an archive. The basic syntax is:

```
ARCF [d:][path]filename[.ARC] [filespecs...] "text" [/B] [/C] [/F] [/Q]
[/S] [/W]
```

The optional switches are used to include binary files, to perform case sensitive searches, to display the name of the file being searched only if text is found within it, to supply a password, to suppress beeps and bells, to suppress displaying the names of files being processed, and, finally, to ignore white space.

ARCFDATE

Norm Patriquin
P.O. Box 8263
San Bernadino, CA 92412
Shareware—$15

ARCFDATE searches an ARC file to find the most recent file, then sets the date on the archive to that date. Basically, this is a way to place a realistic date on your archive files. The program uses various command line options to select specific files, dates, or other parameters. There is even an option that allows you to test the effect of a command without actually updating any files.

Arcmaster 1.0

John J. Newlin
4060 -228 Rosenda Ct.
San Diego, CA 92122
Work—(619) 543-4072
Home—(619) 455-6225
Shareware—$40

*ARC*ing and *deARC*ing have become standard fare for people in the Shareware world, but many have little or no understanding of how to use these programs. For this reason, a program to simplify the use of ARC type programs is a good idea.

Arcmaster is designed as a front end menu system for *PKARC/PKXARC* or *ARCA/ARC-E*. This program allows you to perform many tasks on ARC files that otherwise require a good understanding of the syntax. Among its features are the ability to search any drive for files residing in *ARC*ed files, browse *ARC*ed files using *LIST* (see below), *ARC* and *deARC* to and from any directory, search for files by name, and handle any other ARC related tasks.

Arcmaster makes it easy to manipulate files in and out of ARCs. To retrieve certain files from a particular ARC file, you simply select the ARC file from a listing on screen, then mark and select the files you want to extract. The same easy methods apply when adding to or deleting from ARC files.

People who register Arcmaster will receive a version with additional features including printing of an Archive directory listing, batch file operations, and a few other features.

Many people who are already used to how ARC programs work will not need Arcmaster, but anyone new to using ARC files, or anyone who would like a more user-friendly environment for working with ARC files should look at Arcmaster. It's a fine idea, too long in coming.

Arcplus

GDSOFT
57280 Osage Drive
Goshen, IN 46526
GEnie G.D. Davis
Compuserve 72067,2726

Arcplus is another PKArc utility program. This one will automatically locate PKArc on your disk, and will remember its location after the first time. It will then read and display a listing of every file on your disk with the *.ARC* extension. You can select any of the files from the list, change the current directory path, or even change drives.

Once an ARC file has been selected, you can select files from the current directory and add them to the archive with a simple command. There aren't a lot of options supported in this program, though you can use a command line switch to turn off PKArc's squashing mode which some bulletin boards do not allow. The primary advantage of this program is that it finds all ARC files on your disk and lists them. If you are adding a lot of files to a new or existing archive, you may find Arcplus provides an easy, menu-driven method of doing so.

Arcplus is distributed as FOOLWARE. According to the author, "I'd be a fool if I thought that you would actually send me money, even if I asked for it." This disclaimer notwithstanding, Mr. Davis does like to receive mail, and would probably not complain if you sent money, either.

ARCSWEEP

Dave Evers
2500 Larch Rd. #58
Quincy, IL 62301

So you've been going hog wild on the BBS and have a hundred archived files in your directory and half a million or so files extracted from them. You can't remember what you have in archives and what you have on disk. You desperately need to conserve some disk space, so you go out and find ARCSWEEP.

ARCSWEEP will examine your archives and compare their contents with the files in the current directory. Whenever it finds a file with the same name, same size, and same date/time, it will prompt you to delete the unarchived version of the file (which you can skip or delete). If you have supreme confidence, you can use the No Verify mode which will simply delete all exact matches. Another useful archive utility.

ARCTool2

Paul Nance
Tempe, AZ
Public Domain

ARCTool2 consists of two utility programs. One will list the contents of an archive, even damaged ones. The other will extract files from damaged ARC files. This program is designed to work with files created by System Enhancements' ARC program. We don't know for sure that it will work reliably with files created with other ARC programs, but it seems to do so. This is a fairly advanced utility and some of the listings would confuse novice and beginning computer users.

Lark v. 3r1

Donald K. Schuster
1415 Lemon Street
Clearwater, FL 34616
Shareware—$15 + $2 shipping

Lark is one of the premier PKArc utility programs. It includes a menu driven interface and lets you add or extract files from archives. You can also update archives or freshen the files in an archive by adding files from a directory that has a later date stamp. There are also facilities for copying and moving files between directories (either individually or in batches) or deleting specific files. The main listing shows all archived files in the current directory. You can open a listing of files within an archive by pressing Return with the desired file highlighted.

```
————————————  LARK 3r1  ARCHIVE MANAGEMENT SYSTEM  05/17/88  ————————
ARCHIVE: C:\PKX\1048.ARC                              QTY FILES: 18
TOTAL BYTES: Archived-292966    Unarchived-445741    LATEST UPDATE: 08 Jul 88


        Filename      Sq Size    Length      Type        Date      Time
     =============    =======    =======   ========   =========   =====
     1048.DOC          28172      65995    Crunched   22 Jan 88   16:36
     ORDER.FRM          1024       2552    Crunched   28 Jan 88   20:26
     READ.ME            3699       6581    Crunched   22 Jan 88   14:59
     T87PR.DAT            45       3968    Crunched   28 Jan 88   20:27
     T87PT.SCH            61        533    Crunched   28 Jan 88   20:27
     T87SC.DAT          1033       2944    Crunched   28 Jan 88   20:27
     T87SC.KEY           138        613    Crunched   28 Jan 88   20:27
     TOPTN.DAT           271        271    None       15 Jan 88   22:15
     TP87.EXE         120618     169839    Crunched   27 Jan 88   23:09
     TX87.EXE         137905     192445    Crunched   27 Jan 88   23:09




 ↑↓—Tab up/dn, PgUp, PgDn—Scroll, Home, End—Top, Bottom of list, ESC—Cancel
```

When an archive is shown, the names of all files within the archive are shown as well as their sizes, both squeezed and unsqueezed. The header of the screen shows how many files there are as well as how much space they use, squeezed and unsqueezed. The date of the latest update is also displayed.

If you have Vernon Buerg's List program, Lark will use it to display the contents of any text file in the archive if you choose to do so. You can add, extract, move, update, and delete files in the current archive from this screen.

Help is available at any time, and the program is very nicely put together. It performs many tasks with archives that would otherwise be tedious and difficult. The only drawback, and one you won't have to experience if you register the product, is that you have to enter a temporary six-digit number every time you use the Shareware version. I call this sort of thing "Annoyanceware" because the author has decided to annoy you into registration. On the other hand, you will probably find the product worth the price if you use archives a lot, and won't mind registering. If you use the program and don't register, you'll have to live with yourself, and you'll have to be annoyed.

Narc 2.1

Infinity Design Concepts, Inc.
1052 Parkway Drive
Louisville, KY 40217
(502) 241-4109 (modem)
Shareware—$20 ($35 w/printed manual)

We have Lark, and now we have Narc. Next, maybe Bark, or Quark? Hark, a Shark with a Mark (named Clark) is about to Park a Stark Spark in the Dark.

Seriously, though, Narc is a flashy and useful archive utility that allows you to list *.ARC* or *.ARK* (squashed) files, view their contents in a detailed display, tag and extract files from those files.

```
NARC Ver. 2.1   -   Pathname C:\TEST\1040.ARC
   Name          Length  Disk  Stowage  Ver  Stored  Saved    Date       Time    CRC

 1040   .DOC      65995   65k  Crunched  8    28172   58%  22 Jan 88    4:36p   74B3
 ORDER  .FRM       2552    3k  Crunched  8     1024   60%  28 Jan 88    8:26p   D500
 READ   .ME        6581    7k  Crunched  8     3699   44%  22 Jan 88    2:59p   5B15
 T87PR  .DAT       3968    4k  Crunched  8       45   99%  28 Jan 88    8:27p   6134
 T87PT  .SCH        533    1k  Crunched  8       61   89%  28 Jan 88    8:27p   3600
 T87SC  .DAT       2944    3k  Crunched  8     1033   65%  28 Jan 88    8:27p   6B11
 T87SC  .KEY        613    1k  Crunched  8      138   78%  28 Jan 88    8:27p   467A
 TOPTN  .DAT        271    1k  Unpacked  2      271    0%  15 Jan 88   10:15p   BCFC
 TP87   .EXE     169839  166k  Crunched  8   120618   29%  27 Jan 88   11:09p   E39F
 TX87   .EXE     192445  188k  Crunched  8   137905   29%  27 Jan 88   11:09p   C52A



 (c)87,88                                            Infinity Design Concepts
 Totals    10    445741  439k                 292966   35%     0 Tagged          0
                              F1 = HELP
     Extract    View      Print    ARC-wind   Chg drive  DirTree      Quit
 Extract Single File or Tagged Files.
```

Narc will let you view the contents of a specific ARCed file in ASCII or in hex format. The viewer also contains a search feature and an 8th-bit filter for reading documents like WordStar files. This is very useful for reading document files without unarcing the file. When using programs like Narc and Lark, you can keep documentation for applications in an archive, saving space, and still have access to their contents when you need to refer to the instructions.

Narc's display shows the name of each file, its length, the space used on disk, the compression technique used, a version number, the stored length, the percent of compression achieved, the date and time the file was archived, and the CRC (cyclic redundancy check) number (see figure). You can tag individual files for extraction or printing. When you print a file, you can select various options to format the printout, if necessary. These options can help make a plain ASCII file into a useful printed document.

You can change to any valid drive, or change directories. The change directory feature is especially pleasant in that it displays a directory tree (like T-Shell and other products) and includes options to make new directories or remove existing ones.

There are several other useful enhancements, like direct links to a text editor of your choice, and other time saving features. Suffice it to say that Narc is expertly programmed with excellent use of color and windows, and, like Lark, has a very professional feel. In addition, Narc works well with a mouse if you have one.

PKXtract 2.40

Chris Brown
427 14th St.
Edwards AFB, CA 93523-5000
GEnie address: MAFMPD
Shareware—$5

PKXtract is another utility that can make working with archive files easier. This one works with PKARC files as well as ARCE files. It lists their contents, allowing you to examine the contents of an archive, and extract one or more files from it. The program uses a special configuration file which can be modified in various ways, and a good deal of the disk-based manual is devoted to instructions that detail how to modify the config file. The program itself is easier to use than to configure. It will come up with a list of archive files in the current directory (if no archive file is named on the command line), and allows you to pick one.

Once you pick an archive, its contents are displayed on the menu screen, along with information about their size, creation date, method, and amount of compression used. You can tag individual files for extraction, or tag all files. Also, when you open a file, you can set a disk and directory as the destination for the extracted files, and when you exit the program, it gives you the option of exiting directly to the destination directory. That is a very convenient feature.

```
File         Length   Method    Size  Ratio   Date      ┌─────────────────────┐
1040.DOC      65995   Crunched  28172  58%  22-Jan-88   │ PKXtract - 2.40     │
 ORDER.FRM     2552   Crunched   1024  60%  28-Jan-88   │                     │
 READ.ME       6581   Crunched   3699  44%  22-Jan-88   │ Archive:       1040 │
 T87PR.DAT     3968   Crunched     45  99%  28-Jan-88   │ Files:           10 │
 T87PT.SCH      533   Crunched     61  89%  28-Jan-88   │ Bytes:      445,741 │
 T87SC.DAT     2944   Crunched   1033  65%  28-Jan-88   │                     │
 T87SC.KEY      613   Crunched    138  78%  28-Jan-88   │ Location:         1 │
 TOPTN.DAT      271   Stored      271   0%  15-Jan-88   │ Tagged              │
 TP87.EXE    169839   Crunched 120618  29%  27-Jan-88   │ Files:            0 │
 TX87.EXE    192445   Crunched 137905  29%  27-Jan-88   │ Bytes:            0 │
                                                        │                     │
                                                        │ Destination:        │
                                                        │ C:\TEST             │
                                                        │ Free:     2,625,536 │
                                                        │                     │
                                                        │ Processor: PKXARC   │
                                                        │                     │
                                                        │    Chris Brown      │
                                                        │ Compiled: 12 Jun 88 │
 Commands:                                              └─────────────────────┘
  PgUp,PgDn,Home,End,   T - Tag File      Space - Toggle tag   E - Extract file
  ↑,↓ - Bar Up/Down     U - Untag File    L - Re-Log drive     ALT - More Commands
```

Perhaps in a future version of PKXtract, Chris will add the ability to view text files inside the archives. Then you could actually read the documentation for an archived product before you decide to extract all the files.

PKXtract is an excellent utility for those who don't understand archive command structures, and also for those who would like an easier method of examining and selecting files from archives. The version tested here worked very well, and features an easy interface that anyone should be able to understand. A little work on the configuration options would make this a first-rate product all the way around.

Autosave

Bilogic
11982 Cornerstone Circle, Suite 1622
Manassas, VA 22110
Shareware—$25

An intriguing product, Autosave is a memory resident program that will actually save files from within other applications. Although some programs contain their own routines and commands that save your work periodically, many programs require you to remember to save your work. Many people have experienced loss of data due to power failures, carelessness, or other problems.

Autosave will work with programs like Lotus 1-2-3 and PC-Write which do not automatically save your work. Unfortunately, to use Autosave, you must enter a set of complicated switches at the command line. For instance, to run Autosave with Lotus 1-2-3, you would enter:

```
Autosave -k27,27,27,27,27,27,47,70,83,*,13,82,27 -fsave -i30 -t10
123
```

This complex command structure uses ASCII codes for the keystrokes that might be necessary to save a file. The number 27 stands for the Esc key. The command line above would save to a file called *save.wk1*. The *t10* part of the command sets the minimum time interval to ten minutes. This means that the program waits ten minutes before beginning to look for a period of no activity in which to save. The *i30* part sets the keyboard interval. What this means is that Autosave will wait for a period of 30 seconds without a keystroke before saving the file. These parameters can only be set with the registered version of the product. The default intervals are 5 minutes and 30 seconds.

Although you can create a batch file to run Autosave with its multiple switches and commands, this program could be improved in several ways—notably with a menu driven interface and, perhaps, a "learn" mode that allows you to teach it the necessary commands by performing them.

Autosave is a great idea, and within its limitations, it is a very useful product. With some improvement, it could be a great addition to anyone's system.

Autotest

Unk.
Public Domain

Autotest is a public-domain utility to measure floppy and hard disk access times. It obtains these measurements by performing sequential and random seeks, and reads on the disk. The program will not harm the data on the disk being tested, since the program only reads information and does not write. To run the program, you type the following at the DOS command line:

```
A>autotest
```

The program will then ask for the drive being tested and begin the test. While the program is running, it gives you the results of each type of test being done in a seconds-to-read ratio. When the program finishes, it returns you to the DOS command line. The program is designed for those people who understand what the resulting ratios mean. The program will not tell you if the ratios for your disk are good or bad. Therefore, results obtained using this program would be meaningless to a novice.

AUTOXQT

Rick Ferris
RAF Software Enterprises
707 Woodhorn Court
Houston, TX 77062
(713) 280-0377
Public Domain

This clever utility allows you to define your *AUTOEXEC.BAT* file at the time you boot your computer. Yes, that's right, when you boot! It does this in a fairly clever way by running itself alone (or with whatever you always want) in the *AUTOEXEC.BAT* and then asking you questions about what options and/or applications you want loaded. You will have used an ASCII editor to predefine the questions and the possible results. Those options you choose on boot-up are then incorporated into another batch file called *AE.BAT* which is then executed by AUTOXQT. It's a somewhat convoluted solution, but it does work. The documentation is buried inside a BASIC program, and one suggestion would be that the author produce a conventional document file to accompany the program.

AUTOXQT is a great idea if you like different configurations when you boot, and if you don't mind being quizzed by your computer every time you boot.

BACKSTAT

David J. McLaughlin
Public Domain

BACKSTAT is a utility that reports all the files on a given disk that have not been backed up using the DOS backup command or by some other utility that sets the archive bit of a file. This program uses the status of that archive bit to tell which ones to report. To run the program you type the following at the DOS command line:

```
A>BACKSTAT
```

The program will then list those files that have not been backed up since they were modified. It will include files from all directories on the disk. If you have the ANSI.SYS driver installed in your *CONFIG.SYS* file, the listing is presented in color, making it more appealing. Without the driver, you can see the listing, and also all the escape code sequences intermixed in the listing. This makes the listing difficult to read. Therefore, ANSI is recommended. The program is easy to run, and provides a meaningful report.

BAKER'S DOZEN

ButtonWare, Inc.
P.O. Box 96058
Bellevue, WA 98009-4469
(206) 454-0479   (800) JBUTTON (order line)
Shareware—$59.95 (with quantity discounts available)

Review reprinted with permission from PDN Newsletter

BAKER'S DOZEN is a collection of fourteen utilities (I know, there's only supposed to be thirteen) that perform some very nice functions extremely well. One may not need each of the programs included but I'm sure most of them would prove to be of use to the majority of computer users.

Starting BAKER'S DOZEN is easy enough. Simply type BAKERS12 or DOZEN and you're presented with a complete menu of all available programs. Each program can also be run separately and need not be run as part of the grouping. I will list below each function that's available and highlight any special features I might have noticed.

328

BTTNCALC is a mini (one page) spreadsheet with impressive flexibility. At first glance I expected it to have limited calculating ability, but the list of functions it can perform is far too long to list here and includes standard math as well as and/or/not logic, if/then/else decisions, a full array of trigonometric functions, business related averaging, counts, maximums, minimums, standard deviations, sums, net present values, and a whole bunch of others. There are also date and time functions as well as special functions for random values, selections and cosines, sines, and tangents.

DISKUTIL will look familiar to those who may have worked with Norton Utilities. DISKUTIL has some basic features such as providing disk and file information but it's two major functions involve file handling.

The feature most users would find helpful is it's ability to restore a deleted file. There's no worse feeling than discovering you've deleted a valuable file, maybe one you've invested hours or days building. With DISKUTIL you simply highlight the DISK UTILITY on the menu or invoke DISKUTIL at the DOS prompt. From there you are prompted which key to tap to restore a lost file and DISKUTIL takes you into your disk's File Allocation Table (FAT) where your directory is stored. Simply <TAB> down to the name of the file that's been lost and replacing the first letter of the file name restores the file to the directory. I am sure that there are many people who do not know that DOS does not erase the entire file when the listing is deleted from the directory. What happens is that the first letter of the file name is removed and this tells DOS it can now use that area of the disk to store new data. It's for this reason that if you ever accidently remove a file DO NOT WRITE NEW DATA TO THAT DISK BEFORE TRYING TO RECOVER A FILE. In fact, in the case of a total disaster it's even possible to rebuild your entire File Allocation Table but this is not the way most would choose to spend a free evening. It's far easier to keep backups of important files.

The second valuable feature of DISKUTIL is it's ability to go into a file, locate a string of dates (text or hexadecimal numbers) and make changes. For those who don't appreciate the use this serves, someone familiar with the inner workings of a program might know that a certain set of commands tell the program to perform a certain function. This function may be in conflict with other things going on with the computer. This could be as minor as screen color or may involve a major function in the program. With DISKUTIL one can seek out the location of the desired set of commands and change them. This is not recommended for those new to computing but someone with even moderate experience might find this useful.

CALENDAR is an on-demand calendar with several user-defined options. If desired, it can be loaded into memory and called via a "hot key." Those who have color monitors can set their own colors and special notes can be added as a reminder of special events.

LOCATE does just what the name implies. It can perform a task as simple as finding a single file or it can search files to find specified text. If desired, it can even list the entire line of text that contains the specified text. LOCATE prompts the user for all the needed information and there is no necessity to recall complex parameters.

GKEY provides keyboard information useful to those who write programs. First, there are two tables available to provide both decimal and hexadecimal values for specific letters. In its direct mode GKEY will return the appropriate scan codes for specific keys.

P90 or PRINT 90 rotates text and prints it at a 90 degree angle. This can be especially useful for long spreadsheets and is often referred to as "sideways" printing. The documentation states that P90 may have some problems with non-Epson compatible printers.

FILECOMP compares two ASCII or straight text files and lists variations in content or line numbers. Those who program would probably be the ones who take advantage of this. Programmers don't like to let it out, but sometimes they can get versions mixed up or forget to make a note on something they did in an earlier version. They can then compare the two files and pinpoint the differences that may or may not exist.

PC SORT sorts files containing up to four fields in ascending or descending order. Case sensitivity (UPPER and lower case letters) can also be activated.

PRN FILE does the very useful task of redirecting printer output to a disk file. Some application programs will create very nice printed reports but do not allow these reports to be saved to a disk file in the same format. With this utility you can designate the file name to be saved and then proceed with the normal printing operation of your application program. You will then notice that nothing happens on your printer but, instead, your drives will indicate a lot of disk activity. When the operation is complete you can check the file with any word processor or text editor and you will see the disk file is now identical to what you previously had on paper.

RDIR can be very useful but it can also be very dangerous. RDIR removes a directory or subdirectory along with any files contained in that subdirectory. I'm of the belief that individuals tend to leave subdirectories alone after they're created, and deleting entire subdirectories isn't that common of a practice unless one is doing some major housekeeping. A powerful utility such as this could cause some real havoc especially for those who keep a lot of important information on their hard disk. RDIR requires a path statement (C:\DBASE\FILES) and if not found, works on the currently logged directory. A typo or some good ol' fashioned fuzzy thinking could cause the wrong directory to be removed. RDIR does query to ensure it's removing the right directory but it's still too easy to hit return before realizing you just messed up.

After testing RDIR I called up DISKUTIL to see if it could restore a deleted subdirectory. It had no problem locating the deleted subdirectory but it informed me I had to manually restore this in the File Allocation Table followed by the location where the correction needed to be made. Even though I regard myself as a fairly experienced computer user I get a little nervous about doing work in my File Allocation Table. That's where all the directory and file information is stored and any major errors in there could cause a lot of problems with my hard disk with the worst case solution being the dreaded.FORMAT. RDIR does everything it promises but users might want to regard this with proper caution just because it works so well.

SET SCRN is used to set screen colors. Typing one of three possible keys will adjust text, background or border colors.

SNAPSHOT prints whatever is on your screen to a disk file. SNAPSHOT works only with text oriented screens and will not capture graphic images. This program remains memory resident and the screen is not captured until you press the designated "hot key."

SWCOM12 switches between COM1 and COM2 serial ports for those who operate with two serial boards.

SWLPT12 switches between LPT1 and LPT2 for those with two different parallel printers.

BAKER'S DOZEN maintains the quality and dependability customarily found in all BUTTONWARE products. All programs work as promised and, in many cases, offer more than expected.

—Tim Mullen

BATTIMER

Curtis Harper
LAKELAND RBBS-PC
Benton, KY
Modem # (502) 527-7617
Public Domain

Battimer is a simple program, but some of you may find it useful. It allows you to break out of your Autoexec.bat before it completes. You can press Control-C to break out of any batch file, but sometimes you have to be pretty fast with the keys. Battimer places a short delay into the batch file. With the addition of some supplemental code, you can create a batch file that will quit at a particular point if a key is pressed during execution. Curtis wrote it to allow him to reboot and, if necessary, prevent the loading of his RBBS program. Others may find uses for this program in other kinds of batch files. Though no immediate uses come to mind, this seems like the kind of product that someone will find a great use for. Therefore, we've included it here.

BIBLEV.COM

Jim Morris
Public Domain

This program will display a different verse from the Bible each day, or randomize the verses in its listing. You can add verses to the BIBLEV.DAY file using an ASCII text editor.

What is interesting about this program is that you could also use it to display any other message on a particular day. How useful this facility would be, I don't know, but the program works well, and could display memos or other parables as well as Bible phrases. You might even have it display the sayings of Buddha or any other dogma of interest. If you run a sales force, you might have it display motivational statements. The sky's the limit!

BOOTDUMP ver. 1.0

Neil K. Lauver

BOOTDUMP is a program that reads the boot record parameters of a disk and displays the parameters on the screen in a human-readable format. The program is useful for those interested in knowing the details of the boot record, and how they are stored. This program can also be used for diagnosing problems with a hard disk or diskette that is returning errors.

To run the program you type the following at the DOS command line:

```
A>BOOTDUMP
```

The program then gives a verbose listing of the values found in the boot record. This program can be used by anyone. Even novices who are curious about the inner workings of their machine should enjoy this program.

CATS22

William C. Parke
1820 S Street NW
Washington, DC 20009
(202) 667-4094

program originally written for:

> CHUG (Capital Heath User's Group)
> P.O. Box 16406
> Arlington, VA 22215-1406

If you keep a lot of files on floppy disks, chances are you'd like to catalog them so you could find files quickly. CATS is an excellent utility for doing just that. There are a lot of disk-catalog programs, and we have not done justice to our search for good ones, but this one works very efficiently and quickly, especially if you have a lot of disks to catalog.

You can run CATS with several command-line options, including one that will automatically create sequential numbered volume labels for your disks. It only takes CATS a matter of seconds to read and record the information from a disk to its ASCII file catalog. You can use CATS with different files as well, so if you keep more than one list of floppies, you can catalog them separately.

For people who would like to use CATS with a database, you can force the catalog file to a comma-delineated format useable by most database programs.

A companion file, SORTS, is available to sort the resulting directory listing several ways, though it didn't come with our file, CATS22.ARC.

```
LIST      1              07-11-88 01:28 ♦ CATS.DIR
LILMENU   ARC      88320 88/04-09 17:23 PD1000    \.........................
MS40C     ARC      59648 88/04-09 17:35 PD1000    \.........................
LUCIFER   ARC     101376 88/04-09 17:53 PD1000    \.........................
FASTLIST  ARC      18560 88/04-09 17:57 PD1000    \.........................
DELOUSE   ARC      19584 88/04-09 18:01 PD1000    \.........................
PD1000    V              88/04-20 16:53 PD1000    \.........................
FD        EXE      11264 88/06-22 13:21 PD1000    \.........................
HAIKU     ARC      10477 88/07-04 07:23 PD1000    \.........................
BABYNAME  BAS       2560 88/07-04 07:23 PD1000    \.........................
LIST62A   ARC      26752 88/07-04 07:24 PD1000    \.........................
REBOUND   EXE       1920 88/07-04 07:24 PD1000    \.........................
                  16384 88/07-11 01:21 PD1000    \ <- Free Space...........
PKX-V240  ARC      50048 88/06-22 12:29 PD1001    \.........................
R&R       ARC      24320 88/06-22 13:19 PD1001    \.........................
SQUYNCH   ARC     124288 88/06-22 12:52 PD1001    \.........................
NIOSA     ARC     117760 88/06-22 13:13 PD1001    \.........................
GSETUP    EXE      27716 87/07-19 17:05 PD1001    \.........................
PD1001    V              88/06-24 14:21 PD1001    \.........................
                  16384 88/07-11 01:22 PD1001    \ <- Free Space...........
BATTIMER  ARC      34608 88/06-23 19:20 PD1002    \.........................
EGATREK   ARC     142336 88/06-23 20:42 PD1002    \.........................
LEARN-C   ARC     119936 88/06-23 21:16 PD1002    \.........................
PARAPASS  ARC       9472 88/06-23 19:08 PD1002    \.........................
Command▶-  *** Top of file ***        Options: h8kMpswTalj Keys: X=exit ?=Help
```

The standard format for the catalog file (which can be altered by expert computer users) shows the file name, size, data and time, and the volume it is on. A section is left for optional comments which can be added by using a text editor. In addition, the free space remaining on each volume is displayed, allowing you to see how much room might remain on your disks.

I recommend this program for big jobs—I was able to catalog 23 disks in less than five minutes—RDM

CBIN ver. 2.0

Steve Stern
Public Domain

CBIN is a public-domain utility program which compares two files of any type and reports any differences between the files, as well as where in the files the discrepancy occurred. To use the program, you type the following at the DOS command line:

```
A:>CBIN [filename1] [filename2] [option]
```

Filename1 and *filename2* are the two files to be compared. The option allows you to set the maximum number of comparison errors the program finds before terminating. The program can be useful on a hard disk. For example, suppose you are working in a subdirectory. You find a program called *LIST.COM* and you wonder if its the same version you have in your root directory. You have two choices. Either you can run the program to find out the version number, or you can use the CBIN program to compare the two files.

CDISK ver. 1.1

Graham Systems
238 Germonds Rd.
West Nyack, NY 10994
Shareware—$25

CDISK is a memory resident disk access monitor. Using pop-up menus, you can write protect or enable any disk, make the computer think that the disk drive door is open or closed on any disk, display a disk's status, and view the disk statistics of any disk in the system. These statistics include the number of reads, writes, verifies, formats, errors, and the average speed of the drive. And, since the program is memory resident, this information can be called up at any time. To run the program, you type CDISK at the DOS command line. The program then installs itself permanently in memory. This version of the program does not handle RAM disks very well, nor does it track what drives are where and of what type. The author does promise that in future releases of the program these features will be addressed. This program has a lot of flair and power compared to DPROTECT which is reviewed later. This program is recommended over DPROTECT because it offers more flexibility and features. However, both are good programs and get the job done. Its a matter of choice as to which one has the features you need at that particular moment.

CDTO

Ward Christensen
CompuServe 76703,302
Public Domain

CDTO is a combination of a file search program and a directory changer all in one. If you type in CDTO and a filename, the program searches for a matching name and, when if finds one, changes to the directory where that file resides. You can use wildcards as well, and CDTO will stop on each file found and ask you if that is the one you want. You can answer yes or no at that point. Unfortunately,

CDTO does not show the full path of the files it finds, so, in the case of multiple versions of the same file, you don't know which is which.

When you enter a directory name with CDTO, it moves to the directory that contains that directory. All in all, this is a very good program, especially if you know the name of a file in another directory. It can save several keystrokes.

Using the version of CDTO that we had, the program had a problem when it couldn't find the search file. It wouldn't stop searching, and rebooting was the only option. The documentation indicates that it should stop, leaving you in the root directory, but the version we had did not. There may be more than one version available. In any case, we use it frequently when changing directories where we know the program exists.

CED
Christopher J. Dunford
Public Domain

CED stands for *Command ED*itor, and it does include DOS command stacking like DOS-Edit (elsewhere in this chapter). But *CED* adds some further modifications. In addition to the command stack and command editing features, CED allows you to define substitutions for commands (called aliases). For instance, you can redefine a common command like *DIR* to *D*. Thus, typing *D* *.EXE* would create a directory of all *EXE* files in the current directory.

CED also allows automatic recall of parameters. If you regularly use a command like *EDLIN MYBAT.BAT*, you can first create an alias for *EDLIN*, then use the *PCALL* feature of CED to automatically include the parameter. The syntax would be:

```
CED  SYN E EDLIN
CED PCALL E
```

E is the alias for *EDLIN*.

Now issue the command *E MYBAT.BAT*. *EDLIN* will be run, and the *MYBAT.BAT* file opened. When you finish working with *EDLIN*, you may issue other DOS commands, but the next time you want to use *EDLIN* to process the *MYBAT.BAT* file, all you need to do is type E. The parameter is remembered and inserted automatically. To defeat the *PCALL* function, you simply enter a space after the command (i.e. "E " instead of "E").

CED has several other features, including a way for programmers to define their own DOS resident commands. There are also ways to configure and pre-configure CED, ways to chain CED commands, and ways to use CED from within some applications.

When loaded, CED becomes entirely memory resident, so it isn't dependent on disk drives, directories, etc. It simply becomes a part of DOS.

CED is a fairly complex product, although some of its aspects are simple. Most of what it can do could be simulated through batch files and other utilities, but CED is by far the most interesting and powerful of this type of utility that we have seen.

C-Format ver. 2.1

Chris Patterson
3211 South 58 Street
Omaha, NE 68106-3711
Shareware—requests $10

C-Format is a high speed disk formatting program that can be used as an alternative to the DOS format command. The program is capable of formatting double-sided diskettes only. This program cannot format the AT style 1.2 megabyte floppies; however, the author does promise that in future additions of his program all of these capabilities will exist. It can format a 360k floppy disk in a 1.2 megabyte floppy drive. To run the program, you type the following at the DOS command line:

```
A:>CFORMAT [options]
```

The options tell the program which drive(s) to process, and whether the disk should be verified after the format process. You can also choose continuous formatting which will not stop until a key is pressed. This program also has options that will allow it to be used from within batch files without user interaction. The program works well, and with the enhancements the author promises, this will be a handy program to have when you need to format a floppy disk on the fly and don't have the time to wait for DOS. This program should in no way be used as a complete replacement of DOS, since it does not contain all of the DOS format features.

CHANGE

A simple program, CHANGE.EXE will allow you to change the foreground and background colors used on your DOS screen (assuming you use a color monitor). This program is very simple to use. The command line is simply:

```
CHANGE <foreground> <background>
```

A list of colors is available in the .DOC file. Also, the C source code is included in the ARC file. I like 11 for foreground and 4 for background.

CHGPATH

Scott Mason
4050 Jay Em Circle
Ellicott City, MD 21043
Public Domain but with restrictions on use for profit

CHGPATH will add a new path specification to the PATH end of the path statement, or delete any designated PATH statement. It works from a simple command, and is similar to other programs. In fact, in some ways, this program is like a combination of APATH and DPATH. It is missing the feature that allows you to place a new path spec at any point in the PATH statement (which NEWPATH does), though the author promises that feature in a later version.

CHKDIR

Public Domain

CHKDIR performs the same function on a directory as *CHKDSK* performs on a disk. A typical readout looks as follows:

```
Report on all files for c:\

21178368 bytes total disk space
  1940219 bytes in 199 files
  1902895 bytes in 170 user files
     37324 bytes in 2 hidden or system files
           0 bytes in 27 subdirectories
  2572288 bytes available on disk
```

```
655360 bytes total memory
156544 bytes in use
498816 bytes free
```

CLEAN (unk. version)

Marty Smith
Public Domain

CLEAN is a program to be used with diskette cleaning kits, like those from 3M and Verbatim. It provides a random read across different tracks of the cleaning paper diskette, while at the same time ignoring the DOS read errors. The author claims that his program makes full use of the cleaning surface of the diskette cleaner rather than the 2.5 percent that is normally used. More head movement on the cleaning surface means that the drive head is more effectively cleaned. The program automatically stops the cleaning process after 30 seconds (the amount of time recommended by the cleaning kit manufacturers). The program will work on all drive types, including single-sided and quad density-disks. Of course, it does not work on a hard disk! However, should you accidently run the program on a hard disk, it will not ruin it, since the program only reads and does not write information.

This program may useful for people who use diskette cleaning kits.

Convert

George Fontaine
Public Domain

Though there may be other programs called Convert, this one will convert columnar data into delineated data and back again. Different delineators can be specified to meet different formats. The program was primarily written to help those who want to use Quicksort but have mostly delineated data. Since Quicksort works with columnar data, this program allows conversion to columns, sorting, then conversion back to delineated data. It's handy for changing delineated data to meet formats for other programs (like going from some databases to some spreadsheets or word processors).

Copytree—CT.EXE and ST.EXE

Tridium, Inc.
39 Bowery, Box 979
New York, NY 10002
Shareware—$10

CT.EXE

You can use CT.EXE to copy or move files from a directory/subdirectory to another. You can specify certain options that allow all files to be grouped in one directory, or files and subdirectories to be copied from the source. In addition, you can copy or move only new files (those not already in the target[s]), or update files only if the source files are newer than files in the destination directories. Another option completely wipes out the source files after copying. These cannot be unerased.

ST.EXE

ST.EXE shows the size of a group of files in a directory or directory tree. You can specify files with wildcards (i.e. *.COM) or use a *NOT* operator to eliminate specific files. Various other options make this a useful utility if you are trying to determine how much space a certain group of files uses.

CWEEP 2.31a

Gary M. Berg   or   C/O Chemineer Inc.
3707 Silver Oak St.   P.O. Box 1123
Dayton, OH 45424   Dayton, OH 45401

Compuserve 70106,1624
Public Domain

CWEEP is the CP/M utility SWEEP for DOS machines. It is basically a file utility that lists each file in the designated directory one at a time. You can perform various operations on each file as it is listed, including tagging, viewing, hex dumping, renaming, mass copying, wildcard tagging, modify attributes, calculate CRC, and much more. Most users will probably prefer some of the other file utilities and shells, but CWEEP contains some options not normally encountered in the other programs, especially useful for advanced users.

```
                    CWEEP version 2.31a as of 17-Jan-88
              Copyright (C) 1984-87 by: Gary M. Berg/Chemineer Inc.

   sp/cr Advance to next file          <O>  Output list (-+ only)
    [A]  Again tag '#' files (-+)       [P]  Protected mass copy
    [B]  Back up one file               <Q>  Query files (-+ only)
    [C]  Copy file to drive (-)         [R]  Rename a file
    [D]  Delete a file                  [S]  Sort directory
    [E]  Erase (un)tagged files         [T]  Tag a file
    [F]  Free space on a drive          [U]  Untag a file
    [H]  Hexadecimal display (-+~)      [V]  View a file (-+~)
    [I]  Inquire file size/time (-+)    [W]  Wildcard file tag (-+)
    [J]  Jump to a named entry          [X]  Exit program
    [L]  Log new drive/filename (-+)    [Y]  Modify attributes (-+)
    [M]  Mass copy tagged files         [Z]  Change subdirectory(-)
    [N]  Calculate CRC (-+)             [!]  Goto DOS
 [?],[/]Print this message             [=]  Goto settings menu

  [-?], [+?] other help messages, [@] for printer, [~] for search

     4 files, using 150263 bytes (149K)  -- 2912256 bytes free (2844K)
       Volume label: <OS2>           Path = 'C:\TEMP\'

  2. C:CWEEP   .CIS 18-Jan-1988     1K :[-]
```

DBACK

Eric Gans
French Dept. UCLA
Los Angeles, CA 90024
Public Domain

DBACK.COM will make a copy of the FAT and root directory of a hard disk onto another device and restore it if needed. This is a good way to protect yourself from those unforeseen disasters that sometimes befall our equipment since, often, restoring the FAT will restore what seems to be a destroyed disk drive. A useful insurance policy that is well worth getting. However, it shouldn't be used to replace proper backups of your data.

DELBUT

Scott Pakin
Public Domain

DELBUT allows deletion of all files from a directory or disk, with the exception of specific files named in the command. For instance, the command:

```
DELBUT *.DOC
```

would delete all files except those ending in *.DOC*.

DGM.COM

Bob Jack
Public Domain

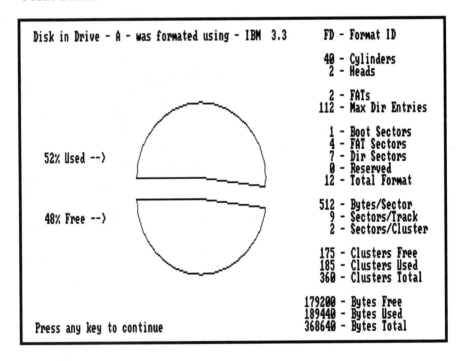

```
Disk in Drive - A - was formated using - IBM  3.3     FD - Format ID

                                                      40 - Cylinders
                                                       2 - Heads

                                                       2 - FATs
                                                     112 - Max Dir Entries

                                                       1 - Boot Sectors
                                                       4 - FAT Sectors
  52% Used -->                                         7 - Dir Sectors
                                                       0 - Reserved
                                                      12 - Total Format

                                                     512 - Bytes/Sector
  48% Free -->                                         9 - Sectors/Track
                                                       2 - Sectors/Cluster

                                                     175 - Clusters Free
                                                     185 - Clusters Used
                                                     360 - Clusters Total

                                                  179200 - Bytes Free
                                                  189440 - Bytes Used
  Press any key to continue                       368640 - Bytes Total
```

This nifty little program (4K) graphically displays the contents of a disk. You type DGM, and a menu of disk drives (A-H) is displayed. Pick a valid drive, and the program then asks if you want a pie chart or a bar chart. Choose the type of chart you want, and you will see a high resolution screen with a chart of disk space used, as well as information about the contents of the disk—boot sectors, FATs, DOS version used to format, and more. This is an attractive and simple-to-use program that is worth having for the fun of it. We found it on Vernon Buerg's board listed as FANCYCHK.ARC.

Diags

Computerwise Consulting Services
P.O. Box 813
McLean, VA 22101
(703) 280-2809

"DIAGS is a tool for the advanced PC user, period."

So begins the on-disk manual for this advanced utility. DIAG.EXE is a program that helps you perform various serial, parallel, and video diagnostics on your PC. It is very technical, but may be very useful for people who wish to examine the operations of these I/O functions.

To quote from the manual again:

"As it now stands, DIAGS is a very powerful facility for:
1) Testing all sorts of asynch communications lines
2) Testing printer handshaking and cable wiring
3) Examining an unknown system's DOS environment, including:
     a) Interrupt vectors
     b) Resident device handlers
4) Directly manipulating the 6845."

If any of that sounds useful to you, get DIAGS.

DIRNOTES

A nice PD file that will allow you to place comments on directory listings. DIRNOTES creates a .DAT file that keeps the comments. Then, whenever you want to see the notes you've entered, type DIRNOTES again. You edit the file descriptions on the screen, moving from one file to another. This is a very clever and potentially useful utility.

```
┌─────────────────────────────────────────────────────────────────────────┐
│                                                                           │
│     Directory of C:\TEST                                                  │
│                                                                           │
│  AFORMAT   BAT      87   7-08-88  10:07p  Format multiple drives          │
│  AFORMAT   DOC    3763   5-11-88   1:12a  Aformat docs                     │
│  APPNOTE   TXT    3695   6-01-88  12:00a                                   │
│  CDTO      COM     574  10-07-87  10:56p  search then move to dir          │
│  CDTO      DOC    1050  10-07-87  11:02p  CDTO docs                        │
│  CMOVE6    COM    9216   9-27-86   6:22a  ▆████████████████████████████    │
│  COPYTREE  DOC   15988   8-29-86  10:22a                                   │
│  CT        EXE   20264   8-29-86  10:48a                                   │
│  DIRN-TES  DAT    1863   7-12-88  11:51aU                                  │
│  DIRNOTES  COM    1704   5-19-87   8:07a                                   │
│  FILL      C     10368   2-15-87   1:27p                                   │
│  FILL      COM    7760   2-15-87   1:28p                                   │
│  FILL      DOC   21377   1-04-88   5:06p                                   │
│  FILL      PIF     369   1-04-88   5:12p                                   │
│  FILL1     DOC    4352  12-10-86   7:38a                                   │
│  FILL1     EXE   43301   1-04-88   3:12p                                   │
│  FILL1     PIF     369   1-04-88   5:12p                                   │
│  FORM-N    BAT       8   5-10-88   3:27p                                   │
│  IL        COM   27240  10-04-87   2:56p                                   │
│  IL        DOC   22136   6-27-88   2:24p                                   │
│  INFO      DOC    2674   6-27-87   2:42p                                   │
│                                                                           │
│           23 Files                        Press Esc to exit               │
│                                                                           │
└─────────────────────────────────────────────────────────────────────────┘
```

Do

Public Domain
Maurizio Ammannato

Do is a simple utility that allows you to perform more than one DOS command at a time. You enter commands in the form:

```
DO DOS cmd; DOS cmd; DOS cmd...
```

Each DOS command is executed in order. If you have ever wished you could do several things at once in DOS, this product may be the answer. For instance, suppose you wanted to erase a file and then run a batch file. You could type the commands one at a time, but you could as easily use Do to accomplish the same effect. You might also wish to print several files to your printer in LPT1. You could do so using a format like the following:

```
DO >lpt1: type doc1.txt; type manual.txt; type listing.txt
```

344

Dpath 3.0

James A. McGreggor, Jr.
Public Domain

Dpath adds a feature to DOS that many think should have been there all along. It allows DOS to access data files along a path the way it currently does with executable files. This capability is necessary when using programs that have overlay or special data files which won't ordinarily be recognized by DOS. WordStar and dBASE are examples of programs that have this problem.

Dpath has another, more problematical use. McGreggor warns strongly against using this feature unless you know what you're doing. The feature in question also allows writing data to data files in other directories. This is not necessary for programs that already allow such abilities, but there are programs that don't allow such writing across directories. However, because of the nature of the search that Dpath performs, there can be complications. Fortunately, you can't accidentally invoke that feature since it requires a specific command line switch. But if you are planning to try it, read the warnings in the Dpath documentation carefully. This program is recommended for people who understand its use and who need it.

DPROTECT ver. 1.0

GEE WIZ Software Company
Public Domain

DPROTECT is a memory resident utility that write protects hard disks and diskettes. Once the program has run, any attempt to modify or write data to a disk will invoke the program. It then prints an error message, and waits for the user to hit any key. The system then resets itself.

The program is a good utility to use when you are testing unknown public-domain programs that could be Trojan horses (see Chapter 3). The program does take a rather drastic approach when it reaches an error condition—specifically, the automatic reset of the entire system. But considering the alternative of having your disk formatted accidently by someone or some misbehaved program, it's only a minor inconvenience.

DRVAVAIL
Lewis Paper
Public Domain

This clever program is designed to work within batch files and return a specific error code after testing if a disk drive is available. For instance, you could write a batch file to automatically copy a lot of files to floppy disks (perhaps using one of the FILL programs mentioned in this chapter). You could use DRVAVAIL to check that a disk is in the floppy drive before continuing. If a disk is not in the drive, you could display a message to the user that requests a disk. This is a simple, but useful program.

EFFIC (unk. version)
TurboPower Software
Public Brand Software

EFFIC is a storage efficiency utility that analyzes how files are stored on either a hard or floppy disk. EFFIC analyzes each file and determines the number of clusters used and the number of non-contiguous clusters. With this information, the program is able to determine what the read/write performance will be for a particular file. For example, a file whose clusters are all contiguous, will have a read/write efficiency of 100 percent. The program is run from the DOS command line by typing:

```
A:>EFFIC [options]
```

The options give the program the flexibility to search for files only in a specific sub-directory, search the whole disk, or display only those files which are non-contiguous.

Though this program is interesting to run, it is not very useful since it does nothing to correct the non-contiguous file problem. Because of this, it is not recommended as an every-day utility. It might be used as a periodic check of disk status, to be followed using a remedial program (like Mace Utilities, for instance) if necessary.

ENVED11

Dennis L. Raney
2612 Castle Drive
Blue Springs, MO 64015
GEnie D.L.RANEY
Shareware donations requested

ENVED stands for Environment Editor, and this handy utility helps you edit the contents of the PC environment variables. Normally, you use the SET command to add or change environment variables, but with ENVED, you can work on a full-screen editor complete with WordStar like commands. It makes modifying the environment variables painless.

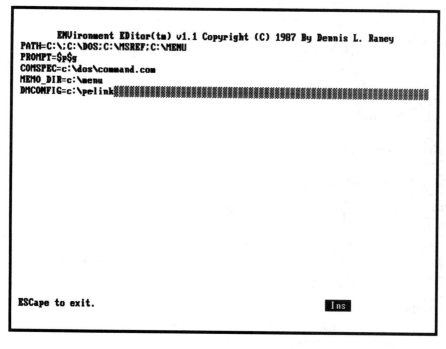

This program, along with NEWPATH (or one of the other PATH modifying programs) is a must on an advanced user's system.

Extended Batch Language

Seaware Corp.
Shareware—$49

If you've ever wanted to control DOS through batch files, but found the interface to be too limited, you'll want to take a look at Extended Batch Language. This is the product that you've been looking for.

The Extended Batch Language (EBL) is a powerful addition to the common DOS batch file language. It brings a lot of processing power to the humble batch file and yet works in the same general format. EBL is full of features and command structures—so full, in fact, that the printed manual you receive with registration is actually a paperbound book full of descriptions and examples of how to use the product.

Extended Batch Language
Seaware Corp.
P.O. Box 1656
Delray Beach, FL 33444
(305) 392-2046

Shareware: $49

Category: Utilities

Recommended use: Adding power and function to DOS batch files

Major Pros: Increased use of variables; greater command set; user input during batch execution; sophisticated parsing and string handling.; stack input for DOS and applications

Major Cons: This is a product for those who want to unleash power in batch files; those who already find batch files enough or more than enough will, no doubt, find this program too much

Sources: Popular BBSs and commercial services, or directly from the author

---

This is a pretty complex product that can be used for simple interactive batch files, for complete menuing systems, or even for complex conditional programs that control how applications will interact with DOS. There are a lot of Basic-like commands that can be used along with DOS commands, and there is greatly improved handling of variables including the ability to declare variables during a script and even accept input from the user during execution of a script. Math functions are also enhanced, including floating point math as an option.

There are also string and color handling commands, various ways to query and to display information, as well as looping, calling other files, and the ability to stack information for later retrieval during DOS or application execution.

EBL works by loading into memory whenever one of its specific commands is issued (although there are ways to force the program to remain in memory during phases of a script). After normal execution of an EBL command, most of the program is released from memory (although a small amount of code remains). The system works quickly and can be made efficient by using careful programming techniques. There are a few potential incompatibilities, but overall, EBL performs many necessary services missing from DOS. If you want to tinker with DOS batch files at a level you never before thought possible, you will want to try EBL. The Shareware version is missing some features, but it has enough to work effectively. We recommend, as usual, that you register the product if you find it useful.

FAKEY

System Enhancement Associates
Public Domain

An improved version of Key-Fake (one of PC Magazine's utilities), Fakey is a very clever program that you can use to initialize an application from within a batch file. For instance, suppose you have a series of batch files designed to load Lotus 1-2-3, but you want the batch file to load different worksheets. Using Fakey and batch variables, you can issue the commands through the batch file that will initialize Lotus1-2-3, and then issue Lotus commands that retrieve the worksheet you specify.

Fakey is available in the public domain. This version includes several new features, including shortcuts for various common commands (like \r for a carriage return), use of hexadecimal numbers, and various mnemonics for common DOS commands. In addition, any key can be represented easily using special characters. Function keys can be represented directly as *Fn* (where *n* is the function key number). *Sn* would represent a Shifted function key *(Cn* and *An*—Ctrl and Alt function keys respectively).

Other special commands include *TOSS* (to clear out all pending keystrokes), *WAIT* *<n>* to pause *<n>* seconds, and *BOOT*, to initiate a warm boot of the system as if the user had typed *Ctrl-Alt-Del*. The documentation accompanying FAKEY includes a full list of ASCII hexadecimal equivalents.

Recommended for advanced users.

Fansi-Console Vers. 2.00i

Hersey Micro Consulting, Inc.
Contact Hersey Micro for registration information, see note below.

Fansi-Console is an amazing program that does a lot of things. First of all, it's a device driver. This means that it must be placed in the *CONFIG.SYS* file and the computer rebooted before it becomes effective. It is a replacement for the *ANSI.SYS* driver that you may already have installed, but it does much more than *ANSI.SYS*. One of the first things you'll notice is the way it speeds up screen handling. Typing a file with the *TYPE* command or using *DIR* on a long listing will show you one of the program's key features.

But screen speedup is only a part of what this program can do for you. It can also blank the screen, allow you to modify DOS colors, create keyboard macros, expand the type-ahead key buffer, remap keyboard, scroll and pause with one key (with retrieval of previously scrolled lines), use one-key typing, control screen snow and flicker, and even force non-color programs into using default DOS colors.

Of particular use to handicapped computer users is the one-key typing option. One-key typing makes shifted keys like the Shift, Alt, and Control keys lock whenever they are pressed (the way the Caps Lock key does now). Pressing the Shift key locks shift on until the key is pressed again. This allows handicapped users to perform two-key operations with one key.

Fansi-Console is fairly technical and involves making some decisions. Installation is simple enough, but the additional features require that you understand something about your computer, its video card, and your monitor. This is not really a good program for computer novices. But the manual isn't lacking. It is excellent, clear, and very detailed; so detailed that only an abridged version is distributed with the Shareware (they like to call it Fairware) version of Fansi-Console—and it is over 300K unsqueezed.

Nevertheless, this program is capable of enhancing DOS to such a degree that it is worth doing some homework. The reading necessary is interesting to anyone curious about his or her computer's internal workings. It would be rough going for the casual user who doesn't want to think about the hardware. For such people, we recommend that you find someone else to study Fansi-Console and install it for you.

Many of the options are difficult to explain in a short space, and are only required for specific hardware setups. Others, like the screen blanking, the scrollback memory, the macro memory allocation, etc., have user definable parameters. For instance, setting the screen blanking to a value of 5000, sets the blanking interval to about 5 minutes. Setting scroll recall to 100 will allow retrieval of up to 100 lines of scrolled information (but at a cost of about 16K of read/write memory). Fortunately, the scroll recall will use expanded memory if available.

The major options must be included in the *CONFIG.SYS* file. A possible line would read:

```
FCONSOLE.DEV /C=1/H=0/L=1/M=1024/R=50/S=5000/W=1
```

This line in the *CONFIG.SYS* would load Fansi-Console with Color What You Can, fast Horizontal Delay, one key Scroll Lock on, 1K macro memory reserved, 50 lines of scroll recall, 5 minute screen blanking, and faster data movement (in this case for the AT).

Some lines modify the appearance of DOS. For instance, the following line in an *AUTOEXEC.BAT* (or other *BAT* file) uses *ANSI X3.64* commands to display the drive prompt in light blue and DOS text in green:

```
PROMPT $e\$e[2;32;40m$e[J$e[1;36m$n$g$e[2;32m
```

Fansi-Console is a fine program despite its technical nature. There are two potential drawbacks to the program. First, it can't be all things to all people—it may not be compatible with all hardware/software combinations, and it may not operate at its best in all environments. The manual has an extensive list of compatible hardware and software as well as another list of programs and equipment with problems.

The second drawback has to do with the amount of environment space required by the *FCONSOLE.DEV* driver when placed in the *CONFIG.SYS*. In our test configuration (using several memory options), Fansi-Console added about 40K to our DOS environment space. In some situations, this amount of space is worthwhile, but when memory is tight, you might want to think twice before implementing this program (simply use an alternate *CONFIG.SYS* and possibly *AUTOEXEC.BAT* for those times when you need more memory, and reboot).

Fansi-Console Vers. 2.00i
Hersey Micro Consulting, Inc.
P.O. Box 8276
Ann Arbor, MI 48107
(313) 994-3259 (voice)
(313) 994-3946 (BBS)

Fairware: $25 ($75 for manual and registration)

Category: DOS enhancement

System Requirements: IBM PC/XT/AT or compatible; DOS 2.0 or higher; uses 32K environment space plus 4K with EGA

Recommended Use: enhance DOS in many ways

Major Pros: speeds up screen handling; allows modifications to BIOS level operations; one-key typing and scroll pause; recall buffer; screen blanking

Major Cons: requires some technical knowledge or dedicated manual reading; uses 32K+ environment space (bad for systems with limited RAM)

Sources: popular BBSs and commercial services, or directly from the author

---

Fansi-Console comes with a complement of associated files. These files range from keyboard remapping programs to utilities that check the kind of monitor and graphics card you have (to see if they produce snow or not). In all, the Fansi-Console package is a sophisticated add-on to DOS, and one that can be used to produce a faster and more useful environment.

Note on Fansi-Console: As of version 3.00, Fansi-Console is no longer considered a Shareware product. The new version has many improvements, and will be sold only with a printed manual. For more information, or to upgrade from the Shareware version, contact Hersey Micro.

FDATE unk. version

Public Domain

FDATE allows the setting or resetting of the date and time stamps of any file on your disk. To use the program you type the following at the DOS command line:

```
A:>FDATE [filename] [date] [time]
```

Filename is the name of the file you wish to modify. The date or time can be optional depending on your needs. If you wish only to modify the time, for example, just enter the new time. The date is optional in this case. The program will trap bad dates and times, but I recommend using normal care and common sense, since this is a program in the public domain.

This program is useful for the software developer who wants to keep track of his application versions by date and time. You may also be able to use this program to defeat copy protection on demo disks that use the date and time stamp to self-destruct.

FID

Bob Halsall
C/O Eastern 'C' Board
Suffern, NY
(914) 368-0658

The author requests that if you like the product, please send a donation of any size to:

The American Cancer Society
90 Park Avenue
New York, NY 10016

FID (File List Generator) is a must-have utility for people who regularly download files from bulletin-board systems. This program will compare the contents of a text file in the form of a typical BBS directory capture with the files in a specified directory Files that are in both lists are displayed, and the output can be routed to disk or printer. This is a great way to tell of you already have files that are on a BBS. The product works well, and has several optional switches that can be set on the command line. Very useful.

FILL.COM and FILL.EXE 2.0

It is rare when two programs perform almost the same function and also use the same name. And it is even more rare when they are both great programs. We found both programs on Vernon Buerg's board. FILL.COM was called FILLFLOP.ARC and FILL.EXE was called FILL20.ARC.

FILL.COM

Dave Rand
72 Longfellow St.
Thousand Oaks, CA 91360

FILL.COM is a simple, effective program that will take files from one or more directories and copy them to another disk (floppy or Bernoulli). The beauty of this program is that it will fill each disk to its maximum capacity, then prompt you for a new disk, if necessary. If you have ever needed to copy a lot of data from your hard disk to another disk, this program may be just what you have been looking for.

You can designate more than one directory "source," each with its own file specifications. For instance, to send all .COM files from the directory \FILES and also send all files from the directory \NEWFILES to drive A:, you would use the syntax:

```
FILL \FILES\*.COM \NEWFILES\*.* A:
```

Whenever the program ran out of space on the A: drive, it will prompt you for a new disk. This program works like a charm. It's small and simple. Can come in very handy.

FILL.EXE 2.0

Jean LaLonde
6667 de Normanville
Montreal, Quebec
Canada H2S-2B8
Compuserve 76606,671
BIX jlalonde
Shareware donation requested. For Logitech Modula-2 source code and libraries—
$25

FILLEXE is a complex program full of great features. Unlike FILL.COM, this program has many options that many users will find useful. Perhaps the greatest benefit over FILL.COM is that FILL.EXE will format a disk if it detects that it is not already formatted. This means that you don't have to worry how many disks you will need before you begin filling floppies. Unfortunately, you can't specify options for the FORMAT command, and you have to be ready to enter N to tell the format command you don't want to format another disk. Too bad FILL doesn't do that for you.

You can also designate more than one target drive, so you could alternate between different drives, further speeding up the copying process.

Other options allow you to define more than one disk drive as a source drive, multiple directories, and even special commands that allow greater selectivity in copying files. Among these options, an AND operator ("FILL \FILES*.COM+*.EXE" copies .COM and .EXE files from the \FILES directory); copy only files whose archive bit is ON; allow for confirmation of each directory and/or file; kill (erase) the source file after copying; log all copied files in a text file for later reference; turn off archive bit for successfully copied files; verify integrity of copied files, and many more.

Though FILL.EXE is a larger file than FILL.COM, its added features make it a much more powerful and versatile product. Which one you prefer is completely a matter of personal preference and specific needs. For really quick, simple copying, FILL.COM may be easier since FILL.EXE prompts you frequently to make choices from among its vast array. On the other hand, FILL.EXE does offer those choices.

Find ver. 1.1

StarSoft Systems
4844 King Edward
Montreal, Canada
Shareware—$20

Find is a Shareware utility designed to replace the *DOS FIND* command. It boasts some added features of the *DOS FIND* command that make it easy to use. With Find you can specify wild-card searches. Command line switches and syntax can be entered in any order. Features of the program include the ability to list all lines in files that do not match the pattern you are looking for, display only a count of the lines containing a pattern match, list relative line number along with the matching line, perform a case sensitive search, and report only when a match is found. You can even search for special characters. This program makes an excellent replacement for the *DOS FIND* command.

Finding Duplicate Files

DDUP

Jean LaLonde
6667 de Normanville
Montreal, Quebec, Canada H2S-2B8
Compuserve 76606,671, BIX jlalonde
Shareware donation requested. For Logitech Modula-2 source code, send $25.

DDUP will find duplicate files on one or more disks with the following options (set from the command line):

- /T (the default) finds twin files with identical name, size, and date-time.
- /N looks for files with identical names but different size or date-time.
- /S looks for files with identical size and date-time, but different names.

In addition, DDUP will find duplicates imbedded in ARC files (though you can exclude those files using the /E switch). Once the duplicates are found, you can delete one or more found files, rename files, compare files, or log filenames to a text file.

DELDUPE 2.2

Vernon D. Buerg

DELDUPE will compare files in two directories, optionally deleting files in one if duplicates are found. Various command line switches control the program. DELDUPE can display file names only, or it can delete older files if duplicates are found. You can also delete files with same names and dates, but different size; or same name, regardless of other parameters. Other options control the display and user prompting.

FD (Find Dupes)

Matt Leber
8851 SE 37th
Mercer Island, WA 98040
Shareware—$5

Sometimes, with today's high capacity hard disk drives, file management becomes an ever more difficult chore—like housework or dishes. One result of this is that you may end up with the same file on your disk in more than one place. FD is a simple, but useful utility that finds duplicate files on your disk. The version I received had no instructions with it, but I was able to figure out that you could send the output to screen, printer, or file. For instance, to send the output to a file, type

```
FD > filename.ext
```

If you have been using a hard disk for some time, and you have moved files around a lot, you may recover a lot of lost space using this program, making its five dollar registration fee more than worth it.

QD ver. 1.5

Claude Biron
103 W.23 Avenue
Vancouver B.C., Canada   V5Y 2H1
Shareware—donation appreciated

We found this file in an ARC file called KILLDUPE.ARC. Like DDUP, it is a Canadian import. This is the only one of the three programs listed here that contains a menu-style interface.

You enter the main command from the command line in the form:

```
QD <d [d]d>
```

where *d* is any drive letter, and *[d]* represents optional additional drives to search. The result is a neatly listed display (in color on a color monitor) that shows all duplicate files found as well as statistics on the disk, percent of duplicates and bytes they consume, etc. You can then store individual or all entries in a .LOG file, compare any two files, print information, or delete a disk file. You can't re-name any files within this program, however.

```
QDups V1.0 Duplicate File Finder Utility - Copywrite (C) Claude Biron 1986.
 — Path Name ——————————————————————————————————————————————

 C:\OS2

 ——— Tally ———     —————————— Multiple Occurrence List ————————
 Directories  47        Name          Size         Date       Time    Atrib.
 Total Files  1109
 Duplicates   66     —————————————————————————————————————————————————————
                       Use [↑↓] [Home] [End] [Pg Up] [Pg Dn] to Select
                       SUBST.EXE       21024 bytes  Feb 11,1988 12:00am ARCHIV
 ——— Drive C ———       SYS.COM          6193 bytes  Sep 16,1987 12:00am ARCHIV
 Size disk 33462272    SYS.COM         34858 bytes  Feb 11,1988 12:00am ARCHIV
 Bytes free 2719744    TREE.COM         3548 bytes  Sep 16,1987 12:00am ARCHIV
    % free 8.13%       TREE.COM        28928 bytes  Feb 11,1988 12:00am ARCHIV
                       UNARC.COM       11482 bytes  Dec 15,1986  0:00am ARCHIV
 ——— Disk Used ———     UNARC.COM       11482 bytes  Dec 15,1986  0:00am ARCHIV
 Bytes dups 1961984    UNARC.COM       11482 bytes  Dec 15,1986  0:00am ARCHIV
   % dups 5.86%        VDISK.SYS        3634 bytes  Sep 16,1987 12:00am ARCHIV
                       VDISK.SYS        4662 bytes  Feb 11,1988 12:00am ARCHIV
                       VERNLIST.ASC     1290 bytes  Jun 30,1988  2:59pm ARCHIV
   Press Shift + F1    VERNLIST.ASC     1290 bytes  Jun 30,1988  2:59pm ARCHIV
   for Help on Keys    XCOPY.EXE       11216 bytes  Sep 16,1987 12:00am ARCHIV
                       Pathname Displayed Top of Screen
 ————————————————————————————————————————————————————————————————
           Press <Esc> or <F10> to QUIT
```

QD is the most attractive and easy to use duplicate file finder/deleter that we've see so far, though DDUP is somewhat more powerful.

Free unk. version

Public Domain

Free is a public-domain utility that reports the amount of free space left on a floppy or hard disk. To use the program you type in *FREE* at the DOS command line, and, optionally the drive letter of the drive you wish to check. Free reports back how much space is free in bytes. Free is an excellent program, and saves a lot of time compared to *DOS DIR* or *CHKDSK* used only to check disk space.

Gravity

John Manning
P.O. Box 278
Auburn, KY 42206
Public Domain

For sheer goofiness, this one is pretty high on the list. It makes everything on your screen fall to the bottom in a heap. Just for fun.

GSETUP

Micro Consulting Associates
868 Ashford Ave. Suite 6B
San Juan, Puerto Rico 00907-1018
(809) 721-3778
Shareware—$15

GSETUP lets you set the CMOS parameters in an IBM AT or compatible without having to reboot with a special diskette. It seems to work on an IBM AT, but I would recommend caution when trying it on other computers. I tried it on a Compaq Deskpro 386, and it trashed the parameters and forced me to rerun Compaq's Setup program. If you want to reset memory, the clock or calendar, or any of the other options that are normally set from the Setup program, and you are using an IBM AT or very close compatible, try this program, but try it at your own risk. Where it works, it is very convenient. *Note: a new version of GSETUP was released at press time.*

HDTEST V3.13

Peter R. Fletcher
1515 West Montgomery Ave.
Rosemont, PA 19010

HDTEST and HDCHEK can help you test the state of your hard disk or floppy diskette. HDCHEK performs a simple, non-destructive test of the hard disk to determine its contents and to see if the HDTEST program will, in all likelihood, work. When you run HDTEST, you will perform a very comprehensive test of the surface of your hard disk, including read/write tests of every cluster on the disk (even those containing data). The test takes several hours (depending on disk size), and is not supposed to destroy any data. However, it is recommended that you back up your disks before running any test like this.

HDTEST claims to perform a much more comprehensive test than other commercial and Shareware products. It will lock out any bad clusters, but will attempt to relocate data that can be recovered.

This is not a program to be taken lightly, and probably is best used by people with some understanding of PCs and DOS. However, it can, potentially, help you prevent unexpected hard disk failures, and so it is worth considering. However, we have not tested this program extensively, and so cannot make recommendations regarding specific system compatibilities. If in doubt, call or write the author.

HOT-DOS 1.18

Robert Best
13681 Dall Lane
Santa Ana, CA 92705
Shareware—$20

HOT-DOS is a memory resident utility that allows you to exit to a DOS shell from within most applications. It uses *Ctrl-Left Shift* as a hot key. As with any DOS shell, there are several limitations on how you can use HOT-DOS, and it may not work from within all applications. In addition, there is a bug that the author warns about, involving typing *EXIT* (the way to return from a DOS shell) when in the primary partition.

Several command line options are available when loading HOT-DOS. You can use the /g option to save and restore CGA color screens. The /x option is for systems using both a color and a monochrome display. It activates HOT-DOS on the monitor not currently active. (Again, the author notes that there are problems using the *x* parameter on a system without a monochrome adaptor). The final command line parameter sets the size of the shell. The program defaults to 64K, but another value can be entered.

Unfortunately, Best hasn't provided a way to remove HOT-DOS from memory—something we wish more programmers of TSR's would do. Since the program appears to use about 76K of memory for a 64K shell, users should be aware of the amount of memory they lose. Still, HOT-DOS can be a pretty interesting utility if used with care.

Interleaves—Two Programs and a Discussion Thereof

IAU.EXE
Dave Bushong
2 S. Spring St.
Concord, NH 03301

INTLEAVE.EXE
Gibson Research Corp.
Box 6024, Dept. C
Irvine, CA 92716
(714) 854-1520

IAU.EXE is used to change the interleave value of your hard disk drive. This is an advanced utility for people who understand what the interleave is, and who need to alter it. The following is a fairly good explanation of the interleave taken from one of the on-disk documents that accompanies this product:

> Your hard disk system reads or writes data on the disk itself as the disk spins. The disk spins at a constant rate. It is similar to the way that a record player works. The head moves from the edge to the center, and the disk spins at a constant rate.

> Your computer can not always accept (or supply) the data fast enough for the disk drive. In such a case, the hard disk system causes your computer to wait until the place for that data comes around again. This takes a little under seventeen thousandths of a second.

If your computer is not able to accept each sector as it comes by, you will notice that the performance of your system is slow. To improve its performance, computer manufacturers shuffle the sectors so that the first one that is requested is never located next to the second one, the second is never located next to the third one, and so on.

You could visualize this by cutting a pizza into seven slices. Using a tag, number each one. Now change their positions so that none is next to the piece that it originally had as a neighbor. If you evenly shuffle them, you might have the arrangement of "1-5-2-6-3-7-4." In this case, the interleave factor is two, since the distance from piece number 1 to piece number 2 is two...

The explanation goes on, but that should be enough to help you understand what the interleave is. Why you should change it is more complicated. If you don't know why to change it, you probably should leave it alone.

If you wish to find out if the interleave factor on your hard disk is optimal, try the programs SPINTEST and SPINTIME from Gibson Research. These programs are explained in the document INTLEAVE.DOC which also explains in greater detail what the interleave factor is, and why it may be causing your computer to work more slowly than it should.

These programs make a good pair, or you can contact Gibson Research for a utility that will reset the interleave. In any case, as we said previously, back up your data.

Intelligent Directory 2.30

John Gaines, Jr.
16 West Deer Park Drive, Apt. C
Gaithersburg, MD 20877
Shareware—$10

This program, found as ID230.ARC is a replacement for the DOS DIR command. What makes this program unique are the number of command line options you can attach to it. You can sort and display files in various formats, display attributes, limit the list to specific files (including hidden files only), list files from more than one directory or disk (each with its own filespecs defined). In fact, this might be the most complex directory program we've seen. By creating batch files of commonly used settings, you could have a series of directory formats pre-defined, or use the environment variables to change ID's defaults.

This is an excellent choice for people who want to list files in a lot of different ways. There are more attractive DIR replacements, and some are easier to use, but none offers such a variety of options.

Janitor

G.S. Cole
Compuserve 71046,1405
GEnie KLUDGE
Public Domain

JANITOR.EXE will erase all .BAK files on the current disk. If you don't need them any more, use the Janitor. But be careful. You may want some of those BAK files later. If you know you will need them later, rename them to something with another extension.

KILLDIR

Amy J. Goebel
#702
5903 Mt. Eagle Dr.
Alexandria. VA 22303
(703) 756-6109 (modem)
Public Domain

Killdir is a useful, but somewhat dangerous program that will erase a directory, all its files (including protected files), and all subdirectories and files within the named directory. This can make short work of an otherwise tedious process, but should be used with some care. The only proviso is that you must be in a directory above the one(s) you wish to erase. Also, the program will prompt you once for the directory, then once again if it encounters any protected files. If you tell the program to continue, it will make short work of the named directory and its files and subdirectories. The version we tested was KILLDIR4.ARC.

LIST ver. 6.2a

Vernon Buerg

LIST is a Shareware utility program that is used to list files on your screen, often saving the time and paper required when printing out document files from a disk. The program has scrolling, positioning, and filtering commands to make displaying documents easy.

Because document files contain different types of data, LIST has several commands to make the file data readable. This is called filtering. For example, LIST can replace all non-text and control characters with blanks, expand tab characters, display line drawing characters, change 8-bit WordStar files to 7-bit text, display hexadecimal values for each character, and remove junk such as control codes and backspaces from documents. In addition, you can change the foreground and background color of the screen to your liking and save the changes permanently. List also contains search and global search features.

```
LIST       1              10-07-87 23:02 ◆ CDTO.DOC

                 LIST - Version 6.2a - 5/07/87
                 (c) Copyright 1987 Vernon D. Buerg
                 456 Lakeshire, Daly City, CA 94015
                 For personal use only. Not for sale or hire.

F1  Display HELP info   a-A  toggle APX/DV/DD    T HOME   go to Top of file
F2  change FIND bg      a-B  mark Bottom line    B END    go to Bottom of file
F3  Find next text      a-C  Clone LIST.COM      D PgDn   forward one page
F4  change FIND fg      a-D  write to file       U PgUp   back one page
F5  change text bg      a-E  toggle EGA 25/43    c-PgUp   list previous file
F6  change text fg      a-F  get new Filespec    c-PgDn   list next file
F7  change 1/25 bg      a-G  Goto DOS            c-left   go to col 1
F8  change 1/25 fg      a-H  toggle Hex mode     7 or 8   strip or leave hi-bit
F9  Find previous text  a-J  Junk filter         *        star filter
F10 Exit to DOS         a-L  toggle preLoading   +/-/#    skip to line #
                        a-M  Mark top line
K   toggle typeahead    a-R  toggle Ruler
P   toggle Printing     a-S  toggle Sharing      If you find LIST of value,
W   Wrap long lines     a-T  toggle Tabs         a gift of $15, or any amount,
/   Scan for exact text a-U  unmark lines        would be greatly appreciated.
\   Find any case text  a-W  freeze top window
X   Exit to DOS (cls)   a-X  exit, orig screen
Command▶-                            Options: h8kMpswTalj Keys: X=exit ?=Help
```

To run LIST, you type LIST [file name] at the DOS command line. Wild cards are accepted. To display all files that end in *.DOC*, you type *LIST *.DOC*. The first *.DOC* file found is displayed on screen. After that, when you press the Escape key (which normally exits List), the next *.DOC* file in line will display, until you run out of valid files. Then you return to DOS.

When you first load a file, its first 21 lines are shown on screen. A set of cursor movement and screen handling commands allow you to move freely through the document (to top, bottom, or page by page). Several other options allow additional control over display and basic formatting of the displayed document. You can even exit to a DOS shell or toggle an 80 column by 43 line EGA mode.

The author requests a $15 donation for his work. This program is a real time-saver, especially when you work with a lot of the programs in this book that contain on-disk documentation.

List is one of the most useful products we know. Not only does it completely replace the *DOS TYPE* command, it does so quickly and conveniently. Its use of wild cards, its ability to strip the 8th bit, its color screens and its search feature make it the best of its kind. It will always be on my DOS Path.

List 6.2a
Vernon D. Buerg
139 Whiteoak Circle
Petaluma, CA 94952
BBS # (707) 778-8944

Shareware: $15

Category: Utilities

System Requirements: none specified

Recommended Use: convenient display of documents on screen

Major Pros: smooth, fast operation; full control over file viewing including cursor key movement, color settings, fast access to any part of document, etc.

Major Cons: no editing features

Sources: popular BBSs and commercial services, or directly from the author

---

Make Label ver. 1.0

George Fontaine
Public Domain

Version 1.0 of Make Label is designed to make repetitive labels of names and addresses. Use them as return address labels, or to label your belongings, disk labels, etc. The program contains special centering algorithms that produce an attractive label for any set of data entered up to 30 characters per line (four lines maximum).

The program at this point has no sophisticated error checking and will not allow commas. It's strictly a fast and dirty program, but one that can be very useful. Future versions may be more elaborate and may contain more formatting, printer, and font support.

MAKEREAD

Ronald Gans Software Company
350 West 55th Street
New York, NY 10019
(212) 957-8361
Public Domain (with restrictions on commercial use)

MAKEREAD is one of those utilities of great potential, and ultimate simplicity. It turns a text file into a self-displaying .COM file. You might use this product to produce self-displaying documentation or notes on disks that must be passed around among many co-workers.

The resulting .COM file displays the entire text file one page at a time. The user can move up or down a page at a time, move to the end of the file, or to the beginning, or even print the file with a simple command. The only odd feature of this program is that it uses the Q key to print a file instead of P. Since Q is often used for Quit, this might be confusing, though the keys you can use are always displayed at the bottom of the screen.

In addition to XWORD (which is reviewed in the Word Processor section), Ronald Gans has written some other utilities including BAAB which converts binary files to ASCII and back, QUERY.ARC which contains utilities to make more interactive batch files, and ULC which will convert words in a text file to various combinations of upper and lower case. All the utilities mentioned here are included with the registered version of XWORD.

MAN

David L. Rick
4000 Ingersoll
Des Moines, IA 50312
Public Domain but with restrictions for commercial use

Have you ever been using one of your favorite Shareware utilities, but then forgot how to use it? And you looked in the directory where you keep that utility and, oops—no .DOC files...

Man can help you. Man will search for and display the .DOC file associated with a particular application. It's that simple. The only restrictions are that the document file have the same name (other than extension, of course) as the application, and that it be somewhere on the DOS PATH or in the path designated as the MANPATH environment variable. Another environment variable is used to specify an editor or file reader (like LIST). Basically, this program will find, then display a document file

Of course, if your document file doesn't have the .DOC extension, or it doesn't have the same name as the application, the program won't work. It's a clever idea, and, with a little foresight, you can arrange to keep your .DOC files in special directories, then use MAN to display them when needed.

MANPREP

Francis X. Guidry
2044 Mallard Drive
Walnut Creek, CA 94596
Public Domain

MANPREP is a program designed to take documentation files that were formatted for printers and prepare them for listing to the screen in anticipation of use with MAN (or some other utilities that list files to the screen). The author gives some examples of batch files that might be used to automate the conversion process.

MasterFile 1.2

Masterware
3213 West Wheeler #177
Seattle, WA 98199
Shareware—$20

MasterFile is a file catalog utility and more. It will allow you to catalog files on a collection of floppy disks, or even catalog files on a hard disk. The program is menu driven and easy to use, and features the ability to add comments up to 75 characters long to any file description. At any time, you can use MasterFile's search facilities to find files based on keywords in the descriptions you enter.

MasterFile has a host of features, including the ability to create a volume label on a floppy disk, add or delete file descriptions (and also delete actual files, as an option), find files by wildcard specifications, etc.

Along with the main MasterFile program is a memory resident program called MASTERPU which you can use to pop-up in the middle of other applications to check the descriptions of cataloged files.

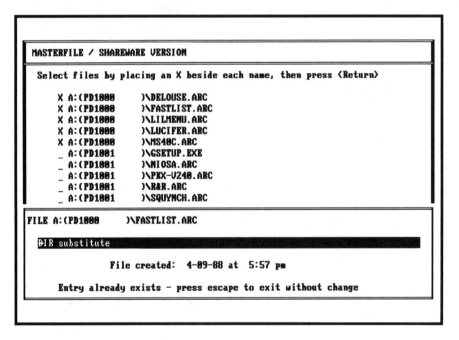

You can use the pop-up program to search the whole MasterFile directory by file name or wildcard as well as by items contained in the file descriptions. You can also add new files and descriptions to the master catalog using the resident program. This feature alone increases the utility of MasterFile over ordinary disk catalog programs. It might not be as fast as some for bulk floppy disk catalog jobs, but it is slick and ideal for the individual who needs to keep records of the contents of floppy or hard disks. At our request, the author added the ability to remove MASTERPU from memory at the user's command. This is a necessary feature of TSRs, but one that is often neglected.

MasterFile can produce an ASCII delimited file of the catalog suitable for use with word processors, ASCII editors, or database programs.

We have used MasterFile and CATS (see elsewhere in this chapter) to catalog our disks, and both have worked well.

MEM.EXE
Harvey Schiffman
Public Domain

MEM.EXE is for OS/2 users only. It allows you to see the largest available block of RAM available, a feature that is not available with CHKDSK running under OS/2. A handy program if you are using OS/2. We found the program under the filename OS2MEM.ARC.

MicroFirm Toolkit Ver. 2.04C
Robert B. Stout
dba MicroFirm
P.O. Box 428
Alief, TX 77411
Shareware—$35

The MicroFirm Toolkit consists of 24 utilities found in six archives—MOV-TOOLS.ARC, DIRTOOLS.ARC, DELTOOLS.ARC, FILTOOLS.ARC, SYS-TOOLS.ARC, and TOOLSDOC.ARC. Here is a summary of what the files do. This is taken from the MicroFirm Toolkit documentation:

> MOVTOOLS.ARC contains the following utilities for moving, copying, piping, viewing, and concatenating files and directory branches:
>
> MV.COM moves, copies, or renames files.

CP.COM copies files.

MB.COM moves or copies entire directory branches.

CB.COM copies entire directory branches.

LYNX.COM concatenates and/or pipes files or streams. It can also encrypt/decrypt, "tee," or replace DOS MORE.

CRYPT.COM encrypts/decrypts streams.

PAWS.COM replaces DOS's MORE.

DIRTOOLS.ARC contains the following utilities for changing directories and displaying information about your directories:

DR.COM displays directories and generates file lists in any of 6 different formats using any of 14 different sorts and allows either interactive browsing or stream outputs.

DU.COM displays a directory's tree structure and the disk space utilized by each branch.

DF.COM displays disk free space.

PWD.COM displays the present working directory for any drive on your system.

AT.COM is a very smart replacement for DOS's CD which allows wildcards and a default home directory.

AA.COM is a special purpose CD replacement used for lateral moves within a directory tree.

DELTOOLS.ARC contains the following utilities for deleting all or part of your files and/or directories:

RM.COM deletes or destroys files.

GOBBLE.COM deletes or destroys directory branches.

TRIM.COM trims excess data from text files past the end-of-file (EOF) mark. It can also add an EOF to a file without one.

FILTOOLS.ARC contains the following utilities for modifying or processing your files:

> RGREP.COM searches files for a specified text string. It can search single files, multiple files, or an entire directory tree. It can display the line containing the match, only the filename, only files not containing a match, or a "window" of lines surrounding the line containing the match. The search string may contain sophisticated wildcards and columnar operators.

> PR.COM prints text files to the printer, screen, or other files, adding headers, optional titles, and page numbers. It can also process file lists or redirected input streams.

> WC.COM displays the number of words, lines, and characters in a text file. Optionally displays a fog (readability) index.

> SPLIT.COM splits large text files into small segments.

> HEAD.COM displays the first 1-9 lines of specified text files.

> DIFF.COM compares text files and documents any differences.

> BCMP.COM compares any 2 files and documents any differences.

SYSTOOLS.ARC contains the following utilities for modifying or measuring your system's functions and/or files.

> SWAP.COM swaps the names of any 2 files.

> TEE.COM allows redirected output streams to be split.

> TIMEX.COM times the execution of any command and displays the resulting error level.

> TOUCH.COM changes the time/date stamp of a file.

> CHMOD.COM changes the attributes of a file.

TOOLSDOC.ARC contains the following documentation and support files for the entire toolkit:

TOOLKIT.DOC is the main documentation file for all the Toolkit utilities.

TOOLKIT.NFO Brief descriptions of the Toolkit utilities.

READ.ME is the release notice for the original version.

READ_ME.1ST is the release notice for the current version.

NEW_IN_2.02A documents changes from the original version.

NEW_IN_2.03C documents changes from the original version.

NEW_IN_2.04D documents changes from the original version.

NEW_IN_3.00A documents upgraded features available only in the commercial version (provided free when you register—see TOOLKIT.DOC).

INSTALL.BAT is the installation program.

PSET-IBM.ARC contains printer setup batch files for use with

PR.COM when using IBM printers.

PSET-EPS.ARC contains printer setup batch files for use with PR.COM when using Epson printers.

PSET-OKI.ARC contains printer setup batch files for use with PR.COM when using Okidata printers.

PSET-CIT.ARC contains printer setup batch files for use with PR.COM when using C. Itoh Prowriter printers.

ADDPATH.BAT is used to add a directory to your PATH.

POP.BAT moves you up directory levels (default = 1).

RESCOL.BAT resets your screen colors to normal (B/W).

SET_MONO.BAT sets up the Toolkit utilities to work in monochrome (B/W) mode.

That about sums it up. Anyone should be able to use at least some of these utilities. The Shareware version is always one step behind the current registered version, and updates are free within the same version number (i.e. 2.04a upgrades to 2.04b, but it is $10 to upgrade to 3.0x).

Move 2.01

Unique Software
P.O. Box 26613
Fort Worth, TX 76126
Shareware—donation requested

This is a simple utility that performs its useful purpose in a minimum of space. At around 1K in size, it is perhaps the smallest file mover we've seen. It will perform the functions of the DOS commands COPY and DELete in one operation. As small as it is, it can use wildcards and contains file handling routines that check for available space on destination drives and also check for duplicate files in the destination directory. It is generally found as MOVE201.ARC.

ND

If you ever wanted to know the date three weeks from now, or 95 days from now, you may like ND.EXE which will tell you the date at any future date. You enter

```
ND X [W]
```

where X is the number or days or weeks forward for which you want the day and date, and W tells the program you want weeks (otherwise it uses days in the calculation).

NEWKEY   Version 4.0

FAB Software
P.O. Box 336
Wayland, MA 01778
Shareware—$30

Reprinted by permission of PDN Newsletter.

For those of you curious about macros and their uses, look no further. NEWKEY Version 4.0 lets you take control of your keyboard in ways that will breathe new life into your keystrokes and software.

A rather unique feature of this disk is the "Guided Tour." After issuing the command "Demo" you will be taken for a test drive that illustrates NEWKEY's major features. After the tour you may refer to the extensive documentation to discover many more details. The complexity of this program will not leave you stranded. Tapping <ctrl>/ will pop up a menu of several items only a keystroke away. These features are all accessible without leaving the current program, since NEWKEY remains memory resident.

Simply stated, macros are redefined keys. NEWKEY lets you choose nearly any key on the keyboard to use as your "hot key," and using a prefix key such as <ctrl> and <alt> adds many more for your use. I'm using this program along with a word processor while writing this review. When I hit 5 on the number pad of the keyboard, "NEWKEY" is automatically typed. Lest you think this is all the program does, read on. NEWKEY has the ability to let you define a key with a variable fill-in-the-blank feature before it continues. An example of this application is a standard business letter that begins:

Dear Mr. _____: Thank you for your letter dated _____.

It's an easy matter to define one key with this type of macro, and when executed you will see typed, "Dear Mr." You can then type in the name, and after hitting the return key the balance will be typed in for you. NEWKEY has a great date/time function that will allow several formats and automatically insert the correct date and/or time. This feature has other variations you will find interesting. Another way to create macros is to use the shorthand mode. Rather than define the number 5 key as used in the above example, I could have used the shorthand method so every time I typed the letters "ne" the word "NEWKEY" would have appeared. The macros, of course, are not restricted in length to just one word, or even 100 words.

NEWKEY is a program that is very compatible and trouble-free. Virtually all aspects of its operation can be customized to suit your own system and needs of a particular program. For instance if the <ctrl>/ command for the menu access conflicts with a program, just rename that parameter.

Besides doing a great job creating macros, NEWKEY has several other options that will help ease the strain on you and your computer. Automatic screen blanking after a defined period of inactivity will protect your monitor from "burn-in." The default time is 5 minutes, but this may be changed to a time from one second to one hour. Hit any key and the screen display is restored to the image you left. An extended keyboard buffer that increases the type-ahead buffer from 16 to 128 keystrokes is also an asset. NEWKEY will also dramatically increase the speed of any key held down for repeat purposes and still eliminate overrun. This "fast key" rate may also be defined by the user for repeats of between 1 and 99 characters per second. Another option is the keyboard click. This is automatically on when creating macros, but may be on or off at all times as desired. Click is hardly the word I would use to describe the sound I'm getting on this particular machine—a rather feeble electronic beep—but it can be quite useful in inputting data and not looking up at the screen to verify keystrokes. There are many other options and customizations you'll discover in using this program.

All your macros, customizations, parameters, commands, and options can be saved. Invocation may be accomplished straight from the program disk or through batch files, of which there are examples. From a file containing Dvorak keyboard customization to a file with Wordstar macros, NEWKEY does many things, and allows you to do even more. To find a top-notch program at an extremely low price is very rare. I'm glad I found this one.

—Gary Breasau

Newpath
Public Domain

There are several utilities to alter the DOS path specification, including APATH and CHGPATH. Newpath is the best one we've seen so far. We found it on Vernon Buerg's BBS, though it is probably available elsewhere. Newpath can add a path specification anywhere in the Path statement, where the other utilities we've seen can only add to the end of the list. In addition, Newpath can delete any existing spec from the Path. Newpath comes with a very rudimentary .DOC file that explains the program's syntax.

Suppose your current Path reads, "PATH=C:\;C:\MENU;D:PARADOX2." To add a new specification, say c:\DOS to your path, you might enter:

```
newpath c:\DOS
```

The new Path would read, "PATH=C:\;C:\MENU;D:\PARADOX2;C:\DOS." However, to add the spec to the third position in the path, you could use the statement:

```
newpath c:\DOS /3
```

Now the Path would read, "PATH=C:\;C:\MENU;C:\DOS;D:\PARADOX2."

If you want to remove the statement, C:\MENU, issue the command:

```
newpath c:\MENU /d
```

This is a very useful utility.

NULL
Public Domain

This PD program will search for any zero byte (null) files on the current drive and ask if you want to delete it. You can also specify a path or another drive (with DOS 3.1 or later). If you think there are null files on your disk, use NULL to eliminate them.

PCSTAT 3.2

PCSTAT provides much the same information as *CHKDSK* (and more), but faster. It gives the date, time, day of week, disk volume label, DOS version, *DOS VERIFY* status, *BREAK* status, statistics for current drive, and a readout of RAM (total and available). A very handy utility.

Pprint Vers. 3.1
Norm Patriquin
P.O. Box 8308
San Bernadino, CA 92412
(714) 369-9766 (BBS line only)
Shareware—$15 ($30 for disk and manual)

Pprint is an extremely useful DOS print utility. It features about 75 different options, many for HP LaserJets, others for dot matrix printers. You can select and customize the printer type you use. You can also select multiple files to print—by file names or by special date parameters. For example, you can select all files that have been modified since a certain date.

You can also set a header and/or footer line, control page numbering, justification, print quality, size, and fonts, and many other features. People who print from DOS will find Pprint a tremendous help, and, although there are many commands, you will soon get used to the ones you use most often and place them in a batch file (or alias—*see* CED) for easy execution. For example, if you regularly print out documents in compressed print, you would use the /C option.

Pprint has some other surprising features. You can use it to force all characters into upper or lower case, skip pages and start at a pre-determined page (great for aborted jobs), and even create a new file using Pprint options to modify parts of the original, then print the new file. You can instruct the program to find duplicate lines and ignore them. You can determine print size, lines/inch, lines/page, select fonts, etc.

Another unique feature of Pprint is its ability to print both sides of the paper using an HP LaserJet. The printer definition files used by Pprint are simple to understand, and can be modified by anyone who has a manual for his or her printer. The list goes on. Pprint raises DOS printing to an art.

Professional Master Key Utilities 2.0

R.P. Gage
RPG Software Farm
P.O. Box 9221
Columbus, MS 39705-9221
Shareware—$25

The on-disk manual for PMK Utilities begins with a registration form, then continues with a healthy dose of disclaimers, including such classic lines as "RPG Software Farm does not warrant that this documentation is accurate, or that any of The Professional Master Key Utilities programs will operate as they were claimed or designed."

Thus it takes a while to reach the point where you can learn about these powerful and potentially useful tools. While disclaimers are necessary protections, they can be taken past a certain point of reason. However some caution should be advised when working with utilities that can alter the contents of files and directories at the sector level.

PMK Utilities contain some of the features of commercial programs like Norton Utilities and Mace Utilities. You can view and edit any sector on any disk, search for text or hex strings, undelete files, modify file attributes, and even show a graphical representation of the disk displaying used and unused space.

```
┌─────────────────────────────────────────────────────────────────────────┐
│  ┌──────────────────────────────────────────┐ ┌───────────────────────┐  │
│  │ To run one of the programs listed, move  │ │ Professional Master Key │  │
│  │ the cursor with ↑ or ↓ to the desired    │ │ Fill Disk             │  │
│  │ program.                                  │ │ UnFormat              │  │
│  │                                           │ │ Zero Disk             │  │
│  │ Press <SPACE> to add arguments and options│ │ Zero File             │  │
│  │ to the command, or press <ENTER> to run it│ │ Quit PMK Master Menu  │  │
│  │ without any additional arguments.         │ │                       │  │
│  └──────────────────────────────────────────┘ └───────────────────────┘  │
│  ┌──────────────────────────────────────────────────────────────────────┐│
│  │ PMK B:-                                                               ││
│  └──────────────────────────────────────────────────────────────────────┘│
│  ════════════════════════ PMK Master Menu ═══════════════════════════    │
│  Professional Master Key, version 2.1a.                                   │
│      View and edit any sector within any file or MS-DOS disk.  Search for a│
│      text string.  Undelete files.  Modify file attributes.  Show a graphical│
│      map of total disk usage and free space.                              │
│                                                                           │
│  PMK [/Mono ON | OFF | AUTO] [/Slow ON | OFF] [d:]                         │
│      PMK /Slow ON B:           — display using BIOS; set working drive to B:│
│                                                                           │
│  Options                                                                   │
│      /Mono (Toggle monochrome).  ON = no colors.  OFF = dispaly colors.    │
│      /Slow (Toggle direct screen writing) ON = use BIOS.  OFF = direct.    │
│      d: (Set working drive).                                              │
│      ═══ Copyright (c) 1986, 1987 by R. P. Gage, all rights reserved. ═══ │
└─────────────────────────────────────────────────────────────────────────┘
```

Another utility is called Fill Disk. This one fills all unused sectors with a particular message or blank all unused sectors. One possible use of this feature is to place a message with your name on every unused sector on a hard disk. If your equipment is ever stolen, this could help identify it, though there are probably better means. Another use of this feature is to be sure that any data that has been erased is completely gone (so that nobody else can ever recover it).

As a corollary to the Fill Disk utility, there are Zero Disk and Zero File which will completely blank a disk or a file respectively.

UnFormat, if properly used, can recover a hard disk in case of an accidental format. Like Mace Utilities, this program could save data lost if someone accidentally (or on purpose) formats you hard disk, but the information must be updated each time you use the computer to remain accurate. The author recommends placing the program in your AUTOEXEC.BAT to keep the regular updates.

Simple Explanation: Unformat programs work because, during a normal DOS format, only certain file headers are reset to make it appear that the disk is empty. In fact, the data is still intact. Restoring the FAT (File Allocation Table) and the boot sectors will generally restore a formatted disk (if nothing else has been done to it).

378

```
┌─────────────────────────────────────────────────────────────┐
│  ╔═══════════ Professional Master Key, version 2.1a ═══════════╗
│  ║                                                             ║
│  To use one of the functions listed below, move the highlighted bar with
│  ↑, ↓, or the first letter in the function name, then press <ENTER>.
│  ────────────────────────────────────────────────────────────
│
│  Alter Files .... Alter any directory or file's attribs, date, or time.
│  Change Disk .... Change the working drive to any available drive.
│  Disk Edit ...... Examine and/or modify the current drive's sectors.
│  Erase Files .... Erase any file that exists on the current drive.
│  File Edit ...... Examine and/or modify any file on the current drive.
│  Information .... Display information about the current drive's data.
│  Locate Files ... Find any file anywhere on the current drive.
│  Map Disk/Files . Show a visual map of the space used the disk & files.
│  Quit .......... Exit Professional Master Key and return to DOS.
│  Rename Files ... Rename any file or directory on the current drive.
│  Undelete Files . Undelete any file or directory on the current drive.
│  ────────────────────────────────────────────────────────────
│
│                   The working drive is B:
│
│  ==== RPG Software Farm   P.O. Box 9221   Columbus, MS  39705-9221 ====
│  ═══════ Copyright (c) 1986, 1987 by R. P. Gage, all rights reserved. ═══
└─────────────────────────────────────────────────────────────┘
```

All PMK utilities can be run from the command line, but the program comes with a menu driven interface to make things easier. You can pick any one of the utilities, and a help screen automatically appears to detail the syntax of the command. Pressing Enter will run the selected utility in its default format. Pressing Spacebar allows you to enter switches and parameters on an edit line. The menu interface is simple, but effective.

How well these utilities work is anyone's guess. We tested some of the utilities, but not all. Those utilities tested worked excellently, and all were accompanied by help screens where needed. These are potentially very useful programs, but we, like the author, want to recommend that you read the documentation carefully before attempting to use these utilities, and that you use them at your own risk.

Psearch Vers. 3.8

Norm Patriquin
Shareware—$15

Psearch is a very versatile search program with a wide range of possible uses. It will locate files on any disk or combination of disks, or in any directory. It will search for text strings within files (even binary files like Lotus worksheets, *COM*, and *EXE* files). It will allow you to view text in files. It will locate files imbedded in *ARC* files. It will take located file names and other data and execute DOS commands with them or place the results in a batch file for editing and later execution. Psearch will even extract specified data and send it to a printer or a file.

```
PS [~][!][;][filespec] /F/DR:xx ... plus other parameters shown below
-------------------- GENERAL COMMAND PARAMETERS -------------------
/F  - Locate file (not text search)   /E  - Show directory tree
/A  - Search all directories          /DR:xyz Scan drives x,y,z
/P  - Pause after every match         /MO - Pause when screen full
/PR - Print output on printer         /PF - Print output to file
/AR - Find Files in .ARC files        /AO - Only process .ARC files
/N  - N:nnn Select files ( n days old /O  - O:nnn Select if ) n days old
/S  - Scan/Peak into file & show words /SO - Set Sound Off
/AT: [U][H][S][R] Select Updated, Hidden, System, or Readonly file files
----------------- TEXT SEARCH RELATED PARAMETERS ------------------
/T  - T:text   Text to be found       /C  - Case sensitive search
/D  - Display matching records        /M  - Show all matches
/FW - Find text as a word             /FP - Find text as word prefix
/FS - Find text as word suffix        /SK - Skip COM,EXE and BAT files
--------------- EXECUTE COMMAND FOR SELECTED FILES ----------------
/X - X:cmd & aa   Execute command for each found file
    The following characters found in command are replaced as follows:
      & - Path name     ! - File name without extension    @ - / for parms
      # - file name     ~ - Name of file in .ARC
/XF:cmd & aa  Like /X to command file   /XP:cmd & aa  Like /X with Pause
```

About the only drawback is the program's potential for complexity. There are so many command-line options that it can take some time to learn to use the product effectively. However, Patriquin has anticipated that problem and built a nice menu-driven interface for Psearch. If you enter PS at the command line with no options, you automatically enter the menu system. Within the menu system there are several help screens that list and explain the command-line options, making it convenient to check the Psearch syntax at any time. The menu system allows you to perform searches directly using almost all the options.

Psearch Vers. 3.8
Norm Patriquin
P.O. Box 8308
San Bernardino, CA 92412
(714) 369-9766 (BBS line only)

Shareware: $15

Category: Utilities

Recommended Use: Search for files and imbedded text

Major Pros: many major features unmatched by other search programs; menu
    driven option for beginners; automatic DOS command execution or batch
    file generation from search results; optional search over multiple drives, or
    on current directory only

Major Cons: could be overly complex for some people's needs

Sources: popular BBSs and commercial services, or directly from the author

Psearch even has some extra power available for text searches. You can perform
Soundex searches (searches for a text string that sounds like one entered). Other
options allow you to ignore vowels in text strings or look for any words containing the characters specified.

You can also search for files based on their DOS attributes. For example, you
can search for files with hidden, read only, and/or updated status, or search for
files by date.

The ability to create and execute DOS commands based on search criteria is potentially powerful. For example, to delete all files in the current directory which
contain references to a specific customer (who may have moved away, died or
gone to a competitor), you would enter the command:

```
PS /T:Roy Smooth /X:DEL
```

A variation on this theme would search for any name that sounds line Smooth,
prompt you before each deletion (allowing you to choose whether to carry out
the DOS command or not), and would search on Drives C:, D:, and E:

```
PS /DR:cde/T:~Smooth/XP:DEL
```

Psearch also works with batch files using batch variables. You can create a batch file that uses % variables in place of some of the Psearch parameters. Using batch files is an excellent way to pre-define Psearch commands while leaving the exact search data open. Another way to pre-define Psearch parameters is to use the DOS *SET* command so that every time you enter *PS*, the command line parameters defined in the *SET* command are assumed.

We found that Psearch is capable of performing the same tasks as both Sfind and Search (found elsewhere in this section), and as such represents a real value. A few of the commands are suppressed until you register, but the program is 99 percent operative without registration. Psearch easily justifies its $15 price, and registration is no hardship.

Psearch is a real value. We highly recommend it, although it does so much that you may also wish to use the other programs like Sfind and Search for simpler situations. But if we were to be limited to one search utility, Psearch would be it.

A Note on Norm Patriquin:

Norm Patriquin has several utilities available. Some of them are included in this book; some are not. Frankly, they are not all of the caliber and complexity of Pprint and Psearch, but you may find them all to be useful. The other programs Patriquin offers are:

PALERT	monitors low disk space conditions.
PATTR	sets DOS attributes for one or more files.
PCOPY	a basic copy utility.
PMOVE	move files between directories.
PDAILY	allows a DOS command to be executed only once a day.
PDELETE	deletes specified files using various command-line switches (works best with batch files for various options).
PTOUCH	modify the date and time for files.
WPGRAB	helps find most recently updated file, designed for use with word processing files to help you find what you were working on.

Patriquin offers his entire line of utilities for $45. Since we think some of the programs he's asking $15 for are worth more, we highly recommend the package option. Even if you don't end up using all the utilities, you will receive a great collection of programs for a great price, and you'll be registered to receive updates, support, and product information.

QSORT ver. 1.2

Ben Baker
Shareware—$10

QSORT is a sorting utility based upon the QSORT algorithm and is meant as a replacement for the *DOS SORT* command. The program features a number of enhancements over the *DOS SORT*. These enhancements include the ability to specify up to 30 keys of different lengths and to sort each key independently in ascending or descending order, to set a record length of up to 3600 bytes, and optionally sort each key in lexical (dictionary order) sequence. QSORT can sort a file of any size, as long as there is enough disk space (10 percent over the size of the actual file) to handle the work files created by QSORT.

To use QSORT, you type *QSORT* at the DOS command line, along with the file name of the file you wish to sort, and the options described above in the form of command-line switches.

QSORT is a superior program for files that have fixed record lengths, and fields that start and end at fixed column ranges. If you have a data file that has fields delineated by commas, for example, and they start and end at different column locations, this program will not work for you. But neither will the DOS SORT command.

Another disadvantage lies in the Quick Sort algorithm itself. Quick Sort has a tendency not to handle equal key values very well. As a result, the author of QSORT states that he cannot guarantee the order of records whose keys are equal. To circumvent this problem, it is recommended that you specify more than one key in a file that has duplicate primary key records.

The advantage to Quick Sort algorithm is that it is very fast. QSORT tries to work in memory rather than disk whenever possible, making it even faster. The author claims that it will sort a 650k file in 40 minutes. However, we didn't test that claim. Benchmarks aside, this is a very good sort utility that far exceeds the performance of the DOS SORT.

```
QSORT ver. 1.2
Ben Baker
P.O. Box 425
Godfrey, IL 62035

Shareware: $10

Category: Utility

System Requirements: no specific requirements given

Recommended Use: sorting fixed length ASCII files

Major Pros: fast, reliable sorts with a number of advanced features

Major Cons: limited to sorting fixed length ASCII files where data starts and
        ends in fixed positions in the file

Sources: popular BBSs and commercial services, or directly from the author
```

RESIFORM unk. version

Lawrence Unger
Public Domain

RESIFORM stands for *RESI*dent *FORM*atter. It is a memory resident formatting utility that allows you to format diskettes while you are working in another program. In addition, the program is capable of formatting floppy disks in about half the time that it takes the DOS format to do the job. Like CFORMAT, which is also reviewed in this chapter, RESIFORM is capable of formatting a 360k floppy in a 1.2 megabyte drive.

To invoke the program, you type in the following at the DOS command line:

```
A:>RESIFORM
```

Each time you want to call up the program, you type the ALT-F1 key combination, and the program pops up. The author has built in a feature that more memory resident programs should have. If you have another memory resident program or an application program that uses ALT-F1, you can reassign the pro-

384

gram to use a different keystroke sequence at start-up. For example, if you want the program to be called up using ALT-F2, when you start RESIFORM you type:

```
A:>RESIFORM 105
```

The 105 is the extended scan code for ALT-F2. You can find more extended scan codes in your DOS BASIC manual. We tested Resiform with several application programs, and it worked beautifully. The author seems to have followed the memory resident convention to allow this program to reside without conflicting with other programs.

This program is perfect for when you find yourself just a few diskettes shy of completing a DOS hard disk backup or some other situation in which formatted disks are need quickly.

SAP300

Don A. Williams
3913 W. Solano Dr. N.
Phoenix, AZ 85019
Public Domain

SAP will sort and condense DOS directories. It condenses by eliminating erased files. This is a relatively simple utility, though it does support options for sorting subdirectories, eliminating erased files (or not), and displaying statistics on the directory to sort. From what we've seen, this program does work, though we suggest caution when trying it.

SCAN ver. 1.0

Dr. Bob's Utilities
Public Domain

SCAN is a utility that scans any binary or ASCII file and displays any ASCII portion of the file. It ignores ASCII sequences of less than four characters. To use the program, you type *SCAN* and the file name of the file you wish to scan on the DOS command line. This program could be used to Scan a *COM* or *EXE* file and redirect the output to a file. The resultant ASCII text might form the basis of a user manual. Another use for this program might be to scan an adventure game file and display all the clues and text.

SEARCH ver. 6.81

Arthur Hill, Jr.
Shareware—$10

SEARCH is a program which will search through text files for words or strings. You may specify up to five different words or strings to search for. The program allows you to specify wild cards for the file names you wish to search through. The program can be run from either the DOS command line using switches, or through a prompted mode in which you are presented with a form to fill out about the current search. The program then runs and displays, in color, the line and corresponding line number on which each word or phrase is found. Each word you specify is highlighted in the line with a unique color so it is easy to find.

SEARCH will also find words imbedded in other words. For example, in a search for the word *FAMILIAR*, SEARCH will show you *UNFAMILIAR* and *FAMILIARITY*. At the end of the search, the program will give you the total number of times it found a word or phrase, how many lines it searched, the total number of lines displayed, and how long it took to search through each line. If you are searching through many files, the program gives you the option of redirecting the search to a output file or to the printer rather than to the screen. As an added bonus, the program includes a replace option, which allows you to replace a word with another. The program does not make a back up of the old file before it does the replace, however.

Other drawbacks of the program include the inability to display whole paragraphs where words were found and the inability to read other file formats like Word-Star, Peachtext, etc. If the program could extract paragraphs and read other files, this program could compete with some very expensive commercial indexing programs, like Zyindex, a commercial program used by many lawyers and other professionals. Even with its drawbacks, this program is still highly re-commended.

Show (unk. version)

Public Domain

Show is a public-domain utility that acts as an enhanced *DOS DIR* command. By typing SHOW at the DOS command line, the program lists all the files in the directory, the size of the file, the actual amount of space the file is taking up on the disk, the date it was last modified, flags (archived, hidden, system, etc.), and the range of clusters that the file takes up. Another option is the ability to check another drive for free space and compare it to the drive/directory you are showing. It then calculates the amount of free space compared to the amount of actual space the files take up, and lets you know if there's enough room on the drive to contain the files.

This program is quite useful. However, a bug does exist when you are using this program with MACE Utilities. For some reason, the program can't handle the *BACKUP.M_U* file that's created in the root directory with these utilities and locks up the system, requiring you to reset it. Aside from this, we had no other problems with this program.

The Software Mechanic Utilities

Hershel Enterprises, Inc.
P.O. Box 832052
Dallas, TX 75083
Public Domain

The Software Mechanic is actually a collection of small utilities. Some of them are similar to other utilities mentioned in this book, but some of them are unique and extremely useful. These 17 utilities are probably most useful for advanced and technical users, though some of them are novice level. Most of them are very simple and require almost no explanation. For instance, NOW.EXE simply displays the current date and time. On the other hand, a few of these utilities have advanced uses, for instance HD.EXE and UHD.EXE will dump a file to an editable hexadecimal format (HD), and then restore the hex dump to a file (UHD).

Other utilities of note are:

- SK.EXE which will show the scan codes of keys pressed from the keyboard
- TP.EXE which will time the execution of a program or DOS operation
- TS.EXE which will search text files for matching strings and extract the results
- CLRLOCKS.EXE which clears Num, Caps, and Scroll locks
- CAT.EXE (like DOS TYPE command with wildcards)
- DM.EXE to dump specific areas of memory
- FO.EXE to format files for printing
- DF.EXE for sorting and listing directories
- RF.EXE for prompted file and subdirectory deletion
- AF.EXE for setting and changing file attributes

- SF.EXE to set the time and/or date stamp on files
- FT.EXE to read test to check integrity of files on any disk
- NOISE.EXE to make noise according to frequency and duration parameters
- LF.EXE to locate files on any or all disks and directories

These utilities all include a help screen, generally read by typing the filename and /h. The help screens give enough information for experienced users to benefit from these programs. If you think any of these utilities are worth having, the price is right, since the whole collection is in the public domain.

SPEEDUP (a.k.a. SPEED41, SP40)
Unknown author
Public Domain

SPEEDUP is a utility program that was designed to speed up the access time of floppy disk drives, yielding a faster performance ratio. Though the program doesn't noticeably improve the speed of your floppy disk drives, it does make them noticeably quieter. To use the program, it is suggested that you place the program in your *AUTOEXEC.BAT* file, so that the program will load when you turn on your system. The program stays memory resident until you turn off your machine, or reset it.

This program is recommended if you can't stand your noisy floppy disk drives and want a slight improvement in their performance.

SWAPNAME unk. version
Vernon Buerg
Public Domain

SWAPNAME is a utility program that allows you to swap the file names of two existing files on your disk. To use the program you type SWAPNAME at the DOS command line along with the two filenames of the files you wish to swap names with. If any errors are encountered, the file names are restored to their original state. This program works well. You'll find it especially useful if you are using multiple CONFIG.SYSs on your computer and want to swap a different configuration in and out without copying.

TSR Utilities Ver. 2.4

Turbo Power Software
Public Domain

Oh, how welcome is this set of utilities. With the proliferation of the memory resident program, or TSR (Terminate and Stay Resident), the need for something to manage these programs is undeniable. How nice to see something in the public domain that does such an important job, and does it well.

TSR Utilities actually consist of 8 programs. The following is a summary taken from the TSR documentation:

- MARK marks a position above which TSRs can be released.
- RELEASE removes TSRs from memory.
- FMARK performs the same function as MARK but uses less memory.
- MAPMEM shows what memory resident programs are loaded.
- WATCH a TSR itself, it keeps detailed records of other TSRs.
- DISABLE disables or reactivates TSRs kept in memory.
- RAMFREE shows how much RAM memory (sic) is available.
- EATMEM uses up memory for controlled program testing.

To use the main feature of the TSR utilities, you first run the MARK program, then the TSR you want to control. For instance, if you were going to load Homebase (see Desk Managers), but thought you might like to remove it later, you would first enter the command MARK, then, after the mark was loaded, you would enter the command to begin Homebase.

To release Homebase and regain the memory it uses, you would issue the command *RELEASE*. This command will release every program residing above the most recent mark. You can issue several marks, thereby gaining control over the number of TSRs separately. Each *RELEASE* command you issue releases programs between the most current mark and the next one.

For more precise control, you can name a mark. For instance, if you enter *MARK HB*, then the command *RELEASE HB* releases all memory above that mark—including any intermediate marks. To prevent accidental release of a mark, a special protected mark can be created by adding an exclamation point to a named mark. For instance *MARK !HB* would create a protected mark. A protected mark cannot be released unless its exact name is used in the *RELEASE* command.

The mark itself takes up a little memory—about 1,600 bytes. Another program *FMARK* actually places most of the mark information in a small file on disk. Using FMARK only takes up about 150 bytes of memory. FMARK requires a file name, and therefore functions much like the named mark described above. FMARKS do not have a specific protected mode, but can only be released by name in any case.

Several other options and complexities to using MARK are detailed in the TSR Utilities manual.

MAPMEM—Often you wish to find out what is residing in memory at any given time. *MAPMEM*, issued from the DOS command line, will show any programs currently in memory, where they reside, any program names recognized, and also any hooked vectors. *MAPMEM* also shows the contents of expanded memory (conforming to the EMS specification). This little program is a great added utility when using *MARK* and *RELEASE*. It gives you the information needed to understand the current state of memory in your machine.

WATCH—This program works with *MAPMEM* and *DISABLE*. It keeps track of various aspects of what is going on in memory. *WATCH* is a TSR, and sits in memory to do its job. *WATCH* is necessary to use the *DISABLE* feature (below).

DISABLE—Many TSRs were not designed to function well with other TSRs, and conflicts are all too common. If you really want to have two conflicting TSRs resident at the same time, *DISABLE* can temporarily suspend one while you run the other, then reverse the process. In conjunction with the other utilities in the TSR collection, this program makes TSR management feasible.

Speaking as one who cringes whenever he learns that a new program is a TSR, the TSR Utilities are a true miracle. Now programs that don't have their own release mechanism don't cause any inconvenience.

MARK and *RELEASE* are easy to use, although some of their aspects can become technical. But the main function of these commands should not daunt anyone reasonably familiar with DOS. The TSR Utilities are a must for people with memory resident programs.

Even though TSR Utilities are public domain, we gave them a databox because we feel that they represent a very important resource in an area where standards are lacking and where the potential for incompatibility is still high.

The TSR Utilities
TurboPower Software
P.O. Box 66747
Scotts Valley, CA 95066
(408) 438-8608 (voice only, Mon-Fri 9AM to 5PM)
CompuServe ID 72457,2131

Public Domain

Category: Utilities

System Requirements: IBM PC or compatible; DOS 2.0 or later

Recommended Use: managing RAM resident programs

Major Pros: solves problems associated with TSRs; basic features are easy to use

Major Cons: some aspects can get fairly technical; not a novice user front end system

Sources: Popular BBSs and commercial services, or directly from the author

VERBACK ver. 1.2 (PD version)
TDS Software

VERBACK is a public-domain utility program that verifies that all hard disk files have been backed up to floppies via the *DOS BACKUP* command. It verifies that the data in all hard disk files is readable; that the data in all the backup files is readable; that the data in the backup files exactly matches the data stored on the hard disk; and that the special files used by the *BACKUP* and *RESTORE* commands are present on the backup floppies. An enhanced version of the program can be obtained by sending $20 to the author.

The program is run by typing VERBACK at the DOS command line. The program then prompts you for certain information, like which drive is the hard disk, and which drive is the floppy disk. The program then runs its verification check, which takes about the same amount of time as running the backup command all over again.

Though the program is useful, it's doubtful that most people will want to sit through the agony of swapping floppy disks all over again after just doing it with the DOS Backup command. On the other hand, nothing could be more disheartening, not to mention disastrous, than to have a serious disk crash, and then find out that your backups are bad.

VERDISK (unk. version)
Public Domain

VERDISK is a utility program that provides a quick and easy way to verify the condition of a hard or floppy disk. The program reads every sector of a disk and reports any errors such as drive seek, controller, CRC (Cyclic Redundancy Check), missing sector, missing address mark, etc. The program will work with all 5.25" floppy disk drives and IBM hard disks. The program was tested using a CORE ATPLUS 72 megabyte hard disk without a hitch. This is a good program to have on a utilities disk.

VOLSER (unk. version)
Public Domain

VOLSER is a public-domain utility that allows you to create or rename the volume label of a diskette or hard disk. The volume label is the name given to a disk when it is formatted. The volume label is displayed when you directory a disk or run *CHKDSK*. This program allows you to create a volume label or change an existing one. To run the program you type the following at the DOS command line:

```
A:>VOLSER [drivespec]
```

Drivespec is the drive designator of the disk that needs to be re-labeled (i.e. C:). The program then prompts you for the volume label which can be up to 11 characters in length.

This is a good utility and can be useful if you lend diskettes to people—you can change the volume label of the floppy to HARRY'S DISK, for example.

Whiz

S.B. Behman
20581 Ashley Way
Saratoga, CA 95070
Shareware—$10

Whiz is a very fast, very useful find-file utility. Like Whereis, Psearch, and Sfind, Whiz will find files on one or more disks based on a file name or wildcard string. Whiz works very fast and find creates a list of files that have been found. You can scroll backward and forward through the list—a feature missing from other find file utilities. Whiz will also compile the list into a file if you wish. Another unique feature is that all files whose archive bit is ON are highlighted. You can set a search to find files only if the archive bit is ON or OFF. Unless you specify a drive to search, the program will search all drives currently on line, including floppy and RAM drives. There can be problems searching some RAM drives, so you can use a special environment variable with Whiz which limits the search to specified drives.

Whiz worked very well on an IBM AT with a 30 megabyte drive, but failed to recognize the 40 megabyte drive on a Compaq 386 Deskpro. Therefore, we recommend this program with some reservations. It does work very quickly and, from what we have seen, works well when it works at all.

Xanadu Utilities

Shareware—$20

The Xanadu Utilities may be found separated, but they are part of a package of excellent system aids. The programs included are *HDIR.COM*, *PCSTAT.COM*, *SFIND.COM*, *QUICKCRT.COM*, *CURSORC.COM* and *CURSORM.COM*, and *HDIRCOLS.BAS*.

HotDIR 2.1

HotDIR 2.1 is a replacement for the *DOS DIR* command. It adds several useful touches. The most obvious touch is its use of color in the directory listing. Each file extension is listed with a different color (which can be defined by the user with the *HDIRCOLS.BAS* program). For instance, all *DOC* files might display in white, while all *EXE* files are blue, *COM* files are green, and *ARC* files are red, etc. Several command line switches are provided to list the directory in different sorted order, with varying numbers of columns across the screen, etc.

In addition to the listing of files, *HDIR* provides the total disk space available, the size of the current file selection (by totaling file size), and the space actually used on the disk by the selected files. Output from *HDIR* can be redirected to a file on disk. You can also run *HDIR* with path names and file names, or wild cards. To list all files a directory named DOS in six columns and sorted by extension you would type:

```
HDIR \DOS /6/e
```

HotDIR makes a pretty colorful addition to any system.

QUICKCRT vers. 1.03

This program didn't actually do anything on an IBM AT (8 MHz) with NEC GB-1 board and NEC MultiSynch. It is supposed to speed up screen handling, but in my test it didn't.
CURSORC and *CURSORM* are small utilities to change the cursor back to its original form after other programs have changed it. The first program is for color monitors, the second for mono.

SFIND ver. 1.02-X
Xanadu Compusoft

SFIND or SuperFIND is a utility to help you locate a file on a hard disk. If that's not enough, it finds files within *ARC* files on your hard disk. To use this program, you type the following at the DOS command line:

```
A:>SFIND [filespec] [options]
```

The *filespec* is optionally a drive letter combined with a file name and extension. Wild cards are O.K. The options tell *SFIND* not to search in *ARC* files, or to pause when the screen is full. As the program finds matching files, it lists them on the screen showing the directory path and ARC file name, if applicable, where the matching file can be found.

This is a useful program, and it works quickly and effectively.

XANADU Utilities 2.0
Tony Overfield and Robert Woeger
911 Enfield St.
Bryan, TX 77802

Shareware: $20

> *Note:* the author also adds an incentive registration deal, where if you pay
> $10 more, you get a special serialized disk. Every time someone registers
> the product with your serial number, the author sends you a check for $4.

Category: DOS Help

System Requirements: IBM PC or compatible or PS/2 computers; DOS 2.0
or later

Recommended Use: enhance DOS

Major Pros: the collection as a whole is excellent, although some specific
programs may not be useful, or may not work (as in the case of
QUICKCRT for us); some of the utilities can be found individually in
various catalogs and BBS listings

Major Cons: they don't work on every system

Sources: popular BBSs and commercial services, or directly from the author

20

Word Processing

This chapter is devoted to word processing tools. These may include style checkers, spelling checkers, outliners, compatibility programs (that make different formats work together), etc. The most important such tool is the traditional word processor. How do you judge whether a word processor will be good for you?

Your first consideration when choosing a word processor has to be, "What am I going to do with it?" If you plan very light duties like short letters, memos, and notes, then it makes little sense to search for the most complex and feature-rich program—no matter how highly it gets rated and recommended. On the other hand, if you are unsure just how far you want to go (maybe there's a great novel lurking in your future, or a book about your area of expertise), you may want to work with a product that allows you to expand.

Not all people need mail merging, even though it is often thought to be an essential part of a good word processor. But if you don't really send out form letters, or you don't intend to create mailing labels from your word processor (there are many fine label-printing utilities), you may not require that feature.

I still remember when, back in around 1981, I was looking for a better Apple II word processor than EasyWriter. I read a magazine review of another word processor making it sound like the ideal product. Based on that review I shelled out close to $200 (it was not Shareware) thinking that I was going to solve all my word processing needs forever. I was dead wrong. Not only did I end up not liking the word processor, but I never used it.

Based on reviews alone, it is difficult to assess a product. The solution? Shareware. Try it before you pay. I never got my money back for that product (although I might have if I had belly-ached enough). With Shareware, I would simply have copied over the disk and not paid.

But the warning about trusting reviews even extends to this book. You may love a product that we have omitted. You may dislike our picks. All we can do is try to indicate the way these programs present themselves. Hopefully, the information here will help you decide. But because each person works in a different way, and because people often form loyalties to programs they use a lot, there is plenty of room for disagreement.

One significant difference between PD and Shareware word processors and commercial programs is that there is less price variation between simpler and more complex products. Commercial products range anywhere from $25 for extremely basic text processing, to several hundred dollars for the top of the line. PD and Shareware range from nothing to maybe $75.

Other features to consider are search/replace, formatting options, screen display, cursor movement and command shortcuts, special effects (bold, underlining, italics, super- and sub-scripts, etc.), cut and paste, headers and footers, multiple document editing (windows), spell checking, table of contents and index generation, math functions, multiple columns, pagination options, document backups, and so on.

In addition to basic word processing, there are those programs which enhance productivity. & is a nifty utility that allows you to preview up to 12 pages at a time on screen before printing. You can see the basic layout in miniature and be sure that the basic format of the document is correct. There are grammar checkers, indexing programs, conversion programs (to convert between commercial word processor formats), and there is even a complete collection of business letter templates for every occasion.

The word processor section of this book contains many examples—more than most sections of the book. This is due in part to the wide variety of people's word processing needs. It also stems from the fact that there are many fairly equivalent word processing programs, each with its own unique qualities, and each finely programmed and presented. We have attempted to look at most, if not all, the significant word processing programs. Some are simple, and some complex. Programs were left out of this chapter for the same reasons they were left out of other chapters: because we felt that they were not the best of the genre, or due to sheer oversight. We feel that there is a use for each program that is included, and that you, as the Shareware consumer, will determine what is best for you.

Galaxy Version 2.3

Omniverse
Shareware—$49.95

For those with simple word processing needs, Galaxy is a very attractive alternative. This word processor features all the essential features: block marking, copying and deleting, search and replace, color customization, automatic repagination, and several cursor movement and Goto options. It is also one of the fastest word processors we've ever seen, comparable in speed to Borland's Sprint.

Galaxy Vers. 2.3
Omniverse
P.O. Box 2974
Renton, WA 98056
(206) 228-7627

Shareware: $49.95

Category: Word Processor

System Requirements: PC or compatible; 192K; at least one disk drive; 80 column display; printer recommended

Recommended Use: simple, but fast and easy, basic word processing

Major Pros: very fast (the program is RAM based); easy to learn and to use; WordStar compatibility; multiple user interfaces; good printer support; runs from any directory on current DOS Path; phone support and 24hr BBS support

Major Cons: lacks advanced features, especially mail merge; manual paragraph reformat (like WordStar)

Sources: popular BBSs and commercial services, or directly from the author

---

Galaxy offers a few bells and whistles, most notably the excellent pull-down menus, extensive printer support, processing of two documents in separate windows (with cut and paste between them), Save As feature to save different file versions, and a set of Preferences easily set from within the program. Starting with version 2.3, they have included the ability to record macros and also to save special default parameter files which can be used to initialize the program differently if called from different directories.

Preferences include EGA 43 line option, show graphics characters (UPPER ASCII) or suppress (which can instantly change a WordStar file from gibberish to readable text), definable undo limit (for restoring altered lines), plus options to set margins, tab size, page length, etc. Galaxy also works with many WordStar commands, its own "quick commands," or the pull-down menus, making it easy for novices, WordStar users, or Galaxy experts. Galaxy can format output documents in WordStar format. You can also set word wrap on or off, and process documents up to 240 columns wide.

Now you can use the directory feature to list the current directory, and highlight and select a file from the list. You can use wildcards to sub-limit the list as well, and Galaxy remembers your last requests, even between sessions, making repetitive typing a rarity. Also, Galaxy does not come with a spell checking program, but it does include a command for accessing Borland's Turbo Lightning with full support of that commercial product.

Although it lacks some of the fancier features like mail merge, math, columns, etc., Galaxy is easy to use and well designed. It makes an excellent, fast and efficient basic word processor.

MindReader 2.0
Brown Bag Software
Shareware—$49.95

When MindReader first came out as a commercial product several years ago, I remember thinking how strange and wonderful a product it was. It combined some solid word processing values with an application of artificial intelligence that is at once brilliant and, at the same time, of limited usefulness.

MindReader contains several fine features, but its major innovation has to do with the way it can, in a sense, attempt to read your mind as you type. When you begin a word, it will offer an on-screen menu of possible words that begin the same way. If you ignore the window and continue typing, MindReader will continue to refine its suggestions based on the letters you have already typed. At any time, you can accept one of the suggested words by typing the character associated with the word you want. For instance, if you type the letter *s*, MindReader displays five choices. The preferred choice is always associated with the semi-colon. In this case, typing the semi-colon selects the word *should*. Other options are numbered 2 through 5. Suppose now you continue to type and enter *stu*. Now the program selects two words, student and study. If you choose to accept the word student, you type the semi-colon. The word is filled in for you, a space is added, and you are ready to continue typing. Remarkably, if you need to punctuate the sentence, you can simply enter a comma, period, or other punctuation mark. The program places the punctuation at the appropriate place, then adds the appropriate number of spaces automatically. Also, whether you use the automatic word fill or not, you can change the suffix of a word. For instance, if the word should be plural, press F2 and it will be made plural. Also, you can make it past tense, or add an -ing extension. MindReader knows the spelling rules and will make appropriate changes. For instance, if you type the word *specify* and want it to be plural, it will be changed to *specifies*. If you wanted a past tense version, it would create *specified*, and adding *ing* would produce *specifying*. The program is not one hundred percent accurate, but it does a credible job of dealing with the irregularities of English spelling.

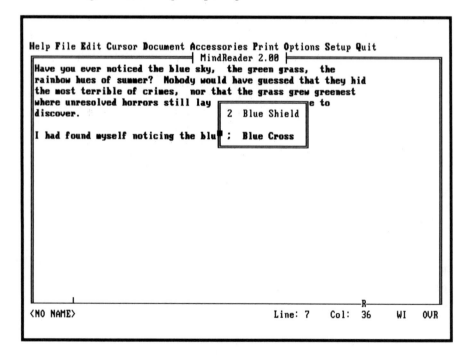

MindReader offers a few enhancements to this system. For one, you can actually define words to add to this Frequent Word option. Therefore, if you often type the word stupendous, you could have it become one of the choices offered. But MindReader is doing more than suggesting words. If you have the AI Learn mode on, MindReader will monitor the words you choose from the Frequent Word windows. In time, it will see that you prefer the word stupendous to the word student, and it will shift their positions. If stupendous is the word you use most, stupendous will become the first choice offered.

All this mind reading is fascinating and works very quickly in the background. The technical achievement of this program is exceptional. However, the usefulness of these features I'm describing is questionable. For fast typists it is more of an annoyance than a benefit. For slow typists, and especially for handicapped users, these features may be a great help.

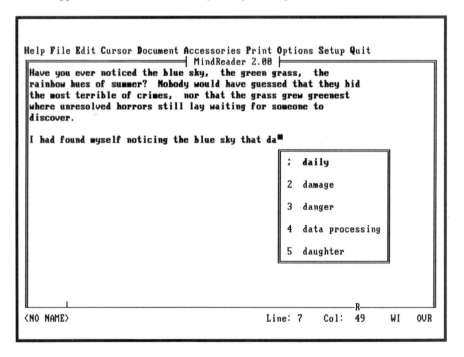

Recognizing that faster typists will not want these features to be fully automatic, MindReader lets you configure it so that the suggestions do not appear automatically. You can turn the feature off entirely, or set it in standby mode. In standby mode, the program waits for you to press a semi-colon in the middle of a word, then makes its suggestions. Of course, this makes typing a semi-colon a little more complex—you have to type it twice.

MindReader has plenty of other good features. It has timed backups, an address book module, user definable page breaks and page headers, a useful line drawing mode, macro recording (with user-defined variables), glossaries, and even a built-in calculator (which can move results to the current document). It has a fairly limited mail merge facility as well as real-time spelling correction, or more conventional spell checking. The built-in dictionary is limited, but it is easy to add to it.

MindReader 2.0
Brown Bag Software, Inc.
2155 South Bascom Ave., Suite 114
Campbell, CA 95008
(800) 523-0764
(800) 323-5335 (in California)
(408) 559-4545 (overseas)

Shareware: $49.95 plus $5 shipping

Category: Word Processor

System Requirements: IBM PC, XT, AT, or compatible; at least 256K
available RAM; DOS 2.0 or higher

Recommended Use: especially great for slow typists, hunt and peck types and
handicapped users

Major Pros: automatically fills in words as you type; macros with
variables;fast execution; WordStar commands; calculator; built-in address
book database

Major Cons: limited mail merge; basic word processing outside the specific
extras; text handling could be improved

Sources: popular BBSs and commercial services, or directly from the author

---

For people familiar with WordStar, MindReader uses many of the familiar WordStar commands along with a set of its own options. It does automatic word wrapping with adjustable ruler line, etc. As a general word processor, MindReader is adequate, but not necessarily our choice. We often found it awkward to work with because it doesn't support the most efficient system of word wrapping. For instance, you can't cursor backward from the beginning of a line to the end of the previous line. Further, if you are inserting text into a line in the middle of a paragraph, it will word wrap correctly, but it will create a new line below the current one, not wrap the line onto the beginning of the following line, even though they should be part of the same paragraph. This may seem a small point, but it is the kind of drawback that you will encounter frequently, and there are plenty of other word processors that handle text better.

There are a lot of features that are present in high-end word processors that are missing in this one, but, again, that does not mean that MindReader can't do the job. It really depends on your needs. Since it is a Shareware product, it might be worth looking at the product to decide for yourself. MindReader is the kind of product that is going to produce a strong response in most people—either they'll like it or they'll hate it. The only real way to tell how you feel is to take a look.

Despite our reservations about MindReader as a general word processor, it is a usable product, and one that has great potential. It is also fun to watch. It has a unique identity in the word processor world.

New York Word Processor version 2.2

Marc Adler
Shareware—$44.95

New York Word is one of the most powerful and versatile word processors anywhere. It rivals the capabilities of commercial word processors, and adds a few unique wrinkles of its own. Starting with Version 2.2, NYW has added a pull-down menu system to make the program more accessible. Despite its very impressive list of features, it is quite easy to use. Like any product of similar complexity, learning to use all its features presents the user with a formidable challenge, but, unlike some feature-laden products, NYW has an easy basic interface that allows novices to become productive almost immediately.

Basic feature list: documents stored in proprietary or ASCII format; automatic backup of documents; periodic backup during editing; docs up to 16000 columns wide; full, practical set of cursor movement options; spelling correction; very sophisticated mail merge and labels; footnotes and endnotes, headers and footers, multiple format lines, multi-column formatter; 10 cut and paste buffers (with sophisticated block functions); two calculator functions for math; index and TOC generation; automatic repagination; up to 26 bookmarks (place markers); up to 12 windows to display the same or different documents (with cut and paste between docs); versatile search and replace features; optional printer codes; special effects (bold, underline, super- and sub-scripts); Macros and Macro libraries; DOS shell; ASCII line drawing mode; user configurable; and a help index.

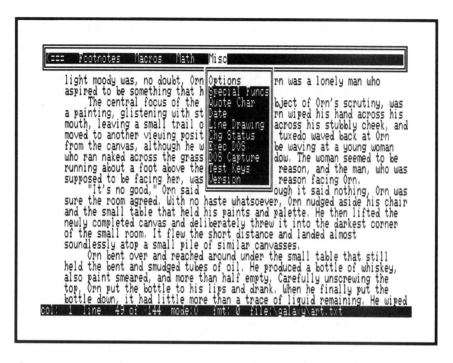

Its cursor movement commands are extremely versatile and easy to use. It features basic movement by character, word, paragraph, page, and line. A Goto command allows movement to specific pages, or line numbers. You can even move up or down a specific number of lines. Other commands move to the beginning or end of a line, to the top and bottom of the screen, next or previous screen, or beginning/end of document. Several exceptional features stand out. Search and replace contains a few versatile options not found in many commercial programs. The most intriguing option is the ability to define several search/replace pairs in one operation. If you wish to change all occurrences of Tom to Harry, and Jane to Debby, and bathroom to washroom, you write a small list as follows:

    Tom=Harry
    Jane=Debby
    bathroom=washroom

Then, in one pass, NYW would make all appropriate substitutions. You could even use wild cards (bath*=wash* would change bathroom and bathtub to washroom and washtub).

NYW contains two math modes. One is a quick and easy calculator that can handle complex arithmetic, including parenthesized expressions. The other mode allows you to add columns and/or rows of numbers, or perform arithmetic operations on numbers in your document.

NYW mail merging (supplied with registered version only) is extremely powerful, although somewhat non-standard. For each form document, there must be a data file and a format file. The data file is simply the letter with the merge variables appropriately inserted. The format file, however, contains more than just a list of records. Each format file begins with a set of variable definitions. Format files can also contain conditional statements. The expression, "if @credit limit@ => $1000 @discount@ == .25," would set a discount variable to .25 only if a particular customer's credit limit was $1000 or more. Other expressions allow you to select which records will print, create calculations based on variables, concatenate variables (for instance, "@name@ = Mr. + @lname@" means add Mr. to each last name). NYWMail can handle addresses consisting of varying numbers of lines, and output of form letters and labels can be sorted in several ways as well.

Another utility only supplied with the registered version is the Multicolumn program. This program allows you to set the document width, the number of columns, and the space between columns. Once the settings are complete, the program creates a columnar version of an ASCII file. This version displays to the screen, but the output can be redirected to a file or to the printer.

Another way to create multicolumn text in NYW is to use its "rectangular block" command. Unlike most block marking commands, this one allows you to cut and paste any rectangular area from the screen. To create multiple column text, you simply format the document with narrow margins, then highlight and cut a page at a time. Paste each page in turn, next to the column that precedes it. In the end, you have a nicely formatted newspaper style document. Editing the finished product later presents new problems, however, as the newspaper style columns do not scroll as one continuous block of text. Adding to or deleting from text formatted this way, then, destroys the formatting. In this sense, NYW does not emulate page layout programs like PageMaker and Ventura Publisher.

The integrated spelling checker is fairly good, but sometimes comes up with nonsensical suggestions. Also, even though suggestions are often accurate, you still need to type in the correct spelling before it will be inserted into the document. Correct words missing from the dictionary can be added to a user dictionary during the spell check.

Creating a table of contents for a document is simply a matter of marking entries with special hidden codes. Multiple codes are used to indicate lower entry levels in the finished table. On command, the TOC is automatically compiled and placed in a separate file, or at the beginning of the current file. Indexing is just as easy. In fact, NYW has one of the best single-level indexing features I've ever seen. All that is required is that you mark a word or phrase with a hidden code once in the document! When the Index command is issued, all pages on which that word or phrase occurs will be entered into the index. Sequential page ranges are automatically formatted with a dash (25-31). Unfortunately, NYW does not create cross references, illustration entries, or sub-heads when generating indexes. Neither the index nor the TOC utility is designed to work with multiple files.

To round out an impressive feature list, NYW offers user-defined macros, multiple documents in separate windows, and several window-related features like Zoom and Shrink, Close, Split, reSize, and Goto windows.

The on-disk manual, and its printed counterpart, are abysmal—in fact typical of Shareware manuals by programmers busy working on a product with little time for writing. The information is there, but poorly formatted and full of typos.

New York Word Processor Vers. 2.2
Marc Adler
Magma Software Systems
138-23 Hoover Ave.
Jamaica, NY 11435
(718) 793-5670

Shareware: $44.95 (plus $2 shipping; $6 overseas)

Category: Word Processor

System Requirements: PC or compatible; DOS 2.0 or later; 384K; 2 drives (hard disk recommended); 80 column display; optional printer

Recommended Use: any word processing

Major Pros: just about any feature a word processor could have; the easiest (but not the most versatile) indexing option we've ever seen; built-in print spooling

Major Cons: a heavy package, not for casual word processing; powerful, but somewhat complex mail merge format; spell checker could be improved

Sources: popular BBSs and commercial services, or directly from the author

---

Help is provided in the form of one Sherman Reinus, a dedicated NYW user who turned his dedication into a new manual. Although the Reinus edition is better organized and comes ready for insertion in an IBM-style binder, it is still not as complete as a product of this size might demand. To get people up and running quickly, Reinus has also created a tutorial disk. Both the manual and the disk are being distributed as Shareware add-ons to NYW, and have the full blessing of Marc Adler, NYW's author. To contact him please write:

> Sherman Reinus
> 4866 73rd Street
> La Mesa, CA 92041
> Shareware—$20 (manual, tutorial disk, and 1 year free updates).

Of course there's more. Suffice it to say that NYW is a versatile word processor that can meet nearly anyone's word processing needs. Some of its procedures might require dedication to learn, but once learned, the product can hold its own with top-of-the-line commercial word processors.

PC-Type
Buttonware
Shareware—$69.95

While PC-Type is not the slickest of the current crop of Shareware word processors, it is a program that offers considerable power and unique features. With customizable color screens, pop-up windows, built-in spelling, mail merge, and label programs, PC-Type is a pretty strong package. Add to that its ability to sort text and to draw ASCII graphics, a Whoops (Undo) key, excellent on-line help, and professionally written manual, and the program becomes a better value. Then add its built-in access to PC-File data, and you begin to see how well this product fits into the ButtonWare line.

PC-Type handles automatic or manual pagination, headers and footers with automatic page numbering, up to ten keystroke macros, block copy, delete, move, search and replace, 100,000 word dictionary for spell checking, ASCII graphics commands, and many more important, more or less expected functions. You can even execute DOS commands without exiting the program.

Its user interface is sometimes awkward. For instance, to split a paragraph, it is necessary to use the unusual command *Control-~*, then type the Enter key (Carriage Return), move to the new line, then press Control-R to reformat the newly created paragraph. By comparison, most word processors would accomplish the same result with the simple pressing of the Enter key.

PC-Type includes a great many keyboard commands, and, while this adds power and flexibility to the program, it also makes learning the product more difficult. Some commands are buried several layers deep (for instance, to invoke a new paragraph without creating a blank line, you must type *F8-F7-F7*).

Still, once you have learned PC-Type, you will be delighted to discover such added features as column addition, newspaper column formatting (including separate formatting of any individual column through the block marking techniques), etc. You can also add printer codes to a document for specific printing effects.

Those who need mail merging, mailing list management, and label printing should find the combination of PC-Type and PC-File a powerful one. Since most Shareware products are created in something of a vacuum, the inter-connectivity of these two products is a pleasant extra.

PC TYPE+ Version 1.0
ButtonWare, Inc.
P.O. Box 5786
Bellevue, WA 98006
(206) 454-0479
(800) JBUTTON (order line)

Shareware: $69.95 (plus $5 shipping per order)

Category: Word Processor

System Requirements: PC or compatible; DOS 2.0 or later; 256K or more; at least one 360K drive; 80 column display; printer recommended

Recommended Use: word processing for those who can use its particular combination of features, particularly merging with PC File+

Major Pros: many power features like columns, simple math, keystroke macros; DOS commands from within program

Major Cons: awkward user interface

Sources: popular BBSs and commercial services, or directly from the author

---

The merge file formats include some powerful and useful options. You can key in information during printout, create some conditional situations, force text into a document, omit blank lines (through the *.GROUP* and *.EGROUP* commands), etc. Files can be included during mail merge, even as the result of conditional expressions, (for example, *IF CITY, "San Francisco", C:\PCT\LETTER2.TXT*). You can even instruct the program to save each set of names and addresses to a special file for later production of mailing labels (with PC-Label, of course). Date and Time stamps and automatic record selection criteria from the PC-File data round out this excellent mail merging product.

We didn't find PC-Type to be the slickest or most easy-to-use word processor, nor did we find it to be the most powerful. But it does have many useful features. Its mail merging and links with PC-File make it worthy of consideration, but its user interface does not compare well with that of other products.

PC-Write 2.71

Quicksoft
Shareware—$89

PC-Write is one of the most successful Shareware products there is. It is also a word processor to rival NYW or any other word processor. For those who may have seen an older version of PC-Write, rest assured—the program has evolved into a powerful, full-featured product.

Among the key features of PC-Write are its printer support (over 300 printers, including several laser printers and Adobe's PostScript). This immense printer support sets PC-Write apart from most Shareware products which may support, at best, a handful of printers. There are separate utilities to manage HP LaserJet fonts, translate to IBM's DCI-RFT standard, and translate to Aldus PageMaker format.

PC-Write also features table of contents and index creation, numerous formatting commands, and a powerful set of options featuring menu-driven and/or command-driven editing controls. PC-Write is very customizable—even the help screens can be customized. Also included is a 50,000 word spelling corrector with optional on-the-fly checking that beeps when you type a word it doesn't know. More conventionally, the spelling checker will suggest spellings for words if requested.

PC-Write allows block cut, copy, and paste; search and replace (including wild card searches); various special effects (bold, italic, underlines, etc.); multiple format lines with tabs and margins; headers and footers; footnotes (with automatic renumbering); split window processing (with the same or separate documents); DOS shell; and much more. You can rename the current file to save a new version. You can also create keystroke macros, and bookmarks to save your place in a document. A complete set of cursor movement keys is provided as well as mouse support. Deleted blocks of text can be undeleted (only to one level, the next deletion replaces the buffer). You can also copy from one file to another.

A new feature called Screen Clip allows you to exit to the DOS shell, copy some text from another program, then return to PC-Write and paste it into the current document.

You can also convert WordStar or DisplayWrite DCA type files, insert current date, repeat the most recent keystroke, count words, etc. One feature that programmers will love is the ability to find a matching bracket, parenthesis, or brace. Word count also provides the number of bytes, characters, letters, and words in a file or block, as well as the average characters per word.

Along with its large set of features, PC-Write has a sophisticated merge utility. It includes the ability to omit blank lines and supports various formats for merge data. PC-Write does not have the conditional features of NY Word's merge feature, however. On the other hand, some people may find PC-Write's merge features easier to use.

Tables of contents and indexes are created by marking words and phrases with special characters. These features work in the same basic way that they do in most programs. Each index entry must be marked, however, unlike NY Word (which allows one index entry to be marked in the file, then compiles the index for the rest of the document).

PC-Write is distributed as Shareware, but the real product includes the Quicksoft support (which is excellent) and the manuals (which are also excellent and extensive). In addition to the main manual, you get two quick reference cards and a quick reference booklet. This is a thoroughly professional product, and Quicksoft is a company run as well as any other software company I've seen.

There are only two major limitations to PC-Write. One is its inability to create files larger than 60K, and the other is its limited WYSIWYG abilities. PC-Write uses an extensive system of dot commands and other imbedded formatting to create finished documents. For this reason, it may not appeal to some users. On the other hand, its extensive formatting abilities include many font-related commands.

```
Esc:cancel.  F1-F1:help.  Alt/Shf/Ctl/Arrow:select.  Fn-key/Letter/Enter:action.
█F1:System/help█ F3.Copy/mark    F5.Un-mark       F7.Paragraph     F9:Find-text
F2:Window/ruler F4.Delete/mark  F6.Move/mark     F8.Lower/upper  F10.Replace
MENU:  help, exit/command, save/unsave;  name text, file load, print;  directory
  work there act. Oh, Ted's all right, but some of the others... God, they

  act like they have all the secrets of the universe locked up in that lab

  of theirs. And Ted's always picking up discarded bits of equipment and

  bringing them home in his lunchbox. So when I say that I never know what

  I'm going to find there, I really mean it.

       What I do with the things I find is put them all neatly in the

  basement. Ted never lets me throw anything away. Then I tell him, "I put

  your gizmos in the basement," and he always gets sort of mad. He hates it

  when I call them gizmos. Then I usually ask him, "What are you going to do

  with all those dealy-bobs down there, anyway?" Dealy-bobs: another word he

  hates. And then he makes me laugh; he always does. He says,
```

Some people may find PC-Write takes some time to learn, but its menu-driven approach soon leads to a familiarity with its command structure, and many WordStar commands are also available. With the excellent manual and quick references, learning PC-Write should pose no great problem.

Version 3.0 of PC-Write is in the works, and should be out by the middle of 1988. Some added features planned are: the end of the 60K file limit, line and page number on the status line, improved spell checking, more integration of the program files (for faster, smoother operation), several enhancements to simulate desktop publishing including a couple of multiple column improvements. Also box moving, menus for entry formatting commands, and more WYSIWYG abilities.

PC Write 2.71
Quicksoft, Inc.
219 First N. #224
Seattle, WA 98109
(206) 282-0452

Shareware: $89 (registration plan means $25 kickback to you if someone
registers and pays for a copy with your serial number)

Category: Word Processor

System Requirements: IBM PC, XT, AT, or compatible; DOS 2.0 or later;
256K (320 with speller); at least one 360K drive; optional printer

Recommended Use: any word processing

Major Pros: very professional packaging (even a DOS tutorial in the manual);
90 day warranty; several user interface options; well established product;
programmer's utilities; extensive printer support; full range of features

Major Cons: memory limit on files is 60K; not completely WYSIWYG

Sources: popular BBSs and commercial services, or directly from the author

PC-Write is a fine product, professional down to its nuts and bolts. That is not to
say it is for everyone, but it certainly holds its own with other word processors
on the market, Shareware or otherwise.

PC Outline

Brown Bag Software
Shareware—price varies

If you've ever had any doubts about whether a Shareware product could be at the
top of its class, you owe it to yourself to look at PC Outline. This is a
completely professional product, a powerful and versatile thinking tool, a full-
featured outliner.

PC Outline can run as a stand-alone application or as a TSR (Terminate and Stay
Resident) program. As a TSR, it requires about 85K of memory, but it may be
85K well used. Since PC Outline can interface with other programs while in

memory, it becomes a handy tool for brainstorming or for moving blocks of data in and out of word processors, spreadsheets, and other programs. PC Outline can even import and export WordStar, ASCII, and database structure files. Use it as a notepad, free-form, or use the outliner to quickly prioritize your thoughts.

PC Outline features a set of commands activated from a series of pull-down menus. Several commands have keystroke equivalents for advanced users. You can create up to nine simultaneous outline windows, cut and paste between them, and zoom a current outline to fill the screen. You can manipulate outline elements in many ways, including promoting and demoting levels or whole families, closing or opening sub-levels, hiding outline elements, changing labels, renumbering lists, etc. You can even use PC Outline as if it were a full-screen editor. You can mark selected entries and then perform different operations only on the marked entries, sort within any level, even create entries that are outside the outline's numbering scheme (as labels, titles, comments, etc.).

Several features are optional, like automatic backups and automatic timed saves of all active outlines. You can even set the time between saves. You can set the current directory, change the default directory from the DOS command line, and also set new default directories for various program and configuration files.

PC Outline is so feature laden, that it can seem a little intimidating, but it is easy to use and the manual that accompanies the shrink-wrapped version is excellent. The program's versatility ensures that almost anyone can find a use for it. Suggested uses range from daily "to do" lists to full book outlines. Anyone writing or planning a project could use PC Outline. It offers so much control that it can be used as an editor or even a simple word processor.

PC Outline also features keystroke replacement macros. You can assign frequently used words, phrases, and even paragraphs to a single key combination. There is even a feature that disables all key redefinitions, even if they were created with outside programs like SuperKey and Prokey.

Print options are varied and allow printing of partial outlines, specialized configuration files for unusual graphic characters, and support of several popular printers. If a printer is not specifically supported, PC Outline allows you to create a special printer configuration file.

The printed manual that Brown Bag will supply with PC Outline contains several sample applications and a tutorial on creating them. Among the applications are a practical to do list, a letter, and a simple project management model.

414

If you think you might have a use for an outline program, PC Outline is well worth considering. We consider it at least equal, if not superior to, any other outliner on the market.

PC Outline
Brown Bag Software, Inc.
2155 South Bascom Ave., Suite 114
Campbell, CA 95008
(800) 523-0764
(800) 323-5335 (in California)
(408) 559-4545 (overseas)

Shareware: price varies with support options. Ranges from $29.95 to $89.95

Category: Outliner

System Requirements: IBM PC, XT, AT, or compatible; at least 128K
available RAM; DOS 2.0 or higher

Recommended Use: amazing outlines; text editing; brainstorming, etc.

Major Pros: has all the features you could ask for in an outline processor;
multiple windows with Zoom feature; full screen text editing; split
numbering, skip, or start new numbering; macros; autosave

Major Cons: none

Sources: popular BBSs and commercial services, or directly from the author

---

Note: With the shrink-wrapped version of PC Outline, you also receive several handy file utilities, including *MEM.COM*, *DIRS.COM*, *GLOBAL.COM*, *MOVE.COM*, *BEEP.COM*, *POPDIR.COM*, *PUSHDIR.COM,* and *CPY.COM.*

MEM.COM provides an instant readout of available RAM.

DIRS.COM gives the total space required by a set of files determined by wild card search.

GLOBAL.COM is used to perform a DOS function on the entire DOS tree starting in the current directory. For instance, to erase all files ending in

.TXT from the entire disk at once, you could type *GLOBAL ERASE *.TXT*.

CPY.COM backs up files to floppies from a file list and prompts you to insert new floppy disks.

MOVE.COM performs a copy and file erase in one command.

BEEP.COM produces a computer beep sound—useful for flagging error conditions in batch files.

PUSHDIR.COM and POPDIR.COM—PUSHDIR is used to store the current directory. Works within a DOS command file (batch file) so that when you issue the companion command *POPDIR* the program returns to that directory. Could also be used for on-the-fly changes between directories.

&

Curtis McKallip
Shareware—$40

& is a useful utility program that displays a reduced view of up to 12 pages of a document at once. It also gives statistics on the word count, line count, character count, sentence count, average characters/word, average words/sentence and words/page. & works with ASCII, WordStar, PC-Write, MultiMate, and Xywrite files (although there are some limitations to its ability to read certain file types).

What is most useful about & is that it allows you to preview a long document several pages at a time. You can search for formatting mistakes as well as widows, orphans, and split tables. Although you can't read the text, & provides some insight into the final form of a document before printing, thereby saving time and paper.

```
&
Curtis  McKallip
P.O. Box 3745
Midland, TX 79702


Shareware: $40 suggested


Category: Page Display


System Requirements: PC or compatible; 128K; at least one 360K drive; 80
    column display; color graphics board recommended


Recommended Use: graphic representation of multiple pages from a
    document, for previewing page breaks, margins, etc.


Major Pros: works with several word processor files; unique look at document
    structure over several pages


Major Cons: lack of on-going support; does not have any other page layout
    features; should support more word processor and page layout formats


Sources: popular BBSs and commercial services, or directly from the author
```

UNWS

Gene Plantz
Public Domain

Another great word processing utility, UNWS strips extra data from WordStar files and turns them into straight ASCII files. This is useful when you want to import WordStar documents into other word processors, use an ASCII-based utility on the document, or import data from a WordStar file into a database or other program that reads ASCII files. This utility can be found under various names.

XWORD

Ronald Gans Software Company
Shareware—$20

You may work in an office that uses more than one word processor, or you may be switching from one to another. In fact, there are lots of reasons why you may need to convert file types from one to another product. XWORD may have an answer for you. This Shareware product will convert between the formats of several commercial word processors. Supported formats include WordStar, WordStar 2000, MultiMate, Word Perfect, Nota Bene, XYWrite III, ASCII, and dBASE III (as an output file only).

The Shareware version of XWORD has been on the market for some time, and we highly recommend that you register it. The registered version is much more up to date, and includes more and better features. Also included on the disk will be some other useful utilities like MAKEREAD (see the Utilities section).

XWORD
Ronald Gans Software Company
350 West 50th Street
New York, NY 10019
(212) 957-8361

Shareware: $20

Category: Word Processor Conversions

System Requirements: PC or compatible; 128K; at least one 360K drive

Recommended Use: Convert files between different word processor formats

Major Pros: works with several major word processor formats; simple command line interface; variety of options; search and replace up to 20 strings

Major Cons: May not work in every case for every need

Sources: popular BBSs and commercial services, or directly from the author

---

The Shareware version of XWORD will also allow you to define one search and replace string to use on a file or list of files (using wildcards). However, the registered version allows you to define up to 20 search and replace strings, and even saving them in a parameter's file for use at a later date. This facility could be very useful to lawyers or other users who must change several details in a list of documents. It is obviously faster than loading each file, then searching and replacing each string one at a time.

XWORD can use wildcards to convert formats for a list of documents in one command. Although the completeness of the conversions may vary somewhat depending on which word processors are involved, the product works very well. It will convert most formatting including margins, tabs, bold, italics, and so forth. It will also convert headers and footers and other parts of most files. We can't test all the conversions that XWORD offers, but we can say that for $20 this program offers a lot of utility. If you need word processor conversions, you owe it to yourself to look at this product.

Style Checkers

Fogfinder
Joey Robichaux
Shareware—$15

Fogfinder tests the readability of your writing using the well-known Gunning Fog Index. Although readability is not the only determining factor in good writing, it is important, especially in business and technical writing. The Fog Index corresponds to the level of education needed to understand a document. An index of 9, for instance, means a ninth grade reading level.

Most successful business and technical writing attempts to achieve a level below 13. This often has as much to do with sentence structure and word usage as it does with the material covered. Restructuring the writing can often make it more readable. Fog Finder analyzes up to 50 sentences of any text file sample. It then produces an on-screen report of its findings. Although there are more elaborate grammar checking programs, many people may find Fog Finder of use.

Fog Finder displays its results along with a graph of values that indicates the general level of writing equivalent to that of several popular magazines. At the top, rating around 12 is *Atlantic Monthly* and *Wall Street Journal*. Below that are ratings for *Reader's Digest, Ladies Home Journal, True Confessions,* and, finally, rating about 6, are *People* and *TV Guide*.

Fog Finder
Joey Robichaux
1036 Brookhollow Drive
Baton Rouge, LA 70810

Shareware: $15

Category: Style Checker

Recommended Use: very basic style checking

Major Pros: interesting comparative look at results vs. familiar sources of
    writing

Major Cons: fairly basic in approach and design; lacks some features of other
    style checkers; standard questions about the usefulness of style checkers in
    general

Sources: popular BBSs and commercial services, or directly from the author

---

A higher rating does not necessarily mean a better document, however. In many
cases, the lower (6 or 7) rating may be preferable.

Fog Finder is a simple look at writing style. PC-Style from ButtonWare gives a
more detailed look.

PC-Style

ButtonWare, Inc.
Shareware—$29.95 plus $5.00 for shipping

PC Style from ButtonWare analyzes text and WordStar files for overall readability
and writing strength. The program counts sentences and words as well as words
per sentence; percentage of long words, personal words, and action words;
syllables per word; and readability index (similar to Fog Finder). As it reads the
file, a series of graphs moves and provides an animated display of the analysis.
When it is finished, the values for the various parameters are displayed, both as
numbers and as graphical data. At the bottom of the screen, a graph displays
overall ratings for readability, personal tone, and action. The graph ranges from
Poor to Excellent.

In PC-Style, a lower readability rating scores a higher rating. The same is true of personal style. The higher the percentage of action words, the higher the rating in the Action category.

Although PC-Style does not make specific suggestions as to how to improve your writing, as some commercial programs do, it does provide a quick way to assess the overall strength of a document. Many people will find that insights from PC-Style can help them in writing more effectively.

PC STYLE
ButtonWare, Inc.
P.O. Box 5786
Bellevue, WA 98006
(206) 454-0479
(800) JBUTTON (order line)

Shareware: $29.95 plus $5.00 for shipping

Category: Style Checker

System Requirements: PC or compatible; DOS 2.0 or later; 256K or more; at least one 360K drive; 80 column display; printer recommended

Recommended Use: check writing style in an entertaining medium

Major Pros: graphic, animated approach to style checking; good breakdown of elements of style

Major Cons: standard questions about the overall usefulness of style checkers in general

Sources: popular BBSs and commercial services, or directly from the author

---

A Note About Fog Finder and PC-Style

I found that Fog Finder and PC-Style did not come up with exactly the same readability index on a file. This may have something to do with the way they read the files. Fog Finder only reads the first 50 sentences. PC-Style reads the entire document. Variations that occur in a long document or toward the end of a work may change the overall rating. In that case, PC-Style is probably the more accurate gauge.

In checking the results of Fog Finder and PC-Style against a commercial grammar checker, I found the results varied somewhat once again. My feeling after doing these comparisons is that any grammar checker should be used with caution and not taken too literally. They provide excellent guides, and can help point out severe writing problems. They do not provide instant answers for weak writing.

Style-Ed
Louie Crew
Shareware—$10

Get Style-Ed, if for no other reason, than to read the manual that accompanies it. The author, Louie Crew, is a verbose, witty, and opinionated gentleman whose documentation is full of odd and intriguing moments. For instance:

> I cringe when I imagine the mindless ways to use this program. For example, the program quantifies transitionals. Transitionals often evidence cohesion, but only if the writers have used them accurately. For some writers, THUS=ALSO, MOREOVER=NEVERTHELESS, etc. This program will not detect their confusion. No program protects us from sophomores. Thank the goddess, most grow up.

> I smile when I imagine those who think these matters completely unimportant. At Breadloaf, Robert Frost used to talk for hours about a minute effect of meter. "But surely you don't think about such things when you write!" allegedly a poetaster exclaimed. Frost teased, "About little else."

Style-Ed helps analyze four categories of your writing—word length, punctuation, syntax, and nominalization. Two programs carry out Style-Ed's mission—STYLED, and STYLLIST. STYLLIST automatically creates an output file in which it compiles a list of long words, forms of *TO BE*, and potential nominalizations. STYLED actually displays a sample of ASCII text with specific formats highlighted. For instance, the word length option displays the file on screen with all words replaced by highlight bars representing the word length. Words longer than 10 characters are displayed in reverse video. At the end of the report, a display shows total word count, percentage of words over 10 characters, and average words per sentence.

The other options produce similar results. Style-Ed seems a good product for quantifying your writing. In conjunction with more conventional style checking programs, it may be very useful. It certainly approaches the subject of writing style from a different viewpoint. And never fear, the manual, for all its loquacity, does explain how to use the program effectively to improve your writing.

Whether you use Style-Ed or not, the manual alone is enough to make you want to send in your Shareware dollars. Maybe Louie will send you a personal letter. It would almost certainly be a good one.

Louie Crew also has some other products, including MUSES, a program to help writers manage their manuscripts; CANTONES, a program to help you learn Cantonese; and a collection of utilities.

STYLED
Louie Crew
P.O Box 64839
Chicago, IL 60664-0839

Shareware: $10

Category: Style Checker

System Requirements: DOS 2.1 or greater

Recommended Use: learn about writing; enjoy the manual

Major Pros: entertaining manual; unusual approach to style education

Major Cons: usefulness of program limited to those who can understand the meaning of its statistics and displays—not for everyone

Sources: popular BBSs and commercial services, or directly from the author

---

One utility will examine a text document to determine the percentage of Basic English words used. Basic English is a list of 850 words that some people early in the 20th century decided were all the words need to communicate in English. This can be a good test for whether your writing has the clearest expression to be understood by the widest range of readers.

Another utility is Poetease, an unusual program that helps you find rhymes, consonance and assonance for selected letter combinations. This generates list of possibilities, including mostly nonsense words. It performs the function that most poets do mentally by simply combining the entered text with a variety of letter combinations. It's up to the user to identify real word possibilities, and, even more, to find the right one.

Other utilities include ADDRESS, a program to help manage addresses; APPLY, which is used to manage and facilitate applications for grants, contests, and other related activities; and HIRE which is the employer's or grantor's version of APPLY.

Maxi-Read 3.0

RWS & Associates
Shareware—$35

Maxi-Read approaches style analysis from yet another angle. It uses fancy graphic screens and an impressive user interface to present its case. It allows you to import an existing text file, or to enter text directly for instant analysis.

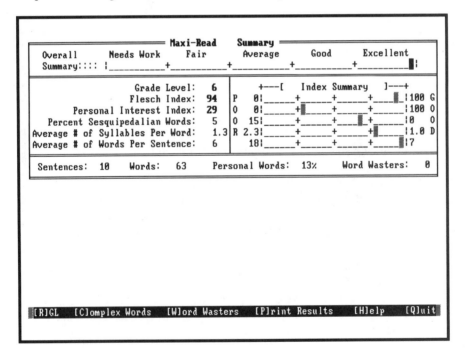

```
←
        ┌─── qwikMR  Results  Summary ───┐
        │ 146 ...Words        10 ...Sentences │   understatement.
        ├──────────────────┬─ Guidelines ┤   entry shortcuts
        │  14 ...Grade Level      │   8-10   │   interface. While
        │  12 % ...Pct. Complex Words │  < 10%  │   d the everyday,
        │  1.7 ...Avg. Syllables/Word │  < 1.6  │   lity -- cutting
        │ 14.6 ...Avg. Words/Sentence │  14-19  │   essing control to
        ├──────────────────┴─────────┤
        │   Overall:   It's Heavy Stuff-See Below │
        │   Words are:   Too many Complex Words │   es the high
        │ Sentences are:   About right for most of us │   dify the vehicle
        └─── Press a key to clear the screen ───┘c, or even a
Volkswagen -- or create your own ideal vehicle that will take you
wherever you want to go. What are you already used to? Or what do
you wish you had? With Sprint, you are in the driver's seat.
Create new menu-key shortcuts on-the-fly, or new formatting
definitions. You can even create your own menus!←            ─
←
←
Sprint features five basic kinds of macros:←
←
    *    Styles (Format Macros)←
←
C:\SPRINT\SPMACROS.SPR          * Ins        11:38pm     Ln.5 of 784   Col0
```

Maxi-Read uses several different criteria (much as PC-Style does), and includes the Flesch Index, number of syllables per word, percentage of personal words, and sesquipedalian words (words of many syllables). It also attempts to assign a grade level for each sample (basically following the Flesch Index). There are a lot of options available, including help with interpretations of the results, a list of common synonyms (to help simplify the sesquipedalian words), and a few options to allow some text to be left out of the analysis (for instance technical words that are well understood by your audience, but might cause the rating system to go slightly berserk). Version 3.0 includes some added features. For one, there is a graphic representation of the readability of a text sample. Also added are word wasters: phrases which should be simplified like "in view of the fact that" instead of "since," or other poor constructions like "irregardless." You can customize the word wasters data file, though the program comes with 150 examples.

Maxi-Read is a serious program. It is very fast, very well documented, and fun to use. In addition, registered users of the program will get a memory resident program, QuickMR, which can actually perform a spot analysis of your writing at any time, even when you are working with your favorite word processor. QuickMR only works with text currently on the screen, however, so for more complete analysis, use Maxi-Read.

If you're a style checking fan, you'll surely love Maxi-Read. It's a lot of fun.

Maxi-Read 3.0
RWS & Associates
132 Alpine Terrace
San Francisco, CA 94117

User-supported: $35 plus $1.50 handling charges

Category: Style Checker

System Requirements: PC or compatible; DOS 2.0 or later; at least one 360K drive; 80 column display (color recommended for full effect); printer optional

Recommended Use: check the readability of documents, the strength of speeches, etc.

Major Pros: flashy programming; enter text from keyboard for instant analysis, or import ASCII file; will strip binary files like WordStar files during import; menu driven and fast; QuikMR with registration

Major Cons: the only question revolves around the usefulness of style checkers in general—extensive documentation helps alleviate potential misuses

Sources: popular BBSs and commercial services, or directly from the author

---

Last Word on Style Checkers

Both PC-Style and Maxi-Read give similar results and offer appealing graphic displays along with their work. Neither is better than another, but rather reflect the programming styles of their authors. Is one more accurate than another? I don't know. I can tell you which one rated my writing higher, but would that be a recommendation or not?

My last word on style checkers is that they probably don't do any harm; they may not do any good, either. It really depends on whether you can respond to their message. If in doubt, find someone who writes well and ask him or her for comments.

Form Letters

Ever get stuck trying to express yourself in a letter? Perhaps you'd like some guidelines on how to write a termination notice, or a resignation letter, a dissatisfied customer letter, etc.

A series of sample letters is available from various sources, and they could save you time and effort in countless ways. These letters are collected under different file names, but should be easy to find by their descriptions in BBS listings and catalogs. Each letter is complete (subject to some personal modifications and editing). You fill in the names, addresses, and key words. The rest is all done. For example, a letter of resignation reads:

```
Dear _____ (name):



        I have just been offered a position that includes a
wider range of responsibilities and that will lead into a
supervisory position



        Therefore, I will be leaving _____ (name of company)
as of _____, 19___ (date). Meantime, I will place my
efforts into training a replacement.



                                         Respectfully,
```

Even though you might write a better letter if you were to take the time, this letter could serve its purpose. There are about 100 different letters in the collection. For anyone who has to deal with a lot of letter-writing situations, this form letter collection is well worth having.

Word Processing Finale

There are a lot of other utilities and programs associated with words. There are little utilities that count words, lines, sentences, and characters. There are utilities to create indexes, to convert file formats, to split files and put them back together again. Perhaps in future versions of this book we'll take a closer look at some of these other utilities. For now, we think the programs mentioned here should help you do almost anything you want with words.

Note: Another product with excellent word processing abilities is Word Plan, but because of its unique Lotus 1-2-3 interface, we've placed it in the Spreadsheet chapter. And for the young users, see Kids Word Processor in the Learning section.

21

Shareware Authorship

The following article was written by Bob Ostrander, the librarian for Public Brand Software. It is written to potential Shareware authors, but it provides excellent insight into what is needed to succeed at Shareware marketing. Because Bob sees hundreds of software packages in a week or a month, he is uniquely qualified to give advice. Because his catalog is very selective about the software they sell, and because Bob is a Shareware author himself, we asked him to write this article.

For potential authors interested in Shareware distribution:

> Bob Ostrander
> Librarian
> Public Brand Software
> 4847 S. High School Rd.
> Indianapolis, IN 46241

If you have written a computer program, or are contemplating writing one and are not sure how to market it, let me offer some words of advice about Shareware distribution.

First, a look at all the alternatives:

Commercial distribution by yourself:

- you get all revenues
- you must do copying, manual printing, distribution
- you must do all advertising (figure $20,000 to get started)
- you keep copyright

Commercial distribution by software house:

- you get a royalty (ranging from 25 cents to 20 dollars—usually about 5 to 10 percent of list price)
- you have no up-front expenses
- you lose copyright

Shareware distribution:

- you get all revenues
- you must do copying, manual printing, distribution
- you do very little advertising (figure about $100 max)
- you keep copyright

Public-domain distribution:

- you get no revenues—just notoriety
- you don't need to copy, advertise, or anything
- you lose copyright

Choose Shareware distribution over the available Commercial alternatives because you don't have the money for an ad campaign. A half page black and white ad in PC Magazine can cost $2000. Even the best packages around must have a lot of luck to get noticed and have reviews written in the major magazines.

Choose Commercial distribution over Shareware distribution if you have a package that addresses a narrow vertical market that can be reached cheaply via trade journals. For instance, an accounting system specific to vending machine companies might be better marketed as Commercial software. It is possible to reach most of your potential customers with an ad in one or two magazines at a reasonable cost.

Choose Shareware distribution over Public-Domain distribution because you lose all say over what happens to your program if you release it to the public domain and you probably won't have any chance to receive money for your work.

Choose Public-domain distribution over Shareware if you have no interest in supporting your product or if you have a small utility or game program that would not be suitable to be paid for. This avenue is great for putting out "Adware"—small programs that serve to advertise your services or bigger systems. For instance, TurboPower Software uses this very effectively to advertise their Turbo Pascal support programs.

Also, programs written under government contracts or by educational institutions are normally suitable for Public-domain distribution since the law often puts the code into public domain anyway. This does not preclude offering to provide telephone support, manuals, quick reference cards, etc. for a fee.

Copyrights are a very important matter. With Shareware, the author retains all copyrights and allows other people only to make copies under specific terms. These terms normally include a prohibition against commercial sale of the software. Sometimes a dollar limit on the distribution fee such as $6.00 or $8.00 is put into the distribution license. The general good that comes of the Shareware concept is that your rights as an author are protected for future sales (PC-Outline, PC-Calc, PC-Graph and others have been bartered after having successful runs as Shareware) and for commercial distribution (PC-Talk is even coming back as a commercial package).

Even when releasing software for Public-Domain distribution, you should put in a copyright message in order to protect your rights for future use of your software as you see fit. If you do this, be sure to include a message that gives others the right to copy your work for non-commercial purposes. This will then become Public-Domain material, but you won't find someone selling it as commercial software without your permission.

A copyright message simply consists of the word COPYRIGHT, the date, and your name (and preferably address). It must be put in a prominent place such as an opening screen, the documentation, or on the main menu. "Copyright, 1987, Bob Ostrander, Public Brand Software, 4847 S. High School Rd., Indianapolis, IN 46241" will do fine; in fact just "Copyright, 1987, Bob Ostrander" will do it, but if there is someone out there who wants to make you rich for your work, they won't be able to find you.

The Shareware concept pays off in the form of registration fees from satisfied users. This pays better on complete packages than it does on small utilities, games, and language aids. PC-Write (Quicksoft—$89) has 14,500 registered users; Eric Isaacson (A86/D86—$80) is receiving one or two registrations a day and his assembler has been out only a few months; the Generic Adventure Game

System ($50) reports dismal registration figures; the PTOOLS Turbo Pascal source code utilities (mine—$20) have received about 50 registrations in the last two years. (I also have received a few job offers).

You will get more registrations if you promise something in return such as telephone support, bug notices, future upgrades, printed manuals, etc.

Don't stint on the program or the documentation. Crippled programs and incomplete documentation don't encourage registrations. People want to see exactly what they are getting, and just because they may already have it, it isn't any less important to have it all. The whole concept of Shareware software is kind of like Public Television. Your local PBS station doesn't put on half a show and then say, "If we don't get 100 new subscribers we won't show you the second half."

Buttonware has for the last couple of years experimented with releasing incomplete documentation for their popular PC-FILE package in hopes of encouraging users to register ($79) for the manual (and other benefits). They have just recently decided that the complete documentation of 200+ pages on the distribution disk is the way to go. There were just too many complaints from people that couldn't use the system to it's full potential without the complete manual and were either too insulted or too apprehensive to register.

Your users first experience your work by reading the documentation. If they feel that your package is worth the money before they even use it, then your registration rate will go up drastically. Peruse some other packages to get an idea of how to write good documentation. A cross-referenced index may not be necessary, but complete instructions on how to use all of the features is.

Target your audience when writing your documentation. If you expect very inexperienced users, be sure to include the basics, right down to how to start DOS. If you are putting out a language support product for programmers, this won't be necessary.

Make your price reasonable. We feel that a registration fee that is about one third to one half of what a comparable commercial program would cost is about right.

This distribution method is by far the most cost efficient available. Bulletin boards, club libraries and the few reputable distribution houses will do a good job of presenting your best side to the potential user and will keep the latest version available to the public. In a couple of un-official, non-scientific studies, it has been found that there is no noticeable difference in the rates of registration traceable to the source of the copy or the geographic area. The user's profession and the age of the copy the user gets seem to make a difference. A new version every six months can spur registrations if there is a significant improvement made to the software.

Also, don't re-invent the wheel. Both the Shareware and Commercial markets are flooded right now with a lot of good packages in the following fields:

- general ledger

- menuing

- text editors

- pop-up desktop utilities

- word processors

- general purposes communications programs

- spreadsheets

- household finances and checkbook balancers

- general purposes flat-file and relational databases

Why butt heads with established software? There are a lot of other untouched areas for you to jump into.

When you launch your Shareware system, don't be shy. Send it to the big Shareware distribution houses. Public Brand Software, PC-SIG, and the Public (software) Library should be the first on your list.

A press release to the major magazines should be also sent out along with a disk of the software. Any publicity you can get at this stage is welcome and a review in *PC Magazine, PC World, Byte,* or *Computer Shopper* can be a real shot in the arm.

Also give it to some of the bigger Bulletin Boards as well as to those in your immediate area. The ARC and PKARC "archive" programs will be invaluable to assemble a disk into one file for uploading to bulletin boards. Many boards will not accept "un-arced" files.

In conclusion, let me quote Bob Wallace, the author of PC-Write:

Shareware is successful for a software package if:

The number of people who buy it because it is shareware outnumber those who don't buy it because it is shareware.

The number who do buy it because it is shareware are those who:

1. are aware of and/or try the package only because it is shareware, and

2. who then register after trying it

Those who take step one but not step two do not affect the analysis.

The number who do not buy it because it is shareware are those who:

1. are aware of and/or try the package only because it is shareware, and

2. who then use the package without registering it, and

3. who would have bought the package, had it not been shareware

Those who take steps one and two but would not have bought anyway (pirates) do not affect the analysis.

We assume shareware is successful if many more people try the software because it is shareware and if the number of them who later pay for it is greater than the number who would have paid for it using conventional marketing.

Shareware can open new markets for you that you can't get without a big advertising campaign. If you think it's right for you, don't hesitate to jump in with both feet.

Part III

Sources

Introduction
to Sources
of PD and
Shareware

"O.K., O.K., it's a great value. I see some programs I can use. I want them. So where are they? How do I get them?"

Getting public-domain and Shareware programs is easy. It's only as far away as your telephone.

There are several ways to get these programs. The first and easiest is from a friend. That's the beauty of this marketing scheme. Your friends are software dealers. They give you the product with their recommendation. What could be easier?

Another good source of programs is a computer user group. There are hundreds of fine user groups all around the country. Among the biggest are the Capital PC User Group, the Boston Computer Society, the Chicago Computer Society, and the Personal Computer User Group (in Salt Lake City). User groups often maintain large libraries of software available to anyone who wants it. There are usually people who can help you find programs and perhaps give you some advice on how to use them. You'll have to spend your time copying, and not all user groups keep a very informative catalog of their disks. You may have to do some weeding. But if you want any of the programs reviewed in this book, at least you'll know what to look for. Find out about local user groups from the newspaper announcements of their meetings, or from computer stores, who usually know about these groups.

For some, it might be easier and/or more exciting to call a local BBS, list its directory, and download. Local BBSs are usually free, and so are the phone calls. Local BBSs often present a large listing of files, but do little filtering of products, and provide very little information about them. You'll be able to find many products listed in this book at the local level, however.

Another source is the commercial bulletin board system. Most systems, like CompuServe, GEnie, BIX, The Source, and Delphi keep large libraries of software. New software often appears on these boards daily, and updates to existing products are often found in these libraries before they appear in other places.

Finally, there are several software libraries that offer excellent service and a wide range of products. These include the PC SIG, Public Brand Software, and The Software Library.

The next few chapters will give you the information necessary to contact and obtain files from BBS or distribution channels like those mentioned above. For more information about telecommunicating and about working with file formats, see Part I of this book.

22

Commercial BBSs

The following entries should give you the information you need to:
- a. establish an account with a commercial BBS
- b. log on to the service
- c. find the IBM file area you need
- d. search for particular files
- e. download what you want

These services have many more features, including electronic mail, airline reservation systems, stock market access, real-time conferencing, and much more. We will limit our scope to the finding and obtaining of public-domain and Shareware files. Most BBSs have special groups which service different computer systems or other interests. When you first begin using a service, you will want to join the groups that interest you. This allows you access to their software libraries as well as their own internal bulletin boards where you can read and write to other group members. You'll find the members of a particular group to be useful sources of information, and reading some of the public messages that are already available may answer many of your questions and suggest to you some good software to download (and some to avoid). The commercial boards also provide you with extra information about files for downloading. For instance, some may display the number of times a file has been downloaded. This gives you some indication of the product's popularity. The file listing may also give the uploader's name, the date it was uploaded, the size of the file, and the exact file name. It may also tell you what library or unpacking program to use (if any).

CompuServe

For information on how to obtain a *free* introductory subscription to CompuServe, call: 800/848-8199 (in Ohio, call 614/457-0802). This introductory subscription contains: a private user ID number and password, a $15 introductory usage credit, and a complimentary subscription to CompuServe's monthly news-magazine, *Online Today*.

On-line connect rate is: 300–450 baud = $6/hour; 1,200–2,400 baud = $12.50/hour; plus a surcharge of 25 cents/hour if you are using a direct CompuServe line.

Some value-added services (identified by a dollar sign on the menu choice) are slightly higher. These include several financial services, some games and entertainment, and reference searches such as Iquest, which is $7 per search. CompuServe has been around for a long time, and contains more than a hundred special interest groups (SIGs) covering a wide range of interests. Establishing an account with CompuServe is easy. Their starter kits are available from bookstores and computer stores, as well as along with various commercial programs. And if none of those options are convenient, calling their toll-free sales support line at (800) 848-8199 will get you started. Once you have a CompuServe starter kit, you get a manual, a starter ID, and some free on-line credit. Using the starter ID will place you in a special area where you can sign up and receive your own ID and password. There are several ways to log on to CompuServe. You can get on via Tymnet, Telenet, or one of hundreds of local nodes around the country that CompuServe has established. For detailed instructions of logon procedures, see the documentation in the CompuServe manual. What follows is an abbreviated instruction list for your convenience.

Logging on via CompuServe Network:

1. use your modem to call the local access number
2. wait for connection
3. after you hear a high-pitched sound, possibly followed by a hissing sound (depending on the baud rate), the connection is ready
4. press Control-C (holding the Control key down and pressing C)
5. pressing Control-C will ask for User ID; pressing (CR) will ask for the Host Name
6. at the "USER ID:" prompt, type your user number in the form, "nnnnn,nnn" (without the quotes) then press Return
7. at the "PASSWORD:" prompt, type your password, then a carriage return

You will not actually see your password appear on the screen, so type carefully. If you make a mistake, you will be prompted to try again. Just follow the prompts.

Logging on via Tymnet:

1. use your modem to dial the local number
2. wait for connection; if you are logging on at 300 baud, you will see a message; otherwise you will see unreadable characters on your screen
3. type the letter A (do not type a carriage return)
4. at "PLEASE LOG IN" type CPS (CR)
5. at "USER ID:" type your user number in the form, "nnnnn,nnn" (without the quotes), then a carriage return
6. at the "PASSWORD:" prompt type your password, then a carriage return

You will not actually see your password appear on the screen, so type carefully. If you make a mistake, you will be prompted to try again. Just follow the prompts.

Logging on via Telenet:

1. use your modem to call the local access number
2. wait for connection
3. after you hear the two high pitched sounds (the carrier tones), and then a third hissing sound, the connection is ready
4. press CR (Return) twice
5. at "TERMINAL =" type D1 (CR)
6. when you see the @ prompt type either of the following:
   ```
   C 202202 (CR)
   C 614227 (CR)
   ```
7. at the "USER ID:" prompt, type your user number in the form "nnnnn,nnn" (without the quotes) then press Return
8. at the "PASSWORD:" prompt, type your password, then a carriage return

You will not actually see your password appear on the screen, so type carefully. If you make a mistake, you'll be prompted to try again. Just follow the prompts. Once you are logged on, you will want to find the IBM file libraries. To reach the IBM forums, type: GO IBMNET

There you will see a menu of possible IBM forums to enter. You may choose one that interests you by following the prompts. If you are new to CIS, you should go to IBMNEW and read the Help files in the DL's first.

```
IBM Software Forum

FUNCTIONS

1 (L)   Leave a Message
2 (R)   Read Messages
3 (CO)  Conference Mode
4 (DL)  Data Libraries
5 (B)   Bulletins
6 (MD)  Member Directory
7 (OP)  User Options
8 (IN)  Instructions

Enter choice !█
```

```
DL 3 - Gen. Utilities (S)



1 (DES) Description of Data Library
2 (BRO) Browse thru Files
3 (DIR) Directory of Files
4 (UPL) Upload a New File
5 (DOW) Download a File
6 (DL)  Change Data Library
7 (T)   Return to Function Menu
8 (I)   Instructions



Enter choice !█
```

Once you choose a forum, you'll be able to enter the Data Library (DL) or 4 on the Functions menu. Next, select one of the available libraries to check out. Here, you may directory, browse, and download files from various libraries of files. Be sure to set the library you want using the Change Data Library command. You can list the directory of files by typing DIR or 3. To find a specific file, or subject matter, type BRO or 2. You will be prompted for a key word which can be a file name or a descriptive word about the files you're seeking. When you find a file you want to download, you can either go back to the menu and type DOW or 5, or press Return for the Disposition Menu from which you can initiate a transfer.

```
    [74045,462]
    DUMP.ARC/binary        23-Jul-87 5120          Accesses: 23
   .DUMP.COM               21-Jul-87 8             Accesses: 7

    [76556,3643]
    XEQ.THD                16-Jul-87 14973         Accesses: 14

    [76010,1025]
    HBINST.ARC/binary      05-Jul-87 50944         Accesses: 20

    [70007,1212]
    ARC-E.COM/binary       03-Jul-87 6496          Accesses: 333
    ARC-E.DOC              03-Jul-87 11556         Accesses: 241
    SORTF.ARC/binary       02-Jul-87 4546          Accesses: 41
    SORTF.DOC              02-Jul-87 0
    SORTF.EXE              02-Jul-87 0

    [74666,511]
    SWDL3.DES              02-Jul-87 32613         Accesses: 199


  Press <CR> for more !
```

CompuServe will prompt you to select a transfer protocol, then instruct you to begin the download using your telecommunication program's commands. When the download is completed, pressing Return will let CompuServe know you're done. That's about all there is to it. Just follow the prompts.

Autosig

For CompuServe users, there is a free product called Autosig. It was written by a team of people (including Vernon Buerg, who also wrote List and ARCE). This product is the ultimate CompuServe utility. It helps automate logons, downloads, message retrieval, etc. Autosig is a complete communications package just for use with CompuServe. This is a very sophisticated product, and is available through the CompuServe IBMCOM. To get Autosig:

1. at the CompuServe prompt, type *"GO IBMCOM"* (you may have to press a carriage return before the next step)
2. select DL (option 4)
3. select the Autosig DL (option 1)
4. (DOW)nload the following files (some of these files are fairly long, so be prepared for a fairly lengthy download session):
   - ATO526.ARC (note that the version number may change)
   - ATODOC.COM (run this to produce the 76 page manual)
   - ATO526.REQ (version number may change, a "required" file)
   - ATONEW.TXT (if it exists)
5. After you've read the .Reg file, you can download the others by typing DOW-file name. CompuServe will then prompt you for information like file name for your computer, etc. Be sure to use an error-checking protocol to DOW these files before downloading others. Read this file to make sure ATO will run on your machine.

You will need an *ARC* file extractor (see the chapter on *ARC*s, *LIB*s, and *ZOO*s). *UnARC*ing the *ATO526.ARC* file produces the *AUTOSIG.EXE* file. When you first run the Autosig program, it will create a special definition file *AUTOSIG.DFN*, which contains your Autosig configuration.

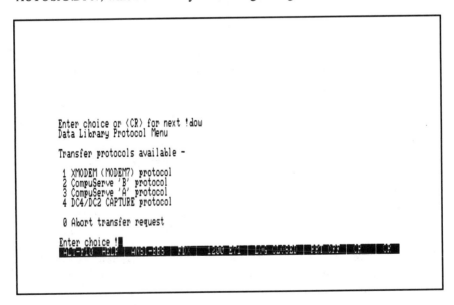

Of course, if you can get Autosig from a friend or colleague, you can save yourself all this trouble. Autosig is free. You may want to make sure that you have the most recent version, however.

From here, you're on your own. It helps to know a little about CompuServe before configuring Autosig, but the manual is quite complete and well indexed. Use the manual and the CompuServe manual as references. Once you begin to use Autosig, you'll be glad you took the time.

GEnie

Prime time is $35 an hour. Non-prime time is $5 an hour, 6 p.m. to 8 a.m., Monday through Friday, all day weekends and holidays, based on your home address local time. There is a one-time $18 sign-up fee.

GEnie is a relative newcomer to the BBS lists, but it is an excellent service that has quickly established itself as one of the leading boards. To establish an account with GEnie, you use a modem to call their toll-free number, (800) 638-8369. At the *U#* prompt type *XJM11999,genie* (CR) and then follow instructions. Within a few days someone will call to help you set up your account.

When you get your account established, you will use one of GEnie's local access numbers to connect with the board. You will log on with your own user number and password in the form *aaannnnn,password* where *a* is a letter, *n* is a number, and password is your private *password*. To go directly to the IBM software library, add another comma and the number 616 to the end of the logon (i.e. *aaannnnn,password,616*). Or, from any GEnie prompt, type *m616* (for move to page 616). Or you can type IBM at any menu prompt.

> *Note*: When you first enter a group on GEnie, you will be asked to join the group. You should follow the instructions presented, then join. If you join the group, you will be able to enter that area again whenever you want. If you do not, you will be presented with the same questions each time, and you won't be able to access the libraries.

Once you are in the software library, you can set specific sub-libraries, or set *all* libraries on. You can then choose to Directory the files (option 2), Search for specific files (option 3), Browse (option 4), or Download (option 6).

The easiest way to download a file from GEnie is to use its record number. Every file has a number, and it is most easily identified using that number. For instance, when you get the *Enter number or name of file to download:* prompt, you will never go wrong entering the number, but names might be ambiguous or inexact. There are several ways to find out the file's number. One way is to download the GEnie library files in a specific format (ASCII, dBASE, or some other formats). This will contain all the files in the GEnie software library up to a certain date. Even though these files are sizable (almost 200K), they allow you to peruse the GEnie file listings at your leisure.

```
    1. IBM PC RoundTable Bulletin Board
    2. IBM PC Real-Time Conference
    3. IBM Software Libraries
    4. About the RoundTable
    5. RoundTable News              870606

    Enter #, (P)revious, or (H)elp?

    GEnie                        Page 616
        IBM PC Software Library
          Library: ALL Libraries

    1. Description of this Library
    2. Directory of files
    3. Search File Directory
    4. Browse through files
    5. Upload a new file
    6. Download a file
    7. Delete a file you own
    8. Set Software Library
    9. Save Current Software Library
   10. Instructions for Software Exchange

    Enter #, (P)revious, or (H)elp?
```

To find the Libfiles files, select option 3 (Search) and enter *Libfiles* for the keyword. Then press CR twice at the next two prompts. One of the files displayed will be appropriate for your use. Note its file number. Now you have to download. When you return to the menu, enter option 6 (Download) and when you are prompted for the number of the file, write the number you got from the Search procedure above. Now a longer description of the file will appear. Confirm that this is the file you want. If it is not, press Return to skip that file. If it is the correct file, then press D to begin the download. When the download is completed, follow the prompts to return to the menu or download another file.

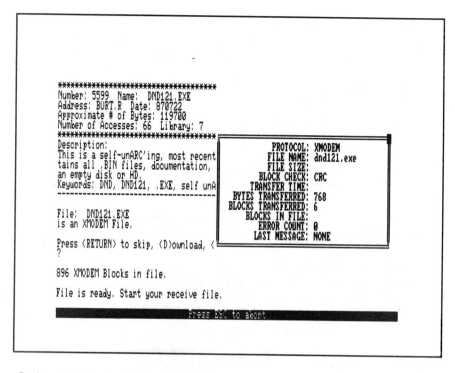

```
************************************
Number: 5599  Name:  DND121.EXE
Address: BURT.R  Date: 870722
Approximate # of Bytes: 119700
Number of Accesses: 66  Library: 7
************************************
Description:                           PROTOCOL: XMODEM
This is a self-unARC'ing, most recent FILE NAME: dnd121.exe
tains all .BIN files, documentation,   FILE SIZE:
an empty disk or HD.                  BLOCK CHECK: CRC
Keywords: DND, DND121, .EXE, self unA TRANSFER TIME:
------------------------------------ BYTES TRANSFERRED: 768
                                    BLOCKS TRANSFERRED: 6
File: DND121.EXE                       BLOCKS IN FILE:
is an XMODEM File.                       ERROR COUNT: 0
                                        LAST MESSAGE: NONE
Press <RETURN> to skip, <D>ownload, <
?

896 XMODEM Blocks in file.

File is ready. Start your receive file.

                Press ESC to abort
```

Option 11 from the library menu allows you to see a listing of the most recent uploads. This is a good place to look for new programs and updates to older ones.

Often I will use option 2 (Directory) to look at what's new because it seems to be more current that option 11. I use Control-S to stop the display and Control-Q to resume. Control-C will abort the listing and return to the menu. Whenever I see a file that interests me, I write down its number. Later, when I begin downloading, I can read the extended file description and decide whether I really want that file or not.

Delphi

To establish an account with Delphi, call (800) 544-4005. The cost is $49.95 for a lifetime membership which includes a Delphi Handbook, and 2 hours free access (evening hours). Rates are $7.20/hour during evening rate periods; otherwise, $17.40/hour.

You can call Delphi directly at (617) 576-0862. To log on to Delphi directly:

1. press Return at the carrier tone
2. at *USERNAME* type your member name and press Return
3. at *PASSWORD* type your password and press Return

To log on via Tymnet:

1. dial the local Tymnet number
2. at the carrier tone type the letter A (no Return; don't worry if you see garbage on the screen)
3. at the *PLEASE LOG IN* prompt, type Delphi (CR)
4. now follow the prompts (as above) to enter your member name and password

To log on via Telenet:

1. dial the local Telenet number
2. at the carrier tone type two carriage returns
3. at the *TERMINAL =* prompt press Return again
4. at the @ type *C DELPHI* and press Return
5. now enter your member name and password as above

Delphi can also be accessed via DataPak from Canada.

Delphi settings are:

- 8 bits
- 1 stop bit
- no parity
- 300, 1200, or 2400 baud
- full duplex
- no auto-linefeed
- *XON-XOFF* or Handshaking enabled

Once you reach the main menu of Delphi, select the Groups and Clubs option, then move into the *MSDOS SIG*. Once you join the *MSDOS SIG*, you can find the software libraries under Databases. You can directory, read an extended description of the file, set different topics, or search for a file or keyword. To use the Read command effectively, you must know the file name you are seeking. Then, after you have read the file description, pressing Return displays the Action> prompt. Here you may choose to see the next file in the list or download the file. There are some options oriented toward ASCII file display, but you will probably want to use Xmodem or Kermit to download the file. Selecting the appropriate command will begin the download process. Select the commands on your telecommunications program and download the file.

Delphi has some sophisticated search routines that allow you to search on keywords and narrow or widen the search parameters. This makes it easy to locate specific files or groups of files.

Some downloads on Delphi may present more than one file for downloading. If you select to download a group under one description, you'll be prompted for each file in the group.

BIX

Byte Magazine runs a commercial service called BIX (Byte Information Exchange). This service contains many interesting conferences and activities as well as articles and programs from Byte. In addition, there are 34 file areas covering a wide range of computer systems. There are 3 specific IBM software libraries divided by file type (1. ARC files; 2. COM, EXE, and unpacked files, and 3. LBR files).

BIX is accessed over Tymnet, and you can call (800) 924-7681 to find your local Tymnet number. BIX also maintains a direct number in the Boston area. Calling the toll free number above will provide the access number in the 617 area. Establishing an account with BIX is easy. Call in and log on as New (in place of a user name). Then follow the prompts which will ask for information about billing (credit cards, etc.) and other registration information. You will be allowed on the system immediately after registration.

There is a one-time fee of $25 to establish an account on BIX. Thereafter, hourly charges are $18/hr for peak times (6 a.m. to 7 p.m. *your* local time), and $11/hr for non-peak hours (all other times, weekends, and holidays).

To log on to BIX via Tymnet:

1. dial your local access number
2. wait for the carrier tones
3. type the letter A (with no carriage return)
4. at the "PLEASE LOG IN" prompt, type BIX (CR)
5. you will be prompted for name and password after the BIX logo has displayed

```
###  #  ###     ### ##
#####   ###    ####   (TM)
###  #  ###    ## ###
##### ###### ##  ###
------------------------
 BYTE Information Exchange

McGraw-Hill Information Systems Co.
Copyright (c) 1987 by McGraw-Hill Inc.

CoSy Conferencing System, Copyright (c) 1984 University of Guelph
    Written by: Alastair JW Mayer

Name? demaria
Password:
You have 1 mail message(s) in your in-basket.
You are a member of 2 conference(s)
From          Memo * Date
dallen        93100   Thu Jul 23 13:48   CC+ review
To            Memo * Date
dallen        93094 R Thu Jul 23 13:41 CC+ review
Conf/Topic              New Messages
System.News/general        236
:join listings
```

Once on the BIX system, you'll want to find the file listings. To do so, look for a prompt that looks like a single colon—:. At the colon, type the following:

```
: join listings
```

Don't type the colon; that's the prompt. Also, whether you type upper or lower case doesn't matter. After a few moments, you'll find yourself in the Listings Conference. Here you can find the main file areas for BIX. In all probability, you will be placed automatically in one of the Byte listing areas. To see a list of available areas, type the letter A (CR). To change directly to one of the IBM file areas, type A and the area name. There are three areas, IBM, IBM.ARC, and IBM.LBR.

For instance, to enter the IBM.ARC area, type: : a ibm.arc

Suppose you want to find Vernon Buerg's ARCE program, but aren't sure if it was an *ARC* file, a *COM* file, or what. To find a file, use the *(F)ind* option, and include the file name or wild cards you are looking for. To *(F)ind ARCE*, type:
```
: f arce.*
```

A listing of all files matching that description will be shown.

```
--------------------- F I L E S   S E C T I O N ---------------------
A..list file Areas, change to new Area         I..message-of-the-day info
B..list Subareas, change to new Subarea        R..receive file from BIX
D..switch file Description (long<-->short)     S..send a file to BIX
L..list all files in Area/Subarea             T..type a file (as text)
LD.list all files in Area/Subarea by date     P..set default preferences
F..find files using filename with wildcards    ?..help files, including this one
K..keyword search of files                     Q..quit, return to BIX
--------------------------------------------------------------------

Additional help:
   Experienced users can type the single-letter command and its argument(s)
and bypass the text prompting (e.g. 'f meta*.*' to find all files of the form
'meta*.*'. This works with all the commands that prompt for an argument.
   A wildcard filename may contain "*", which stands for any combination of
characters, and "?", which stands for exactly one character. For example,
"???.bas" asks for all 7-character files that end in ".bas".
   You can use the word "all" as a valid subarea name. If you respond to the
"f" (find files) command with the filename "all", BIX will return *all*
the files in that area/subarea combination.
   For more information, read 'readme.lis' in any of the 'frombyte' Areas.
File Area: FROMBYTE87   Subarea: ALL   File Description: SHORT
File: A B D F I K L LD P Q R S T or ? for help:
```

```
Attempting to change to Area 'IBM.ARC'....

File Area: IBM.ARC   Subarea: ALL   File Description: SHORT
File: A B D F I K L LD P Q R S T or ? for help: f arce.*


--- Find file(s) using filename with wildcards ---

Searching for 'arce.*'....   Found 1 file.
Loading descriptions...
Now calling up individual description...

arce.com       6528  BINARY Vern Buergs utility to remove files from archive

--- end of descriptions ---
File Area: IBM.ARC   Subarea: ALL   File Description: SHORT
File: A B D F I K L LD P Q R S T or ? for help: r arce.com

--- Receive-file subsystem ---

arce.com       6528 bytes

File transfer protocol to be used:
A K X XC Y YC Q or ? for list:
```

Now, to download a file, you use the *(R)eceive* command. Type *R* and the file name you want, i.e.:: `r arce.com`

You will be prompted for the file protocol. You will probably use Xmodem, but BIX supports several other protocols including Ymodem and Ymodem/CRC. Future enhancements of BIX will also support batch file downloads (using wild cards), but at the time of this writing, that has not been implemented.

To finish a downloading session, type (Q)uit, then, at the main BIX prompt, type BYE to log off.

The Source

The Source is one of the original commercial BBSs. Its IBM software library consists of over 2000 titles. To establish an account with The Source, call (800) 336-3366. The account can be established over the phone. The sign-up fee is $49.95. There's a $10 monthly minimum fee that will be applied to time spent. There's a special $95 annual fee with no minimum monthly charges. Prime-time access at 300 baud is 36 cents a minute; 1,200 baud is 43 cents a minute; 2,400 baud is 46 cents a minute. The non-prime time rate at 300 baud is 14 cents a minute; 1,200 baud is 18 cents a minute; 2,400 baud is 20 cents a minute. Prime time is 7 a.m. to 6 p.m. on weekdays. All other times are non-prime time (local time) in the area. Some value-added services like certain financial services contain a surcharge. Chat mode (where users type messages to each other on-line) is somewhat cheaper.

To log on to The Source via Telenet, follow the standard Telenet log on (see CompuServe above), then enter the terminal identifier given to you when you registered. Once you have entered the terminal information, enter name and password at the prompts. You will be placed at the Entry Menu.

To go directly to the *IBM SIG*, type *Q* to drop to the command mode. Now type *IBMSIG*. To search for specific files, type *IBMSIG LIBRARY SEARCH*. You will be prompted for a keyword or file name. Once the files have been located, another menu prompts you to Scan or Read the files. When you Read a file, you will see a longer description of the file, and then a menu of choices—Display, Xmodem, or Kermit.

To download a file, select the appropriate download method (Xmodem or Kermit for most files) by typing the first two letters of the options (i.e. *XM* for Xmodem). Then set up your communications program to download.

To find a file by file name, type *FI* (file name or partial file name).

For more information, contact the particular service you wish to use. We know for sure that, for Canadian users, CompuServe and Delphi can be accessed through DataPak.

23

Sysop in a Lamp

Rub Three Times and Say the Magic Word

Charles Strom is one of the sysops of GEnie's IBM RoundTable. His experience with PD and Shareware stretches back many years, and as a sysop on a major commercial service, he sees a tremendous amount of the creative activity in today's PD and Shareware. We thought you might enjoy hearing from one of the sysops from such a large system.

Charles H. Strom
NYU Department of Chemistry
4 Washington Pl.
New York, NY 10012

I became involved in public-domain software in the early days of microcomputing. Single user RCPM (remote CP/M) systems were already well established in the late 1970s. The prototypes were run by fellows such as Keith Petersen, Dave Hardy and Bruce Ratoff. My phone bill soon went through the roof, downloading from one system and uploading to another. A typical upload was accompanied with full source and was clearly designated in the public domain. Indeed, the authors encouraged others to improve upon their efforts. I cut my teeth on 8080 assembly language by occasionally doing just this.

A new service emerged, CompuServe Information Service. CIS offered not only local telephone access charges, but I was attracted by the notion of dozens of users accessing public-domain CP/M files. There was no such thing as a special interest group (SIG) at this time, and I distributed files gleaned from the RCPM's by uploading them to my private disk space, lowering their protection, and announcing their availability through the one and only system bulletin board (called BULLET). Interest grew rapidly, and CIS asked if I had any interest in running a SIG on CompuServe based on some software developed by Chuck Sandoian, another subscriber. I got together with two other interested individuals (we met one evening on-line) and the CP/M SIG, or CP-MIG, was born.

As CP-MIG grew, so did public-domain software. Our weekly real-time conferences were a gathering place for many of the luminaries of the day. Others preferred to use the bulletin-board system as their communications vehicle. The great bulk of usage, however, was devoted to downloading files from our software library. For each user on the BBS, there were dozens and dozens of anonymous subscribers combing the software for the newest versions of a super directory program, an improved MODEM7 overlay, or perhaps a ZCPR utility.

We were probably the largest single source of CP/M software in terms of users and downloads, if not sheer volume of software available. This in no way detracted from the small, single-user systems which continued to flourish. Indeed, many sysops used CP-MIG as a source for software and we even had a section devoted to sysop concerns.

As everyone knows, for whatever reason, IBM embraced the Microsoft operating system and turned their backs on Digital Research and CP/M. From then on, the days of CP/M as a large market force were numbered. We continued to proselytize the virtues of CP/M and the spirit of public-domain software, RCPM's, source code availability, and the other hallmarks that made our involvement with the hobby so satisfying.

In the summer of 1985, I was contacted by a former CIS manager who had convinced General Electric's computer services company, GEISCO, that the time was right to challenge CompuServe's industry domination. As CompuServe grew, it became more lumbering and bureaucratic and less responsive to our needs. I felt that there was less humanity in the operation than in the early days.

To be fair, another significant factor in my mind was that I sadly felt that CP/M was at a dead-end, and there were no areas on CIS into which I could expand. Most sysops of single user systems run their service for the enjoyment of the hobby. We enjoy what we do, but it is a business as well as a hobby. There is significant income to be derived from running these services, and my migration to GEnie (General Electric Network for Information Exchange) allowed me to move into the expanding IBM-compatible field. I saw a gigantic market waiting to be tapped as opposed to the shrinking interest in CP/M. Therefore I decided to shift emphasis to the IBM compatible arena, and GEnie's IBM RoundTable, hosted by David Kozinn, Paul Homchick and me, was born in the autumn of 1985.

GEnie's IBM RoundTable is a consuming avocation. Our activities consist of three areas—a bulletin board, real-time conferences and a software library. The bulletin board is divided into various categories of interest which are further sub-divided into topics and messages addressing those topics. A nice feature is that our messages are permanently available and do not roll off into the bit-bucket as on other services. Hence the BBS serves as a useful repository of technical hints and tips, mini-reviews of software or equipment, etc. If a new subscriber asks for information previously covered, we need only point him to the topic of interest. This encourages our members to take a little more effort to address questions in detail since they need not do it repeatedly. Of course the permanency of the bulletin board messages also means that the sysops need to exercise care in maintaining the system, cleaning out material of limited interest, moving messages from inappropriate areas, etc. We feel the advantage this structure affords makes the extra housekeeping worthwhile. Our real-time conferences are in large part a social event. Most commonly, we have a "random access" format where participants are free to discuss anything. One evening a week, we sponsor a PC-VCO conference. VCO is a computer conferencing program originally developed for the Macintosh computer and adapted to the IBM-compatibles by Scott McGuiness. VCO presents a "conference table" on the participants' screens, surrounded by icons of each of their faces that were previously prepared and uploaded to the service. My face is downloaded by each of the others and when STROM speaks, the program highlights my icon on each screen. The party atmosphere is enhanced by control over facial expressions, sound effects, etc.

More formal conferences are held at irregular intervals when we arrange for a celebrity in the computer industry to field questions from the group. These are structured rather rigidly and are controlled using tools available to the meeting leader so we don't have the anarchy of a free-for-all.

By far the largest activity on the IBM R/T is the software library. IBM-compatible computing brought with it the concept of shareware, a term coined by the late Andrew Flugelman. Better than 90 percent of the contributions to our software library is shareware, and much of it is uploaded by the authors themselves who are then available on-line for user support.

In spite of the existence of hundreds of single user, free, and low cost systems nationwide, we are able to offer something more for our subscribers—a local, toll-free telephone access number, virtually infinite disk space for file storage, and the GE name and its implied assurance of quality. We screen every file for trojans and pirated software unlike some sysops who have *laissez-faire* policy and do not take pains to minimize their users' exposure.

Most importantly, a large service such as GEnie assures our members of a large pool of expertise. True, the sysops are deeply involved in computers and are particularly experienced in the area of telecommunications, but we also have a large group of other experts on which to draw. Thus, when a problem arises related to the operation of a program downloaded from our software library, there are many brains to pick for a solution. Of course, this pool of expertise extends to all facets of the RoundTable and we are all able to learn from the experiences of others. This is certainly one of the most significant advantages of a large multiuser interest group like GEnie's IBM R/T.

We enjoy our work as sysops, and always have. Make no mistake about it—it is work. We must invest several hours a day to stay on top of the files and messages, be available for helping new users get comfortable with the new environment, and also to aid the GEnie staff in their continuing efforts to improve the utility and ease of use of the system as well as identifying and developing new areas that complement our interest group. It is great to enjoy one's work, and even more gratifying to have strangers come up to us at shows introducing themselves as users of our service and thanking us for our efforts. It makes the long hours worthwhile.

24

Catalogs and Other Resources

Several major catalogs distribute public-domain and Shareware programs. Although they charge a nominal fee for disk copying and mailing, their services are often more convenient than modem transfers. For instance, a file transfer can be interrupted by bad line conditions or other vagaries of the phone system. Nothing is as discouraging as having the phone line disconnect for no apparent reason after half an hour of downloading.

Catalogs also provide information about updates, and often they have full time librarians whose only job is to screen and test hundreds of products a year. This service can be invaluable and makes these catalog services very worthwhile.

PC SIG

One of the original PD and Shareware catalogs is still distributed by the PC SIG. This group has kept a historical record of PD and Shareware in its 700+ disks of software. Its publications, the PC SIG Library catalog, and the monthly PC SIG Magazine, (now renamed *Shareware Magazine*) are important sources of information. The PC SIG Library is in its fourth edition. It is over 400 pages long and contains several indexes.

In addition to their other sources, PC SIG has placed its entire library of disks on one CD ROM. This disk contains an almost complete history of PD and Shareware programs for the PC, and is an exceptional (if somewhat overwhelming) source. Many programs included in this book were taken from the SIG's CD.

PC SIG charges $6 per disk plus $4 shipping (per order). California residents must add 7 percent sales tax. The SIG directory is $12.95. The CD ROM is $295 (or $495 with 3 updates spaced about 3 to 4 months apart). The CD ROM requires a CD player, and is compatible with Sony, Hitachi, or Philips drives. Drivers and software to run the drives are included with the CD ROM.

You can reach the PC SIG at:

> PC SIG
> 1030 East Duane Avenue, Suite D
> Sunnyvale, CA 94086
> (800) 245-6717
> (800) 222-2996 (in California only)
> (408) 730-2107 (FAX)
> (408) 730-9291 (foreign orders or technical support)

Comments about the PC SIG:

The PC SIG library may be the greatest historical archive of PD and Shareware there is. The people are enthusiastic about their subjects, and aim to please. My only comment is that, perhaps due to the sheer volume, you may not get the best product in its class. Sometimes the product supplied will not be the most recent version. Because PC SIG takes a more open approach to its library than some other services, it is necessary to choose programs with care to get the best.

On the other hand, if you want a comprehensive source of information about PD and Shareware, we highly recommend obtaining a copy of the PC SIG Library book (currently in its fourth edition).

The Public (Software) Library

Nelson Ford is the force behind Houston's Public (Software) Library. His commitment to the PD and Shareware ideal have made him a respected expert on the subject. He personally weeds through each program, submits it to rigorous testing and personal scrutiny, and only chooses the software that meets his standards.

Ford's monthly newsletter contains information about new products he's seen, problems and comments he's received from users, and other information germane to the industry. The newsletter also contains the file listings for the library. These are divided into sections (for instance, Spreadsheet Programs), and often subdivided (for instance, DOS Menu Programs under Utilities). Each listing has an associated disk number by which it can be ordered.

Each program in The Public (Software) Library catalog has Nelson Ford's personal stamp of approval, and is therefore certain to be of high quality.

Subscriptions to The Public (Software) Library Newsletter cost $12 per year (Texas residents must add $.87 tax). A single issue costs $1. Yearly collections of the newsletter are available on disk.

Each disk is sold for $5 plus $4 shipping (per order). To order, call (713) 721-5205 or write:

>   The Public (Software) Library
>   P.O. Box 35705
>   Houston, TX 77235-5705

PC Blue

PC Blue is a library run by the New York Amateur Computer Club. PC Blue keeps a large library of disks on file, including a lot of CP/M and Lotus 1-2-3 utilities.

To join the NYACC, write to the address below. You will receive a form to fill out and a request for a $20 membership fee. Forms can also be found on some BBS services, along with listings of files available from PC Blue.

Disks from the PC Blue libraries are available for $10 each ($16 for foreign orders). A yearly automatic update service is offered for $200 ($350 foreign).

The NYACC holds monthly meetings in New York, but otherwise does not offer any access number or other support.

You can reach the PC Blue libraries by writing to:

> Public Domain SW Society
> P.O. Box 2085
> Clifton, NJ 07015-2085

Public Brand Software

Bob Ostrander operates Public Brand Software. Bob is also the company's librarian. Like Nelson Ford, Ostrander is a meticulous critic of software, only including in his catalog those products which meet his standards. He also seeks out good software and encourages its entry into Shareware. In addition, Bob has written some of his own utilities and has funded the development of several other projects.

The Public Brand catalog is small, but large in value. It contains categorized file listings with short, informative descriptions. Ostrander has developed a ratings system. Especially good disks receive a trophy. A top rated program or disk receives four stars. Another rating indicates the level of expertise required to make full use of a disk. This rating system includes Beginner, Intermediate, and Expert.

The Public Brand catalog shows particular care and attention to the customer's needs. Often you may find a program or utility in this catalog that you won't find anywhere else. And the addition of a toll-free number makes ordering a breeze.

Disks cost $5 each. Shipping for standard air mail is $5 per order, but extra charges can be added for other shipping methods if needed. Indiana residents must add 5 percent sales tax. Public Brand also sells blank disks for $1 each, and disk cases of various kinds. Updates are also available as well as whole library purchases.

Public Brand Software
P.O. Box 51315
Indianapolis, IN 46251

(800) IBM-DISK

or for those who don't like telephone number acronyms,

(800) 426-3475
(317) 856-1001 (in Indiana)
(317) 856-4144 (business phone)

The order line is open 24 hours.

PDN Newsletter

P.O. Box 42441
Cincinnati, OH 45242-6799
(513) 831-6799
CompuServe 70217,3264
GEnie PDN-42441
Editor/Publisher Tim Mullen

The PDN Newsletter is full of interesting news about PD and Shareware. Each issue contains lots of new information about what's going on in the Shareware world as well as full reviews of products. Some of those reviews have been reprinted in this book, so you can see what they are like. We think you'll get a lot out of PDN Newsletter. In addition, PDN keeps a relatively select group of programs available in its catalog (around 400 applications) and charges a copying fee that ranges from about $3 to about $10, depending on the program. The PDN Newsletter is published bimonthly, and each issue contains the entire current catalog.

Catalog Summary

The PC SIG Library catalog, even at $12.95 is an excellent source of information. It is potentially confusing due to its historical nature and the sheer number of programs. The PC SIG Magazine extends an on-going effort to examine, review, and report on the state of PD and Shareware.

Nelson Ford's newsletter may be one of the best sources of new information and colorful opinion. His software catalog contains many excellent products, and his reputation and hard work lend credibility to PD and Shareware in general.

The Public Brand catalog is one of the best selective collections of software (along with Ford's), and it is one of the most convenient to use. It's ratings and brief, but informative descriptions make the catalog an excellent reference as well as a source of products.

For those really interested in maintaining a high awareness of PD and Shareware products, we recommend all the services listed in this chapter. There's something to learn from each of them.

User Groups

In the first edition of this book, we didn't tell you much about user groups, an omission we regret. We wish to rectify that situation now.

User groups may be one of the best ways for people to find out about computers, telecommunications, and PD and Shareware. There are groups all around the country. Some of them are megalithic conglomerations of users from major metropolitan areas. Others are smaller and more intimate. Most of them will have much to offer—ranging from a hefty library of PD and Shareware disks, to experts in various fields who can act as advisors, to other users trying to find out how to do all those many things we are always trying to do on computers.

We mailed out a letter to some of the larger user groups and asked them to give us current information about themselves. The following is a list of top user groups around the U.S. as compiled by us with some help from Marshall Magee (for ASP) and Roger Shanafeld (from Microsoft). Groups are in alphabetical order:

Albuquerque PC Users Group—708 11 St NW Albuquerque NM 87102

Anchorage IBM PC Users Group—3605 Arctiv Blvd. #1320 Anchorage AK 99503

Athens IBM PC User Group—255 S. Milledge Avenue Athens GA 30605

Baltimore IBM PC Users Group—1910 Trout Farm Road Jarrettsville MD 21084

Baton Rouge PC Users Group—P.O. Box 3564 Baton Rouge LA 70819

Big Apple User Group—P.O. Box 490 New York NY 10274

Birmingham IBM PC Users Group—P.O. Box 19248 Birmingham AL 35219

Boeing Employees Computing Society—P.O. Box 3707 Seattle WA 98124

Boise PC Users Group—779978 Fairview Ave. Boise ID 83704

Boston Computer Society—One Center Plaza Boston MA 01059 (617) 367-
8080

Buffalo IBM PC User Group—4242 Ridge Lea #23 Buffalo NY 14226

Business Computer Club of Charlotte—2109 S. Tryon Street Charlotte NC
28203

Capital PC User Group—P.O. Box 3189 Gaithersburg MD 20878

Central Connecticut User Group—P.O. Box 964 Glastonbury CT 06033

Central Illinois PC Users Group—P.O. Box 10053 Springfield IL 62706

Central Pennsylvania IBM PC Association—P.O. Box 634 Lemont PA 16851

Central Virginia IBM PC Users Group—P.O. Box 34446 Richmond VA 23234

Chicago Computer Hobbyist—10249 S. Ewing Chicago IL 60617

Chicago Computer Society—P.O. Box 8681 Chicago IL 60680-8681 (312) 794-
7737 President: Mary Dolce

Cincinnati Personal Computer Users Group—P.O. Box 3097 Cincinnati OH
45201 President: Bill Radock

Colorado Springs PC Users Group—P.O. Box 25481 Colorado Springs CO
80396

Columbia PC Users Group—1560 Daniel Boone Blvd. Columbia MO 65201

Des Moines Area IBM PC Users Group—1876 SE Park Avenue Des Moines IA
50320

Diablo Valley PC Users Group—P.O. Box 8040 #117 Walnut Creek CA 94596
(415) 943-1367

Grand Forks IBM PC Users Group—717 Ives Street Buxton ND 58218

Greater Cleveland PC Users Group—30704 Royalview Drive Willowick OH 44094

Greater Rhode Island IBM PC Satellite Group—Univ. of Rhode Island Academic Computer Center/Tyler Hall 048 (401) 792-2301

Hawaii PC Users Group—P.O. Box 22967 Honolulu HI 96822

Houston Area League of PC Users—P.O. Box 61266 Houston TX 77208-1266

PC-HUG—P.O. Box 2173 Huntington WV 25722-2173 (304) 526-5189

IBM PC Users Club—315 Cutler Hall Ohio Univ. Athens OH 45701

IBM PC Users Group—of Ashville 142 Edwin Place Ashville NC 28801 (704) 684-2241 (days) President Bruce Rogers

IBM PC Users Groups of St. Louis—P.O. Box 837 St. Louis MO 63188

IBM Users Group of California—P.O. Box 4136 Los Angeles CA 90078

IBM Users Groups—2906 Montauk Ct. Falls Church VA 22042

Indianapolis Computer Society—P.O. Box 2532 Indianapolis IN 46206 (317) 862-5967 President: Bob Sanborn

Int'l Business Schools Computer Users Group—Bently College Waltham MA 02254

Kentucky-Indiana PC Users Group—P.O. Box 3564 Louisville KY 40201

Madison IBM PC User Group—P.O. Box 2598 Madison WI 53701-2598

Miami PC Users Group—2500 E. Hallandale Beach Blvd. #707 Hallandale FL 33009

Milwaukee Area IBM PC User Group—P.O. Box 2121 Milwaukee WI 53201

Montgomery PC Users Club—3505 McGehee Road Montgomery AL 36111

Music City IBM PC Users Group—P.O. Box 121633 Nashville TN 37212

New Orleans Personal Computer Club—P.O. Box 1131 Metaire LA 70004

New York IBM PC Users Group—80 Wall St. #614 New York NY 10005

North Orange County IBM PC Users Groups—P.O. Box 3616 Orange CA 92665

North Texas PC Users Group—2025 Rockcreek Drive Arlington TX 76010

Northeast Ohio PC Club—P.O. Box 16194 Rocky River OH 44116

PC Users Group—of Boca Raton 2583 NW 23rd Way Boca Raton FL 33431

PC Users Group—of Colorado P.O. Box 944 Boulder CO 80306

Pacific NW IBM PC Users Group—P.O. Box 3363 Bellevue WA 98009 (206) 525-3452

Pasadena IBM PC Users Group—711 E. Walnut St. #306 Pasadena CA 91101

Philadelphia Area IBM PC Club—2041 Harbour Drive Palmyra NJ 08065

Phoenix IBM PC Users Group—P.O. Box 44150 Phoenix AZ 85046

Portland PC Users Group—P.O. Box 1727 Beaverton OR 97075-1727

Portsmouth IBM PC Group—57 S Street Portsmouth NH 03801

Quad Cities PC Users Groups—P.O. Box 464 Bettendorf IA 52722

Sacramento PC Users Group—P.O. Box 685 Citrus Heights CA 95611-0685

San Diego Computer Society—P.O. Box 81444 San Diego CA 92138

San Francisco PC Users Group—3145 Geary Blvd. #155 San Francisco CA 94118

Silicon Valley Computer Society—2464 El Camino Real #190 Santa Clara CA 95051 (408) 286-2969 Executive Director: Kent Safford

South Florida Computer Group—P.O. Box 5684 Fort Lauderdale FL 33310 (305) 484-3130 President: Gaetano Tata; Secretary Merrell Evancik

Southwest Michigan PC Users Group—2320 Crosswind Drive Kalamazoo MI 49008

Space Coast PC Users Group—P.O. Box 396 Titusville FL 32781

Stanford-Palo Alto Users Group—for IBM PC P.O. Box 3738 Stanford CA 94305

Tampa IBM PC Users Group—5118 N. 56th St. Tampa FL 33610

Terre Haute PC Users Group—100 S. 22nd St. Terre Haute IN 47803

Tidewater PC Users Group—P.O. Box 5105 Virginia Beach VA 23455 (804) 481-1254

Tucson Computer Society—P.O. Box 1489 Tucson AZ 85702

Twin Cities PC User Group—P.O. Box 3163 Minneapolis MN 55403

Utah Blue Chips—P.O. Box 510811 Salt Lake City UT 84151 (801) 521-7830 Dana B. Snow

Washtenaw IBM PC User Society—P.O. Box 7508 Ann Arbor MI 48107

25

The Private BBS

Aside from the commercial services that were discussed earlier in this book, there are a multitude of privately owned BBSs available in every state of this country. In fact, they probably number in the thousands. What are these private BBSs and why do they exist?

Private BBSs are usually run from someone's house, with a dedicated private phone line attached to a personal computer. They usually support one user at a time and provide such services as electronic mail, public-domain and Shareware software, and in some cases, on-line games and entertainment. These computers usually operate using BBS software. Some of the more popular BBS programs are RBBS, FIDO, and EBBS.

BBSs are run by very dedicated people known as SYSOPs or SYStem OPerators. The SYSOPs maintain the system, answer questions, post files and generally keep things running. Most SYSOPS's are the owners of the BBS they operate. Since they do all of this work for free, they usually expect users to figure things out on their own. They view themselves as hobbyists, and expect their users to understand that fact. The learning process is part of that hobby.

Because these services are privately run—free of charge in most cases—and require the use of a dedicated computer and phone line, they tend to come and go. However, they can still be an excellent source of software and utility.

The major problem with most BBSs is that they are single user. If a BBS is any good, it's usually busy 24 hours a day. Some people have reported putting their computers on automatic redial for days to access some of the best systems in the country. So why go to all this trouble? Because it's free—except for the cost of the phone call.

We will discuss the basic features of a BBS system. We will give some command examples of an RBBS system, which are pretty much generic to all BBS systems that you might encounter. We will also explain how to access these systems for the first time.

BBSs are usually broken down into three main sections: mail, files, and utilities. Mail is usually found at the main menu when you first log in. Most systems tell you if you have any mail waiting or not, and then give you a main menu prompt with a list of possible commands. Here is a list of some of the commands you might encounter, and an explanation of each:

A)nswer Questionnaire — answer questionnaires on multiple topics

B)ulletin listing — see general system bulletins

C)omment for SYSOP — private message to RBBS operator

D)oors—run non-RBBS programs

E)nter message — leave mail for someone or everyone

F)iles menu — files are downloaded/uploaded here

G)oodbye — log off this system

H)elp — help for any command, section, topic

I)nitial welcome message — repeat of logon welcome message

J)oin a conference — change to a new message base

K)ill a message — erase a message you left before

O)perator page — pages SYSOP for 30 seconds

Q)uit — go elsewhere in system—disconnect, to files or utilities

P)ersonal mail — list messages directed to you by name

R)ead message(s) — select messages to read

S)can messages — check messages (date/from/to/topic)

T)opic scan — check messages for topics

U)tilities — (baud rate, case, graphics, line feeds, msg. margin, nulls)

As you can see, the commands are diverse. From the main menu you can enter the file's subsystem, or the utilities menu which is where you can modify your user settings like page length and default file transfer protocol. Since the focus of this book is on software and not RBBS, we will leave the description of the utilities section at that. If you are having a problem seeing your screen, or transferring files, the utilities menu is where you want to check first. Review your user settings and compare them to the settings in your terminal program. Most problems can be resolved by following this step.

The files section provides the directory listings for all the files the BBS has to offer, as well as the facilities to accomplish a transfer. The following is a list of commands you will most likely find in the file menu:

D)ownload — you get a file from here

G)oodbye — exit this system — DISCONNECT

H)elp — help with any command, section, or topic

L)ist directories (categories) of files available for download

N)ew files — get list of files new since specified date

Q)uit — go elsewhere—to main menu, utilities, off system

S)ubstring search — list files with specified text in name/description

U)pload — you send me a file

V)iew ARC Contents — look to see what is in an .ARC file

X)pert — expert mode on/off

The file subsystem permits you to move files between your system and the BBS. Downloading refers to moving files from a BBS to your computer, and uploading is moving files from your computer to the BBS.

The transfer of data can either be done in ASCII or by using a protocol such as *XMODEM*. The *XMODEM* protocol is common to CP/M and DOS based systems, and was originally developed by Ward Christiansen. Please refer to to the protocols chapter for more information on this subject.

To list the names of the files that are available on the disks for downloading to your system, enter the *<L>*ist command at the Files Menu. The full names of the files will be listed along with a short description of each file. Usually there is a document file that accompanies most of the program items on the system. These document files usually use the *DOC* or *TXT* file extension.

The basic steps in downloading are:

1. tell the BBS you want to download

2. tell the BBS exactly which file you want to download

3. tell the BBS what protocol you want to use

4. after the BBS says it is ready, tell your communications program to save the incoming file

   Note: The first three steps can be specified on a single line in the format *d;<filename>;<protocol>*. (e.g. *D;PCWRITE.LBR;X* will download the file *PCWRITE.LBR* using *XMODEM* protocol.)

   Note: if you set a default protocol when you first signed up with the BBS, you will *not* be asked by the BBS what protocol to use. If you want to override the default protocol, do the first three steps above on one line. For example, to download *LOVE.DOC* using ASCII when the default is XMODEM, enter *D;LOVE.DOC;A* at the file function prompt. If you want to reset the default protocol, enter the utilities section, select *F* for F)ile protocol, then N)one.

ASCII Data Capture

You can transfer files in ASCII mode if your system is capable of data capture. To download a file using the ASCII method, follow the sequence of steps listed below.

1. List the files available for download using the L)ist command and either capture the list to your printer or write down the exact names of the files you want to receive.

2. After returning to the Files Menu, select D)ownload.

3. When the BBS asks for the file name you wish to select, input the exact file name, including a period between the file name and extension.

4. When the BBS asks for the type of download you want, input A for A)SCII method. (Only if you have default protocol set to None will you be asked this question.)

5. When the BBS tells you to open your capture file and enter a carriage return to start the download, you should do so. (For instance, opening your capture file in QMODEM would use the CTRL-HOME command sequence.) After setting up to receive the file on your end, you have to send the BBS one carriage return so that it knows you are ready to start.

6. The file will be sent a line at a time until the entire file is sent. You will see the lines of ASCII code (readable text and numbers) on your screen as they flow to your system. If you wish to suspend the transmission temporarily, your system should send the BBS a Ctrl-S (XOFF). A Ctrl-Q (XON) will restart the temporarily halted transfer. A Ctrl-X (ASCII CAN [cancel]) can be sent anytime to abort the transmission of the data; because of the output buffering performed automatically by the BBS, there may be up to 120 characters transmitted before the output stops.

7. When the file transfer is finished, the BBS will normally send you an End Of File Marker (Ctrl-Z) followed by some kind of alarm or bell. You should close your capture file (QMODEM CTRL-HOME) as soon as you hear the bells or you will get garbage at the bottom of the file. If you go away for a cup of coffee and end up getting the "end of file" sign attached to the bottom of the capture file, you can delete it from the file later using a text editor.

8. After the file transfer is complete, you will be returned to the File Menu. You should look at the capture file at this point to be sure you got it ok. (For instance, use the QMODEM Alt-V command to do this.) Do not list the entire file unless it is short; most BBSs will give you only so many minutes to remain off-line before they assume you have left for the day, recycle, and drop you off line.

XMODEM File Transfer

Files with *EXE* and *COM* extensions and tokenized BASIC files can be moved to your system. Files containing the IBM PC special ASCII characters (ones with ASCII values above 128) can also be transferred with XMODEM. These include WordStar files. These files cannot be transferred in ASCII mode, since ASCII transfer is only 7 bit and these types of files require the full 8-bit transfer of the data, with no translation of the contents of the file.

XMODEM also offers the advantage of a block check to assure that the data sent contains no errors. It does this by adding a checksum byte to the end of each block of data. The receiver calculates its own checksum and compares it to the one received. If an error is detected in the transmission, XMODEM will request that the BBS retransmit the block of data. Please refer to the protocol chapter for more information on XMODEM.

To perform an XMODEM file download, follow the instructions shown above for ASCII DATA CAPTURE, but select X)modem instead of A)scii when the BBS asks what file download type you want (step 4 above). The XMODEM file transfer steps are as follows:

5. If you called in using *EVEN* parity the *RBBS-PC* will tell you to switch to NO parity and 8 data bits. If you called in using 8 data bits, the system will not give you this message. You should then open your capture file (for instance, *QMODEM,* in the *PgDn* command) and start the XMODEM receive process.

6. The file will be transferred automatically by XMODEM. You may abnormally abort the transfer by sending the BBS an ASCII CAN code (*Ctrl-X*). QMODEM will do this for you if you press the *PgDn* key during the file transfer.

7. When the file transfer is finished, XMODEM automatically closes your capture file for you. XMODEM also ensures that no garbage gets into your

file; binary files and text files are just as they were sent to you with 99.6 percent error free transmission. WordStar files should transfer without extra hard carriage returns being added.

8. XMODEM transferred files cannot be listed on your monitor unless they are actually ASCII files. Binary files will appear as symbols rather than human-readable text. You will have to test these files after you exit your communications program.

File Uploading

File uploading to the BBS is very similar to downloading. After you have downloaded a few files, you might want to share one of your favorite programs or files with the other users just to test your ability to upload.

Uploading of ASCII files can be done without interruption between lines. Most systems can handle data uploading at 300 baud without any problem. If the transfer is done at 1200 baud, however, there may be a data overrun if the file is over 20K. If the system falls behind during a file upload operation, it will send an XOFF (Ctrl-S) to your system. If your system supports XON/OFF file transfer speed-matching, data transmission will be suspended until an XON (Ctrl-Q) is sent to you, indicating that the BBS is ready to accept data again.

Before sending a file, be sure the system has enough disk space to take the file. When you ask for U)pload at the File menu, the system will tell you how much disk space is free on the upload drive. If the system runs out of disk space during an upload function, it will issue a cancel request. This will be in the form of a data stream of one or more ASCII CAN (Ctrl-X) characters. Your system will abort transmission if it supports XON/OFF file transfer speed-matching protocol. If your system does not support XON/OFF, the data overflow will be lost and the BBS, in most cases, will recycle, dropping you off line.

Most systems have ground rules about uploading files to the system, so it is important that you follow these rules. For example, some systems will not accept any games. Generally speaking, no system will accept a commercial program that is not Shareware or public domain. Uploading this type of file usually results in being locked out of the system, so be careful!

Glossary

Acoustic coupler—a more old fashioned kind of modem on which you place a voice-type telephone receiver in a special cradle where information is sent and received. Acoustic couplers have largely been replaced by internal and external modems (see below).

Alias—like a macro (*see* macro) or a batch file (*see* batch file) in that it is a redefined command used to execute a series of operations. For example, the letter *d* could be redefined as an alias for the DIR command.

Archive—In computerese, an archive is a backup of data. An archive file is one that was created with one of the library file programs, particularly ARC.

Archive bit—a flag place on DOS files that indicates whether the file has been backed up or not. Some directory programs in this book will display the status of the archive bit.

ASC—sometimes used as a file extension to denote an ASCII file.

ASCII—stands for American Standard for Coded Information Interchange. What it is: a standard set of computer codes to represent letters and graphic symbols. ASCII is recognized by many different types of computers, and can be reliably used to transfer text-only messages.

ASM—a file extension that indicates an assembly language file.

Asynchronous—a data communications protocol that does not require a fixed timing between characters when transmitted.

Auto-answer—a feature on some modems that allows them to pick up the phone when it rings.

Auto-dial—a feature on so-called intelligent modems that allows them to place a call on command, then connect the call when the other end answers.

Auto-linefeed—automatically inserts a linefeed at the end of each line of data. This setting does not need to be on normally.

BAS—a file extension that represents a BASIC file.

BAT—a file extension that represents a batch file (*see* batch file).

Batch file—a special kind of DOS file that can execute a set of other DOS commands, including running application programs. Batch files are often used to control processes that require running several different programs.

Baud—a measure of data transfer speed (bits per second). Common baud rates in telecommunicating are 300; 1,200; and 2,400.

BBS—a bulletin board system; generally a public- or private-access host computer system that people access by modem (*see* Part III, Sources).

Binary—having to do with base two systems (i.e., on/off, 0/1, etc.). Computers think in binary terms, but most human interaction with computers is translated by the Operating System, by specific programming languages, or by applications.

Bit—a standard unit of computer measure; a single on/off, 0/1 setting (*see* Byte).

Boot—from bootstrapping; an antiquated term for starting a computer. Retains the same meaning, although the original bootstrapping process is long gone. Some people use it to mean starting an application, but this is a confusing variant. Boot means to start up a computer. Cold Boot means to turn on the switch. Warm Boot means to reset the computer while it is still running.

Boot Sectors—invisible information used by the system to determine the information needed to boot the computer.

Browse—used in databases and on BBSs to indicate looking through data one item at a time. On a BBS, for instead, Browse usually allows you to see a file listing (or subset of files one listing at a time) with verbose descriptions.

Buffer—a space in memory or on disk where information is temporarily stored. Often word processing programs use buffers to store cut material to be pasted late, or to store deleted material in case you change your mind. Programming languages use buffers to save information temporarily, too.

Bug—a part of a computer program that does not work correctly.

Bulletin Board (BBS)—a service accessed by modem on which you can leave and receive messages, exchange software, and perform a variety of activities ranging from accessing stock market information to playing a game.

Byte—usually defined as 8 bits (see bit, above). For instance, a byte might be made up of eight on or off states (signified by ones and zeros) as follows: 10001101. A byte is a standard unit of computer measurement. 1024 bytes constitutes a kilobyte; 1,024,000 bytes is a megabyte.

CAD—Computer Aided Design (graphic design on computer systems).

Carrier tone—the high-pitched tone emitted by a modem when it detects a connection on the other end of a line. When the carrier tones are matched at each end, a hissing sound is heard, signifying that a connection has been made.

Carrier detect—one of the pins on the modem that signals detection of a carrier tone.

CD ROM—a high capacity read-only disk (typically around 200 megabytes or more).

CGA—Color Graphics Adaptor (medium resolution color display standard for IBM computers).

Character string—a specific word or phrase as defined in a program is called a string.

Checksum—an algorithm used to verify the integrity of data often used when transferring files by modem.

Circular dialing queue—a list of numbers that will be called in sequence from a telecommunications program.

COM—a file extension for an executable file. COM files can be run by simply typing the first part of the file name; i.e. to run *PROGRAM.COM*, type *PROGRAM*.

Compatible—a computer substantially compatible with the IBM PC, XT, or AT. Compatibility varies, but most so-called clones run most software designed for the IBM series of personal computers.

Concatenate—to link together; a computerese mumbo-jumbo word.

CP/M—Control Program/Microcomputer; a precursor to DOS, and source of many of the original public-domain and Shareware programs.

CPU—the Central Processing Unit; the "chip." In a PC or XT, the CPU is an Intel 8088 chip. In an AT, it is an 80286 chip, and in the Model 80, it is the 80386.

Cursor—point which marks the current location of input to the computer. There are often different types of cursors, depending on the application. Most of the time it marks the spot where entry from the keyboard will have effect. Sometimes it marked where mouse movements and clicks will have effect.

Data—information.

Database—a collection of data organized in categories (records and fields). Databases range from simple mailing lists to complex accounting data.

dBASE—a popular database from Ashton-Tate. Versions of dBASE include dBASE II, dBASE III, and dBASE III plus.

Default drive—the current drive; sometimes called the currently logged drive. The default drive is where the actions will take place unless another drive is specifically mentioned.

Dialing queue—*see* circular dialing queue.

DIR—DIRectory; the DOS command used to obtain a list of files in the current drive and directory.

Directory—a sub-divided area on a disk where programs may be stored. Directory names are separated by using the backslash (i.e. *\DOS\MENU*). (*See* root directory.)

Disk drive—a mechanism for reading and writing information to and from disks. A disk drive can be of several types including floppy disks (both 5.25" and 3.25") and hard disks. There are also removable hard disks like the Bernoulli drives that allow high storage capacity with removable media.

Disk (or diskette)—usually refers to a floppy disk (*see* disk drive).

DOC—a file extension that represents a document file. Some word processors use this extension for proprietary file types, but some people place this extension on ASCII files, too (also *see* TXT and ASC).

Documentation—the instructions that accompany a program.

DOS—the Disk Operating System developed for IBM by Microsoft. This is the language that the computer and the disk drives share. DOS is up to version 3.3 so far, but shows little sign of stopping despite the impending emergence of OS/2, the next operating system.

DOS shell—two possible interpretations exist. A program that replaces the DOS commands (like Command, Directory Scanner, Tshell, etc.) is sometimes called a shell program. The actual DOS shell is a partition taken out of memory to run a second COMMAND.COM. Many programs that allow exiting to DOS from within the application use a DOS shell. Some care needs to be taken when running a DOS shell. Particularly, do not run BASIC, and do not attempt to run a TSR within the shell (*see* TSR). To return to the program that called the shell, you always type EXIT at the DOS prompt. If you type EXIT and nothing happens, you were probably not in a DOS shell.

Download—to receive data from another computer.

Dump—sending raw data out to a device like a printer or modem.

Duplex—a designation of the ability to communicate concurrently or one at a time (*see* full duplex and half duplex).

Echo—controls the appearance of typed characters to the local screen during telecommunication.

Editor—usually refers to a program designed to edit and compose text. Editors are often used by programmers when writing computer programs as they often contain features useful for that work. Word processors are more useful for general writing tasks.

EGA—Enhanced Graphics Adaptor. This is a high resolution color display.

Electronic mail—also known as E-Mail; messaging via computers. All BBSs allow some form of E-Mail, although Fido boards have perfected E-Mail to an art, and services like MCI, CompuServe, GEnie, etc. all contain sophisticated E-Mail facilities.

Embedded command—a command placed in a document that affects the output of the document when it is printed or specially formatted for screen or file, but which does not take effect immediately.

Emulate—to simulate the environment of another system. Many telecommunication programs can emulate different types of terminals used on mainframes and other systems.

Environment variables—certain special information can be passed to the DOS system using the SET command. These are called environment variables because they operate within the total DOS environment. A common environment variable is the COMSPEC variable which sets the location of the *COMMAND.COM* if it is to be different from the original boot location. For instance, if you boot from a floppy disk, but wish to have the computer consider the *COMMAND.COM* on your hard disk as the main system, you might issue a statement such as SET *COM-SPEC=C:\COMMAND.COM* which will cause DOS to recognize the C: drive as if you had booted from it.

EXE—a file extension used on an executable file. Typing the first part of an EXE file name is enough to run the file, i.e. typing *PROGRAM* will run a file called *PROGRAM.EXE*.

External modem—a device that stands outside a computer and is connected by a serial cable (see below). One disadvantage of external modems is that they can be shared by several computers. One disadvantage is that they usually cost a little more than internal modems (see below).

FAT—File Allocation Table. A system file used to keep a list of all directories and files, and their locations on the disk.

File—a unit of information storage on a disk. Files come in many types ranging from binary (coded) files like COM and EXE files, to text files like TXT files, to data files used by specific programs.

File name—a DOS file name consists of up to 8 letters and/or numbers with a period and three character extension, i.e. *PROGRAM.EXE*.

File name extension—helps determine the type of file (*see* EXE, COM, TXT, etc.).

Floppy disk—a computer storage medium. Two formats are in common usage, 5.25"and 3.25" disks.

Format—magnetic information placed on a disk to allow DOS to read and write data to it. Until a disk is formatted, it is useless magnetic particles without form. Formatting arranges the disk into special areas called sectors where the computer files can go.

Form feed—moves the paper in a printer to the top of the next page.

Full duplex—a telephone is a full duplex device because two people can talk at the same time. In telecommunications, full duplex indicates that both sides can communicate at the same time.

Garbage—bad telephone lines are sometimes referred to as dirty or noisy lines, or as containing "garbage" on the line.

Half duplex—a walkie talkie is a half duplex device because one person must be receiving while the other transmits, then they "Roger, over" to each other to exchange roles. In telecommunications, half duplex indicates the same type of arrangement. Xmodem is a half duplex protocol.

Hard copy—a printout to printer or plotter.

Host computer—the computer that other computers call. The host computers of large BBSs like CompuServe are mainframe computers. Host computers of many local BBSs are PCs and ATs.

Hot key—generally refers to the key combination used to invoke a TSR program (*see* TSR).

I/O—Input/Output. Any information sent from the computer to a peripheral device (modem, monitor, printer, keyboard, etc.) is considered I/O.

Internal modem—an internal modem resides in a computer's internal slot. Internal modems can only work with one computer at a time, but they cost less than external modems.

K—the abbreviation for kilobyte (i.e. 64K means 64 kilobytes).

Kermit—one of the major transfer protocols (*see* Chapter 2).

Keyboard—Basic input device similar to a typewriter keyboard.

Kilobyte—1,024 bytes (*see* K, bytes, bits).

Language—in computers; a way of translating the computer's binary code into something human beings can read and write; a set of rules and commands for creating computer programs.

Laser Printer—a printer that uses a laser engine to produce very high quality output.

Line feed—moves a printer carriage one line.

Logon—signing on to a remote system.

Logon script—a program automatically executed on connection that answers any logon questions (i.e. name, password, etc.).

Lotus 1-2-3—benchmark spreadsheet from Lotus Development Corp.

Macro—a set of commands which are triggered from a single keystroke or command; conceptually similar to DOS batch files, but generally occur within applications.

Megabyte—1,024,000 bytes (*see* kilobyte, byte, bit).

Memory—*see* RAM and ROM.

Menu—in computer applications, menu has several meanings. Menus are used within applications to list choices. Pop-up menus are small windows of choices that appear on the screen in various locations. Pull-down menus are windows that appear from a menu bar at the top of a screen, pulling down as if they were Venetian blinds. Pull-down menus have been popularized by Apple's Macintosh computers, and have begun to gain acceptance in IBM applications.

Merge—placing organized database information in other text files; usually used for creating form letters and mailing labels.

Microcomputer—a small computer. PCs are all microcomputers, but today's PC has the power of mainframes of the past.

Microprocessor—*see* CPU.

Minicomputer—more powerful (and more expensive) than a microcomputer; smaller than a mainframe.

Modem—MOdulator DEModulator; a device for linking one computer with another (usually over phone lines, but not always).

Modem7—a variation of Xmodem.

Monitor—CRT or display screen. Monitors come in color and monochrome. They also come in various sizes and resolutions.

Motherboard—the main processing board of a computer with CPU and other components. A large printed circuit.

Mouse—a hand-held input device.

MS-DOS—Microsoft's DOS for compatibles (*see* DOS).

Multi-user—ability to process more than one computer terminal; concurrent access from multiple computer operators.

Nulls—a way of slowing down the interchange during telecommunications when one system is processing faster than the other; sometimes necessary when using a printer to record data on-line.

Off-line—not connected via modem.

On-line—connected via modem.

Operating system—the interface between the computer and virtually everything else (*see* DOS, PC-DOS, MS-DOS).

Output—data going out to something (a modem, a printer, a screen, etc.).

Parallel—another I/O method that sends simultaneous streams of information, generally used with printers.

Parity—a method of error checking during data transmission.

Path—1. a list of drives and directories searched by the system when it can't find a file during execution of a command. The path is created using the DOS PATH statement. Several utilities in the Utilities chapter can help modify the path. 2. the path is also the full description of the location of a file. For instance, a file on the C: drive, in the *FILES* directory, is notated as *C:FILES\FILENAME.EXT*. That is the full path of the file, *FILENAME.EXT*.

Pascal—a high level computer language.

PC—a microcomputer.

PC-DOS—IBM version of DOS (*see* DOS).

Peripheral—a device connected to a computer such as a modem, disk drive, printer, plotter, monitor, mouse, graphic tablet, etc.

Pixel—a specific dot on a CRT screen.

Plotter—a high resolution printing device designed to produce graphic output.

Printer—an output device for text and graphics hardcopy.

Program—computer instructions that implement the completion of a specific task.

Programmer—person who writes computer programs and drinks a lot of coffee late at night.

Protocol—a specific set of rules for controlling communications sessions.

Public domain—read the book!

RAM—Random Access Memory. RAM is the memory used when the computer is on. It is cleared whenever the computer is turned off. This is called volatile memory.

RAM disk—a pseudo-disk driver created in RAM. Contents disappear when the computer is powered off.

Resolution—a measure of the amount of detail that can be displayed on a monitor. Measurement is in pixels (dots on the screen—640 x 200) or line and columns (25 x 80).

ROM—Read Only Memory. Memory that cannot be changed and does not disappear when the computer is turned off. It is called non-volatile memory.

Root directory—the directory highest up in the directory tree, from which all other directories branch (*see* directory).

Serial—a method of transferring data in a stream of packets (like boxcars on a train).

Set—for information on the DOS SET command, *see* Environment Variables.

Shareware—read the book!

Shell—*see* DOS shell.

SIG—Special Interest Group. Areas found on BBSs that specialize in forming dialogs on specific subjects.

Software—computer programs.

Sort—arrange organized data in order. For instance, when working with databases, you can sort information by name, zip code, amount, etc.

Source code—computer program for an application. Often source code is available from an application's author, and the application can be modified (with permission) to customize the application.

Spooler—temporary storage buffer to allow an application to continue while the printer works in the background.

Spreadsheet—a computer application designed for manipulating numbers and playing "what-if" with figures. Spreadsheets are organized in columns and rows, with each intersection called a cell. A cell can contain numbers, text, or formulas.

Stop bit—used during telecommunications to signal the end of a character or letter.

Syntax—rules governing the structure of a language or operating system.

SYSOP—SYStem OPerator. The person responsible for maintaining a BBS or a SIG. Pronounced "Sissop," not "Sizop" or "Sizeop."

Terminal—a computer node.

Text file—an ASCII file (*see* ASCII).

TSR (Terminate and Stay Resident)—programs that, once loaded, remain in memory for instant retrieval (also *see* Hot key).

Turbo Pascal—popular version of the Pascal language from Borland International.

TXT—common file extension used with ASCII files.

Upload—sending files or data to a remote computer.

Word processor—an application for manipulating text.

WordStar—a popular word processor from MicroPro.

Xmodem—the most common file transfer protocol (*see* Chapter 2).

XON/XOFF—Special control characters sometimes used to handle flow control during data transfers. Like a traffic cop at an intersection telling drivers when to go and when to stop.

Wxmodem—file transfer protocol (*see* Chapter 2).

Ymodem—file transfer protocol (*see* Chapter 2).

Ymodem batch—file transfer protocol (*see* Chapter 2).

Zmodem—file transfer protocol (*see* Chapter 2).

About the Authors

Rusel DeMaria is a freelance writer and columnist. His weekly computer column appears in *The Maui News* and another column appears in Island Computing. He has written articles and reviews for many major computer magazines, including *Business Software Magazine*, *DBMS*, *PC Week*, *BYTE*, *Macworld*, *Mac User*, *A+ Magazine*, *ST-LOG*, and *The Whole Earth Catalog*. He is MS-DOS Editor for the *MACazine,* a columnist for *Nikkei Byte* in Japan, and co-sysop of the RHS RBBS. In addition to computer writing, DeMaria is a novelist and flamenco/classical guitarist.

George R. Fontaine is a programmer and writer. He has been programming for over eleven years. He is currently a Detective Sergeant in the Maui Police Department. Fontaine holds a degree in Administration of Justice. He is the Sysop of the RHS RBBS.

Index

How to Order the Public-Domain Software and Shareware Disk

The **Public-Domain Software and Shareware** utilities disk (MS-DOS format) contains an excellent collection of useful utilities and entertaining games. Because the files are archived, you actually receive several diskettes worth of programs. Included are such programs as Arcmaster, a full-featured archive file management system; DPROTECT, a disk drive directory listing to the screen, printer, or disk file; Privacy, an encoder/decoder program that allows you to encode your files; SWAPNAME, a file that allows you to swap the file names of two existing files on your disk; the game Spacewar; and much more.

The disk price is $20.00. California residents must add the appropriate sales tax. Order by sending a check, or credit card number (VISA, MasterCard, or American Express) and expiration date, to:

M&T BOOKS

Public-Domain Software and Shareware disk
M&T Books
501 Galveston Drive
Redwood City, CA 94063

Or, you may order by calling our toll-free number between 8 A.M. and 5:00 P.M., Monday through Friday, Pacific Standard Time; 800/533-4372 (800/356-2002 in California). Ask for Item **#48-8**.

New York Word is a professional quality **Shareware** word processor. Its features include :

Multi-window editing
Column cut and paste
Automatic Table-of-Contents and Index generators
Automatic hyphenation
Two calculators
Spelling Checker
Capture DOS output in a window
Mail Merge with Arithmetic and Conditional Processing

To order your copy, fill out the registration form on the other side and mail your payment of **$45** plus **$2** shipping per copy (**$7** overseas) to:

Marc Adler
Magma Software Systems
138 - 23 Hoover Avenue
Jamaica, New York 11435

NEW YORK WORD
Registration Form

Name _____

Address _____

City _____ State _____ Zip _____

Please send me one copy of the New York Word word processor. I will receive the latest version, printed manual, various utilities, and phone support. Please enclose **$45.00** plus **$2** shipping per copy. (**$7** overseas). Checks should be made payable to **Marc Adler** and must be in US funds, payable to a US bank.

Your support of the Shareware concept will enable authors to continue to develop high quality, low-cost software.

Marc Adler is a member of the Association for Shareware Professionals

If you would like to order New York Word, please detach the above card and mail it with your payment to Marc Adler, 138-23 Hoover Ave. , Jamaica, New York 11435.

Quicksoft, Inc. 219 First N. #224, Seattle, WA 98109

To order by mail, detach and complete this coupon and mail to Quicksoft. Orders must include check, money order, credit card information, or an additional $5 for UPS C.O.D. Offer is valid for U.S. and Canadian shipments only. This coupon may not be combined with other coupons or discounts. If you are using a registered copy of PC-Write from a friend, and you want them to earn credit for your order, don't use this coupon - please call.

Take advantage of this special $10 discount and order a Full Registration Package, today! You'll get documentation, full support, updates, and the right to earn commissions when you share PC-Write. Or, save $4 on our shareware diskettes and <u>try</u> PC-Write before you <u>buy</u> it.

90-day money-back guarantee!

Subtotal	_____
Tax (7.9% WA only)	_____
Rush Fee **$5**	_____
PO/COD Fee **$5**	_____
Total	_____

Name: _____

Company: _____ Day Phone: _____

Address: _____

City, State, Zip: _____

VISA/MC Number: _____ Expires: _____

Signature: _____

MTB.M *Quicksoft, Inc.* 219 First N. #224, Seattle, WA 98109   1-800-888-8088

"Everyone ought to have a copy."
- Jerry Pournelle, Byte

The Public *(Software)* Library

EXPERTS ALREADY KNOW IT'S THE BEST:

"Where to get the best and most current free and shareware software and where to get good information about that software? The answer is easy on both counts: it's the Public (Software) Library." - Steve Cummings, August, 1987 *Computer Currents Magazine*

"Having just gone through the ordeal of looking at the 700 disks of PC-SIG, I can appreciate as never before the incredible amount of work put into maintaining the P(s)L collection." - Alfred Glosbrenner, author *How to Get Free Software*

" The P(s)L library is regularly updated and cleaned out and documentation added or improved when necessary. The library's copying and handling charges are also among the lowest of any group." - Steven Rosenthal, *PC Week*

NOW FIND OUT FOR YOURSELF:

Call or write for a FREE sample newsletter and catalog listing of all the 1,000+ disks in the library, carefully arranged by category.

The Public (Software) Library
P. O. Box 35705
Houston, TX 77235-5705
713-721-5205 or 713-721-6104

˙The Public *(Software)* Library Newsletter

WHAT OUR READERS SAY:

"I must compliment you on the high quality of your monthly newsletter. I found it easy to read, very informative and truly enjoyable." - R.D., New Jersey

"We ordered a copy of your newsletter because the price is right and was I pleasantly surprised!! You've gained a new subscriber." - T.S. San Francisco

"...a welcome surprise." - J.D., MD, Houston

"...entertaining and informative." - Z.G., Brooklyn

"...informative, fun and very useful!!" - J.H., Miami

"...incredibly valuable to me." - N.R., Michigan

"...LOVE your newsletter." - D.W., Ontario

NOW FIND OUT FOR YOURSELF:

Call or write for a FREE sample newsletter and catalog listing of all the 1,000+ disks in the library, carefully arranged by category.

The Public (Software) Library
P. O. Box 35705
Houston, TX 77235-5705
713-721-5205 or 713-721-6104

Automenu™

Try Automenu™ and you'll quickly see why it's becoming the industry standard for a menu system. Here are a few of the reasons: ☆ Network compatible ☆ Multi-level password protection ☆ Ability to prompt for information to be passed as parameters to programs and batch files ☆ Automatic execution of any menu selection at a pre-selected times ☆ Unlimited number of menus and menu selections ☆ Non memory-resident ☆ Mouse, light pen and voice support ☆ Fast and Small. Assembler-based and fits in less than 20K.

Try Automenu™ at our risk. It's only $40 for a complete, registered version with this coupon, and we offer a money-back guarantee. Call or write to place your order now. Dealer inquires welcome. Visa and MC accepted.

Automenu™ - the first menu system and still the best.

Automenu™ is a trademark of Magee Enterprises.

MAGEE ENTERPRISES
Post Office Box 1587
Norcross, Georgia 30091 USA
404-446-6611 / CompuServe 70167,2200
FAX 404-446-7434 / BBS 404-446-6650

If the card below has been removed, please call **Public Brand Software** at 1-800-IBM-DISK for an informative catalog detailing their complete library of Public Domain software and Shareware.

FREE DISK	# Public Brand Software	FREE DISK

has an offer for you:

1. Call 1-800-IBM-DISK* for a free 80+ page catalog detailing our complete library of Public Domain software and Shareware.

2. Wait a few days for the catalog to be delivered by first class mail.

3. Browse thru the catalog (it's pretty interesting reading) and use this coupon as a **DISK CERTIFICATE** to get a disk of software (your choice) free* – no strings attached.

If you don't like the phone, write to us at: P.O. Box 51315
Indianapolis, IN 46251

*This coupon good for a free disk – no strings attached. But there always is an asterisk, right? Ok, here goes
Not affiliated with IBM Corporation, regardless of what our phone number is – so there.
And, by the way, that's 317-856-1001 in Indiana.

MAGEE ENTERPRISES

Automenu M&T Coupon Offer
Post Office Box 1587
Norcross, Georgia 30091 USA

The card below has a brief description of **Public Brand Software**. If it's no longer there, call (**1-800-IBM-DISK** – 317-856-1001 in Indiana) or drop us a line at **PO BOX 51315, Indianapolis, IN 46251**. Thanks.

Public Brand Software

may be just what you are looking for:

This book told you about Shareware and the many places you can get it. Let us tell you about ourselves. We formed back in early 1985 to distribute Public Domain software and Shareware and have since pleased over 50,000 customers with our services. Our full time librarians and completely descriptive catalog make the difference. Our quick service, full disks, rapid updating, and many "exclusives" also set us apart from the crowd.

We test, review, <u>and rate</u> everything in our library and only offer what we feel is the best tool for the job. Our disks hold as much as we can put on them; often even more than 360k since we "archive" to squeeze as much as possible on each disk. We use only first quality DS/DD BASF, 3M, SONY, etc. brand name disks and ship orders in handy plastic SRW disk caddies to avoid bent-in-the-mail problems. We always ship out orders in the very next day's UPS; no waiting for checks to clear or backorders to be filled. We always have the newest updates available from the authors.

It's the least we can do (and more than anyone else does). All this for a $5 per disk librarian and copying fee. ($6 on 3.5" disks). Support your Shareware authors. Thank you.

**Join the list of satisfied ButtonWare customers.
500,000 users agree,**

ButtonWare is #1!

**ButtonWare, Inc.
P.O. Box 5786
Bellevue, WA 98006**

_____

_____

_____

Brown Bag Software
® 2155 South Bascom Ave. #114
Campbell, CA 95008
U.S.A.

More Programming Tools from M&T Books

Programming Languages

C

Graphics Programming in C
Roger T. Stevens
Item #019-2 $39.95 (book/disk)
Item #018-4 $24.95 (book)
Details the fundamentals of graphics processes for the IBM PC family and its clones. All the information needed to program graphics in C, including source code, is presented. The provided source code will enable the user to easily modify graphics functions to suit specific needs. Both Turbo C and Microsoft C are supported. Available September 1988.

C Chest and Other C Treasures from *Dr. Dobb's Journal*
Edited by Allen Holub
Item #40-2 $24.95 (book)
Item #49-6 $39.95 (book/disk)
This comprehensive anthology contains the popular "C Chest" columns from *Dr. Dobb's Journal of Software Tools*, along with the lively philosophical and practical discussions they inspired, in addition to other information-packed articles by C experts. The software in the book is also available on disk with full source code. MS-DOS format.

Turbo C: The Art of Advanced Program Design, Optimization, and Debugging
Stephen R. Davis
Item #38-0 $24.95 (book)
Item #45-3 $39.95 (book/disk)
Overflowing with example programs, this book fully describes the techniques necessary to skillfully program, optimize, and debug in Turbo C. All programs are also available on disk with full source code. MS-DOS format.

A Small C Compiler: Language, Usage, Theory, and Design
James E. Hendrix
Item #88-7 $23.95 (book)
Item #97-6 $38.95 (book/disk)
A full presentation of the design and theory of the Small C compiler (including source code) and programming language. The author has implemented many features in this compiler that make it an excellent example for learning basic compiler theory. Some of these features are: recursive descent parsing, one-pass compilation, and the generation of assembly language. Here is a look into a real compiler with the opportunity for hands-on experience in designing one.

Dr. Dobb's Toolbook of C
Editors of *Dr. Dobb's Journal*
Item #89303-615-3 $29.95
From *Dr. Dobb's Journal of Software Tools* and Brady Communications, this book contains a comprehensive library of valuable C code. *Dr. Dobb's Journal of Software Tools'* most popular articles on C are updated and reprinted here, along with new C programming tools. Also included is a complete C compiler, an assembler, text processing programs, and more!

The Small-C Handbook
James E. Hendrix
Item #8359-7012-4 $17.95 (book)
Item #67-4 $37.90 (book and CP/M disk)
Also from *Dr. Dobb's Journal of Software Tools* and Brady Communications, the handbook is a valuable companion to the Small-C compiler, described below. The book explains the language and the compiler, and contains entire source listings of the compiler and its library of arithmetic and logical routines.

Forth

Dr. Dobb's Toolbook of Forth
Edited by Marlin Ouverson
Item #10-0 $22.95 (book)
Item #57-7 $39.95 (book/disk)
This comprehensive collection of useful Forth programs and tutorials contains expanded versions of *Dr. Dobb's Journal of Software Tools'* best Forth articles and other material, including practical code and in-depth discussions of advanced Forth topics. The screens in the book are also available on disk as ASCII files in the following formats: MS/PC-DOS, Apple II, Macintosh, or CP/M: Osborne or 8" SS/SD.

Dr. Dobb's Toolbook of Forth, Volume II
Editors of *Dr. Dobb's Journal*
Item #41-0 $29.95 (book)
Item #51-8 $45.95 (book/disk)
This complete anthology of Forth programming techniques and developments picks up where the Toolbook of Forth, First Edition left off. Included are the best articles on Forth from *Dr. Dobb's Journal of Software Tools,* along with the latest material from other Forth experts. The screens in the book are available on disk as ASCII files in the following formats: MS-DOS, Macintosh, and CP/M: Osborne or 8" SS/SD.

BASIC

The New BASICs: Programming Techniques and Library Development
Namir Clement Shammas
Item #37-2 $24.95 (book)
Item #43-7 $39.95 (book/disk)
This book will orient the advanced programmer to the syntax and programming features of The New BASICs, including Turbo BASIC 1.0, QuickBASIC 3.0, and True BASIC 2.0. You'll learn the details of implementing subroutines, functions, and libraries to permit more structured coding. Programs and subroutines are available on disk with full source code. MS-DOS format.

QuickBASIC: Programming Techniques and Library Development
Namir Clement Shammas
Item #004-4 $34.95 (book/disk)
Item #003-6 $19.95 (book)
This book provides the reader with the opportunity to learn the details of creating subroutines, functions, and libraries to permit more structured coding.The remainder of the book is dedicated to an in-depth discussion of building original libraries and functions to fulfill individual programming needs. Programs and subroutines are available on disk with full source code.

Turbo BASIC: Programming Techniques and Library Development
Namir Clement Shammas
Item #016-8 $34.95 (book/disk)
Item #015-X $19.95 (book)
Advanced programmers will be introduced to the flexible Turbo BASIC environment, programming framework, data types, and the use of libraries, functions and subroutines to permit more structured coding. As with the QuickBASIC book,

the techniques discussed in this volume are then put to use building a selection of useful libraries. All programs and subroutines are also available on disk with full source code.

HyperTalk

Dr. Dobb's Essential HyperTalk Handbook
Michael Swaine
Item #99-5 $39.95 (book/disk)
Item #99-0 $24.95 (book)
Well-known columnist Michael Swaine provides a complete analyses of Hyper-Talk in this new book. Complete coverage of topics such as the move from authoring to scripting, concepts and components of the language, programming style considerations, full language exposition and discussion, and more, are presented. Programs available on disk.

Turbo Pascal

The Turbo Pascal Toolbook
Edited by Namir Clement Shammas
Item #25-9 $25.95 (book)
Item #61-5 $45.95 (book/disk)
This book contains routines and sample programs to make your programming easier and more powerful. You'll find an extensive library of low-level routines; external sorting and searching tools; window management; artificial intelligence techniques; mathematical expression parsers, including two routines that convert mathematical expressions into RPN tokens; and a smart statistical regression model finder. More than 800K of source code is available on disk for MS-DOS systems.

MIDI

C Programming for MIDI
Jim Conger
Item #86-0 $22.95 (book)
Item #90-9 $37.95 (book/disk)
For musicians and programmers alike, here is the source that will help you write programs for music applications. The author begins by outlining the features of MIDI (Musical Instrument Digital Interface) and its support of real-time access to musical devices. An introduction to C programming fundamentals as they relate

to MIDI is also provided. The author fully demonstrates these concepts with two MIDI applications: a patch librarian and a simple sequencer.

MIDI Programming for the Macintosh
Steve De Furia and Joe Scacciaferro, Ferro Technologies
Item #022-2 $37.95 (book/disk)
Item #021-4 $22.95 (book)
This book equips the musician and programmer alike with the background necessary to program music applications and to take advantage of all the Macintosh and the MIDI interface have to offer. Specific examples are presented and all source code is available on disk. Available November 1988.

Business

PC Accounting Solutions
Editors of *PC Accounting* (formerly *Business Software*)
Item #008-7 $37.95 (book/disk)
Item #009-5 $22.95 (book)
This anthology serves as a well-rounded source of expert information for managers who want to implement a PC-based accounting system or to gain better control of their existing system. From choosing and maximizing your accounting systems and software to building better spreadsheets and budgets, this book is an immensely valuable source that will improve your ability to analyze the information that is critical to the success of your business.

Public-Domain Software: Untapped Resources for the Business User
Rusel DeMaria and George R. Fontaine
Item #39-9 $19.95 (book)
Item #47-X $34.95 (book/disk)
Organized into a comprehensive reference, this book introduces the novice and guides the experienced user to a source of often overlooked software—public domain and Shareware. This book will tell you where it is, how to get it, what to look for, and why it's for you. The sample programs and some of the software reviewed is available on disk in MS-DOS format. Includes $15 worth of free access time on CompuServe!

Time and Task Management with dBASE III
Timothy Berry

Item #09-7 $49.95 (manual/MS-DOS disk)

Like an accounting system for time and tasks, this package helps users organize hours, budgets, activities, and resources. Providing both a useful time-management system and a library of dBASE III code and macros, this package has practical as well as educational value. To be used with dBASE III. Source code and documentation is included. MS-DOS disk format.

Sales Management with dBASE III
Timothy Berry

Item #15-1 $49.95 (manual/MS-DOS disk)

Sales management works with dBASE III to provide a powerful information system that will help you to keep track of clients, names, addresses, follow-ups, pending dates, and account data. This system organizes all the day-to-day activities of selling and includes program files, format files, report files, index files, and data bases. Documentation and full source code is included.

Programming Tools and Source Code Libraries

C

Small-Windows: A Library of Windowing Functions for the C Language
James E. Hendrix

Item #35-X $29.95

Small-Windows is a complete windowing library for C. The package includes video functions, menu functions, window functions, and more. The package is available for MS-DOS systems for the following compilers: Microsoft C Version 4.0 and 5.0; Small-C; Turbo C 1.0 and 1.5; and Lattice C 3.1. Documentation and full C source code is included.

Tools

Small Tools: Programs for Text Processing
James E. Hendrix

Item #78-X $29.95 (manual/disk)

This package of text-processing programs written in Small-C is designed to perform specific, modular functions on text files. Source code is included. Small Tools is available in both CP/M and MS/PC-DOS versions and includes complete documentation.

Small Assembler: A Macro Assembler Written in Small C
James E. Hendrix
MS-DOS version: Item #024-9 $29.95 (manual/disk)
CP/M version: Item #77-1 $29.95 (manual/disk)
Here is a full macro assembler which was developed primarily for use with the Small-C compiler. It provides an excellent example for learning the basics of how assembler works. The manual provides an overview of the Small Assembler, documents the command lines that invoke programs, and more. The accompanying disk includes both the executable assembler and full source code.

NR: An Implementation of the UNIX NROFF Word Processor
Allen Holub
Item #33-X $29.95
NR is a text formatter that is written in C and compatible with UNIX's NROFF. *NR* comes configured for any Diablo-compatible printer, as well as Hewlett Packard's ThinkJet and LaserJet. Both the ready-to-use program and full source code are included. For PC compatibles.

Turbo Pascal

Statistical Toolbox for Turbo Pascal
Namir Clement Shammas
Item #22-4 $39.95 (manuals/disks)
Two statistical packages in one! A library disk and reference manual that includes statistical distribution functions, random number generation, basic descriptive statistics, parametric and nonparametric statistical testing, bivariate linear regression, and multiple and polynomial regression. The demonstration disk and manual incorporate these library routines into a fully functioning statistical program. For IBM PCs and compatibles.

Turbo Advantage
Lauer and Wallwitz
Item #26-7 $29.95
A library of more than 200 routines, with source code sample programs and documentation. Routines are organized and documented under the following categories: bit manipulation, file management, MS-DOS support, string operations, arithmetic calculations, data compression, differential equations, Fourier analysis and synthesis, and much more! For MS/PC-DOS systems.

Turbo Advantage: Complex
Lauer and Wallwitz
Item #27-5 $39.95
This library provides the Turbo Pascal code for digital filters, boundary-value solutions, vector and matrix calculations with complex integers and variables, Fourier transforms, and calculations of convolution and correlation functions. Some of the *Turbo Advantage: Complex* routines are most effectively used with Turbo Advantage. Source code and documentation included.

Turbo Advantage: Display
Lauer and Wallwitz
Item #28-3 $39.95
Turbo Advantage: Display includes an easy-to-use form processor and thirty Turbo Pascal procedures and functions to facilitate linking created forms to your program. Full source code and documentation are included. Some of the *Turbo Advantage* routines are necessary to compile *Turbo Advantage: Display*.

Operating Systems

OS/2

The Programmer's Essential OS/2 Handbook
David E. Cortesi
Item #82-8 $24.95 (book)
Item #89-5 $39.95 (book/disk)
Here is a resource no developer can afford to be without! Cortesi succinctly organizes the many features of OS/2 into related topics and illuminates their uses. Detailed indexes and a web of cross referencing provide easy access to all OS/2 topic areas. Equal support for Pascal and C programmers is provided. *The* essential reference for programmers developing in the OS/2 environment.

UNIX

UNIX Programming on the 80286/80386
Alan Deikman
Item #83-6 $24.95 (book)
Item #91-9 $39.95 (book/disk)
A complete professional-level tutorial and reference for programming UNIX and XENIX on 80286/80386-based computers. Succinct coverage of the UNIX program environment, UNIX file system, shells, utilities, and C programming under UNIX are covered. The author also delves into the development of device drivers;

some examples of these are video displays, tape cartridges, terminals, and networks.

On Command: Writing a UNIX-Like Shell for MS-DOS
Allen Holub
Item #29-1 $39.95
Learn how to write shells applicable to MS-DOS, as well as to most other programming environments. This book and disk include a full description of a UNIX-like shell, complete C source code, a thorough discussion of low-level DOS interfacing, and significant examples of C programming at the system level. All source code is included on disk.

/util: A UNIX-Like Utility Package for MS-DOS
Allen Holub
Item #12-7 $29.95
This collection of utilities is intended to be accessed through SH but can be used separately. It contains programs and subroutines that, when coupled with SH, create a fully functional UNIX-like environment. The package includes a disk with full C source code and documentation in a UNIX-style manual.

MS-DOS

Taming MS-DOS, Second Edition
Thom Hogan
Item #87-9 $19.95
Item #92-5 $34.95
Described by reviewers as "small in size, large on content," and "fun." The second edition promises to be just as readable and is updated to cover MS-DOS 3.3. Some of the more perplexing elements of MS-DOS are succinctly described here with time-saving tricks to help customize any MS-DOS system. Each trick is easily implemented into your existing tools and for programmers, Hogan includes many complete source code files that provide very useful utilities. All source code is written in BASIC.

Program Interfacing to MS-DOS
William G. Wong
Item #34-8 $29.95
Program Interfacing to MS-DOS will orient any experienced programmer to the MS-DOS environment. The package includes a ten-part manual with sample program files and a detailed description of how to build device drivers, along with the device driver for a memory disk and a character device driver on disk with macro assembly source code.

Other

Tele Operating System Toolkit
Ken Berry

This task-scheduling algorithm drives the Tele Operating System and is composed of several components. When integrated, they form an independent operating system for any 8086-based machine. Tele has also been designed for compatibility with MS-DOS, UNIX, and the MOSI standard.

SK: THE SYSTEM KERNEL
Item #30-5 $49.95 (manual/disk)

The System Kernel contains an initialization module, general-purpose utility functions, and a real-time task management system. The kernel provides MS-DOS applications with multitasking capabilities. The System Kernel is required by all other components. All source code is included on disk in MS-DOS format.

DS: WINDOW DISPLAY
Item #32-1 $39.95 (manual/disk)

This component contains BIOS level drivers for a memory-mapped display, window management support and communication coordination between the operator and tasks in a multitasking environment. All source code is included on disk in MS-DOS format.

FS: THE FILE SYSTEM
Item #65-8 $39.95 (manual/disk)

The File System supports MS-DOS disk file structures and serial communication channels. All source code is included on disk in MS-DOS format.

XS: THE INDEX SYSTEM
Item #66-6 $39.95 (manual/disk)

The Index System implements a tree-structured free-form database. All source code is included on disk in MS-DOS format.

Chips

Dr. Dobb's Toolbook of 80286/80386 Programming
Edited by Phillip Robinson
Item #42-9 $24.95 (book)
Item #53-4 $39.95 (book/disk)
This toolbook is a comprehensive discussion of the powerful 80X86 family of microprocessors. Editor Phillip Robinson has gathered the best articles from numerous key programming publications to create this valuable resource for all 80X86 programmers. All programs are available on disk with full source code.

Dr. Dobb's Z80 Toolbook
David E. Cortesi
Item #07-0 $25.00 (book)
Item #55-0 $40.00 (book/disk)
This book contains everything users need to write their own Z80 assembly-language programs, including a method of designing programs and coding them in assembly language and a complete, integrated toolkit of subroutines. All the software in the book is available on disk in the following formats: 8" SS/SD, Apple, Osborne, or Kaypro.

Dr. Dobb's Toolbook of 68000 Programming
Editors of *Dr. Dobb's Journal*
Item #13-216649-6 $29.95 (book)
Item #75-5 $49.95 (book/disk)
From *Dr. Dobb's Journal of Software Tools* and Brady Communications, this collection of practical programming tips and tools for the 68000 family contains the best 68000 articles reprinted from *Dr. Dobb's Journal of Software Tools,* along with much new material. The book contains many useful applications and examples. The software in the book is also available on disk in the following formats: MS/PC-DOS, Macintosh, CP/M 8", Osborne, Amiga, and Atari 520ST.

X68000 Cross Assembler
Brian R. Anderson
Item #71-2 $25.00
This manual and disk contain an executable version of the 68000 Cross Assembler discussed in *Dr. Dobb's Toolbook of 68000 Programming,* complete with source code and documentation. The Cross-Assembler requires CP/M 2.2 with 64K or MS-DOS with 128K. The disk is available in the following formats: MS-DOS, 8" SS/SD, and Osborne.

General Interest

Interfacing to S-100/IEEE 696 Microcomputers
Mark Garetz and Sol Libes
Item #85-2 $24.95
This book helps S-100 bus users expand the utility and power of their systems. It describes the S-100 bus with unmatched precision. Various chapters describe its mechanical and functional design, logical and electrical relationships, bus interconnections, and busing techniques.

Building Local Area Networks
Patrick H. Corrigan
Item #025-7 $39.95 (book/disk)
Item #010-9 $24.95 (disk)
The specifics of building and maintaining PC LANs, including hardware configurations, software development, cabling, selection criteria, installation, and on-going management, are described in a detailed, "how-to" manner with numerous illustrations and sample LAN management forms.

Dr. Dobb's Journal Bound Volume Series

Each volume in this series contains a full year's worth of useful code and fascinating history from *Dr. Dobb's Journal of Software Tools*. Each volume contains every issue of *DDJ* for a given year, reprinted and combined into one comprehensive reference.

Volume	1: 1976	*Item #13-5*	*$30.75*
Volume	2: 1977	*Item #16-X*	*$30.75*
Volume	3: 1978	*Item #17-8*	*$30.75*
Volume	4: 1979	*Item #14-3*	*$30.75*
Volume	5: 1980	*Item #18-6*	*$30.75*
Volume	6: 1981	*Item #19-4*	*$30.75*
Volume	7: 1982	*Item #20-8*	*$35.75*
Volume	8: 1983	*Item #00-3*	*$35.75*
Volume	9: 1984	*Item #08-9*	*$35.75*
Volume	10: 1985	*Item #21-6*	*$35.75*
Volume	11: 1986	*Item #72-0*	*$35.75*
Volume	12: 1987	*Item #84-4*	*$39.95*
Volume	13: 1988	*Item #027-3*	*$39.95*

To order any of these products send your payment, along with $2.95 per item for shipping, to M&T Books, 501 Galveston Drive, Redwood City, California 94063. California residents, please include the appropriate sales tax. Or, call toll-free 800-533-4372 (in California 800-356-2002) Monday through Friday between 8 A.M. and 5 P.M. Pacific Standard Time. When ordering disks, please indicate format.

Public Domain and Shareware Survey

You can help make this a better book. Please take a moment to fill out the this postage-paid survey and mail it back to M&T Books.

1. Which sections of the book did you benefit from the most?

2. Was the Telecommunications Primer useful?

2a. Was it sufficiently complete?

3. Was the Applications section useful?

3a. Was it sufficiently complete?

3b. Are there some applications you would like to see more of?

4. Did you find the Sources section of the book useful?

4a. Was it sufficiently complete?

5. Did you enjoy the articles from Shareware professionals?

6. Name your ten favorite public domain or Shareware programs:

	Name	**Category**	**Source**
a.	_____		
b.	_____		
c.	_____		
d.	_____		
e.	_____		
f.	_____		
g.	_____		
h.	_____		
i.	_____		
j.	_____		

NAME (optional)_____

ADDRESS (optional)_____

CITY_____

STATE_____ ZIP_____

BUSINESS REPLY MAIL
FIRST CLASS PERMIT 871 REDWOOD CITY, CA

POSTAGE WILL BE PAID BY ADDRESSEE

M&T Books

501 Galveston Dr.
Redwood City, CA 94063

——————————— PLEASE FOLD ALONG LINE AND STAPLE OR TAPE CLOSED ———————————